EX LIBRIS

MARC MORRIS

THE
ANGLO-SAXONS
A HISTORY OF
THE BEGINNINGS
OF ENGLAND

HUTCHINSON
LONDON

1 3 5 7 9 10 8 6 4 2

Hutchinson
20 Vauxhall Bridge Road
London SW1V 2SA

Hutchinson is part of the Penguin Random House group of companies
whose addresses can be found at global.penguinrandomhouse.com

First published in the United Kingdom by Hutchinson in 2021

www.penguin.co.uk

A CIP catalogue record for this book is available from the British Library.

ISBN 9781786330994

Maps and family trees designed by Martin Lubikowski

Typeset in 12/14 pt Bembo
by Integra Software Services Pvt. Ltd, Pondicherry

Printed and bound in Great Britain by Clays Ltd, Elcograf S.p.A.

The authorised representative in the EEA is Penguin Random House Ireland,
Morrison Chambers, 32 Nassau Street, Dublin D02 YH68.

Penguin Random House is committed to a sustainable future for
our business, our readers and our planet. This book is made from
Forest Stewardship Council® certified paper.

To my father

TOM MORRIS

CONTENTS

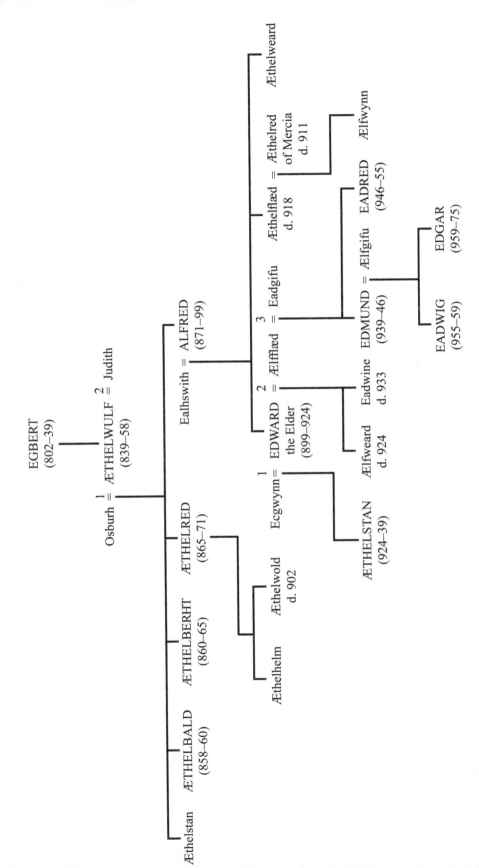

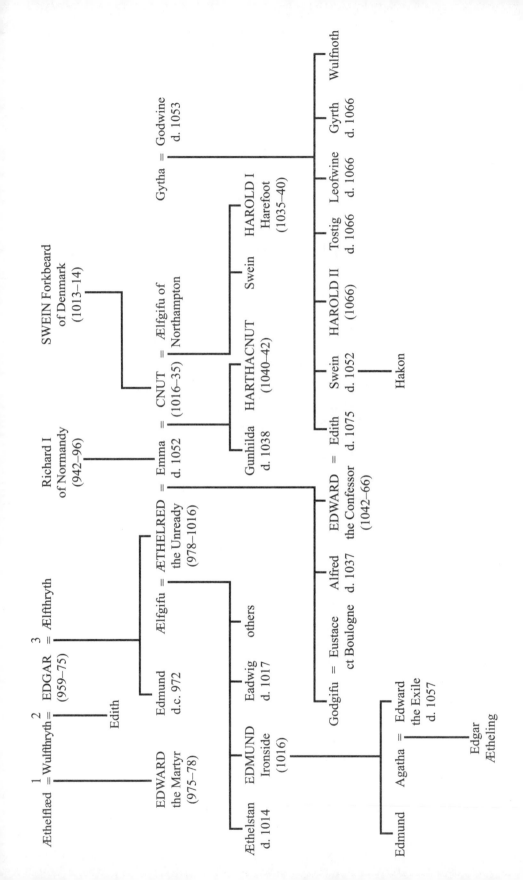

Acknowledgements

My thanks to everyone who helped with the creation of this book. To Sophie Ambler, Mark Edwards, Helen Gittos, Ryan Kemp and Melanie Marshall for supplying advice, articles and translations, and to Rory Naismith for his expert assistance in tracking down images of coins. I should particularly like to thank Richard Abels, Guy Halsall, Charles Insley, John Maddicott and Howard Williams, who kindly read various chapters of the book in draft and offered valuable criticisms. Most especially, I must thank Levi Roach, who read almost half the whole book, and patiently answered many emails over the years it took me to write it.

At Hutchinson it has been a great pleasure to work with Anna Argenio, who edited the book with rigour, intelligence and good humour, and with David Milner, who copy-edited the finished draft with his usual keen-eyed professionalism. My thanks also to Josh Ireland for proof-reading the whole text, to Martin Lubikowski for drawing the maps, and to Rose Waddilove for her patient pursuit of all the pictures. I am very grateful to Sarah Rigby and Jocasta Hamilton for commissioning the book back in 2016, and to my agent, Julian Alexander, for almost twenty years of guidance and friendship.

Lastly, thanks to Cie, Peter and William, for their love and support.

List of Illustrations

Integrated images

1. The Sutton Hoo helmet. © The Trustees of the British Museum. All rights reserved.
2. Detail of the Bayeux Tapestry: the death of King Harold. With special permission from the City of Bayeux.
3a. Richborough Roman fort, reconstruction, circa AD 120. © Historic England Archive.
3b. Richborough Roman fort, reconstruction, mid-third century. Artist: Ivan Lapper (English Heritage/Heritage Images/Getty Images).
3c. Richborough Roman fort, aerial photograph. © Historic England Archive.
4. Three coins from the Hoxne Hoard. Photograph taken by Chris Keating during British Museum/Wikipedia workshop. Public domain.
5. Cadbury Castle. © Historic England Archive.
6. Prittlewell barrow burial. © Museum of London Archaeology, reproduced with permission.
7. Excavation of the Sutton Hoo ship. © The Trustees of the British Museum. All rights reserved.
8. Great hall at Cowdery's Down. Artist: Simon James. Used with kind permission.
9. Lindisfarne aerial photograph. Northumberland County Council. Used with kind permission.

Colour images

Figures on p. 32

INTRODUCTION

I n the course of writing this book, I asked numerous people to name the first thing that came to mind when they thought about the Anglo-Saxons. Naturally there were a wide variety of answers, but two in particular were mentioned over and over again. The first was the Sutton Hoo treasure, discovered in 1939, and now kept in the British Museum. The second was the death of King Harold at the Battle of Hastings, famously fought in 1066.

Neither of these was surprising: the Sutton Hoo treasure, placed in a ship with its original owner in the early seventh century and then concealed under a giant mound, remains the most impressive collection of Anglo-Saxon objects ever unearthed. Even if you're not familiar with it by name, you would almost certainly recognize its most famous items. The helmet, with its distinctive face-mask, has featured on the cover of countless books and magazines. King Harold's death at Hastings, meanwhile, is well known because it led directly to the Norman Conquest, and because it is depicted on the Bayeux Tapestry, another of the world's most famous artistic survivals.

But what did these two most popular 'Anglo-Saxon' associations have in common with each other? They were separated by almost half a millennium, during which there had been an enormous amount of change. Harold was the ruler of a single kingdom, which contemporaries called England, with boundaries very close to where they are today. It was peaceful and prosperous, with an expanding economy, an abundant silver coinage, and dozens of towns, cities and ports. It was also a Christian country,

1. The Sutton Hoo helmet.

with sixteen cathedrals, around sixty monasteries, and thousands of local churches.

At the time of the Sutton Hoo burial, the picture was very different. What would eventually become England was a gaggle of smaller kingdoms, all vying against each other for temporary advantage. None of them had a settlement of more than a few hundred people, or silver coins, or much in the way of trade.

2. The Bayeux Tapestry: the death of King Harold.

Nor was there much organized Christianity, which had arrived only a generation earlier, and had so far made very little progress: almost everyone was still pagan, worshipping gods like Thunor, Frig and Woden. King Harold, who lived in a world of bishops, boroughs, shires and sheriffs, would probably have felt far more at home with the English of the later Middle Ages than the people who had buried their lord in a boat over four centuries earlier. Those intervening centuries had been ones of fundamental transformation.

Generalisations about 'the Anglo-Saxons' are consequently difficult, and, unless made at the most simplistic levels, fairly redundant. It is as meaningful to talk about 'Anglo-Saxon warfare', for instance, as it would be to generalize about military tactics between the fourteenth and the nineteenth centuries. In this book, therefore,

I have for the most part avoided wide-ranging discussions, and tried to chart major social and political developments as they occurred. Each chapter seeks to explore the dominant theme of a particular era. Chapter 3, for example, discusses the second half of the seventh century, which saw the dynamic expansion of Christianity, and the foundation of monasteries and bishoprics. Of course, there were other important things happening in Britain during this time, and these are also discussed, but only as secondary concerns. This approach has meant that a lot of material has inevitably ended up on the cutting-room floor, but it is impossible to write about a period that spans more than seven centuries, from Roman Britain to the Norman Conquest, without being selective. By confining myself to one major theme per chapter, my hope has been to create a clearer story.

In the case of most chapters, I have also concentrated on one particular historical character. Four are focused on individual kings, two on individual bishops, and one on an individual family (the Godwinesons). Again, this was primarily in the interests of narrative clarity, and because biography is a way of framing events in relatable, human terms. At the same time, I wanted the book to be more than just a series of unrelated portraits, so there is plenty of non-biographical material included in each chapter, exploring the book's wider themes and linking one chapter to the next. This is not intended as a series of potted histories, but as an account of the emergence of the English and the development of England.

Sadly, none of the chapters is focused on a woman, because there is simply not enough evidence to sustain such an extended treatment. In the case of certain kings and bishops, we are lucky to have contemporary accounts of their lives, but in the case of queens or abbesses, no such source material has survived. The Venerable Bede provides a few brief sections on particular religious women in his mammoth *Ecclesiastical History*, written in the early eighth century. After that, there are no narrative sources about women until the mid-eleventh century, when two queens, Emma and Edith, commissioned political tracts that touched on aspects of their careers. Yet even these late sources, valuable as they are, contain insufficient material to support an entire chapter. Frustratingly, there are periods where we can discern that certain women were playing a pivotal political role. On several occasions in the tenth century, young kings come and go in quick succession, while their mothers continue at court from one reign to the next, appearing as the leading witnesses to royal charters. But powerful though these women were, their activities are otherwise unrecorded, and their personalities and careers are unrecoverable.

This gap in the evidence might seem surprising, given that the Anglo-Saxon era is often thought of as having been a golden age for women. Since the late eighteenth century, it has been a commonplace that women in England had better rights before the Norman Conquest than they did afterwards, and were held in higher esteem by society. Before 1066, said one eminent historian in the mid-twentieth century, men and women enjoyed 'a rough and ready partnership'.[1] As so often with golden ages, however, this picture rests on a selective reading of very limited and debatable evidence. One of its principal props is an account of German women written by the Roman historian Tacitus towards the end of the first century AD. These women, claimed Tacitus, were virtuous, frugal and chaste, and supported their sons and husbands by encouraging them to acts of valour. But this was simply a Roman praising 'barbarian' society in order to criticize his own. German women were portrayed as laudable because, unlike their Roman counterparts, they did not conduct adulterous affairs or waste their time at baths and theatres. The reality, unfortunately, seems to be that the status of women in first-century Germany and Anglo-Saxon England was no better than it was in later centuries.[2]

The same is largely true in the case of Anglo-Saxon men. The argument that the pre-Conquest period was a golden age for people in general has an even longer history. When England broke with Rome in the sixteenth century, scholars sought to prove that the Anglo-Saxon Church had originally been a pristine, home-grown institution, unsullied by papal influence. During the

Civil War of the seventeenth century, Parliamentarians argued that the freedoms and representative powers they were fighting for had once belonged to their Anglo-Saxon ancestors and been lost in 1066. Almost all of this was myth, but it was enduring and pervasive. In the late nineteenth century it took on a sinister edge when people began to extol the supposed racial superiority of the Anglo-Saxons, leading some scholars today to suggest that the use of the term 'Anglo-Saxon' should be abandoned.[3]

Needless to say, given the title of this book, I do not agree with that suggestion. The term 'Anglo-Saxon', it is true, was not much used by the people we refer to by that name, who tended to think of themselves as either 'Angles' or 'Saxons'. But it was used in the late ninth century by Alfred the Great, who commonly styled himself 'king of the Anglo-Saxons', and also by several of his tenth-century successors. In addition, the use of the term 'Anglo-Saxon' as a convenient means of describing the various English-speaking peoples who lived in lowland Britain between the departure of the Romans and the arrival of the Normans has a long-established history, stretching back at least 400 years.

What is important is that we attempt to see these people as they were, and try to shed the misconceptions about them that have developed in later centuries. This is not easy, for they come laden with much accumulated baggage. The enthusiastic revival of Anglo-Saxon personal names in the nineteenth century makes it hard not to think of the various Alfreds, Ediths and Harolds in this story as honorary Victorians. The reality, of course, is that they were very different, both to us, and to our more immediate forebears. In looking at their lives we will see many things that may strike us as admirable: their courage, their piety, their resourcefulness, their artistry, and their professed love of freedom. But we will also find much that is disconcerting: their brutality, their intolerance, their misogyny, and their reliance on the labour of slaves. Their society produced works of art that continue to dazzle, and institutions that are still with us today, but it was highly unequal, patriarchal, persecuting and theocratic. Their difference to us, even though they possessed certain similarities, is what renders them fascinating. We need to understand them, but we do not need to idolize them.

Our understanding of the Anglo-Saxons must ultimately rest on the historical sources, but for most of the period these are extremely meagre. For the first two centuries after the end of Roman rule, we have virtually no written records of any kind, and are almost entirely reliant on archaeology. The situation improves as the period progresses, and richer material survives, but there are still huge gaps in our knowledge. Sometimes major events are known to us only because of an allusive reference in a charter or a single excavated coin. Often they can only be surmised, because we have no direct evidence at all.

The less evidence, the more contention. The fact that so much is debatable means that the academic arguments are endless. Engaging with them is like navigating a huge, fast-flowing river, fed by a thousand streams of scholarship, and attempting to summarize them is as foolhardy as trying to freeze a waterfall. A definitive history of this period is impossible. What follows is the reading of the evidence that seems most plausible to me, and the arguments I have found the most persuasive. I have tried to show my reasoning whenever possible, without compromising the course of the story, because the story ought to seem remarkable. Like an old reciter of tales, called on by the king to relate the events of earlier times, I hope my audience will be entertained.

1

THE RUIN OF BRITAIN
The Fall of Rome and
the Coming of the Saxons

In November 1992 a farmer named Peter Whatling lost his hammer in a field near the village of Hoxne (pronounced 'Hoxen') in Suffolk. Unwilling to accept that it was gone forever, he enlisted the help of a friend, Eric Lawes, who had been given a metal detector as a retirement gift. Lawes, obtaining a strong signal, began to dig, and made a discovery so startling that he immediately contacted both the police and the local authorities. The next day a team from the Suffolk Archaeological Unit arrived and completed the excavation in conditions of considerable secrecy.

What Mr Lawes had found turned out to be one of the most spectacular hoards of Roman treasure ever unearthed in Britain. It included twenty-nine pieces of gold jewellery – bracelets, rings, necklaces and an extremely rare body-chain, decorated with precious stones. There was also a rich array of silver tableware – bowls and dishes, ornately wrought pepper pots in the shape of animal and human figures, and almost a hundred spoons and ladles. Most significantly, there was a vast quantity of coins – 584 of gold and over 14,000 of silver. This alone made it a truly exceptional discovery, at a stroke nearly doubling the number of coins that have come down to us from late Roman Britain. They also found Mr Whatling's hammer.

A find like the Hoxne Hoard (colour picture 1) – now in the keeping of the British Museum, along with the celebrated hammer – immediately raises all sorts of questions. Who owned it? Who buried it? When, and why? Usually such questions cannot be answered with any certainty, but in this particular case there were some useful clues. Several of the spoons have names inscribed on them, and by far the most frequently occurring name is Aurelius Ursicinus. Unfortunately we have no idea who he was, since he is not mentioned in any of the written sources for Roman Britain, but presumably he was the owner of the spoons and therefore possibly the owner of the entire treasure. What we cannot say for sure is whether he was still alive at the time it was buried. But when it comes to determining when that time was, we are on firmer ground, thanks to the presence of the coins. These can be dated from the images of the emperors that appear on them, and the latest examples in the hoard were minted between AD 407 and 408. How soon after that date the hoard was buried is another matter.[1]

That leaves the most crucial question of all: why was this rich selection of precious objects and vast amount of money hidden in the earth? Experts these days are generally cautious on making definite pronouncements on such matters, and will point to a variety of possible motives. Sometimes such treasures are buried with their former owners and therefore constitute grave goods. Other times the context of the site might indicate a votive offering – if, for instance, treasure had been thrown down a well, or buried near a shrine. But while such ritual explanations are always possible, there is one paramount factor that consistently prompted people in all periods to conceal their valuables in the ground, and that was fear – fear that those valuables might otherwise be taken from them by force. When the numbers of known hoards in the British Isles across the centuries are plotted on a graph, the greatest spike by a very long margin occurs during the Civil War of the 1640s, but there are also sharp increases at the time of the Norman Conquest and the viking invasions. In 1667, the diarist Samuel Pepys was sufficiently spooked by a

Dutch raid on the Thames that he grabbed all the gold coins he had in London and sent his wife to bury them on their country estate in Cambridgeshire.

Fear was always balanced by hope. Those who concealed their valuables in the ground when danger threatened evidently did so in the hope of recovering them once the threat had passed, and it seems likely that this was the intention of whoever buried the Hoxne Hoard. The treasure had been carefully packed into an oak chest, which decomposed apart from traces of its hinges and locks, and within the chest some items had been stowed in smaller wooden boxes or wrapped in fabric. Clearly this was no robber's swag. The person who deposited it had done so with great care, almost certainly intending to return and dig it up when they judged conditions were safer, just as Samuel Pepys did with his coins in the autumn of 1667. Unlike Pepys, the owner of the Hoxne Hoard never got to do so.

Hoards, then, in the words of the historian John Maddicott, are 'reliable barometers of unrest'. Perhaps the most surprising thing about the Hoxne treasure to non-experts is that it was far from unique: well over a thousand other hoards have been unearthed from all over Roman Britain. Few are as rich as the one found at Hoxne, though several of similar quality have been uncovered in the same region of East Anglia, at Mildenhall, Eye and Thetford. The majority of these finds are datable to the fourth century AD, and the rate of deposit increases markedly as that century progresses. By AD 400, based only on those that have been found and recorded in the modern age, the wealthy elite of Roman Britain were between them burying hoards at an average of ten a year.[2]

The reason for their behaviour is not hard to comprehend, for by that date the Roman Empire was in a deeply disturbed state, and no corner of it more so than its northernmost province, Britannia.

By the time the Hoxne Hoard was buried, the Romans had been involved with Britain for almost half a millennium. Julius Caesar had led the first military incursions in 55 BC, but had failed to annex any territory. It was not until nearly a century later, in AD 43, that a full-scale conquest was launched by the emperor Claudius, who obtained the submission of the island's southern rulers, impressing them with the might of a military that could transport war elephants across the Channel. It took a further forty years of campaigning to subdue the remainder of the lowlands, interrupted by the famous revolt of Boudicca in AD 60, but by the end of the first century the contours of power in what was now Roman Britain had been established.

In that same period, and into the second century, all the familiar hallmarks of Roman civilization were introduced. Towns and cities appeared in Britain for the first time, laid out to rigid grid-plans, and within them bathhouses, theatres, temples, monuments and basilicas, all built expensively in stone, some of them faced with marble. The greatest city of all was London, founded soon after Claudius' invasion to serve as an administrative hub for the newly acquired province. With walls some two miles long and enclosing an area of 330 acres, it was home to a population of perhaps 50,000 people, and its forum was the largest north of the Alps.

Linking the thirty cities and seventy or so towns was an infrastructure so extensive and impressive that it would not be replicated in Britain for more than a thousand years. Roads connected the new urban centres to each other and to their agricultural hinterlands, bridges were built over major rivers, and rivers were linked together by the construction of canals. These feats of engineering were designed principally for the benefit of the army, but they also facilitated trade with the rest of the empire. Ships came to Britain carrying produce and products from across Europe and beyond, on a scale that would not be matched until the end of the Middle Ages.[3]

Life for some in Roman Britain was therefore extremely good. In the countryside, and in the towns, the rich lived in villas that had dozens of rooms, frescoed walls, mosaic floors, indoor plumbing and underfloor heating. They drank imported wine and cooked with imported olive oil, enjoying a level of luxury that any British aristocrat before the eighteenth century would have envied. But for many others, life cannot have been nearly so pleasant. Because of its obvious grandeur and sophistication, the Roman Empire has traditionally excited admiration, but latterly some experts have emphasized that the extreme wealth of the elite depended on the aggressive exploitation of the majority of the population, who are for the most part absent from the archaeological and written records. In the 1960s, a cemetery was discovered at Poundbury in Dorset, just outside the Roman town of Dorchester, containing the remains of over 1,200 ordinary fourth-century Britons. The majority of bones showed signs of wear and tear associated with years of hard labour and long-term malnutrition. In the estimation of the historian David Mattingly, 'for every winner under Roman rule there were a hundred losers'.[4]

That said, for those at the bottom of the ladder, life in Britain before the arrival of the Romans was not necessarily any nicer, for slavery was an equally common condition in Celtic society. Moreover, other historians would argue that the immense sophistication and complexity of the Roman economy brought benefits to everybody, albeit not to the same degree. The sheer amount of ceramic found in archaeological digs of Roman sites shows it was produced on an industrial scale, turned on potter's wheels and fired in high-temperature kilns, meaning everyone had access to good-quality plates, bowls and jugs, and even humble buildings like barns and cowsheds had tiled roofs. It is a reasonable assumption that more perishable items – ironmongery, leather goods and textiles – were also being mass-produced. The Romans also improved agricultural productivity by introducing a heavy plough that turned the soil, replacing the inferior kind which merely scratched the surface. Fens were drained and forests were cleared. The population grew to somewhere between 2 million and 6 million, a density that even at the lowest estimate would not be reached again until the time of the Norman Conquest. Roman towns and cities, being carefully designed with drains and sewers, had better sanitation than their medieval successors. The Britons had known coin before the coming of the Romans, but nothing like the volume that was in circulation afterwards. And this level of sophistication demanded literacy. At one time it was a requirement that every soldier in the Roman army should be able to read. That requirement was eventually dropped, but in order for international trade to flourish, and government to function, a great many people had to be literate.[5]

The Romans – and from the start of the third century, everybody living in the empire was considered a Roman citizen, whatever their ancestry – assumed all this would last forever, for the empire was eternal. And yet, within the space of a single lifetime, it was all gone. The towns and cities crumbled and fell into ruin, the coinage ceased to be minted, and the most basic commodities disappeared, leaving people to scratch and scavenge for a living, or to prey on the more vulnerable.[6]

So what went wrong?

The prosperity of the Roman Empire depended on peace, and that peace was provided by its army – a soldiery that was well trained, well paid, and well equipped, armed with mass-produced weapons and ingenious machines of war. In Britain, having quelled the population of the lowlands within a few decades of Claudius' invasion, the army found itself permanently stationed against the upland regions of the island, which were harder to conquer and economically less worth the effort. Legionary fortresses, each capable of accommodating thousands of men, were established at Caerleon, Chester and York, and from these main bases an extensive network of garrison forts was spread through the hills and valleys beyond, in order to subdue or exclude the peoples that lived to the north and west – the Celtic inhabitants of what are now Scotland, Wales and Ireland. In AD 122, the emperor Hadrian visited Britain and decided to mark the northern limit of the empire by building his famous wall, which stretched from the Irish Sea to the North Sea and was studded with forts along its seventy-three-mile length (colour picture 2). According to Hadrian's contemporary biographer, its purpose was 'to separate the Romans from the barbarians'.

At its maximum in the second century, the number of soldiers stationed in this extensive frontier zone was massive – something like 50,000 men, over ten per cent of the entire imperial army. In the following century these numbers were drastically reduced, falling to around a third of their peak before AD 300. This reduction in military expenditure had knock-on economic effects for Britain as a whole. Across the province towns shrank in size, and their public buildings and monuments fell into disrepair and decay. London in particular was badly hit – its population plummeted and many of its buildings were dismantled.[7]

Meanwhile, by the middle of the third century, a new threat had emerged, as raiders from across the sea began attacking and plundering the southern and eastern coasts. They came from Germania, which was the catch-all Roman term for the region of Europe that lay outside the empire, north of the River Rhine and the River Danube, and west of the River Vistula. The particular German people that were raiding Britain were known as Saxons.

But in spite of these cutbacks and menaces, peace in Britain was preserved. Though army numbers had been slashed, there was heavy investment in physical defences. Greater sums than ever before were spent on town walls, and a string of new fortresses was constructed along the southern and eastern coasts. At Richborough in Kent, for example, the bustling port that had grown up since the Roman invasion presumably came under Saxon attack, for in the mid-third century its size was drastically reduced, and its central area was ringed with triple lines of ditches that cut unsparingly through shops and warehouses. By the end of the century the whole town had been transformed into a formidable fortress, with stone walls twenty-six feet high and over ten feet thick. Similar structures were built elsewhere at places like Portchester, Pevensey and Caister-on-Sea, and were collectively known as the forts of the Saxon Shore. Meanwhile, life in the towns and cities went on in some style. New villas were built, and former industrial zones were transformed into gardens and orchards. In the countryside, some of grandest villas yet were constructed in the early fourth century.[8]

3. The changing appearance of Roman Richborough. A prosperous port around AD 120 (a), reduced to a small fort in the mid-third century by the addition of ditches (b), and finally enlarged and walled in the late third century (c).

16

As we move further into the fourth century, however, the situation starts to seem less sanguine. We begin to hear about a warlike people in the north of Britain called the Picts, and as the decades progress we can discern a growing anxiety about their attacks. The defences of Hadrian's Wall were repeatedly rebuilt, and in 343 the emperor Constans personally led an expeditionary force against the Pictish menace. By the 360s there were also invaders crossing the sea from Ireland – the Scots and the Attacots. The crisis became so acute by 367 that it provoked a widespread mutiny among the army, requiring another military expedition from the Continent to restore order.[9]

Modern historians are divided about this restoration. Some see it as a success, returning Britain to the sort of prosperity it had previously enjoyed, with continued investment in grandiose villas and civic defences. Others, however, are less convinced, and see the events of 367–8 as a blow from which the province never truly recovered. An analysis of all the known Roman sites in Britain, counting the number of rooms occupied from one generation to the next, suggests that the country had been in decline since the early fourth century. By 375 the occupancy of villas had fallen by a third, and in towns it had fallen by a half. Such figures suggest that the property-owning classes had indeed been hit hard by repeated barbarian incursions.[10] But what really sealed Britain's fate were similar attacks on the other side of the empire.

The Roman Empire was famously vast, stretching from the Atlantic in the west to Arabia in the east, and encompassing all the lands that surrounded the Mediterranean – the 'Middle of the World' sea. So vast, indeed, that it eventually proved impossible to administer from a single centre, and in AD 286 it was split in two: a western half comprising Italy, Spain, Gaul and Britain, and an eastern half that included the Balkans, Greece, Palestine and Egypt. From that point onwards, apart from a couple of exceptional periods, there were always two emperors, ruling two separate empires, with two separate armies.

There is no single agreed explanation of what caused this colossal political system to unravel, but one factor generally accepted as a catalyst was the appearance of the Huns. A nomadic people who originated on the wide grasslands of central Asia, the Huns were, in the words of a contemporary Roman writer, a 'wild race, moving without encumbrances, and consumed by a savage passion to pillage the property of others'. By 376 those others included the Goths, a more settled people who lived on the frontier of the eastern empire. That year, because of Hunnish attacks, many thousands of Goths sought and received permission to cross the Danube and settle in imperial territory. But relations between the refugees and their Roman hosts soon soured, leading to rebellion and eventually a full-scale battle at Adrianople (now Edrine in modern Turkey). It was a colossal disaster for Rome: two-thirds of the army of the eastern empire – perhaps 10,000 men – were wiped out, and the eastern emperor, Valens, was among those killed.[11]

The catastrophe in the east had immediate consequences for the west. Probably some western troops were sent eastward to compensate for the losses at Adrianople, but more consequential still was the decision to relocate the western capital. For the previous century, the western empire had been governed from the city of Trier, now in Germany, then in the Roman province of Gaul. But in 381 the emperor Gratian, probably because of the ongoing crisis in the Balkans, abandoned Trier for Italy, and removed his court to Milan. This was bad news for Gaul, because the presence of the emperor was a source of patronage for the local elite, and an important prop to the regional economy.[12]

It was also bad news for Britain, for the island was equally enmeshed in the empire's political and economic systems. Several Roman writers noted that grain was shipped from Britain to feed imperial troops on the Rhine, and we can therefore reasonably assume that other British commodities were also being exported to Trier. When the court was removed, therefore, it is likely that Britain was hit hard. Just two years later, in 383, the army in Britain revolted, and proclaimed its leader, Magnus

Maximus, as the new emperor of the west. He promptly invaded Gaul, defeated and killed Gratian, and restored the imperial court to Trier.[13]

This attempt to reverse the direction of travel, however, was short-lived. Five years later Maximus was himself defeated and killed in battle by the new eastern emperor, Theodosius, and the western court was once again removed to Italy. The blow to Britain was compounded by the fact that, in order to effect his usurpation, Maximus had removed troops from the province, and they had either perished with him, or else stayed on the European mainland. A contemporary survey known as the *Notitia Dignitatum* (List of Dignities) suggests that by the 390s soldiers who had earlier been stationed in north Wales at Caernarfon were serving in the Balkans, while the legion formerly at Caerleon in south Wales had been relocated to Richborough, a fort less than ten times the size of their previous barracks. Archaeological evidence at such sites also suggests the military presence in Britain was rapidly diminishing.[14]

Meanwhile, in the heartlands of the empire, the crises continued to mount. Theodosius, who had ruled both east and west since 392, died three years later, dividing the empire between his two sons. Both were young and inexperienced. Arcadius, who ruled in the east, was seventeen years old; Honorius, who succeeded to the west, only ten. Feuding and civil war between competing factions followed, while the barbarian menace continued to increase: in 401 and 402 Italy itself was invaded by the Goths.[15]

These tumultuous events must have had an impact on Britain, but precisely what that impact was we cannot say. What we do know is that 402 is the last year in which Roman coins appear in Britain's archaeological record in any significant quantities. The minting of coins in London had ceased after the death of Magnus Maximus in 388, and since then the province had been reliant on new supplies from the mainland, principally from Milan. But in 402 Milan was deemed to be too close to the fighting on the other side of the Alps, and production was moved to Ravenna. After this relocation, the bulk import of coin to Britain suddenly ceased.[16]

This was probably the final straw for the army in Britain: nothing is likelier to have created discontent among the soldiery than not being paid. Of course, there would still have been an existing currency in circulation, but without regular transfusions from the Continent it cannot have been enough. The British authorities evidently tried their best to cope. The vast majority of coins recovered from late Roman Britain show signs of 'clipping' – that is, of having had some amount of silver sheared from their edges. In the case of the Hoxne Hoard, 98.5 per cent of its 14,500 silver coins had been mutilated in this way, some of them losing almost a third of their original weight. This is likely to have been an official attempt to make the existing currency go further: after 402 we find coins struck in Britain that are imitations of genuine imperial issues, suggesting that at least some of the silver clipped from older coins was being recycled to make new ones. The Hoxne treasure contains 428 such copies, and all of these copies had themselves been clipped.[17]

4. Three coins from the Hoxne Hoard, showing
the reduction in size due to clipping.

Thus by the start of the fifth century the people of Britain were being paid in coin which was visibly shrinking from one year to the next, and presumably in many cases not being paid at all. By 406, the army had clearly had enough. In the summer of that year, they rose in rebellion, proclaiming a man named Marcus as their new emperor. By the autumn he had been deposed in favour of a certain Gratian, who was in turn murdered after only four months and replaced by an ordinary soldier called Constantine. This rapid turnover of leaders suggests that the issue went beyond personalities, and that a struggle was taking place between rival factions in pursuit of different policies, particularly Britain's relationship with the rest of the empire. These debates acquired added urgency after the end of 406, at which point a number of barbarian tribes – the Vandals, the Alans and the Sueves – crossed the Rhine frontier and invaded Gaul, reportedly causing alarm among the Britons that they might be next.

The replacement of Gratian with Constantine, which happened soon after, suggests the triumph of those who believed the best form of defence was attack. Immediately after his elevation, the would-be usurper set out for Gaul, intent on deposing the sitting emperor. His name, we are told, gave people hope, presumably because it evoked the memory of Constantine the Great, who had been proclaimed emperor in Britain almost exactly a century earlier, and had gone on to reunite a divided empire. But the new Constantine, alas, did not measure up to his illustrious namesake. After some initial successes, he incurred the implacable enmity of his rival, Honorius, by executing some of his relatives, and was in turn captured and beheaded by loyalist imperial forces.

What proved to be a personal disaster for Constantine was an even greater calamity for the country he had left behind. In pursuit of victory on the mainland he must have taken with him many of the troops stationed in Britain, further reducing its already depleted defences. If any voices had cautioned against his all-or-nothing strategy, they were soon proved right. Soon after his departure, probably in 408, the province was devastated by an invasion of Saxons.[18]

Now it was the turn of the rest of the population to rise in rebellion. According to the Greek historian Zosimus, writing in the early sixth century, the barbarian attacks drove the Britons 'to revolt from Roman rule and live on their own, no longer obedient to Roman laws'. It was an extraordinary step prompted by the dire condition to which events of recent decades had reduced them. The whole point of the Roman state was to guarantee peace for its citizens with a well-trained army. If that army was absent, or so inadequate that it could not prevent the violent incursions of seaborne raiders, what was the point of paying taxes, or obeying a law that forbade civilians from carrying weapons? Self-defence was synonymous with self-rule. The Britons, says Zosimus, 'armed themselves, and ran many risks to ensure their own safety, and freed their cities from attacking barbarians ... expelling the Roman magistrates and establishing the government they wanted'.[19]

This makes the revolt of 409 sound like a great success – plucky little Britannia throwing off Roman rule and beating the barbarians into the bargain. In fact, this was the event that tipped the province over the precipice. Once its economic and political links with the empire were severed, Britain went into free fall. The archaeological record, previously so abundant, becomes almost undetectably thin. Good quality pottery vanishes, as do everyday items of ironmongery such as nails. Their sudden disappearance indicates not only that these industries had failed soon after 410, but that within a generation the villas and towns of Roman Britain had been almost completely abandoned. The implication of this data is unavoidable: society had collapsed. It was, in the words of one modern historian, 'probably the most dramatic period of social and economic collapse in British history'.[20]

The further implications of this are appalling. The abandonment of towns and villas means huge numbers of people must have been on the move in search of shelter and food. The failure of normal trade and distribution networks indicates that food would have been in short supply. The absence of an army would have led to the rise of looting, pillaging and robbery. The rich could use their existing wealth to hire armed protection, but were evidently unable to remain in their luxurious but unfortified residences. Everyone else would have had to fend for themselves.

One way or another, as happens when modern states fail and civil society dissolves, people must have perished in huge numbers, through famine, disease and violence.[21]

This was the period in which the Hoxne treasure was hidden. The very latest coins in the hoard, only eight in number, bear the face of Constantine, the British usurper proclaimed in 407, and were minted before the death of his eastern counterpart, Arcadius, in 408. The fact that all eight were clipped and showed other signs of wear suggests they must have circulated for some time after their issue, meaning that the hoard might have been buried a decade or two later. During these decades there were no longer occasions for dining with ornate silver salt cellars or donning gem-studded jewellery, and an ever-increasing likelihood that such items would be stolen or seized by violence. Hence, presumably, the decision to secrete them in the ground.[22]

The hope must have been that the bad times would eventually end, and that Roman rule would be restored, as it always had been in the past.

Nothing is more likely than that, during these years, Britain also continued to suffer from repeated barbarian raids. Hard proof is lacking, because raiders, unlike settlers, leave little behind in the way of archaeological evidence, and where the record does reveal towns and villas destroyed by fire, the tendency of late has been to assume the causes were accidental rather than deliberate. But, given the lack of soldiers to man the coastal forts, and the breakdown in co-ordination and communication, barbarians who had been trying their luck in Britain for decades were now presented with a much softer target. The social chaos unleashed in the wake of the revolt, the hordes of displaced and vulnerable people, made the former province a perfect hunting ground for invaders in search of treasure, cattle or slaves. Later tradition has led to the assumption that the worst threat was posed by the Picts and Scots, and doubtless this was true the further one travelled north. But in southern and eastern Britain the primary menace was the Saxons.

Although there are no contemporary descriptions from Britain, Saxon raiders are described in a few sources from across the Channel in fifth-century Gaul. In 455, for example, a Gallo-Roman aristocrat and poet named Sidonius Apollinarius made a passing mention of 'the Saxon pirate, who deems it sport to furrow in British waters with hides, cleaving the blue sea in a stitched boat'.[23] Some years later, the same writer provided a fuller picture in a letter to a friend who was responsible for repelling raids along the Atlantic coast. 'The Saxon', he wrote, 'is the most ferocious of all foes. He comes upon you without warning; when you expect his attack he slips away. Resistance only moves him to contempt; a rash opponent is soon down … Shipwrecks to him are no terror, but only so much training. His is no mere acquaintance with the perils of the sea; he knows them as he knows himself.'[24]

It was not only the Saxon's ferocity and fearlessness that perturbed his opponents, but his paganism. The Romans had once worshipped a pantheon of different gods, but in the course of the fourth century they had abandoned them for Christianity. During the reign of Constantine the Great (306–37) the persecution of Christians had ceased and their creed had become the official religion of the empire. In every province new churches had sprung up, and a new hierarchy of priests, headed by bishops. Sidonius, who had begun his career as a diplomat, eventually became bishop of Clermont-Ferrand.[25] He was consequently appalled by the heathenism of the Saxon pirates who, like most of the peoples beyond the empire's northern frontier, had not experienced conversion and clung stubbornly to their pagan beliefs.

'When the Saxons are setting sail from the Continent,' he explained, 'it is their practice, thus homeward bound, to abandon every tenth captive to a watery end.' This custom, he continued, was all the more deplorable because it was prompted by sincere belief. 'These men are bound by vows which have to be paid in victims; they conceive it as a religious act to perpetrate this horrible slaughter, and to take anguish from the prisoner in place of ransom.'[26]

Pagan pirates such as these must have been attacking Britain in the early fifth century, ravaging far inland, profiting from and contributing to society's collapse. In 429, another Gallo-Roman bishop, Germanus of Auxerre, was asked to cross the Channel to combat an outbreak of a heresy, and ended up helping a besieged community of Britons against a horde of Picts and Saxons – a struggle he won by baptising the defenders and commanding them to chant the Alleluia as a battle cry. This story comes from a life of Germanus written half a century later to establish his sanctity, and is therefore unlikely to be true in every respect, but it establishes two important fundamentals. First, that there were still some people in Britain in 429 trying to uphold public authority, sufficiently anxious about the spread of heresy to send for overseas help. Second, that these British authorities were engaged in an existential struggle against barbarian invaders, and – notwithstanding Germanus' stalwart assistance – they were finding it increasingly difficult to cope. In the words of the bishop's later biographer, they were 'utterly unequal to the contest'.[27]

This brings us to the most well-known part of the story. It is well known because it was told by the Venerable Bede, whose *Ecclesiastical History of the English People* is without question the single most important and influential work of the whole Anglo-Saxon period. According to Bede, the Britons, 'ignorant of the practice of warfare', were reduced to such a wretched state by Pictish and Scottish attacks that they held a council, in which they decided to employ foreigners to fight on their behalf. At the invitation of their king, Vortigern, a force of Saxon warriors came to Britain in three ships and was granted a place to settle in the eastern part of the island. In the first instance these mercenaries acquitted themselves well, winning a victory against the Britons' northern enemies.

But, as Bede goes on to explain, the Saxons secretly intended to conquer the whole country for themselves. After their initial success they sent word back to their homelands that Britain was fertile and the Britons were cowards. Very soon a much larger fleet of Saxons arrived and joined together with the original cohort to form an invincible army. It was not long before the inevitable denouement. The Saxons suddenly made peace with the northern peoples they were supposed to be fighting and turned their weapons against their British hosts, demanding greater rewards for their service, and threatening to devastate the whole island if their demands were not met. When no more supplies were forthcoming, the Saxons burned and ravaged Britain from sea to sea. 'Public and private buildings fell into ruins,' says Bede, 'priests were everywhere slain at the altars, prelates and people alike perished by sword and fire regardless of rank, and there was no one left to bury those who had died a cruel death.'[28]

Famous as it is, Bede's story cannot be taken at face value. The main problem is that as a source it is very late: Bede was writing in the early eighth century, a full 300 years after the events he purports to describe, and during that time the tale of the coming of the Saxons had taken a legendary turn. The assertion, for example, that the initial force arrived in three ships, aside from being inherently improbable, is a common trope found in the origin stories of other northern European peoples. Similarly, the mention of a British leader called 'Vortigern' is suspect, because the name itself meant something like 'High Ruler' in Brittonic. Bede also named the leaders of the Saxons as a Hengist and Horsa, and says they were brothers. This was apparently a local tradition from Kent, and is even less likely to have any basis in historical reality: their names translate as 'gelding' and 'horse', and brothers with alliterative names are another frequent feature of European foundation myths. Hengist and Horsa are no more likely to have existed than Romulus and Remus.[29]

But while bits of Bede's account are clearly folklore, his main source was a written one. The story of the arrival of the Saxons was originally committed to parchment by a British author called Gildas, who wrote a tract known to posterity as *The Ruin of Britain*. It is an extremely problematic text, not least because we know almost nothing about Gildas himself. Historians have spilled vast amounts of ink arguing about his possible dates on the basis of a few debatable words in his work. On balance, it

seems likeliest that he lived in the early sixth century, and probably wrote his famous tract at some point in its second quarter.[30]

The main problem with *The Ruin of Britain* is that it is not
really a work of history – it is an open letter addressed to the
British rulers of the author's own day, criticizing them for their
manifold failings and sins, and exhorting them to mend their
wicked ways. Gildas *does* include a historical introduction to
explain how the society of his own day had come to be in such
a sorry state, but he was hampered by a lack of reliable sources.
As he explained at the outset, earlier books about Britain's history
had either been burned by barbarian raiders or carried off into
exile, forcing him to rely on the works of foreign writers that
gave him only a very incomplete picture. Accordingly, he provides
no dates whatsoever, and commits some howling errors. To take
one egregious example, he asserts that Hadrian's Wall was built
in the context of Pictish attacks in the early fifth century, misdating
its actual construction by almost 300 years.[31]

And yet, when all these caveats have been lodged, *The Ruin
of Britain* remains the most valuable account of the island's fifth-
century history, and the only one that can be regarded as even
remotely contemporary. The main event – the ultimate cause,
according to Gildas, of all Britain's subsequent misery – was the
arrival of the Saxons. His story is more or less identical to its
later reiteration by Bede: the Britons, plagued by Pictish and
Scottish attacks, convened a council, and decided to employ a
force of Saxons as mercenaries. These warriors initially arrived
in three ships and settled on the east side of Britain, but were
soon joined by a second and larger contingent. Gildas, unlike
Bede, makes no mention of the Saxons engaging the Scots and
Picts – in his account they simply become ever more demanding
and aggressive towards their British hosts, before finally revolting
and ravaging the whole country, an event that Gildas describes
in the same apocalyptic terms that Bede later borrowed.[32]

Is this story credible? Gildas lived much closer in time to these
alleged events than Bede, but he was still writing almost a century
after they took place, and his mention of the Saxons arriving in

three ships suggests that the story had already been infected by legend. Moreover, is it really plausible that the Britons would have sought to employ Saxons as mercenaries, given the evidence, both direct and circumstantial, that the Saxons themselves had been raiding and plundering Britain for decades with the same fury as the Scots and Picts? Gildas evidently thought not, for he makes no mention of Saxon attacks prior to this episode. In his account, the Saxons appear only after the Britons made the fateful decision to invite them – a decision that Gildas furiously condemned as the height of folly.[33]

Perhaps surprisingly, the answer to these questions is yes: it is perfectly reasonable to believe that the Britons would have decided to employ barbarians to fight on their behalf, because this was a long-established Roman practice. Throughout the fourth century such warriors had been routinely recruited into imperial armies, some of them rising to the highest rank. Flavius Stilicho, for example, the most senior general in the western empire, and its effective ruler during the minority of Honorius, was of Vandal descent. It was a practice that worked well while recruits were integrated into the regular army and effectively Romanized. What worked altogether less well was a new policy, introduced towards the end of the fourth century, which saw entire barbarian armies hired under the command of their own leaders. These 'federate' troops often proved much less dependable, and were liable to switch sides suddenly with disastrous consequences. But by that time matters were becoming desperate, and such desperate experiments could be contemplated.[34]

Such was the situation in which the Britons eventually found themselves in the wake of their break with Rome. The country was in chaos and under constant assault from Picts, Scots and Saxons. The legions were long gone, and a civilian population, previously forbidden from carrying weapons, could not learn the arts of war overnight. In these circumstances, it becomes easy to understand how those in authority might seek to remedy the problem by recruiting one group of barbarians to fight against the others.

When did these events take place? Bede, who was much more concerned with chronology than Gildas, placed them during the rule of the emperor Marcian, whose accession he dated to 449, and eventually that date was adopted (and indeed celebrated) by later writers as the official year of the Saxons' arrival. But Bede was misled by a mistake in his principal source, *The Ruin of Britain* – a paraphrase of a letter that was almost certainly written *after* the Saxon revolt, but which Gildas had carelessly placed in his story at a point *before* the Saxons had even arrived. Bede, who was able to adduce from the letter's contents that it could not have been written before 446, was thus led to believe the Saxons must have arrived in Britain after that date.[35]

In fact, other evidence, unavailable to Bede, indicates that he was about twenty years out, and that the first arrivals had taken place a generation earlier, around the year 430. It is around that date that we find the earliest archaeological indications of Saxon settlement: burials, artefacts and buildings of a kind that were utterly unfamiliar in late Roman Britain, but entirely common-place in northern Germany and southern Scandinavia. We also have another written source besides Gildas. *The Gallic Chronicle of 452*, as its prosaic modern title implies, is a set of annals composed in Gaul in the mid-fifth century. It says nothing about the coming of the Saxons, but it suggests that their revolt took place around 441. Its entry for that year says 'The Britains [*sic*], up to now afflicted by various disasters and vicissitudes, were widely reduced to the rule of the Saxons.'[36]

Naturally, one wishes that this anonymous writer, composing his chronicle only a decade later, could have been a little more garrulous. What, for example, did he mean by 'widely' (Latin: *latae*)? The most we can conclude is that he knew the Saxons had seized control of a substantial area of Britain, but evidently not all of it. This accords with Gildas' description of what happened to the Britons after the Saxon revolt. Gildas, as a prophet chiding his people, emphasized the catastrophic consequences. Some of them were caught and killed, he says, and some surrendered and were enslaved, while others fled into foreign exile or hid in the hills and forests. But Gildas then goes on to describe what was clearly a significant and celebrated British fightback. After a time, he says, the Saxons went home – presumably meaning their original settlements in Britain, rather than their homelands on the Continent – and God gave strength to the Britons. Gildas names their leader as Ambrosius Aurelianus, who he indicates was a Roman of high birth. Under this man's direction, we are told, the British people regained their confidence and defeated the Saxons in battle. After the Saxon revolt, therefore, Britain was evidently divided, with the newcomers in control of some areas and the pre-existing population in control of others.[37]

How it was divided is worth investigating in more detail. Gildas portrays the split as the result of a straightforward binary struggle, and historians have tended to picture it that way ever since: Saxons in the east, Britons in the west, with only bloody battles if ever the twain should meet. To be fair to Gildas, this was probably how it seemed from his perspective in western Britain in the early sixth century. But there are several indications that, in the immediate wake of the Saxon revolt, and for much of the rest of the fifth century, the situation was rather more complicated.

As we already noted, from around 430 we start to find archaeological evidence in Britain of new settlers from the Continent. Cremation of the dead is the most obvious and clear-cut example. It had not been practised by the Britons since the third century, but was typical among the Saxons. The custom was to burn the body of the deceased on a funeral pyre, sometimes along with the bodies of animals, and then bury the ashes in an urn. In the Saxon homelands – the region between the rivers Elbe and Weser in north Germany – we find very large cremation cemeteries with thousands of urns dating back several centuries before 430. After that date, we begin to find them in Britain too. One of the largest and most thoroughly excavated is that at Spong Hill in Norfolk.[38]

The other new practice that suddenly reveals itself around this time is the inclusion of grave goods – personal items such as jewellery, combs or weapons that belonged to the deceased in life and were buried with them after death. Sometimes they are found in cremation cemeteries, buried along with the ashes in the urns, but other times they are included with non-cremated individuals who had simply been buried in the ground – a custom which archaeologists refer to as 'furnished inhumation'. This too had been practised in Saxony, but had been introduced there only a few decades earlier, around the year 400. Its appearance in Britain a generation or so later was clearly connected to the coming of the Saxons, and many of the grave goods contained in such burials have close parallels with items found in their homelands.

Both these two new funerary practices are found in eastern Britain from the second quarter of the fifth century, and their distribution seems to reveal a significant regional split. Cremation cemeteries are almost exclusively concentrated in the northern part of this zone – the areas defined by rivers that flow into the Wash or the Humber (Figure 1.1). Furnished inhumations, by contrast, are found everywhere, but some of the items found within them reveal a similar division. To the north we find brooches and other metalwork decorated in a distinctive manner (dubbed the 'Saxon Relief Style' by art historians) which was clearly imported from the Saxon homelands. To the south, meanwhile, in an area defined by the River Thames, we find metal items worked in a different fashion – the so-called 'Quoit Brooch Style' – which appear to be Romano-British in origin (Figure 1.2).

What the archaeological evidence seems to reveal, therefore, is not a simple two-way split between Saxons and Britons, but a situation that was more complex, with the east divided into two quite distinct zones. In the more northerly zone there was a burial and artistic culture that clearly advertised a continued attachment to the Saxon homelands. In the southern zone, however, the situation seems more ambiguous. Some of the grave goods found in this region are Saxon, but others proclaim continuity with the imperial past. The occupants of these graves may have been continental newcomers, but in some cases they look

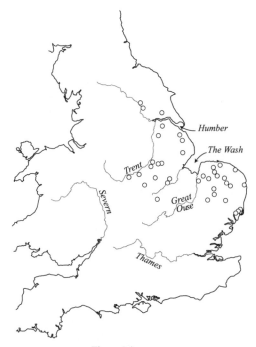

Figure 1.1
Cremation cemeteries

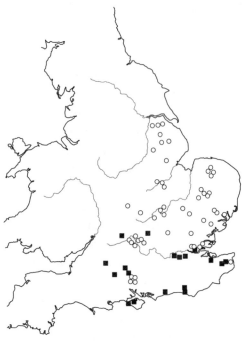

Figure 1.2
○ Saxon Relief Style v.   ■ Quoit Brooch Style

Figure 1.3
Roman provinces, with capitals and
conjectured boundaries

Figure 1.4
Anglian wrist-clasps

like Romano-British people who had simply adopted a new and more demonstrative form of burial.[39]

Could these apparent cultural divisions reflect political ones? This is altogether more speculative, but there is one intriguing possibility. Late Roman Britain had been divided into four (possibly five) provinces, each with its own governor and capital city. The locations of the capitals are known to have been London, Lincoln, Cirencester and York. The boundaries between the provinces are a matter of conjecture, but some historians have been inclined to draw the line between the London and Lincoln provinces in much the same position as the cultural watershed apparent in the archaeology of the mid-fifth century (Figure 1.3).[40]

Highly speculative as it is, therefore, it could be that these provinces continued to have some sort of function after Britain's break with Rome.[41] Perhaps their governors even came together in a council, as Gildas says, and agreed to hire Saxon mercenaries, who were then settled in various locations in the east, and ended up ruling some part of the island for themselves. On the basis of the archaeological evidence, we would probably locate that area as the zone in eastern England where the evidence of Saxon culture is strongest – the province governed from Lincoln. The London province must also have received significant numbers of new settlers, but here the evidence for a wholesale Saxon takeover is not so readily apparent. In this region, at least some people of Romano-British ancestry remained in positions of social significance. They were content to adopt a new way of being buried that advertised that significance, and wore dress fittings that announced their connections with the empire. Perhaps they still hoped that one day the empire would return.

This reading of the archaeological record leads us to the vexed but crucial question about the scale of Saxon immigration. Traditionally it was assumed that, wherever the newcomers settled in Britain, they simply replaced the indigenous peoples who had been living there before. Gildas, as we've seen, portrays the Britons as being either killed or enslaved, or else fleeing into exile, and this was the majority view well into the twentieth century. It was reinforced by archaeology: how else could the abundant quantity of Saxon material, and almost total absence of Romano-British finds, be explained? The Saxons, it was widely held, must have migrated to Britain in vast numbers, occupying a landscape that had already been almost emptied by warfare, famine and social collapse, and expelling or exterminating any remaining Britons with the edges of their swords.[42]

Beginning in the 1960s, this view was subjected to a thorough-going re-evaluation. Doubts were expressed in general about the scale of barbarian migrations in fourth- and fifth-century Europe, and it was argued that the numbers involved must have been much smaller than those given by contemporary writers. For Britain, in particular, historians pointed to the difficulty of transporting large numbers of people across the sea with the rudimentary ships available at the time. Instead of a mass migra-tion, scholars developed the idea that Britain was invaded by only a few Saxons who were disproportionately powerful. The Britons were not massacred or expelled en masse by this minority but remained in place, and eventually adopted the language, religion and culture of the newcomers. Historians call this an 'elite transfer' model. Such a model, of course, serves to confound the traditional interpretation of the archaeology, for it raises the possibility that people found buried with Saxon grave goods might not be migrants at all, or even the descendants of migrants, but Britons who have embraced Saxon culture.[43]

Latterly the pendulum has swung back in the other direction, and the scale of migration is now once again generally reckoned to have been very sizeable. This revisionism has little to do with DNA. The scientific analysis of bones, and especially teeth, from fifth- and sixth-century burials can sometimes indicate where their owners grew up, and in some cases we find people buried in Britain who had grown up in northern Germany. While this is helpful in individual cases, however, it tells us nothing about the overall size of the population movement. The other approach, which involves collecting the DNA of modern persons – and on this basis making sweeping conclusions about their ancestry – is much more problematic, and has generally been regarded with scepticism by historians.[44]

The case for a substantial movement of people across the North Sea in the fifth and sixth centuries rests more on a reconsideration of traditional evidence. There is a strong argument, for example, based on language. It is inherently unlikely that the majority of people in Britain would have ended up speaking English – a Germanic language – had there not been a great many immigrants from Germania.[45] Historians have also refuted the idea that a mass migration was technically impossible. It is sometimes objected that the Saxons could not have crossed the sea in large numbers because their ships lacked sails, but the evidence suggests that this was not the case.[46] As we've seen, Sidonius Apollinarius, a contemporary witness, described how Saxon pirates would sacrifice every tenth captive they had seized in Gaul on their homeward voyage, implying a minimum of ten captives per boat was possible. Presumably captains with willing passengers would have been able to carry even more. It does not require that many crossings from Saxony to Britain to reach a substantial number of migrants. If one boat could ferry just ten passengers and made five trips in a year, that would mean fifty new arrivals. A hundred boats doing the same would mean 5,000. A hundred boats doing the same for fifty years would bring the total to a quarter of a million.[47]

Sizeable as this hypothetical number is, however, it would take an awful lot more boats and crossings to imagine that there could have been more Saxons than Britons. Even if we take the lowest population estimate for late Roman Britain – 2 million – and imagine a fifth century so catastrophic that half the population perished, we are still left with a scenario in which Britons would have outnumbered Saxons by a factor of four to one. Such numerical speculation therefore still begs the question: why did British culture not triumph? Other parts of Europe – Gaul, Spain and Italy – were invaded by barbarian peoples, but in these provinces it was Roman culture that won out: the newcomers learned to speak languages based on low Latin, and quickly converted to Christianity. Yet in the parts of Britain settled by the Saxons, the direction of travel was all the other way. The Britons who remained in these areas adopted a new Germanic tongue, and began to worship pagan gods. In French the days of the week *mardi, mercredi, jeudi* and *vendredi* are named after the Roman gods Mars, Mercury, Jupiter and Venus. In English Tuesday, Wednesday, Thursday and Friday are named after the Germanic gods Tiw, Woden, Thunor and Frig.[48]

The likeliest answer is that, by the time the Saxons came to settle in Britain, they found little that was worth preserving. Across the Channel in Gaul the towns and cities had been battered by invading barbarians, and had shrunk in size as a result, but most of them ultimately survived, and the survival of urban life meant the continuity of organized Christianity, based as it was on cathedrals and bishoprics. But in Britain, as we've seen, civic life had collapsed completely in the early fifth century, before the earliest Saxon settlers had arrived. As for organized Christianity in Britain, the evidence suggests it had never been very strongly established in the first place. Mosaic floors with Christian iconography in several late Roman villas show that some aristocrats had converted during the fourth century, but there is almost no evidence for urban churches of the kind we see on the Continent.[49] Some very basic elements of Roman social organization may have been adopted by the Saxons – the boundaries of existing fields, for example, would have survived the collapse and would have been laborious to alter. But the cities, the industries, the commerce and the culture – all these had already gone, or were wrecked beyond repair. The broken Britain that the Saxons found consequently had no allure, and in British culture they saw nothing they wished to emulate.

This is not to say that every group of Saxon settlers had nothing to do with the Britons. There cannot have been one single migration experience that applied across the whole country, and there must have been lots of regional variation. North of the

River Humber, where Saxon settlement was thinner, it may be that there was something like an 'elite transfer' model, with the settlers taking over a functioning society. In the Midlands, meanwhile, certain cemeteries suggest we might be looking at a migration of male warriors who married local British women, and in the south and south-east, as we've seen, there may have been interaction that went beyond one group slaughtering or enslaving the other.[50] Overall, however, and especially in the east, the Saxons seem to have preferred to keep to themselves. They established their own communities on new sites, constructed buildings in an imported style, and maintained their traditional funerary practices. That they had little interaction with Britons is suggested by the remarkable fact that only around thirty words in Old English are reckoned to have been borrowed from Brittonic. Such a low figure makes it as good as certain that it was not just Saxon warriors who came to Britain, but whole communities of men, women and children, who did not mix and intermarry with the locals.[51]

So far we have spoken only of Saxons, the catch-all term used by Gildas and others to describe the immigrants who came to Britain. But when Bede came to retell Gildas' story around two centuries later, he felt compelled to add more nuance. 'They came', he said, 'from three very powerful tribes – the Saxons, the Angles and the Jutes', and he went on to explain how each of the three had settled in Britain to form the various kingdoms of his own day. Thus the people of Kent were Jutes, the peoples of East Anglia, Mercia and Northumbria were Angles, and the peoples of Wessex, Sussex and Essex were Saxons. And for a long time, historians assumed that Bede was correct, and that these tribes, as he called them, had migrated in discrete groups from their homelands: the Jutes from Jutland, the Saxons from Saxony, and the Angles from the region in the middle, Angeln.[52]

In fact, Bede was only half-right. You can, it is true, find a lot of material evidence – ceramics, jewellery and so forth – to support his assumption. Some artefacts unearthed in East Anglia, for example, are undeniably similar to those dug up in Angeln, and the same goes for the other regions mentioned by Bede. But – and here is the point where Bede was wrong – you also find a lot of material within those regions that *doesn't* conform to his assumption. Saxon brooches, for example, are found everywhere in Britain that saw barbarian settlement, from Yorkshire to the south coast. Britain was settled not by three separate 'tribes' who carefully maintained their identities during the migration process, but by a steady flow of peoples from all around the coasts of northern Europe and southern Scandinavia. Saxons, Angles and Jutes were certainly among their number, but so too were Frisians, Swedes and Franks, all mixing together, forming communities, and combining their artistic cultures to create new ones. Bede himself, in a later but less celebrated passage, acknowledged this point, saying 'there were very many peoples in Germany from whom the Angles and Saxons, who now live in Britain, derive their origin'.[53]

The notion that *everyone* in a particular region was 'Anglian', 'Saxon' or 'Jutish' was therefore one that must have developed at some point after their arrival, probably in the last quarter of the fifth century. During that time Britain witnessed a new wave of migration from Scandinavia. This is revealed by a distinctive form of female dress accessory, the wrist clasp, which originated from western and southern Norway. The earliest examples in Britain are found around the Humber and the Wash, which must have been the points of entry for their wearers, and from there the fashion quickly spread across the whole of the Anglian zone – but no further. The distribution of wrist clasps stops abruptly at the line identified earlier as a cultural frontier between the more barbarian and more Romanized regions of eastern Britain (Figure 1.4). It looks therefore as if the people of this Anglian zone had already developed a common group identity by the end of the fifth century, and that one way of expressing it was in the form of female dress. We see a similar development in the southern zone. The earlier Quoit-Brooch Style disappears, and with it perhaps the desire on the part of its wearers to present themselves as Roman. It was replaced by a new style which made heavy use of geometric animal forms, and originated from beyond the empire's northern fringes. This suggests that the people in this region, whatever their origins, were now identifying as 'Saxon'. More of them must have started speaking in a Germanic tongue, and begun to worship pagan gods.[54]

Those who still wished to cling to the vestiges of the Roman past, and in particular to Christianity, would have had to head west. Here, in what is now Wales and Cornwall, were the hills and forests that Gildas said had offered the Britons refuge. Gildas himself is the best evidence that in these western regions there was still a literate, Christian culture, and that those at the very top of society were still striving to lead a Roman lifestyle. At Tintagel in the far south-west, archaeologists have discovered the remains of amphorae that had once contained wine or olive oil, and fragments of high-quality tableware, imported from the eastern Mediterranean in the late fifth and early sixth centuries. Similar finds have been made at other high-status sites in Wales and the West Country.

But the amount of material being imported in this way was vanishingly small compared to the enormous quantities that had previously been shipped to Britain when it was an imperial dominion. Only a few got to indulge in the pretence that they were part of a Roman elite. For most people, even basic items were extremely hard to come by. At Cadbury Congresbury, an Iron Age hill fort near the estuary of the River Severn, reoccupied towards the end of the fifth century, the only quality items of pottery or glass were ones that had been made a century earlier. Some of the pots used for cooking were cremation urns, excavated from ancient Roman cemeteries and emptied of their human remains. This was in every sense a degraded society, sifting through the detritus of an earlier civilization, in which life for the majority was almost impossibly grim. These Britons may have been living in an Iron Age hill fort, but in technological and material terms they had slipped back to the Bronze Age.[55]

Cadbury was one of several hill forts reoccupied and refortified around this time, a reminder that the kind of basic security that the Britons had previously enjoyed was also a thing of the distant past. Besides any looters and robbers in their own midst, the people of western Britain also faced continued assault from Irish raiders (and indeed, some colonisation, as inscribed stones found in Wales attest).[56] The principle security threat, however, were the Saxons to their east. After the successful resistance led by Ambrosius Aurelianus, says Gildas, the Britons and the Saxons were engaged in a long war of attrition – it lasted forty-three years, apparently – with victory going to one side then the other. This state of affairs continued until the Britons defeated the Saxons at a place called Badon Hill (*Mons Badonicus*).[57]

5. Cadbury Castle in Somerset, one of the many Iron Age hill forts reoccupied in the second half of the fifth century.

The Battle of Badon Hill is celebrated because it is said to have been one of the battles fought by King Arthur. Most people know that 'King' Arthur, with his court at Camelot and his Knights of the Round Table, is a fantasy concocted hundreds of years later by storytellers following in the footsteps of Geoffrey of Monmouth, a mischievous twelfth-century monk. The real Arthur, they will tell you, was actually a rather less exalted figure, a warrior who led the Britons against the Saxons at the turn of the fifth and sixth centuries and won them a temporary reprieve. The evidence for any sort of Arthur, however, king or otherwise, is hopelessly thin and inadequate. The first mention of him that can be reliably dated occurs in a text written in the early ninth century. This source describes Arthur as *dux bellorum* ('leader of battles') and lists a dozen engagements in which he is supposed to have participated, ending with Badon Hill. None of them are locatable and the suspicion is that the whole passage is a literary fiction. It is, of course, impossible to prove that Arthur *didn't* exist, and those who wish to imagine him battling against the Saxons can certainly do so without fear of contradiction. Believing in his existence on the strength of the evidence we have, however, is like insisting that a lost thousand-piece jigsaw puzzle must have been a picture of steam train because one of the three surviving pieces appears to show a puff of smoke.[58]

Arthur or no Arthur, the Battle of Badon Hill marked the end of a period of constant warfare between the Britons and the Saxons. It was, says Gildas, 'pretty much the last defeat of the villains'. It also takes us up to Gildas' own day, for he reveals in passing that he was born in the same year that the battle was fought – without, needless to say, taking the trouble to state which year this was. At a rough guess, based on the few clues in his text, we might suppose it was around the year 500. Since Gildas tells us he had been contemplating the composition of his text for a decade, he was most likely writing in the second quarter of the sixth century.[59]

It was apparently a time of comparative peace – he refers at one point to 'the calm of the present'. But in the same paragraph he laments the state to which Britain has been reduced. 'The cities of our land are not populated even now as they once were; right to the present they are deserted, in ruins, and unkempt.' Archaeology reveals the truth of this statement. Wherever experts have peered under the surface of post-Roman Britain, they have found the same evidence of dereliction and decay. London, Lincoln and York were now ghost towns, with crumbling walls, grass growing tall in the streets, and large areas flooded and returned to marsh.[60]

Having completed his erratic historical review, Gildas turned to his main task, which was to excoriate the current leaders of the Britons, both secular and religious. External wars had stopped, he said, presumably in reference to the end of hostilities with the Saxons, but civil wars were ongoing. Here he must have been referring to conflicts between the various rulers who had emerged in western Britain since the break with Rome. They called themselves kings, explained Gildas, but actually they were tyrants. They plundered and they terrorized, they had multiple wives and concubines, and they loved and rewarded the robbers who sat with them at table. 'They despise the harmless and humble,' he added, 'but exalt to the stars, so far as they can, their military companions, bloody, proud and murderous men.'[61]

To some people in the east of Britain, this all sounded like an excellent idea.

2

WAR-WOLVES AND RING-GIVERS

The Emergence of Kings and Kingdoms

To understand the earliest Anglo-Saxon kings, it is perhaps best to begin with a story about their contemporaries in Scandinavia. Around the start of the sixth century there was a Danish king called Hrothgar, who ruled for many years with great success, but was brought low by a monster that repeatedly attacked his mead-hall and massacred all his men. Eventually, after twelve years of despair and devastation, he and his people were saved by a young hero from the neighbouring land of the Geats, who defeated and killed the monster with his bare hands, and for an encore went on to dispatch its vengeful mother, who lurked in a lair at the bottom of a lake. Such was the hero's amazing prowess that he later became king of the Geats, ruled for fifty years, and died in old age defending his people against a dragon.

As a historical source, this story has the disadvantage of being completely made up – the monsters and the dragon are something of a giveaway. The above is a very bald summary of a long poem, known since at least the eighteenth century by the name of its heroic protagonist, Beowulf. Although set in Scandinavia, it is written in Old English by an anonymous author. It survives in only a single manuscript, badly damaged by a fire in 1731.

From the style of its script we can discern that it was written around the year 1000, but most historians think that the poem itself was composed considerably earlier. Based on its content, it cannot have been written before the middle of the seventh century, and despite lots of robust academic debate in recent decades, the majority view remains that it is probably a product of the eighth century. Given that lay literacy at that time was highly restricted, the likelihood is that it was the work of a priest or a monk.[1]

Early students of *Beowulf* were disappointed that it was preoccupied with monsters and said almost nothing about real historical events or people. Its only apparent link to reality is Beowulf's uncle, King Hygelac, who has been tentatively identified as the man who invaded Frisia around 523, which is how we deduce that the poem is probably set in the sixth century.[2] But these early scholars rather missed the wood for the trees, because while *Beowulf* is all but useless for reconstructing the politics of sixth-century Scandinavia, it is peerless in illuminating the society of the earliest Anglo-Saxon kings and their subjects. It vividly brings to life a world in which kings dwell in great wooden halls, feasting with their followers, drinking mead, and listening to poets harping about the heroes of old; an era of restless warrior bands in search of adventure, and wandering royal exiles, hoping one day to win back their ancestral thrones. They carry swords richly worked with precious metals, to which they give names and ascribe mystical protective powers. They fight against each other for glory, but especially for gold, which they prize above all else. A great lord like Hrothgar will deck the interior of his hall with golden tapestries, and decorate its exterior with a golden roof. He will reward his loyal followers with golden war-gear and gold torques. He will be a giver of gold rings.

Much of this world is already familiar to many of us through the novels of J. R. R. Tolkien, and the films of those novels directed by Peter Jackson. Tolkien was a professor of Anglo-Saxon at Oxford, and made his own translation of *Beowulf* in the early 1920s. Consequently, when he later came to write his famous books, he drew heavily on the poem for inspiration, reworking some of its scenes, borrowing ideas, themes and elements of plot. The people of Rohan in *The Lord of the Rings*, for example, are essentially Anglo-Saxons as Tolkien imagined them. Their king, Theoden, lives in a golden great hall, and the scene in which he receives Gandalf, Aragorn, Gimli and Legolas closely mirrors a similar scene in *Beowulf*. Meanwhile, in *The Hobbit*, Bilbo disturbs Smaug the dragon by stealing a golden cup from his hoard, and the dragon in *Beowulf* is woken by a thief who does exactly the same.[3]

But while Tolkien borrowed much from *Beowulf*, he also drew on other sources of inspiration, not least his own Catholic faith. Characters in his novels therefore exhibit Christian virtues such as pity and forgiveness. There is nothing of this in *Beowulf*. Although the poem is ostensibly Christian – it speaks of a single God, to whom successful characters occasionally give thanks – almost all of the attitudes it celebrates are those of a pagan past. It exalts the loyalty of warriors to their lord, even to the extent of being willing to die for him, and its heroes are overwhelmingly concerned with their earthly renown. When Beowulf, for instance, is fighting against his second monster, it is not faith that sustains him, but belief in his own reputation, and a desire to win everlasting fame. When Hrothgar's hall is attacked, Beowulf says it is better to avenge the dead than indulge in mourning. When one brother kills another, their father is sad, but recognizes that it has been done 'in accordance with the law of the blood-feud'. This is, in short, a highly unstable world, full of betrayal, vengeance and violence – not just because monsters lurk on its cold, windswept fringes, but because of internal disputes that can be resolved only through bloodshed. The kings and warriors crave success, but they know that it will always be fleeting, and that death and destruction is their ultimate fate.[4]

Beowulf is a much better guide to the earliest Anglo-Saxon kings than some seemingly more sober and bona fide sources. Take, for example, Henry of Huntingdon, who wrote *The History of the English* in the early twelfth century. 'Now when the Saxons subjected the land to themselves,' Henry tells us, 'they established seven kings, and imposed names of their own choice on the kingdoms.' He goes on to list these kingdoms in what he implies was their order of creation: Kent, Sussex, Wessex, Essex, East Anglia, Mercia and Northumbria.[5]

It is hard to overstate the enduring impact of this statement. Henry's confident declaration that there were originally seven Anglo-Saxon kingdoms quickly became an established fact, and gave rise in the sixteenth century to the word 'heptarchy', a term that still finds its way into school curriculums today, despite academics suggesting for the past half-century that it should be given a decent burial. Their reason for doing so is that Henry's assertion rests on no authority at all – he simply listed the more prominent kingdoms he found in his early sources. Bede, for example, mentions all seven of the kingdoms listed by Henry, but he also names several more, bringing his own total to around a dozen. And, as we shall see, Bede's total was far from comprehensive.[6]

Another source on which Henry of Huntingdon drew heavily was the *Anglo-Saxon Chronicle* – or *Chronicles*, as some historians prefer. These were initially compiled at the end of the ninth century by scholars working at the court of Alfred the Great, and relate the history of Alfred's kingdom – Wessex – and its neighbours from the earliest times. The compilers presumably drew on older annals and sources that are now lost, for some of the information they record is demonstrably true. Among the entries for the fifth century, for instance, we find dates for the accession of popes, emperors and bishops which are tolerably accurate. Thus the *Chronicle* gives the impression of being a credible source even for the earliest period, and for centuries historians were inclined to treat it as such.

The problem is that the entries for the earliest Anglo-Saxon kings look much less credible. Under the year 449, for example, the *Chronicle* repeats the story told by Bede, about how the

Saxons came to Britain in three ships at the invitation of King
Vortigern, and were led by the brothers Hengist and Horsa. The
Chronicle, though, adds more to the story, describing how Horsa
was subsequently killed in a battle against Vortigern, and how
Hengist became king of Kent. It also provides similar stories, not
mentioned by Bede, about the foundation of other kingdoms.
Sussex, we are told, was founded in 477 when Ælle landed with
his three sons in three ships, killed many Britons and drove the
survivors into the woods. Wessex, meanwhile, was apparently
founded by Cerdic and Cynric, a father-and-son team who beat
the Britons, having also arrived in three ships, or possibly five
– the *Chronicle* is confused on this point and has them arriving
twice, in both 495 and 514.[7]

What the *Chronicle* has to tell us about the origins of the
Anglo-Saxon kingdoms therefore is clearly legendary. In each
case, the founding fathers come to Britain in three ships, and in
two instances they do so in alliterative pairs (Hengist and Horsa,
Cerdic and Cynric). Sometimes they also give their names to
locations associated with their conquests. The place of Cerdic's
landing is said to have been *Cerdicesora*, and the place of Ælle's
landing was *Cymensora*, after his son, Cymen. The *Chronicle* insists
that Portsmouth was named after a certain Saxon warrior called
Port, and the Isle of Wight after Cerdic's kinsman, Wihtgar.
Since we know that both Portsmouth and Wight were place
names current in the Roman period (Portus, Vecta), we can say
with some confidence that the formation actually occurred the
other way round: the personal names were concocted from the
places, and not vice versa.[8]

As well as being inherently implausible, the stories that suggest
Anglo-Saxon kingdoms were being founded from the middle of
the fifth century are flatly contradicted by the archaeological
record. As we've seen, by the end of the century settlers had
formed distinct regional identities as Angles, Saxons and Jutes,
and it is possible that these may represent some sort of political
groupings. But we search in vain within these regions for any
evidence of elites. When we look at the remains of early

settlements, for instance, what we find is all relatively modest. Buildings are either fairly humble halls that look to be residences, or else an even more basic type, constructed over a shallow pit, and hence known to archaeologists as sunken-featured buildings (SFBs); these were probably used as workshops or stores. A typical settlement might therefore resemble the one at West Stow in Suffolk, where such buildings have been excavated and reconstructed. There is nothing on such sites to suggest much in the way of social differentiation.[9]

It seems that the earliest Anglo-Saxon settlers had set themselves up as free, independent farmers. They took – or were granted by whoever was in charge – enough land to support their family, an amount that they called a hide. Bede helpfully describes a hide as 'the land of one family', and its Germanic root, *hiwisc*, implies a married couple. This family would have lots of dependants to help work the land who were not free – slaves, probably in many cases Britons who had remained *in situ* or else been rounded up by their new masters. Such divisions of status seem to be reflected in the earliest cemeteries, in which around half of all adult males were buried with some form of weapon. Since in barbarian societies the bearing of arms was equated with freedom, it seems likely that these were the graves of freemen, or *ceorls*. By implication, those males buried without weapons would have been their slaves.[10]

In the latter part of the sixth century, however, several changes happen at once. From around 570 there is a sudden and dramatic drop in the number of furnished burials, both male and female – enough to suppose that the practice had been deliberately restricted. At the same time, we find a minority of individuals being interred in extremely ostentatious ways, buried with extravagant quantities of costly items under giant mounds of earth. Such barrows burials had been common enough in Bronze Age Britain, but had seldom been carried out in the intervening 1,500 years. Their reintroduction in the late sixth century signalled the emergence of an elite determined to advertise its superiority. Similarly, when we look at the building record, there is a sudden desire on the part of some to build on a much grander scale, constructing dwellings that dwarfed the modest homes of others.[11]

These changes in the archaeological record accord well with the evidence of place names. Among the commonest types of Anglo-Saxon place names are those ending in -ing or -ingham, elements which mean 'the people of' and 'the settlement of the people of'. A place name like 'Reading', for example, means 'Reada's people' in Old English, and similarly 'Wokingham' means 'the settlement of Wocca's people'. In the nineteenth century, and for a long time into the twentieth, scholars were happy to believe that these names had been introduced into the landscape by the earliest Saxon settlers, and that men like Reada and Wocca must simply have been among the first off the boats. It has since been shown, however, that this was an unfounded assumption, because such place names do not coincide with the earliest archaeological evidence of settlement. It now seems likely that the first examples of -ing and -ingham names date to the late sixth century – the same moment we see signs of rapidly rising elites.[12]

This timing might alter the way we think about such names. There is a tendency to picture places ending in -ing as rather cosy communities, living together because of bonds of kinship – little more than extended families. *Beowulf* begins with a brief history of King Hrothgar's people, who are called the Scyldings, after their founding father, Scyld, and it assures us how much they loved their leaders past and present. But it also makes clear that these leaders were lords, and the way they had achieved their dominance was far from benign. Scyld, we are told, had started life as a foundling, but rose to greatness by robbing the halls of others and laying fear upon them, forcing them to pay tribute.[13]

We may suspect that something similar was occurring in late sixth-century Britain, and that men like Reada and Wocca were not necessarily benevolent father figures, but rather men with strong right arms, violent proclivities and boundless greed, asserting control over others, demanding tribute in the form of goods and services. *Ceorls* who had previously been independent, farming their single hides of land, lords of their own little communities of family and slaves, now found themselves bound to contribute to the upkeep of one particular individual or family that was lording it above the rest.

To see what this might mean in practical terms we have to jump forward a century or so to the time of King Ine of Wessex, who ruled from 688, and laid down the law about what his subjects owed him. From every group of ten hides under his rule, Ine expected an annual render of ten vats of honey, 300 loaves of bread, twelve 'ambers' of Welsh ale, thirty of clear ale, two full-grown cows or ten goats, ten geese, ten hens, ten cheeses, an amber of butter, five salmon, twenty pounds of fodder and a hundred eels. The king would have expected this annual render to be delivered to one of the several centres across his domain where he had a dwelling, and presumably the facilities to store it until he and his followers were ready to consume it. We can imagine similar burdens being introduced, to a greater or lesser degree, everywhere in the late sixth century, as ambitious new lords coerced their weaker neighbours into economic and political subservience. And it was from the most successful of these lordships that the earliest kingdoms grew.[14]

If this model is correct, it meant that originally kingship was open to anyone with enough ambition and muscle – even a foundling like Scyld could quickly create a lordship that covered a large territory. And it implies that initially there may have been quite a lot of kingdoms – a good many more than the seven immortalized by Henry of Huntingdon in the twelfth century. A better idea of the plurality of powers in the early Anglo-Saxon period is revealed by a document produced during that time, probably in the late seventh century. It is a list of different peoples, or tribes, each followed by a number of hides: historians today refer to it as the Tribal Hidage. Its purpose is obscure, but it is generally reckoned to have been composed to calculate how much each tribe owed in the way of tribute to some superior lord. Since it includes all of the kingdoms of 'the heptarchy' except for Northumbria, some scholars contend that it must have been drawn up by a Northumbrian king demanding tribute from all the others – a circumstance which would suggest a late seventh-century date.

Whatever it was for, and whoever compiled it, the Tribal Hidage sheds some light on territorial situation at the end of the intensely competitive period in which the Anglo-Saxon kingdoms came into being. We see some tribes that are evidently large and well established: Wessex, assessed at a punitive 100,000 hides; Mercia and East Anglia, both assessed at 30,000; and Kent, pegged a little lower at 15,000. Beneath them are a further six tribes reckoned at 7,000 hides each: the familiar names of Sussex and Essex are found in this group, but so too are the now-forgotten peoples known as the Wrocensætna, Westerna, Lindesfarona and Hwinca. Moving on through the list we find a further six tribes answering for more than a thousand hides each, but a far greater number – seventeen out of a total of thirty-five – are assessed at only a few hundred hides a piece.[15]

The most common assumption is that all kingdoms probably began as such small-scale affairs, and that some had grown larger by bullying others into a state of dependence. Having secured the submission of his neighbours, an ambitious warlord could call upon them to fight in his ranks, enabling him to take on bigger contenders, until eventually he established his supremacy over a wide region. At what stage such a man might start styling himself as 'king' must have varied from case to case. The modern word derives from the Old English *cyning*, meaning something like 'son of the kin'.[16]

It is impossible to say for certain why kings suddenly emerged in the later decades of the sixth century, but the middle decades had been notably catastrophic. Trouble began in 536, when a number of writers noted that something was very wrong with the weather. 'During the whole year,' said the Byzantine historian Procopius, 'the sun gave forth its light without brightness … it seemed exceedingly like the sun in eclipse, for the beams it shed were not clear.' Another Mediterranean writer spoke of a year-long eclipse, and remarked that this led to 'a winter without storms, a spring without mildness, and a summer without heat'. Even the *Anglo-Saxon Chronicle*, generally unreliable as it is for the sixth century, noted two eclipses around this time.[17]

What these writers were all describing was a 'dust-veil' event caused by volcanic eruptions. It was first detected in the data in the early 1980s, but scientists have only recently pinpointed the culprit as a volcano that erupted in Iceland in 536, and then again in 540 and 547. On each occasion it spewed enough ash into the sky to obscure the sun across the whole of the northern hemisphere, causing a dramatic drop in temperatures: recent analysis has identified 536–45 as the coldest decade in the past 2,000 years.[18]

The consequences were obviously calamitous: crops failed everywhere and famine swiftly followed. 'Failure of bread', wrote an Irish annalist in 536, and again in 539. After the famine came bubonic plague. It began in the east, devastating Constantinople in 541, spreading to the western Mediterranean in 542, and eventually reaching Ireland in 544, where it must have torn through a population already weak from hunger. It is extremely unlikely, as some have suggested, that this plague did not also spread to Britain. The communities of south-western Britain, as we have seen, had trading links with the Mediterranean in the early sixth century – the same links that had presumably carried the plague to Ireland – but the high-status sites where Mediterranean artefacts have been found were suddenly abandoned in the mid-sixth century. From this we can reasonably infer, in spite of the absence of documentary evidence, that the Anglo-Saxon communities in the east of Britain must also have been affected. Even if, by some unlikely fluke, they managed to avoid the worst ravages of the disease, they would still have faced the same climate downturn and famine during these terrible decades: you cannot dodge a dust-veil event.[19]

All over the British Isles, across Europe and beyond, populations must have been devastated in the middle years of the sixth century. In Ireland the calamities kept on coming until the mid-570s, with the earlier plague followed by a wave of further epidemics, including smallpox. The unknown factor is how quickly these societies recovered from what one chronicler called 'the great mortality'. The south-west of Britain appears to have been hit very hard and to have remained depopulated for decades, possibly centuries. Other British areas, such as the north-west, seem to have recovered quite quickly, to judge from the archaeological record. Precisely how the Anglo-Saxon communities to the east were affected will probably never be known, but it is hard not to imagine that the shocks of the mid-sixth century could have caused society to be severely shaken and radically reshaped. Acute shortages of food must have led to increased violence, with desperate communities raiding each other. Devastated survivors may have been willing to surrender their independence and submit to the rule of others if that was the only way of guaranteeing their sustenance. (The word 'lord' derives from the Old English *hlaford*, meaning 'loaf-guardian', or 'bread-giver'.) Amid all the death, violence and chaos, there must have been a few individuals who emerged as winners, and were able to turn the desperation of others to their own advantage.[20]

Who were the earliest kings? Is there any way of disentangling myth and reality in the early sections of the *Anglo-Saxon Chronicle*? Here our best guide is once again the Venerable Bede, writing in 731, a century and a half before the *Chronicle* was composed and hence unaffected by its distortions. In a famous passage, Bede provides a list of the most powerful early Anglo-Saxon kings – those who exercised power not only over their own peoples but also over neighbouring rulers. He begins with three kings who, he claims, ruled over the kingdoms of southern Britain, up as far as the River Humber.

The first king in Bede's list is Ælle, king of the South Saxons, or Sussex – the same man that the *Chronicle* has landing in Sussex in 477. As we've seen, the *Chronicle*'s story has all the hallmarks of legend, but Bede's mention of Ælle may indicate that he was indeed a real person. Since we have no archaeological evidence to support the idea that Sussex had kings at such an early date, it may be that Ælle actually ruled at some time around the middle of the sixth century, at the start of the period when kings were beginning to emerge. Beyond that, nothing is known of him.[21]

We are on slightly firmer ground with Ceawlin, king of the West Saxons, or Wessex, who is the second name in Bede's list of southern overlords. Ceawlin appears in the *Chronicle* between 560 and 593, and these dates may give a tolerably accurate indication of the years in which he flourished, even if regnal lists from Wessex suggest his actual reign may have been somewhat shorter. According to the *Chronicle* he was the grandson of Cerdic, the leader who had arrived with three boatloads of followers on the Hampshire coast half a century earlier. This last part is again legendary, and the West Saxons may have had more reason than most for wishing to obfuscate their past, for Cerdic is not a Germanic name. It appears to derive from the British name 'Caradoc', suggesting that the house of Wessex may have had mixed Saxon and British roots. According to Bede the West Saxons had originally been called the Gewisse and, far from landing on the coast of Hampshire, they seem to have been based initially in the upper Thames Valley, where there is abundant archaeological evidence of early Saxon settlement. That was certainly the area where Ceawlin was throwing his weight around in the 570s and 580s, according to the *Chronicle*, 'capturing many villages and countless spoils'. If these annals have any basis in truth, he was driven out of his kingdom in 592 and died the following year.[22]

By this point, if not before, supremacy in southern Britain had passed to King Æthelberht of Kent. We are much better informed about Æthelberht because he was the first Anglo-Saxon ruler to convert to Christianity, which obviously endeared him to the author of the *Ecclesiastical History*. 'He was the third king to rule over all the southern kingdoms,' says Bede, 'but the first to enter the kingdom of Heaven.' Æthelberht's origins, however, are scarcely any better documented than those of his South Saxon and West Saxon predecessors. Bede tells us that the convert king was the son of Eormenric, son of Octa, son of Oisc, and adds that the dynasty was known as the Oiscings. Less credibly, he also informs us that Oisc was the son of Hengist, which is probably the point where reality fuses with legend.[23]

The true origins of the kings of Kent therefore remain a matter of speculation. Bede, as we've seen, asserted that the region had been settled by a people called the Jutes, who came from Jutland in southern Scandinavia, and his statement finds some support in the archaeological record. Grave goods unearthed in the east of the modern county of Kent are quite different from the 'Saxon' items discovered across the rest of southern Britain. At Finglesham, close to the Roman coastal fort at Richborough, some of the earliest barrow burials from the Anglo-Saxon period were found to contain Scandinavian-style gold pendants, many of which bore images of Woden. The name 'Finglesham' derives from the Old English *Pengelsham*, meaning 'prince's settlement', so perhaps the earliest rulers of Kent really did hail from the direction of Jutland.[24]

But the amount of Scandinavian material in these graves was nothing compared to the quantity that came from Gaul – or Francia, as it had become known.[25] The Franks were one of the barbarian peoples who had crossed the Rhine frontier in 406, and by the end of the fifth century they had conquered three-quarters of the old Roman province, establishing a large and powerful kingdom. The practice of building a barrow over a burial chamber was probably introduced to Britain in imitation of their ostentatious precedent. When the Frankish king Childeric died around 481, he was entombed at Tournai with more than eighty kilograms of treasure, including gold coins, gold and garnet jewellery, and a signet ring inscribed with the extremely helpful legend CHILDIRICI REGIS.[26] The emerging kingdom of Kent was clearly heavily influenced by its powerful neighbour across the Channel. King Æthelberht's father, Eormenric, had a Frankish name, and the likeliest explanation for that would be him having a Frankish mother. A long-standing dynastic relationship would also explain how, probably in the late 570s, Æthelberht himself came to be married to a Frankish princess called Bertha.[27]

An important condition of this marriage was that the bride be allowed to practise her own religion. In the course of conquering Gaul the Franks had adopted much of its Roman culture, learning to speak a version of low Latin that eventually became French, and abandoning their pagan gods for Christianity. In order to meet Bertha's spiritual needs, Æthelberht provided her with an ancient church that stood outside the ruined Roman city at the centre of his kingdom. Originally known as Durovernum, it was now referred to as Canterbury (*Cantwara-burh* – 'the stronghold of the Kentish people'). After two centuries of neglect, most of its original street plan was lost under a thick layer of loam and rubble, but new routes had subsequently been cut through the debris to converge on the site of its old theatre, a towering stone structure capable of seating up to 7,000 people. For Æthelberht this may have been Canterbury's main attraction – an ancient arena that could be used for royal ceremonial.[28]

The story of how Æthelberht came to convert to Christianity is a famous one. According to Bede, it began in Rome, with some boys from Britain being brought to market to be sold as slaves. A passing monk named Gregory, struck by their fair complexions and beautiful hair, asked what race they were, and was informed they were Angles. 'Good,' he replied, 'they have the face of angels, and such men should be fellow heirs of the angels in heaven.' The monk went on to become Pope Gregory the Great, and dispatched a mission to Britain with the aim of converting its pagan inhabitants.

As Bede himself recognized, this was only a story, probably much improved by repeated telling. It included other laboured Latin puns besides Angli/*angeli*, and he only inserted it in his history as an afterthought because it was hallowed by long tradition. It may have arisen from one of Gregory's own letters, dated 595, in which he asked a papal official in Gaul to buy some Anglian slave boys so that they could be baptised in Rome and trained as monks. But however Gregory's interest in the pagan Angles was piqued, the following year he put together a mission, headed by a Roman monk named Augustine.[29]

After some prevarication, Augustine and the forty other monks who made up the mission arrived in Kent, probably in the spring of 597, landing on the island of Thanet. As Bede tells the story, their arrival came as a surprise to Æthelberht, who furnished them with supplies but ordered them to stay put. A few days later the king and his leading companions came to meet the newcomers, taking care to do so outdoors, in case they tried to deceive them with any magic. Having listened to them preach, Æthelberht conceded that their religion seemed reasonable, but explained that he could not lightly abandon his existing beliefs. He did, however, grant them a dwelling in Canterbury and licence to preach within his kingdom. For their worship Augustine and his missionaries made use of the church previously given to Queen Bertha, now dedicated to St Martin. (It still stands, rebuilt, but using earlier Roman material.) Very soon they had achieved impressive results. The following year, Pope Gregory was rejoicing in his letters that Augustine had already baptized more than 10,000 of Æthelberht's subjects.[30]

Even allowing for a large amount of papal exaggeration, the fact that the mission had met with any degree of success presupposes that the king himself, despite his initial hesitation, must have been among the first to convert. And who could blame him? 'Almighty God', the pope assured him in a letter of 601, 'raises up certain men to be rulers over nations, in order that he may, by their means, bestow the gifts of righteousness upon all those over whom they are set.' Christianity offered the king not only the promise of future paradise and life everlasting, but the immediate prospect of being elevated above his Anglo-Saxon peers. Rome provided the ideological authority to accompany the cultural and economic clout he already possessed thanks to his Frankish connections. Æthelberht had a Christian queen and a renovated Roman city as his capital. Soon after his conversion he also issued a written law-code, aided by the literate churchmen who now formed part of his entourage, and founded a brand new church (St Augustine's Abbey, outside the walls of Canterbury) where he and Bertha were eventually buried.[31]

Æthelberht also stood above other Anglo-Saxon kings on account of his immense wealth. Gold had been in short supply in Europe since the fall of the western empire, but in the last decades of the sixth century large quantities flowed into Francia from Byzantium (the later name for the eastern empire, which existed for another millennium). Some clearly found its way across the Channel, enabling the king of Kent to become a ring-giver extraordinaire. Being a more ductile metal than silver, gold encouraged the development of a new artistic style. Out went the fragmentary, disembodied animal forms of old, known to scholars as Style I; in came new designs, composed from sinuous, interlaced serpentine creatures, known as Style II – the style we tend to think of as characteristically Anglo-Saxon. The gold brooch, inlaid with glass and garnet, found in a very rich female grave at Kingston Down near Canterbury (colour picture 4), is a particularly fine example of the type, showing the kind of splendour Æthelberht's contemporaries (in this case, perhaps one of his relatives) could afford.[32]

To some degree the distribution of such finds can be used to chart the extent of Kentish royal power. In the last years of the sixth century the archaeology characteristic of the eastern heartlands of the kingdom spread westwards, suggesting that Æthelberht had probably annexed the region beyond the River Medway. His influence may have extended even further. The princely barrow burial at Taplow in Buckinghamshire, excavated in the nineteenth century, contained items so similar in style to those found in Kent that its male occupant has been proposed as a 'Kentish puppet king'. Bede described Æthelberht as a 'very powerful monarch' whose authority stretched as far as the River Humber, and by the end of his reign Kentish fashions had indeed spread over most of southern Britain.[33]

But other evidence suggests Æthelberht's power was in reality more circumscribed. In 601 Gregory the Great, encouraged by the success of Augustine's mission, concocted a plan for the Christianization of the rest of the Anglo-Saxon kingdoms. It involved the creation of two archbishoprics, one in London, another in York, each responsible for superintending a dozen diocesan bishops. Æthelberht's attempts to put it into effect, however, were distinctly limited in their success. He established a bishopric in west Kent at Rochester, reinforcing the impression that he had brought the region under his direct control, and another in London. The ruinous Roman capital lay in the neighbouring kingdom of Essex, and the Kentish king evidently exercised some degree of political influence there, perhaps amounting to overlordship: the king of Essex, Sæberht, was his nephew, and Æthelberht had induced him to convert. For the time being, however, two additional bishops was as far as the pope's ambitious scheme was able to progress, and his command that London be the seat of the archbishop was never fulfilled. Canterbury, Æthelberht's own capital, retained that distinction, with Augustine serving as its first incumbent.[34]

If you wanted to meet a king who was really expanding his authority at the start of the seventh century, it was necessary to venture north of the Humber. 'At this time,' explains Bede, 'Æthelfrith, a very brave king and most eager for glory, was ruling over the kingdom of Northumbria.' There was, in fact, no single Northumbrian kingdom at the moment Bede was describing – the term gained currency only towards the end of the century, and was possibly an invention of Bede himself. But Æthelfrith, whose appetite for power does indeed appear to have been almost insatiable, effectively laid its foundations.[35]

At first his rule was restricted to the kingdom called Bernicia – he succeeded there around the year 592. The earliest Anglo-Saxon settlements in the region appear to have been around the River Tyne, but Æthelfrith's ancestors had soon spread their power along the north-east coast, dominating the areas now known as Northumberland and County Durham. His shadowy grandfather, Ida, was credited by the *Anglo-Saxon Chronicle* with building a fortress on the great rocky outcrop at Bamburgh, the site on which Bamburgh Castle now sits. Bede supplies the unlikely story that it was named after Æthelfrith's first wife, Queen Bebba.[36]

From Bamburgh, Æthelfrith fought and conquered in all directions. In the first instance this was at the expense of the British kingdoms that bordered his own. 'He ravaged the Britons more extensively than any other Anglian ruler', says Bede. The British people immediately to the north of Bernicia, known as the Gododdin, must have been among his first targets, and it may be that the ancient poem *Y Gododdin*, lamenting their defeat at Anglo-Saxon hands, relates to a real event in Æthelfrith's reign. According to Bede, Bernician conquests against the Britons were so sweeping that it caused alarm even in the distant Gaelic kingdom of Dal Riata, in what is now western Scotland, prompting its ruler, Ædan, to march against Æthelfrith 'with an immensely strong army'. The two sides met at the unidentified location of *Degsastan* in 603, where Æthelfrith was again victorious, cutting Ædan's army to pieces and forcing him to flee with only a few survivors.[37]

It was apparently soon after his bloody triumph at *Degsastan* that Æthelfrith turned his attention south and took over the neighbouring Anglo-Saxon kingdom of Deira. Almost nothing is known about its rulers prior to this point, so precisely how Æthelfrith gained control remains a mystery. Some have assumed he did so with characteristic brutality, on the grounds that Deira's previous ruler, Æthelric, appears to have died around the same time. But it might be that the Bernician took power by a more peaceful arrangement, for his second wife, Acha, was the daughter of an earlier Deiran king named Ælle. On balance, however, some form of coercion or aggression on Æthelfrith's part seems likely, since he fell out violently with Ælle's son (and Acha's brother), Eadwine, who was obliged to flee into exile in fear of his life.[38]

After a decade or so of wandering, during which he dodged repeated assassination attempts, Eadwine ended up at the court of Rædwald, king of the East Angles. Soon messengers began arriving from Æthelfrith offering the East Anglian king large sums of money in exchange for ending the life of his house guest, and eventually threatening war if the offer was refused. Rædwald at one point almost succumbed to the pressure, says Bede, but was dissuaded from carrying out such a dishonourable act by his queen. Instead he chose to go on the offensive, raised a large army, and surprised Æthelfrith in battle, catching the northern king before he had time to call up his whole host. They fought on the east bank of the River Idle, a tributary of the Trent, on the border that now divides Yorkshire and Nottinghamshire, and there Æthelfrith was slain.[39]

The fallout from this clash was far-reaching. With Æthelfrith dead, the dynastic tables in Northumbria were reversed: Eadwine returned home to rule both Deira and Bernicia, sending the sons of his erstwhile tormentor into flight. Meanwhile, in the south, victory against such a formidable adversary increased the standing of Eadwine's protector, Rædwald. According to Bede, Rædwald was regarded as the coming man in southern Britain even during the supremacy of Æthelberht, the fabulously wealthy king of Kent. Coincidently, Æthelberht died in 616, the same year that Rædwald won his famous victory at the River Idle, enabling the East Anglian king to assume his place as the pre-eminent southern ruler – the fourth in Bede's list of over-kings.[40]

Our written sources tell us very little about East Anglia and its earliest rulers. According to Bede, Rædwald was the son of Tytil, son of Wuffa, and their dynasty was known as the Wuffings. If later regnal lists can be trusted, Wuffa died in 578 and Tytil in 599, at which point Rædwald's reign must have begun. How much territory they ruled within what is present-day East Anglia is even more of a mystery. The fairly obvious etymology of the county names 'Norfolk' and 'Suffolk' has invited specu-lation that they might reflect a primal division between northern and southern tribes that existed from some early date, but neither name is recorded before the eleventh century. Bede mentions a royal residence at Rendlesham in south-east Suffolk, and archaeology suggests that this may well have been the Wuffings' original zone of operation – a region of winding tidal inlets that had proved readily accessible to the first seaborne settlers.[41]

Like the early kings of Kent, the Wuffings appear to have been caught between two cultural tides. Historically, they looked across the North Sea to Scandinavia, but latterly they had felt the irresistible pull of Frankish power, and the Christianity that went with it. Bede explains that Rædwald had been initiated into the new faith during a visit to Kent – presumably King Æthelberht, in his capacity as overlord, had a hand in trying to convert him. Once he was back home, however, Rædwald's commitment was diluted by his queen and other advisers. Much to Bede's disgust, the king ended up hedging his spiritual bets, with two altars in his temple: one for celebrating the Christian rite, and another on which he continued to offer pagan sacrifices.[42]

But when it came to being buried, Rædwald – or perhaps his more conservative wife and family – swung decisively in favour of tradition. The king appears to have died around 625, at which point the fashion for princely burials was at its peak. In the neighbouring kingdom of Essex, for example, a tomb was created around the start of the seventh century at Prittlewell, now a suburb of the seaside town of Southend. Rediscovered in 2003, its chamber was four metres square, and it had been covered by a mound (long since vanished) that was ten metres in diameter. No body was found inside – it had dissolved over the centuries due to the acidity of the soil from the collapsed barrow – but there was an outstanding array of grave goods, including two small gold crosses that implied that its occupant had embraced Christianity. Given its location, there is a fairly strong case for supposing he was a member of the royal family of Essex who had died around the year 600.[43]

6. A reconstruction drawing of the barrow burial at Prittlewell in Essex.

Essex was very much an also-ran kingdom – even Henry of Huntingdon, who included it in his famous heptarchy, recognized as much. But it was the southern neighbour of East Anglia, and the whole point of burial on such an extravagant scale was competitive display directed at others. When the Wuffings came to bury their own king a few years later, therefore, they determined on something even more spectacular. A few miles downstream from their royal residence at Rendlesham, close to the banks of the River Deben, they had an existing burial ground where earlier members of the dynasty had been cremated and buried in bronze bowls. In Rædwald's case they decided to dig a giant trench, into which they dragged a ship, twenty-seven metres in length. At its centre, in a specially built chamber, they placed their dead king, surrounded by all his finery. They then covered the entire assemblage with soil, raising a mound thirty metres across and perhaps five metres high.[44]

The ship burial at Sutton Hoo, discovered thirteen centuries later in 1939, is sufficiently famous that there is a danger of forgetting the truly exceptional nature of the treasure it contained. But there was a reason the archaeologists who excavated it came away with sweaty palms and in need of a stiff drink. Here for the first time was a hoard that seemed to come direct from the world of *Beowulf*, full of items of such richness that they still dazzle despite their familiarity. The helmet, with its haunting, empty eyeholes, usually attracts the most attention, but some of the smaller items are even more beguiling: the belt buckle is perhaps the finest surviving example of Style II metalwork in existence, a masterpiece woven from gold (colour picture 5). Other items found in the tomb are too numerous to list, but they included all manner of war-gear, including a mail shirt, a sword with a gold pommel and a shield with a gold boss; a vast array of dining equipment, including drinking horns, cauldrons and bowls, and a silver dish that came from Constantinople; and a collection of more personal items, including knives, combs, bottles and a cloak.[45]

Admittedly, we cannot say with absolute certainty that this was Rædwald's treasure – his body was absent, erased by acid like the occupant of the tomb at Prittlewell, and sadly there was no ring with the words RÆDWALDUS REX. Some historians would therefore urge caution and end up sowing doubt. But this remains by far the richest and grandest princely burial ever discovered in Britain, which presupposes it contained not only a king, but a very great one. Given its location we can confidently assume it was a king of East Anglia, and given the presence of coins that date to the mid-620s, we can be fairly certain that it was indeed Rædwald. Sometimes archaeology and history fit together well enough that the most tempting conclusion also happens to be the correct one.[46]

7. The excavation of the Sutton Hoo ship burial in 1939.

Just as the king's body had vanished over time, so too had his ship – its outline was only discernible from the rivets that had held its timbers together. It was the largest ship ever excavated in Europe that pre-dates the viking era, but not the only one discovered at Sutton Hoo. Another mound on the site, sadly robbed of its treasures, was identified in 1998 as a more conventional chamber burial that had been sealed by having a ship placed on top of it – a somewhat smaller vessel measuring twenty metres. If this burial predated the larger and more famous one, it might perhaps have been the tomb of Rædwald's son, Rægenhere, who was killed fighting alongside his father at the Battle of the River Idle. Either way, the practice of using ships to bury the dead was virtually unparalleled in Britain, but was a fairly common practice in Sweden, suggesting that the Wuffings had ancestral connections to that region that they were keen to advertise.[47] It is probably going too far to suggest on the basis of these connections that they were the descendants of Beowulf, and responsible for the transmission of his legendary tale. But the parallels between Sutton Hoo and the famous poem certainly resonate. Although Beowulf himself was burned on a funeral pyre, his remains were interred under a mound 'that sailors could see from afar', and the same must have been true of the mounds that rose beside the Deben at Sutton Hoo. Stronger still are the echoes from the start of the poem, when the dying King Scyld, founding father of the Danish royal house, insists on travelling to the next world by being borne across the sea.

> They stretched out their beloved lord in his boat
> laid out by the mast, amidships,
> the great ring-giver. Far-fetched treasures
> were piled upon him, and precious gear.
> I never heard before of a ship so well furbished
> with battle-tackle, bladed weapons
> and coats of mail. The massed treasure
> was loaded on top of him: it would travel far
> on out into the ocean's sway.[48]

By the time Rædwald sailed to the halls of his ancestors, his power had already been eclipsed by that of his sometime protégé, King Eadwine of Northumbria. In the decade since his accession in 616, the former exile had established himself as the most powerful Anglo-Saxon ruler to date, dominating not only the lands north of the Humber but also those to the south. 'Like none of the Angles before him,' said Bede, 'he held under his sway the whole of Britain, both the Anglian kingdoms and those of the Britons as well.'[49]

This hyperbole encouraged later writers to even greater excess. A ninth-century contributor to the *Anglo-Saxon Chronicle* copied Bede's list of over-kings and dubbed them *bretwaldas*, apparently meaning 'rulers of Britain' (a variant manuscript calls them *brytenwaldas*, meaning 'wide-rulers'.) This led historians in more recent times to argue that *bretwaldas* may have enjoyed some sort of formal status, and perhaps even a degree of institutional power. Bede further encouraged such speculation by describing how Eadwine always had his battle standard carried before him, even in peacetime, when he was riding through the towns and countryside with his entourage. 'Even when he passed through the streets on foot,' Bede added, 'the standard known to the Romans as a *tufa*, and to the Angles as a *tuf*, was borne in front of him.' The fact that the ship-burial at Sutton Hoo was found to contain the remains of such a standard, and also a sceptre, suggested that Eadwine was not alone in comporting himself in this manner.[50]

Few historians nowadays, however, would argue that there was any institutional basis to 'bretwaldaship'. It might have pleased Eadwine and Rædwald to march around with Roman-style banners, but they were merely aping an ancient tradition, not maintaining one. The reality was that there were no rules in this game of thrones, and kings did not defer to other kings out of respect for some universally recognized high office. Compulsion through force was all, and subservience was expressed in the form of tribute.[51]

Tribute could take various forms – gold, for example – but the most common was probably cattle. Cows and oxen had the advantage that they could be driven on the hoof to royal collection centres and kept alive until it was time to kill them. The prime time for doing this was November, so there were fewer animals to feed throughout the winter. As Bede explains in his book *The Reckoning of Time*, the Anglo-Saxons' word for November was 'Blodmonath', 'for it was this month that the cattle which were to be slaughtered were dedicated to the gods'. Kings were expected to take a hands-on role in this ritual, reinforcing the sacral nature of their rule. The axe-hammer found in the royal tomb at Sutton Hoo has recently been reinterpreted as an instrument used for the sacrificial dispatch of a cow or ox with a single blow to the head.[52]

Cattle were a vital commodity for Anglo-Saxon rulers, not just because of their mighty appetite for meat, but because of their abundant need for leather and hides. Leather in particular was required for a vast array of essential items: shoes and boots, bags and purses, bottles and flasks, as well as all manner of equestrian equipment and war gear – saddles, harnesses, straps, scabbards, armour and tents. There was virtually nothing that could not be improved with leather and a great many things that simply could not be made without it. It was, in the memorable phrase of one historian, 'the plastic of the Middle Ages'.[53]

If only because of their need for its by-products, therefore, Anglo-Saxon kings were required to feast on an epic scale. At the start of *Beowulf*, no sooner are we introduced to King Hrothgar than we are told about his hall, Heorot, built to be the wonder of the world: a throne room in which the king could dole out torques and rings, and also a venue for eating, drinking and entertainment. The hall symbolizes the king's power, and when it is ruined by the attack of the monster, Grendel, that power is visibly diminished.[54]

Eadwine had just such a mighty hall at a place called Yeavering. It stood on the northern frontier of his kingdom, twenty miles inland from the fortress at Bamburgh, in the foothills of the Cheviots. Bede informs us that the king had a royal residence there, and happily this is another occasion where history and archaeology touch hands, for the site was identified by an aerial survey in 1949 and subsequently excavated.[55]

The location had clearly been occupied by the kings of Bernicia because of its long-standing political and ritual significance. It sits just below an Iron Age hill fort, the largest in Northumbria, and had been used as a burial ground in prehistoric times. Powerful Anglo-Saxons routinely made use of ancient landscape features in this way, appropriating cult sites and barrows in the hope of inheriting their numinous power. More recently Yeavering had been used by British rulers as a centre for collecting tribute: one of the site's most distinctive features was a raised earthwork that formed a giant enclosure, plausibly interpreted as a place for corralling cattle – over ninety-four per cent of all the animal bones found there were from cows or oxen. It was presumably taken over by Eadwine's predecessor and bête noire, King Æthelfrith, in the course of his expansive wars against the Gododdin, for the earliest buildings on the site appear to have dated from around 600. They included a structure that was devoid of any evidence of habitation but next to a pit filled with the skulls of oxen, suggesting it was a pagan temple used for the kind of ritual killings described above. Excavators also found the footprint of a curious structure shaped like a segment of a Roman amphitheatre, seemingly built with the purpose of seating several hundred people for an outdoor audience with the king.[56]

As for the hall itself, it turned out that several different ones had stood on the site, succeeding each other in turn as they were either destroyed by fire or deliberately demolished. The largest, apparently dated to the reign of Eadwine, was eighty feet long and forty feet wide, and the uniform measurements of its postholes indicated that it had been built with precision. It must have stood very high, as its supporting timbers had been sunk into holes over two metres deep. Some idea of how high it might have risen is suggested by the cauldron found at Sutton Hoo, to which was attached a chain that measured 3.75 metres – the distance, presumably, between the brazier on the floor of Rædwald's hall and the lowest rafters of its roof. A building on this kind of scale indicates that Eadwine, like Hrothgar, was aiming to inspire awe among onlookers.[57]

Impressive as it was, the hall complex at Yeavering was far from unique. Eadwine himself had several others in Bernicia alone, at Sprouston, Doon Hill and presumably Bamburgh, and he must have had several more in Deira. And what was true of Eadwine must also have been true of other Anglo-Saxon kings: halls of similar size have been excavated at Lyminge in Kent and at Cowdery's Down in Hampshire, and another has been identified at Rendlesham. Only a few such halls have been rediscovered, because as wooden buildings they have left little discernible trace. They were by their nature ephemeral structures, as likely to be burned down by accident as by torch-wielding enemies. The Anglo-Saxons knew that their world was transitory. Even as the *Beowulf* poet first describes the splendour of Heorot, he reminds us that it is ultimately doomed to burn. Bede concludes his description of Yeavering by noting that it was abandoned by Eadwine's successors, who built a new hall at nearby Millfield.

It was not merely that individual halls did not last long; the desire to build on such a scale was also short-lived. There is a tendency to imagine, because of their prominence in *Beowulf* and the novels of Tolkien, that such buildings were the normal form of royal residence across the whole Anglo-Saxon period. But from our present perspective they can seem almost a passing fad, beginning around 600 and lasting for little more than half a century. This of course means they coincide closely with the fashion for ostentatious princely burials. Both were manifestations of the same underlying phenomenon, the rise of kings, and the fierce, even desperate competition between them.[58]

The importance of the hall, its protection and its comforts, are evoked in a famous passage in Bede's *Ecclesiastical History*, when one of Eadwine's chief men invites the king to picture himself feasting with his followers in the middle of winter. 'The fire is burning on the hearth in the middle of the hall, and all inside

8. A reconstruction drawing of the great hall at Cowdery's Down in Hampshire.

is warm, while outside wintry storms and snow are raging.' Then suddenly a sparrow flies through the building, in one door and out the other. 'For the few moments that it is inside,' says the king's adviser, 'the storms and tempest cannot touch it, but after the briefest moment of calm, it vanishes from sight, into the wintry world from which it came.' The image was offered to Eadwine as a metaphor for the limits of their understanding. As pagans, all they knew about was man's short life on Earth – what came before, and what came after, was a total mystery. Perhaps, the speaker concluded, they could obtain surer knowledge about these matters if they embraced Christianity.[59]

During the first decade of Eadwine's reign, the Christian mission to Britain had been almost completely snuffed out. As soon as Æthelberht of Kent had died in 616, the other rulers he had persuaded to convert reverted to paganism. (Or, in

Bede's borrowed biblical phrase, 'returned to their vomit'.) In East Anglia, as we've seen, Rædwald was talked out of Christianity by his wife and advisers. King Sæberht of Essex was succeeded by his pagan sons, who grew angry with the bishop of London when he refused to let them eat Communion bread unless they were first baptized, and chased him into exile. Even in Kent itself, the new faith faltered and almost failed. Æthelberht's own son, Eadbald, not only refused to embrace Christianity but, to Bede's disgust, followed the heathen custom of marrying his father's widow (i.e. his stepmother). The bishop of Rochester, like the bishop of London, deserted his post and fled to Francia, and even Augustine's successor as archbishop of Canterbury, Laurence, was ready to do the same, until St Peter appeared to him in a vision and angrily exhorted him to stay put.[60]

It was therefore a small but significant development when Eadwine, by now the most powerful Anglo-Saxon king, married Eadbald's sister, Æthelburh, for she, unlike her brother, had remained a Christian. At some point before 624, like her Frankish mother half a century earlier, the Kentish princess travelled north into a heathen kingdom, accompanied by a Christian priest, on the understanding that she would be allowed to practise her faith. Once the marriage had been celebrated, she and her priest set to work on converting Eadwine, encouraged by exhortations from the pope. 'Illustrious daughter,' said Boniface V in a letter, 'persevere with all your might to soften his hard heart', and enclosed a silver mirror and a gilded ivory comb as gifts for the new queen. In a similar letter to her husband, accompanied by a gold-embroidered robe, Boniface urged the king to destroy the graven images he and his people were currently worshipping. Such an uncompromising stance might seem unlikely to meet with much success, but one of the notable aspects of the Gregorian mission was its pragmatic willingness to accommodate existing rituals. Gregory the Great himself, in a letter of 601, had noted the Anglo-Saxons were 'in the habit of slaughtering much cattle as sacrifices to devils', and suggested that, while the devil-worship would obviously have to go, those who converted ought to be allowed to carry on slaughtering cows and having feasts. So long as they did it in praise of God, let them eat steak.[61]

Whether he was swayed by his wife's words, the pope's gifts, or the reassurance that beef was still on the menu, by 627 Eadwine was ready to take the plunge. At Easter that year he was baptized in York, in a wooden church that had been specially erected for the purpose amid the ruins of the Roman city. The ceremony was performed by the queen's priest, Paulinus, who afterwards became York's first bishop. Other members of the royal family were baptized soon afterwards, as were lots of ordinary Northumbrians. According to Bede, on one occasion Paulinus spent more than a month at Yeavering, immersing people from the surrounding countryside in the River Glen every day from sunrise until sunset. Meanwhile, in York, Eadwine had commissioned a new stone church, dedicated to St Peter, to replace the makeshift one used for his own christening. As Bede ruefully noted, however, its walls had not been raised to their full height before the king was 'slain by a cruel death'.[62]

Eadwine's extensive overlordship meant that he had lots of potential enemies. The year before his baptism, according to Bede, he was nearly killed by an assassin sent by the king of Wessex, who rushed at him with a poisoned sword, wounding him and killing two of his retainers. Once he had recovered, Eadwine had retaliated by leading an army into Wessex and laying it to waste, an action that would have satisfied contemporary expectations of honour and vengeance but done nothing to lessen the likelihood of future reciprocal violence.[63]

In the event the king's nemesis was Cadwallon, ruler of the British kingdom of Gwynedd. Like Æthelfrith before him, Eadwine had evidently made war against the Celtic peoples to his west, for Bede informs us that he had extended his rule to the islands of Man and Anglesey 'which lie between Britain and Ireland, and belong to the Britons'. Anglesey was effectively the offshore granary of mountainous Gwynedd, and its loss must have been a highly damaging blow for Cadwallon. In 633 he sought revenge, invading Northumbria and engaging its king in battle. The two armies met at a place called *Hæthfelth*, usually reckoned to be Hatfield Chase near Doncaster, and there Eadwine was killed on 12 October, dying at the age of forty-seven. With him perished many other Northumbrians, including one of his own sons. His severed head was brought to York and placed in the unfinished church of St Peter.[64]

As Bede remembered with great bitterness, this was merely the beginning of Northumbria's suffering. After his victory Cadwallon raged through the defeated kingdom, 'meaning to eradicate the Angles from the land of Britain'. The widowed Queen Æthelburh and her two young children managed to escape by boat to her family in Kent, along with her sometime priest, Bishop Paulinus, but few others were so lucky, as the invaders spared 'neither women nor innocent infants'. Bede blamed this on Cadwallon's bestial cruelty and barbarism, but in truth the British king's behaviour was probably no different to that of any seventh-century warlord: Eadwine himself must have done much the same when he had harried Wessex a few years earlier. In the world of *Beowulf*, this was the fate people expected after the death of their lord and protector. As Beowulf's body burns on its funeral pyre at the end of poem, a Geat woman sings in despair

> of her worst fears, a wild litany
> of nightmare and lament: her nation invaded,
> enemies on the rampage, bodies in piles,
> slavery and abasement.[65]

As its conqueror, Cadwallon was free to reorder Northumbria as he saw fit, and his first move was to split it in two, breaking apart the thirty-year-old union of Deira and Bernicia. To this end he permitted the sons of Eadwine's predecessor, Æthelfrith, to return from their long exile, and set up the eldest of them, Eanfrith, as Bernicia's new ruler. Deira, meanwhile, lacked a leader after the destruction of Eadwine's family, so the kingship was handed to his cousin, Osric. Neither lasted a year. Given Cadwallon's military dominance he must have expected both men to act as his puppets. The first to resist was Osric, who in the summer of 634 besieged the British king when he was staying in a fortified town – rashly, in Bede's opinion, because his new overlord suddenly rushed out with his army and slaughtered all the besiegers, including Osric. After this, says Bede, Cadwallon simply occupied both kingdoms and ruled them like a tyrant. When Eanfrith came from Bernicia to make peace, the British king had him killed.

Northumbria stood in desperate need of a saviour, and that role was filled by Eanfrith's younger brother, Oswald. The second son of Æthelfrith, Oswald had returned to Bernicia the previous year with the rest of his family, having spent more than half his life in exile. Now around thirty, it fell to him to assume the mantle of leadership and avenge his brother's murder. Bede depicts his clash with Cadwallon as a David-and-Goliath struggle: Oswald advancing at dawn 'with an army small in numbers' against 'the abominable leader of the Britons and the immense force which he boasted was irresistible'. They met near Hadrian's Wall, at a place called Deniseburn, not far from Hexham, and there Oswald's doughty little band defied the odds, killing Cadwallon and vanquishing his army. So miraculous was their victory that the site of battle later became a place of pilgrimage, and was known as Heavenfield.[66]

And so Oswald became the new ruler of Northumbria, reuniting the kingdoms of Bernicia and Deira. (It must have helped that his mother, Acha, had been a member of the Deiran dynasty.) He erased the shame of defeat and devastation at Cadwallon's hands, and restored the northern kingdom to its former glory and primacy. This by itself would probably have been enough to endear him to Bede, but the historian was particularly delighted that Oswald was a Christian, having converted during his time in exile. (His older brother, Eanfrith, had done the same, but then despicably reverted to paganism.) Bede names Oswald as the sixth in his line of overlords, and enthused that 'although he wielded supreme power over the whole island, he was always wonderfully humble, kind and generous to the poor and to strangers'.[67]

This was pure hagiography on Bede's part: in reality Oswald must have been no less ruthless and bloodthirsty than any other *bretwalda*. In discussing the fate, for example, of the young children who had fled into exile with Queen Æthelburh – her own son, Uscrea, and Eadwine's grandson, Yffi – Bede reveals that the queen subsequently sent them across the Channel to her family in Francia, 'fearing King Oswald' – the implication evidently being that the Northumbrian king would not have hesitated to have these children killed. Nor was Oswald any less violent as a conqueror than his predecessors. Although Bede makes no mention of it, we know from Irish annals that the king expanded his power northwards as far as the Firth of Forth, destroying the Gododdin and seizing their fortress at Edinburgh. He also made war on his southern neighbours, invading the Anglo-Saxon kingdom of Lindsey (Lincolnshire) where, as Bede cannot help admitting, he was long-despised by the locals. Like his tyrannical father before him, Oswald carried war and destruction in all directions, and was merciless in his pursuit of his enemies. It was no surprise, therefore, that he should eventually come to blows with Penda, the king of Mercia.[68]

Mercia was the last of the major Anglo-Saxon kingdoms to emerge. Its name comes from the Old English *mierce*, and equates to the later word 'march', indicating that the Mercians were at first a border people, dwelling on the frontier between the Anglian kingdoms in the east and the British ones to the west. Bede informs us that their kingdom was divided by the River Trent, and archaeologists have found lots of early pagan cemeteries along the Middle Trent Valley, albeit later and poorer than ones found elsewhere. To judge from the subsequent importance of Tamworth and Lichfield as royal centres, the kingdom's heartlands were probably in the vicinity of these places.[69]

As for King Penda, all we know about his ancestry comes from an eighth-century genealogy of dubious worth. He was said to be the son of Pybba, and their dynasty was apparently descended from the more distant Icel. Penda himself was the first of their line to leave his mark on history and was clearly the man who transformed the Mercians from being a marginal people into what was for a long time the mightiest Anglo-Saxon kingdom of all. His reign may have begun as early as 626: the *Anglo-Saxon Chronicle* noted his arrival that year, and two years later recorded a battle between Mercia and Wessex after which their rulers 'came to terms' – almost certainly a euphemistic way of describing a defeat at Penda's hands. Five years later he impressed himself on the collective memory of the Northumbrians as the junior partner of their British conqueror, Cadwallon, fighting along-side him at the Battle of Hatfield and participating in the devastation of Northumbria that followed. Bede, reserving most of his vitriol for Cadwallon, dismissed the Mercians as ignorant idolaters, but nonetheless noted that Penda was 'exceptionally gifted as a warrior'.[70]

What became of Penda after Cadwallon's destruction by Oswald the following year is uncertain. The fall of his ally and the restoration of Northumbrian power must have arrested the Mercian ruler's rise and perhaps even temporarily reversed it. We cannot say, therefore, why Oswald and Penda subsequently locked horns, beyond a long-standing mutual hostility. Bede says they clashed at a place called Maserfelth, which is traditionally said to be Oswestry in Shropshire. If true, this would indicate that Oswald was operating well beyond his own borders and suggest he was the aggressor, perhaps hoping to revenge himself on a weakened Mercian king. But the identification of Maserfelth as Oswestry was not made until the twelfth century, allowing plenty of room for doubt. It may have been that Penda was already restored to his former power and was menacing Oswald somewhere closer to home. Wherever it took place, the great battle that was fought between them was decisive. Oswald was killed and then, on Penda's orders, ritually dismembered. Just as Beowulf proudly displayed the severed arm of Grendel after vanquishing the monster, so the pagan Mercian king celebrated his victory by chopping off his opponent's head and hands and hanging them on stakes.[71]

Penda's bloody triumph must have made him the most feared and powerful ruler in Britain. Bede, writing eighty years later, could get away with refusing to acknowledge this superiority, but those who did so at the time quickly came to regret it. Cenwalh, for instance, who became king of Wessex around the time of Maserfelth, was initially married to Penda's sister, but then repudiated her so he could marry someone else. The Mercian king avenged this affront to his family's honour by invading Wessex and deposing Cenwalh, who was forced to flee into exile in East Anglia. There was little love lost between the Mercians and their East Anglian neighbours: Penda had already invaded the eastern kingdom once and killed two of its kings, and a few years after Cenwalh's flight he did so again, slaying a third East Anglian ruler. Despite Bede's determination not to include him in his list of overlords, Penda was undoubtedly the most brutal and successful warlord of his age.[72]

His relationship with the kings of Northumbria, by contrast, may have been somewhat better than expected. Bede, it is true, describes two further occasions on which the Mercian ruler devastated the northern kingdom, the first of which probably occurred in the immediate wake of Maserfelth. It saw him advance as far as Bamburgh, which he would have burned to the ground by means of a massive bonfire, had a providential wind not driven the flames in the opposite direction. Penda also capitalized on his victory, like Cadwallon before him, by splitting Northumbria in two: Bernicia passed to Oswald's younger brother, Oswiu, while Deira was given to a kinsman of the late King Eadwine. Significantly, however, after rearranging Northumbria to his liking, Penda sought to improve relations with its new rulers by orchestrating a pair of royal weddings: his son married one of Oswiu's daughters, and one of his daughters was married to

Oswiu's son. This second match took place in 653, indicating that relations between Mercia and Northumbria may have been warily cordial for as much as a decade.[73]

We do not know what caused them to collapse so spectacularly during the two years that followed, but in 655 Penda was once again on the warpath, devastating Northumbria for a third time. The army he led on this occasion was truly massive, and shows just how powerful he had become in southern Britain. Bede says it contained the legions of thirty other leaders, a number reminiscent in scale of the thirty-four peoples listed in the Tribal Hidage. Some of these leaders were other kings: one was the new king of East Anglia, no doubt mindful that resisting Penda's will had cost his three immediate predecessors their lives. If ninth-century sources are to be believed, the Mercian also had British kings marching behind his banner.[74]

It seems that this enormous host ravaged all the way across Northumbria to its northern frontier on the Firth of Forth before its beleaguered king finally came to Penda in search of terms. 'Oswiu was at last forced to promise him an incalculable and incredible store of royal treasures and gifts as the price of peace,' says Bede, 'on condition that he would return home and cease to devastate.' Although Bede was at pains to deny it, it seems likely that Penda must have accepted this offer, for he had retraced his steps to somewhere in the vicinity of Leeds when, on 15 November, Oswiu unexpectedly fell upon his army. The two sides fought on the banks of a river that Bede names as the Winwæd, which gave its name to the battle. As with Heavenfield a generation earlier, Bede stresses the smallness of the Northumbrian force compared to the combined immensity of their foes, so as to render their eventual victory all the more heroic and miraculous. 'The heathens were put to flight or destroyed', he rejoiced, noting that the river had burst its banks due to heavy rains, so that more men drowned while fleeing than were cut down during the actual fighting. Many of the southern kings in Penda's army were among those killed, including the great Mercian leader himself. Bede depicts it as a glorious Christian victory, but nonetheless reveals that Oswiu celebrated by cutting off Penda's head, presumably in revenge for the earlier dismembering of his brother Oswald. We do not know whether it ended up similarly impaled on a stake.[75]

Penda's passing marked the end of an era. He was, in the words of one modern historian, 'the last great pagan king of Anglo-Saxon England'. By the time of his death the royal dynasties of Kent, Wessex, East Anglia and Northumbria had committed to Christianity decisively, and it was only the small-fry kings of Sussex and Essex who wavered for another generation. Bede recognized that Penda's destruction was a watershed moment, not only because it freed Northumbria from his depredations, but because it also enabled the Mercians to become Christian. The rapid progress of Christianity in the second half of the seventh century coincided with a sharp decline in the princely barrow burials and huge mead-halls, as the Church provided new ways for rulers to monumentalize their power.[76]

Before we part company with Penda, however, one question remains. What became of the 'incalculable and incredible' treasure he was offered by Oswiu? Bede says that the Mercian king refused to accept it because he wanted to destroy Northumbria completely, but Bede was not above altering the facts when it suited, and the suspicion is that he did so here, so as to acquit Oswiu of the charge of attacking a man with whom he had just made peace. According to the ninth-century *History of the Britons*, Penda *did* accept the treasure, and went on to distribute it among his British allies.[77]

In 2009, a metal-detectorist named Terry Herbert made an astonishing discovery in a field in the Staffordshire village of Hammerwich – a hoard of Anglo-Saxon treasure containing over five kilograms of gold items and about a third of that weight in silver, making it the largest such hoard ever discovered (colour picture 6). Unusually, nothing within it was feminine jewellery – it consisted almost entirely of war gear, or rather the parts of war gear that were made from precious metal. They included a fragmented gold helmet, and the gold, silver and garnet fittings of almost a hundred swords. Every piece was of the very finest quality, decorated with Style II designs of interlaced animals, exhibiting the kind of craftsmanship that could have been obtained only by the highest members of the elite. The few non-military items in the hoard were objects of Christian devotion: some crumpled gold crosses, parts of a shrine, and a gold strip with the biblical inscription, 'Rise up, Lord, and may your enemies be dispersed, and those who hate you flee from your face.'

Could the Staffordshire Hoard, as it immediately became known, have been part of the peace offering handed over to Penda in 655? It is certainly the right style and period, dated to between 650 and 675, with marked similarities to other items of precious metalwork from early Christian Northumbria. If this wasn't the war gear of Oswiu and his fellow warriors, it is exactly what their war gear would have looked like. The place of the hoard's discovery is also highly suggestive, for Hammerwich lies in the very heart of Mercia, just a few miles from Lichfield.[78]

Sadly, of course, for all the tantalizing possibilities the treasure presents, we will never be able to say for sure where it came from. Nor will we ever know why it was buried. Was it carried from the battlefield at Winwæd by one of the few Mercian warlords fortunate enough to escape? Was it subsequently secreted because of some later threat, with the hope of future recovery? Or was it perhaps consigned to the ground in circumstances like those described in *Beowulf*, when an unnamed individual, the last survivor of a vanquished race, buries their treasure with words of despair, intending that it should be forgotten?

> Now, earth, hold what earls once held
> and heroes can no more; it was mined from you first
> by honourable men. My own people
> have been ruined in war; one by one
> they went down to death, looked their last
> on sweet life in the hall.[79]

3

GOD'S CHOSEN INSTRUMENT

St Wilfrid and the Establishment of Christianity

There are few places in Britain where you can stand in a room that has remained essentially unchanged since the seventh century. For this reason alone, the Northumbrian town of Hexham is well worth a visit. It lies roughly halfway between Carlisle and Newcastle, just to the south of the River Tyne, about thirty miles from where the river runs into the sea. To the modern visitor, accustomed to the distorting gravitational pull of London, this might make it seem fairly remote, but to a person living in seventh-century Northumbria, it lay at the very heart of a powerful and expanding kingdom.

Back then, Hexham's architectural glory was its abbey church, and that remains the case today. In the intervening 1,300 years it has been rebuilt several times – most recently at the start of the twentieth century, when its late medieval nave was heavily restored. In the centre of the nave, however, behind a modern wooden gate, is an opening in the floor, from which a dozen steps descend. At the foot of this narrow stairwell is a tiny antechamber, and beyond that, a small, windowless room, only thirteen feet long and eight feet wide. Now evenly illuminated by electric light, it would originally have been lit by flickering lamps placed in the two niches in the walls on either side.

This is the crypt of the Anglo-Saxon church (colour picture 8). It was created in the 670s, and it brings us as close as is physically possible to the world of its creator, St Wilfrid.

Wilfrid was one of the towering figures of his age, if not the whole Anglo-Saxon period. Born into a well-connected Northumbrian family, he rose through the ranks of the Church to become, for a time, the most powerful bishop in Britain. At certain points his authority extended not only over Northumbria itself but also over the Pictish lands to the north and the other Anglo-Saxon kingdoms to the south. He was a figure of enormous controversy, whose behaviour was on many occasions far removed from what is typically regarded as saintly. He founded scores of churches and converted many thousands of people, but was quite happy to see Christianity imposed by bloody conquest. While other churchmen strove for humility, Wilfrid comported himself like a king, revelling in the pomp of his position, feasting and drinking on a grand scale, surrounded by a large household of young warriors. As such he clashed with his ecclesiastical peers, who had different ideas about how bishops should behave, and with actual kings, who regarded him as a threat to their own authority. His quarrels with consecutive kings of Northumbria led to long periods of exile, and multiple trips to Rome, during which he battled against angry pagan mobs and dodged assassination attempts by fellow Christians. In some respects his career resembles that of another turbulent priest, Thomas Becket, but whereas Becket's story famously ended in martyrdom, Wilfrid outlived all his rivals and died at an advanced age, surrounded by his adoring acolytes. As a consequence, he is far less famous today, which is a pity, for his long and dramatic life reveals all the themes, ideas, personalities and conflicts during the crucial period in which the Anglo-Saxons converted to Christianity. It is a story worth telling from beginning to end.

A biographical treatment of Wilfrid is made possible by the fact that a contemporary account of his life has survived. Written after his death by one of his supporters, Stephen of Ripon, the *Life of Wilfrid* is a work no less controversial than its subject, clearly intended to refute or else to gloss over the allegations of misconduct made by the bishop's many critics. As such it is more like a piece of political propaganda than a work of conventional hagiography, and has to be read against the grain. That said, it provides an invaluable alternative narrative to the one supplied by Bede, and helps to give a fuller, rather less roseate picture of seventh-century Britain.

A towering figure like Wilfrid necessarily demanded towering buildings. The crypt at Hexham may be modest, but it was intended only as an inner sanctum, for the display and worship of holy relics. The church that stood above it was altogether bigger, probably over a hundred feet long, large enough to rival the great hall of any seventh-century king. And while secular halls were built from perishable timber, Wilfrid's churches were fashioned in permanent stone, intended to last for eternity. In Hexham's case, the stone was sourced from various Roman sites along the Tyne Valley: altogether, his continental masons recycled something like 7,000 tonnes for its construction. The bishop's biographer thought there was nothing like it north of the Alps, and described it as a 'vast structure', with 'walls of remarkable height', foundations of great depth, and 'crypts of beautifully dressed stone'.[1]

Wilfrid was born in 634, amid scenes of conflagration. According to Stephen of Ripon, the house in which the future bishop was delivered burst into flames at that very moment, a disaster which the biographer retrospectively interpreted as a fiery visitation of the Holy Spirit. It was in any case a particularly perilous time to be a newborn Northumbrian, for the kingdom had recently been invaded by the British ruler, Cadwallon, whom Bede accuses of massacring mothers and infants. As we've seen, Cadwallon also killed Northumbria's first Christian king, Eadwine, and caused his widow and children to flee to Kent, along with Paulinus, the first bishop of York. The situation was retrieved only by the return of Oswald, the son of Eadwine's predecessor, who slaughtered Cadwallon in battle that same year at Heavenfield, and went on to become Northumbria's new king. Bede regarded this as a providential victory, for Oswald was a Christian, who erected a cross on the site of the battle, and was later venerated as a saint. Oswald, however, had not been converted by the Roman missionaries, like Paulinus, who had landed in Kent with St Augustine almost forty years earlier. He had been baptized during his long years in exile, which he had spent among the Irish.[2]

Christianity had been introduced to Ireland during the fifth century by missionaries from the remnant of the Roman Empire in western Britain – the most famous being St Patrick. Its success in the first instance was limited by the nature of Irish society. Elsewhere in Europe the new religion had spread using the apparatus of the Roman state, with bishops establishing themselves in cities and towns, but Ireland had never been part of the empire, and had no such urban centres, so its bishops had no obvious locations in which to base their activities.

Towards the end of the fifth century, however, and especially during the sixth, a new form of organized Christianity began to flourish in the west of the British Isles. We are so accustomed to thinking of monasteries as ancient, crumbling and ivy-covered, it is hard to imagine a time when they were a new phenomenon, but in sixth-century Britain and Ireland, they were exactly that, and monasticism was an alluring, alternative lifestyle. The trend – craze, even – had begun in third-century Egypt, where some Christians had voluntarily retreated into the desert, in order to escape persecution, temptation, or reality, intending to lead a life of contemplation, hopeful that it would bring them closer to God. The earliest pioneers lived as hermits, and were hence known as monks (from the Greek, *monos*). Soon, however, many of them decided it was more convenient to live in communities, under the rule of a father figure, or abbot (from *abba*, Aramaic for father).

From Egypt the practice had spread westwards across the empire, reaching Gaul by the late fourth century and the Christian parts of the British Isles by the end of the fifth century. By the middle of the sixth century it was already extremely popular. In Ireland in particular, monasticism sat more comfortably with a non-urban society than the episcopal traditions that had been introduced by the earliest Christian missionaries. In their search for solitude, Irish monks often set themselves up on islands off the mainland. One monastery that may have existed as early as the sixth century was that founded on Skellig Michael, an island seven miles off the coast of Kerry, now best known as the location of Luke Skywalker's retirement. Its surviving stone huts give a good idea of the austere conditions in which early Irish monks existed.[3]

At the same time that monasticism was making great headway in Ireland, the Irish were starting to colonize the western seaboard of what is now Scotland, creating a new kingdom called Dal Riata – a maritime empire that spread across the North Channel, and included hundreds of tiny islands and craggy peninsulas. It was on one such island, a dot in the sea called Iona, that a well-connected Irishman named Columba founded a new monastic community in 563 with the blessing of Dal Riata's rulers. Soon it became the pre-eminent Christian centre in the kingdom, a base from which other monasteries were founded, and a destination for pilgrims and penitents.[4]

It was to Dal Riata that Oswald's family had fled when he was in his early teens. During his seventeen-year stay in the kingdom he had learned to speak Irish and converted to Christianity, probably being baptized on Iona. Unsurprisingly, therefore, once he had returned to Northumbria in 634 and found he needed to replace the churchmen who had fled the previous year, he looked to his own spiritual alma mater rather than to distant Canterbury. Immediately after his accession, he sent to Iona requesting a new pastor for his people, and received in return a monk named Aidan, who became Northumbria's new bishop. Aidan, raised in the Irish tradition, had no desire to reside, like his predecessor, in the old Roman city of York, and so the new stone church that Paulinus had begun to build there was abandoned. The new bishop instead sought out an island on which he might found a monastery, and settled on Lindisfarne, just off the Northumbrian coast, but conveniently close to Oswald's royal palace at Bamburgh. Here he raised a church in the modest Irish manner, with walls of wood and a roof of reeds.[5]

9. An aerial view of Lindisfarne. The abbey is situated on the island's south-western tip, to the left of the cluster of buildings.

As the fledgling community at Lindisfarne grew, so too did the young Wilfrid. As a boy, says his biographer, he was handsome, well proportioned, gentle, modest, self-controlled and sensible. We are told next to nothing about his parents, but his father was of sufficient status to rub shoulders with Northumbrian noblemen, on whom Wilfrid waited when they came to visit. These connections were enough to secure the boy an opening at the court of Oswald's successor, King Oswiu, and at the age of fourteen he was presented to Oswiu's queen, Eanflæd. His biographer would have us believe that Wilfrid was already determined on a career in the Church by this point, which may well be true, but we are also informed that he left home because his stepmother was cruel, and that he set out for court not only well dressed but also armed and mounted, so there is room for doubt. Perhaps it was Eanflæd, a pious Christian herself, who pointed him in a more contemplative direction. Whatever the case, it was she who assigned Wilfrid the job of assisting one of the king's companions, Cudda, who had somehow become paralysed, and intended to spend the rest of his days living as a monk on Lindisfarne.

So, in the late 640s, the teenaged Wilfrid found himself living on a small island in the North Sea, attending to the needs of the disabled Cudda, and no doubt thinking that life might be marginally more exciting. During this time he also learned the fundamentals of the Christian faith, reading and memorizing texts that probably fired his enthusiasm to be elsewhere. After a year or two on Lindisfarne, he announced his wish to visit Rome. Around 650, with the blessing of his master and the sponsorship of Queen Eanflæd, he set out. Eanflæd sent him in the first instance to the court of her cousin, the king of Kent, with instructions that he was to remain there until a suitable travelling companion could be found. Eventually, after a year of 'tedious waiting', Wilfrid was paired with another pious young Northumbrian named Biscop Baducing, with whom he crossed the Channel and continued his journey.[6]

When they reached Lyon in southern Francia, the pair parted company, Biscop continuing towards Rome, Wilfrid for a while staying put. Lyon was an attractive Roman city, far larger than anything a first-time traveller from Britain would have previously experienced, and its archbishop, Annemund, was keen for Wilfrid to extend his stay indefinitely. According to Stephen of Ripon, the archbishop took such a shine to his new house guest that he offered him a large province to govern and his niece's hand in marriage. Such an offer implies that Wilfrid must have spent a considerable period in Annemund's company demonstrating his worthiness, and underlines the fact that despite his time on Lindisfarne he had not yet been tonsured as a monk – the possibility of a secular career was still open to him. Wilfrid decided to decline the archbishop's generous proposal and pressed on with his pilgrimage. It was perhaps around 653 that he finally arrived in Rome.[7]

It is hard to imagine the impact that a visit to Rome must have had on an impressionable young mind that until recently had known only Northumbria. The 'eternal city' was nowhere near as large as it had been at its peak in the second century when that phrase was first coined, and perhaps a million citizens had jostled in its crowded streets and piazzas. Since the empire's collapse its population had plummeted, and probably stood at no more than 100,000 people at the time of Wilfrid's visit. But to a boy from Britain, where no towns or cities had survived the fall, and even the largest communities were reckoned only in hundreds, Rome must have seemed a teeming metropolis. And even though the number of inhabitants had dwindled, the architecture remained. The city was surrounded by twenty-two miles of walls, within which the monuments of its imperial heyday still stood, ruinous in places, intact in others, awesome in every instance. A visitor in the seventh century could still see triumphal arches, baths, palaces, theatres, bridges, aqueducts and fountains, many of which have now vanished, as well as those monuments that still stand today, such as Trajan's Column, or the Mausoleum of Hadrian. During his stay in Kent Wilfrid would have doubtless seen Canterbury's Roman theatre, which could seat perhaps 7,000 people. In Rome he would have seen the Colosseum, capable of holding an audience ten times as large.[8]

Impressive as these relics of empire were, Wilfrid had come to Rome because of its more recent emergence as the headquarters of Christianity. The city was filled with untold numbers of churches and chapels, which he spent every day visiting to pray at their shrines. The largest and most important was St Peter's, the great basilica built by Constantine the Great in the early fourth century, 350 feet long and able to accommodate around 3,000 worshippers. Peter, the first apostle, was also said to have been Rome's first bishop, and his successors had therefore always claimed a certain pre-eminence, though it was not until the late fourth century that they started styling themselves as 'pope' (*papa*). Gregory the Great's project to convert the pagan Anglo-Saxons at the end of the sixth century had bolstered that claim and raised the prestige of the papacy, but even then the bishops of Rome still had equally prestigious and ancient rivals in the east, at Alexandria, Antioch and Jerusalem. Only fifteen or so years before Wilfrid's arrival, however, these Byzantine cities had been conquered by the armies of Islam, leaving the authority of Rome in the Christian west unchallenged.[9]

After several months of patient waiting, Wilfrid at last gained a papal audience. During his daily visits to churches and shrines he had befriended an archdeacon, Boniface, who became his mentor, making him learn the Gospels by heart and instructing him in matters of law and doctrine. Eventually Boniface was able to present his young protégé to St Peter's successor, probably at the Lateran palace, another architectural wonder that had been donated to the papacy by Constantine. Pope Martin I placed his hand on Wilfrid's head, said a prayer and blessed him, sending him away in the peace of Christ. Wilfrid gathered up the relics he had collected during his stay and retraced his steps to Lyon.[10]

His visit to Rome had a profound and lasting impact on Wilfrid, exposing him to a form of Christianity that was a world away from the kind he had experienced on Lindisfarne. This was most obviously true in the contrast between thatched wooden churches and soaring stone basilicas, but it also applied to matters of religious practice and even points of doctrine. Irish monks, for example, had a form of tonsure which seems to have involved shaving the back of the head, whereas in Rome the top of the head was shaved, leaving a circle of hair in the shape of Christ's crown of thorns. Back in Lyon, Wilfrid asked Archbishop Annemund to tonsure him in the Roman manner. He was now convinced of his monastic vocation, and committed to Roman orthodoxy.[11]

Wilfrid was also heavily influenced by the behaviour and bearing of continental bishops. Irish bishops advertised their humility by walking almost everywhere. Bede tells us that when Bishop Aidan of Northumbria was given a splendid horse by the king, he almost immediately gave it away to a beggar. On the Continent, bishops did not spurn such creature comforts, and regarded splendour as an essential prerequisite of their public role. In Gaul, it was the bishops who had in many cases filled the political vacuum created by the collapse of Roman civil authority. They were not simply spiritual advisers to secular rulers, or even administrators. Often they themselves were rulers, defending their cities during sieges, and sometimes called upon to lead armies. They therefore took expensive horses as their due, along with palaces, households of warriors, wide estates, and well-stocked wine cellars. A bishop like Annemund evidently had the power to offer a young pilgrim from Northumbria his own province to govern, and he reportedly promised to make Wilfrid his successor after the latter's return from Rome. Wilfrid clearly found this a seductive proposition, for he remained in Lyon for the next three years.[12]

The downside for bishops who wielded as much political power as Annemund was that it occasionally landed them in the soup. In the later 650s, the archbishop was one of several prelates who clashed with Bathilde, queen of King Clovis II, and as a result ended up being executed. According to Stephen of Ripon, Wilfrid accompanied Annemund to his trial and was apparently ready to join him in his martyrdom, but was spared on account of his foreign origins. With his glittering prospects in Lyon gone, Wilfrid packed up his Roman relics and made his way home to Britain.[13]

Much had changed in his absence. In the first place, the Roman mission of St Augustine had come to an unofficial end with the death of the last of the saint's companions, Honorius, in 653.

Honorius had been archbishop of Canterbury for twenty-six years, and it had taken eighteen months to find a suitable replacement. Secondly, and partly as a consequence of Canterbury's eclipse, the influence of Lindisfarne had spread far beyond the confines of Northumbria. Bishop Aidan's successor, Finan, soon found himself called upon to baptize rulers from neighbouring kingdoms. At some point before 655 King Sigeberht of Essex had journeyed north to be christened in a ceremony near Hadrian's Wall, as had Peada, king of the Middle Angles, son of Penda of Mercia. A short while later Penda himself, the great pagan overlord of most of Britain, had perished in battle at Winwæd, enabling the conversion of Mercia to begin in earnest. Missionaries from Lindisfarne moved swiftly into all three kingdoms. Bede describes how one of their number, Cedd, was appointed as the new bishop of Essex, and began preaching, baptizing and building churches, the most important of which was the one he founded in an abandoned Roman coastal fort at Bradwell-on-Sea. Remarkably, it stands intact today and is still used for worship (colour picture 9).[14]

Wilfrid, with his new-found zeal for all things Roman, now saw much at fault with Lindisfarne's form of Christianity, and can only have viewed these developments with disdain. It was probably for this reason that on his return to Britain he seems to have gone in the first instance to Wessex, where the Church had both a strong Roman tradition and close connections with Francia. Its first bishop, Birinus, was a Frank who had arrived in the 630s as a Roman missionary and established his episcopal seat at Dorchester. His successor, Agilbert, who was also Frankish, now took Wilfrid under his wing. Wilfrid's intention, supported by Agilbert, was evidently to return to Northumbria and eradicate Irish customs in favour of Roman ones. The problem was how to achieve this while Northumbria was ruled by King Oswiu, who was just as attached to Irish traditions as his late brother Oswald had been. The solution was found by introducing Wilfrid to the king of Wessex, Cenwalh, who in turn recommended him to his friend Alchfrith.[15]

Alchfrith was King Oswiu's eldest son, and a king in his own right – Oswiu had made him the ruler of the southern part of Northumbria, the former kingdom of Deira. Like many an heir apparent throughout history, he did not always see eye to eye with his father, and their fractious relationship provided Wilfrid with the entree he needed. On Cenwalh's recommendation, Alchfrith summoned the well-travelled monk before him and quizzed him about the mysteries of the Roman Church. Such was Wilfrid's eloquence that the young king was immediately won over, and the two of them soon became firm friends.

The most visible demonstration of Alchfrith's enthusiasm for Wilfrid's cause was his gift to him of the monastery of Ripon, which came with a generous endowment of forty hides of land. The *Life of Wilfrid* enthuses about the size of the king's grant and all the wonderful works of charity that Wilfrid was able to carry out as a result, but fails to mention that Ripon had previously been given to some monks from Lindisfarne, who were unceremoniously evicted on Wilfrid's arrival and replaced with new recruits willing to adhere to his preferred Roman standards. In the early days of monasticism there were no universally recognized rules, and individual abbots were free to devise their own regimes, leading to a great deal of variety. But one of the most popular in Roman circles was the rule devised in the sixth century by the Italian abbot Benedict of Nursia, and it was this Benedictine Rule that Wilfrid introduced to Ripon.[16]

With Wilfrid installed in Northumbria, and his enthusiastic promotion by Alchfrith, a clash with Lindisfarne was inevitable. There were many differences of style and behaviour between the Roman and Celtic traditions, from their tonsures to their feelings about the use of horses, but there were also crucial differences when it came to doctrine. The most important of these doctrinal differences concerned the celebration of Easter.

Surprisingly, perhaps, the argument had nothing to do with the use of the word 'Easter' itself to refer to the festival of Christ's resurrection. Everywhere else in Christendom at this date used a variant of the word 'Pascha', the Aramaic for Passover, the Jewish festival on which Christ had been executed. But, as Bede explains in his book *The Reckoning of Time*, the Anglo-Saxons had always called the fourth month of the year 'Eostremonath', after a pagan goddess named Eostre, and persisted in using that name to refer to the new Christian ritual.[17]

In the seventh century, the controversy surrounding Easter turned on the question of when it should be celebrated. Passover began on the fourteenth day of the Jewish month of Nisan, which meant it could fall on any day of the week. By the fourth century, however, Christian theologians had decided that Easter should always be on a Sunday, and ruled that it should be the Sunday immediately after Passover. Anyone who continued to follow the old rule was to be condemned as a heretic.

This ruling, however, left an unanswered question: what if Passover fell on a Sunday? Some Christian theologians, anxious to avoid any connection with the Jewish festival, subsequently decided that Easter must always be on the Sunday that followed. This was the thinking in Rome. But other Christians were less bothered if Passover and Easter coincided, so long as Easter was on a Sunday. This was the attitude in the west of Britain, adopted by the monks of Iona, and hence the practice of their associates at Lindisfarne.[18]

To modern ears, especially on non-religious heads, this can sound arcane and complicated, as indeed it was, but to contemporary Christians it was absolutely crucial. Easter was the holiest day in their calendar, so it seemed ridiculous if they could not agree on which day it ought to be celebrated. According to Bede it had been a source of bitter controversy among the monks of Lindisfarne in the 650s, and in the early 660s their arguments became even worse. It also led to an absurd situation at the Northumbrian court, because King Oswiu adhered to the teachings of Lindisfarne, whereas his queen, Eanflæd, who was from Kent, followed the Roman tradition in which she had been raised. This meant that in some years Oswiu would be celebrating Easter Sunday and feasting with his courtiers while his wife and her circle were still observing their Lenten fast. This may not have bothered Oswiu very much, since he had apparently done nothing to remedy the situation despite being married to Eanflæd for two decades, but what had been a doctrinal debate among monks became a political issue when his son Alchfrith began agitating for the Roman Easter, egged on by his new adviser Wilfrid.[19]

Eventually, in 664, Oswiu moved to resolve the conflict by arranging a conference. The venue was Whitby, an abbey on what is now the north Yorkshire coast, where the River Esk meets the sea. It had been founded six years earlier by Hild (known to posterity as St Hilda), who was the great-niece of King Eadwine, with whom she had been baptized as a girl. Having taken the habit of a nun some twenty years later, Hild had become Northumbria's foremost holy woman. As abbess of Whitby, says Bede, everyone called her 'mother', on account of her exemplary grace and devotion. This included a great many young men who would go on to become bishops, for Whitby was an abbey for both men and women. Such 'double-monasteries', as modern scholars have dubbed them, were quite common in both Francia and Britain, and a popular choice for aristocratic women who wished to retire, to study, or otherwise to shape their own destinies. Naturally not everyone approved of the mingling of the sexes in a single institution, even if chastity was the watchword. Wilfrid, as an advocate of the Benedictine Rule, is unlikely to have commended such an arrangement.[20]

The Synod of Whitby assembled in the early months of 664 – perhaps around Easter time. Presiding over the debate was King Oswiu, but Alchfrith was also present. Defending the Irish tradition were the monks of Lindisfarne, led by Bishop Colman, who had succeeded Finan three years earlier. Arguing the case for Rome was Bishop Agilbert of Wessex, lately arrived in Northumbria having fallen out with King Cenwalh. Part of the reason they had parted company, according to Bede, was that Cenwalh spoke only Saxon, and his Frankish bishop could not speak the language very well. Language was evidently a factor that hampered communication between the Roman and Irish churches. One of those present at Whitby was Bishop Cedd of Essex, who acted as interpreter for both parties. But what Agilbert really needed was someone to present the Roman case on his behalf in Old English. Wilfrid, therefore, was the perfect weapon – a native Northumbrian converted to the Roman cause, blessed with eloquence and a firm grasp of the arguments. Shortly before the synod assembled, Agilbert had ordained Wilfrid as a priest, a promotion that rendered him able to preach and baptize, but also gave him the authority to act as the bishop's mouthpiece.[21]

Oswiu opened the proceedings by declaring that it was essential that they should all follow the same rule, and called on Colman to present the Irish case. Colman responded with the straightforward argument that their Easter was traditional: the monks of Lindisfarne were following the custom of Iona, established by Columba, and Columba was following the teaching of St John the Evangelist. The king then asked Agilbert to put the opposing argument, but the bishop explained that his new disciple would be better able to put the case in English. Wilfrid rose to speak.[22]

According to his biographer, he was the model of politeness and humility. According to Bede he was combative and insulting. In both versions Wilfrid began by observing that the Roman method for calculating Easter was followed more or less everywhere, whereas the alternative mode of reckoning was used by only a few people – the British, the Picts and the followers of Columba. In Bede's account he added that such people were fools. When Colman asked if this meant that St John the Evangelist was a fool, Wilfrid parried that in the early days of Christianity it had been necessary to accommodate the Jews by allowing that Easter and Passover could coincide. Nowadays, he maintained, this was no longer important. Wilfrid then further raised the temperature by arguing that Colman's predecessors could be forgiven their ignorance about these matters on account of their 'rude simplicity', but cautioned that anyone who persisted in rejecting Rome's teaching would be committing a sin. 'Do you think', he asked, 'that a handful of people in a corner of the remotest island is to be preferred to the universal Church of Christ which is spread throughout the world?' Concluding his case, Wilfrid quoted the words of Christ on which Rome's authority rested: 'Thou art Peter, and upon this rock I will build my Church.'[23]

At this point, King Oswiu intervened. Is it true, he asked Colman, that Christ said these words to Peter? The bishop had to admit that it was. In that case, the king announced, he had best side with Rome, since Peter was the keeper of the keys to the kingdom of heaven. The matter was therefore settled. Colman was told he must accept the Roman method of reckoning Easter, and also the Roman tonsure, or else resign his office. The bishop chose to resign. He left Lindisfarne and returned to Iona, taking those monks who wished to go with him, and some of the bones of their founding father, Aidan.[24]

The outcome of the Synod of Whitby was thus a victory for the Romanist party, but not quite the outright one they craved. Oswiu's unexpected pivot had conceded that they were right in principle, but it simultaneously defanged the opposition of his son. A political stand-off with Alchfrith had been avoided. Now everyone was ostensibly singing from the same song sheet, and Oswiu retained the conductor's baton. It had clearly been the hope of Alchfrith and Agilbert that their protégé Wilfrid would replace Colman as Northumbria's new bishop. Wilfrid's performance during the proceedings, however, had provoked a lasting bitterness, not only among those who remained on Lindisfarne, but also at Whitby itself, for Hild and her young acolytes had also been champions of the Celtic cause. Oswiu had more sense than to appoint such a divisive figure. Instead he selected a bishop from southern Ireland named Tuda, whom Bede describes as 'a good and devoted man'. The southern Irish had long accepted the Roman Easter and tonsure, but Tuda probably had more empathy with the existing Northumbria clergy than the abrasive winner of the Whitby debate. And so, with a new bishop of Northumbria installed, the synod broke up, with the arguments of Rome vindicated, but Wilfrid's personal ambition frustrated.[25]

In the summer of 664 there was a sudden and devastating outbreak of plague. Unlike the previous visitation a century earlier, its impact on Britain is well attested. Bede tells us that it began in the south: among its first victims were the king of Kent and the archbishop of Canterbury, both of whom died on 14 July. From Kent it spread to Essex, where it led to a rejection of Christianity, as people began restoring derelict temples and worshipping graven images, hoping to placate the fury of their old gods. Tens of thousands, perhaps hundreds of thousands, must have perished, as the plague ripped mercilessly through communities across the whole country. The south, says Bede, was depopulated, while in the north, the disease raged 'far and wide, with cruel devastation, laying low a vast number of people'. Among those it carried off was the kingdom's new bishop, Tuda.[26]

The death of Tuda just a few months after his appointment gave Wilfrid a second chance – no doubt, in his mind, a God-given one. There was, however, a complicating factor. So many bishops had died that there were not enough survivors to consecrate a new one. When Gregory the Great had laid down the rules for the Anglo-Saxon Church, he had declared that no new bishop should be created unless there were three or four others present. By the end of the year, the plague had killed the bishops of Essex, Northumbria and Rochester, as well as the archbishop of Canterbury. Only the bishops of Wessex, Mercia and East Anglia remained. Three bishops might have technically been sufficient to appoint a successor for Tuda, but Wilfrid and his supporters evidently felt that this particular trio was inadequate – the absence of an archbishop may have been an overriding concern.[27]

Alchfrith therefore sent Wilfrid overseas, to be consecrated in Francia. He set sail, says his biographer, with a vast sum of money, so that he might arrive in great state, and grandeur was very much the leitmotif of his visit. After his reception at the court of King Chlothar III, a convention of no fewer than fourteen bishops was assembled at Compiègne, fifty miles north-east of Paris, presumably in the royal palace there. Among them was Wilfrid's former mentor, Agilbert, erstwhile bishop of Wessex, who had returned to Francia earlier in the year, and no doubt took the lead in arranging the ceremony. As the choir sang, Wilfrid was carried into the church on a golden throne, borne aloft by nine of the bishops.[28]

Such a splendid assembly must have taken some time to orchestrate, and Wilfrid showed no hurry to return home once it was over, apparently lingering on the Continent for almost a year. When he finally decided to do so, the ship that carried him across the Channel was blown off course by a storm, and ended up beached on the coast of Sussex, a kingdom that had not yet converted to Christianity. Wilfrid and his companions were soon confronted by a mob of pagan locals who showed no deference to his episcopal dignity, but plenty of interest in his rich possessions. Happily, Wilfrid had God on his side (and a cohort of well-armed warriors he had prudently brought with him), so they escaped from the skirmish with only five dead, and eventually found their way back to Northumbria.[29]

It was there that Wilfrid received a second and even more unpleasant shock. During his absence, another man had been promoted in his place. It had been Alchfrith, the king's son, who had sent Wilfrid to be consecrated in Francia. Whether or not his father, King Oswiu, had given his approval is unclear. If so, the old king had evidently changed his mind in the meantime, and nominated a priest called Chad, brother of Cedd, the bishop of Essex. With no archbishop of Canterbury to carry out the consecration, and perhaps a shortage of willing collaborators among the three remaining Anglo-Saxon bishops, a certain amount of creative thinking had been necessary to effect this promotion. Chad had eventually been invested by the bishop of Wessex and two bishops 'of the British race'. As Bede noted with disapproval, the Britons still stubbornly used the old reckoning for Easter, meaning, as far as he was concerned, that they were schismatics and sinners. Wilfrid would have felt exactly the same, and regarded Chad's appointment as invalid, but he also found on his return to Northumbria that he no longer had a champion. Alchfrith disappears from the historical record at this point. Presumably he had died during Wilfrid's absence, though neither Bede nor Stephen of Ripon provides any details. He may have been another victim of the plague, though it is also possible he died in rebellion against Oswiu. Bede at one point says that Alchfrith had wanted to go to Rome but was forbidden from doing so by his father, and on another occasion says that Oswiu was attacked by his son. A stone cross at Bewcastle in Cumbria seems to have been set up a few years later in Alchfrith's memory, but its inscription says nothing about the circumstances of his death.[30]

Without a patron to push his case, Wilfrid retired to the monastery Alchfrith had given him at Ripon, a bishop without a bishopric. He was, however, well placed to offer his services elsewhere, since so many bishoprics still lacked bishops. With no archbishop of Canterbury and no bishop of Rochester, the king of Kent called upon Wilfrid to ordain new priests. So too did the king of Mercia, and in return rewarded him with land on which to found new monasteries. Despite his rebuff in Northumbria, Wilfrid's elaborate consecration in Francia meant he was the best-qualified bishop in Britain, and he played this card to its fullest advantage.[31]

Perhaps perturbed by the amount of power Wilfrid was accumulating as an unofficial metropolitan, King Oswiu took steps to try to resurrect the archbishopric of Canterbury, which had remained defunct since the plague had carried off its previous incumbent two years earlier. He interceded with the king of Kent, and together the two of them selected a priest named Wigheard to become the new head of the Church. A native Anglo-Saxon, well versed in ecclesiastical affairs, Wigheard seemed an ideal appointment. The two kings packed him off to Rome for consecration, laden with rich gifts of silver and gold. After a journey which probably took about two months, the archbishop-elect presented himself before the pope, explained his purpose in coming, and then almost immediately dropped dead from plague, along with most of his companions.

In his letter of condolence to Oswiu, Pope Vitalian promised to find a replacement archbishop as soon as possible. This was no easy task, for nobody in Rome seems to have wanted the job. The first person the pope approached turned him down, and the second was not fit enough to undertake the long journey. In the end, perhaps in some desperation, Vitalian was persuaded to pick Theodore, who by any reasonably reckoning was an unlikely candidate. There was no question that he was a very learned man, but, at sixty-six years old, it must have seemed doubtful whether he would live long enough to impart much of this learning to his Anglo-Saxon flock. He was also an easterner, a native of Tarsus in modern Turkey, and the pope felt compelled to send to send him with a Roman chaperone to ensure he did not introduce any unorthodox customs. At the time of his selection Theodore still had the eastern form of tonsure, and it was therefore necessary to wait four months for his hair to grow so he could be given the correct Roman crop. It was not until the summer of 668 that the newly invested archbishop set out towards Britain, and the journey took him many months, with delays due to sickness, suspicious Frankish rulers, and the onset of winter. He finally arrived in Canterbury in May 669, a whole year after his departure.[32]

Though he was no one's first pick, Theodore proved to be a highly successful head of the Anglo-Saxon Church, and set about restoring it to order with exemplary swiftness and energy. Immediately after his arrival he embarked on a tour of every kingdom. His first task was to restore the depleted episcopate, which he did by appointing new bishops to Rochester, Wessex and East Anglia. When he arrived in Northumbria he deposed Chad on the grounds that his appointment had been uncanonical, but soon afterwards, recognizing Chad's suitability for the role, appointed him as the new bishop of Mercia. As the new bishop of Northumbria, Theodore appointed Wilfrid.[33]

Finally installed in the position he had craved for almost a decade, Wilfrid announced his arrival by ringing the changes, distancing himself from the Celtic traditions of Lindisfarne and aligning himself with those of Rome. In his view bishops should be based in cities, not on islands, and to this end he embarked on the restoration of the abandoned church in York begun more than forty years earlier by Bishop Paulinus. The building was in a very sorry state, its walls running with rainwater and befouled by the birds that flew in and out through its empty windows. Wilfrid's craftsmen set about re-leading the roof, glazing the windows, and whitewashing the walls until they shone. As a result, says his biographer, the new bishop of Northumbria was loved by the whole nation.[34]

As we noted at the outset, the *Life of Wilfrid* is a work of propaganda, so how much impact the new bishop actually had on ordinary Northumbrians is a question worth considering. Wilfrid was clearly a dynamic force, adept at convincing the powerful to part with large amounts of land in return for the promise of salvation and life everlasting. He was also a brilliant organizer, able to arrange the import of foreign craftsmen with the necessary expertise to build and beautify new stone churches. But, in common with those founded by other bishops and pious individuals, these churches were almost all monastic. This did not mean that they were entirely closed-up, cloistered communities, as would have been the case in later centuries. Many early monasteries contained priests as well as monks or nuns. A religious retreat for some, for others they were more like a mission station, from which they could go out into the world to preach and convert. For this reason, to differentiate them from what came later, some historians avoid using the word 'monastery' to describe these early communities, and use its Old English equivalent, *minster*.[35]

The fact remains, nevertheless, that whether a minster was a closed-up institution for a few pious aristocrats, or a large community with considerable outreach, its church, however splendid, could be used by only a small number of worshippers. Churches for ordinary people – parish churches – were at this date unknown. How, then, did such people come to hear about Christianity? Perhaps a priest or even a bishop would come wandering into their settlement once in a while to preach and baptize. In lieu of a church they might erect a wooden cross, like the one at Heavenfield, as a symbol of veneration, and to mark the place where the faithful might congregate. In time this might be replaced with something more elaborate: beginning in the late seventh century, carved stone crosses, with designs originally enhanced with paint of different colours, were raised on such sites, especially in Mercia and Northumbria.[36]

When it came to the lives of ordinary people, however, the elite were better at telling them what they were not allowed to do, rather than what they should be doing instead. King Eorcenberht of Kent, who ruled from 640 to 664, drew praise from Bede for being the first Anglo-Saxon ruler to order the destruction of idols across his whole kingdom, and also for ordering people to fast during Lent. But while the authorities were trying to eradicate pagan practices, most people were left in the dark about the nature of Christianity. One of the few stories told by Bede to feature ordinary folk is extremely revealing in this regard. He describes how some monks were using rafts to move wood down the River Tyne, when a sudden storm blew up and swept them out to sea. Other monks who were watching from the monastery were distressed, but the peasants who observed the spectacle simply stood and jeered. When they were rebuked for this, they replied with further insolence. Let the monks drown, they declared, 'for they have robbed people of their old ways of worship, and how the new worship is to be conducted, nobody knows'.[37]

Such was the situation that confronted Archbishop Theodore at the time of his arrival in 669. During his tour of the Anglo-Saxon kingdoms, he must have seen much to alarm him. A text that was later drawn up in his name imposed penances for all sorts of pagan practices: offering sacrifices to devils; burning grain to preserve the purity of a house with a corpse in it; mothers placing their daughters in ovens, or on rooftops, in order to cure them of fevers. He also found that, given the scale of the problem, some senior churchmen were too pedestrian for his liking. Chad, for example, was in the habit of walking everywhere, in imitation of Aidan, and other Irish holy men before him. In redeploying him to Mercia, Theodore made it clear that he wanted the bishop to make more frequent use of a horse. When Chad demurred, the archbishop, who was approaching seventy, heaved him into the saddle with his own hands.[38]

What the situation demanded, Theodore soon decided, was not simply swifter bishops, but more of them to go around. Gregory the Great's original plan for Britain, it may be remembered, was for two metropolitans, one in London, the other in York, each of whom would have twelve bishops beneath him – a total episcopate of twenty-six. What had actually happened was that a bishop had been adopted by each of the major Anglo-Saxon kingdoms: Essex, East Anglia, Mercia, Wessex and Northumbria all had just one prelate apiece. Only Kent, with Rochester and Canterbury, had two, and that was rendered more explicable by Canterbury's extraordinary status as the sole archbishopric. The bishops clearly favoured this state of affairs, for the greater the size of a diocese, the greater the amount of money that found its way into the episcopal coffers.[39]

When, therefore, Archbishop Theodore floated the idea of dividing their dioceses not long after his arrival, it met with very little enthusiasm. The occasion was a general council, or synod, of the Church, which took place at Hertford in the autumn of 672. The fact that such a meeting took place at all was something of a triumph: Theodore, as Bede notes, 'was the first of the archbishops whom the whole Anglo-Saxon Church consented to obey'. All those present agreed with Theodore's opening proposal that they should be bound by the law of the Church laid down in ancient times (canon law), and they achieved consensus on several specific chapters he had tabled for discussion: Easter, they reaffirmed, should be kept according to the Roman reckoning, and monks and priests should not be allowed to wander at will. They also approved of Theodore's plan to hold synods on a regular basis, though it was collectively felt that meeting twice a year was impractical, and that annual assemblies would suffice. But when Theodore raised the idea of creating more bishops, the consensus evaporated. 'This chapter received general discussion,' states the official record of the synod, 'but at the time we came to no decision on the matter.'

In the list of bishops attending the Synod of Hertford, one name is notably absent. 'Our brother and fellow priest Wilfrid, bishop of the Northumbrian people,' noted Theodore in his preamble, 'was represented by his proctors.' These men doubtless carried back to Wilfrid a report of the topics that had come under discussion, several of which seem to have been chosen with his own behaviour in mind. It can hardly have been an accident that Theodore invited the synod to affirm the law which forbade any bishop from intruding into the diocese of another, or the one which decreed 'that no bishop shall claim precedence over another bishop out of ambition'. Now that Canterbury's authority was restored, Wilfrid was being tacitly informed that his freelance activities in other kingdoms were expected to come to an end. Whether he paid any heed to such thinly concealed admonitions is doubtful. As his contemptuous absence from the meeting at Hertford suggests, the bishop of Northumbria's attention was engaged elsewhere. He was by this point busy carving out his own ecclesiastical empire, aided by the north's new king.[40]

Old King Oswiu had died on 15 February 670, a few months after Theodore's arrival and Wilfrid's appointment as bishop of his kingdom. He was fifty-eight years old, and is the first Northumbrian king we know of who didn't die in battle. The new king's name was Ecgfrith, and he was the second of Oswiu's legitimate sons. Ecgfrith was about twenty-five years old at his accession, and proved to be a highly capable ruler, ready to continue his predecessors' policy of aggressive territorial expansion. His father had apparently pushed Northumbrian power beyond the River Forth and imposed a tribute on the Picts, and when they tried to throw off this burden at the start of Ecgfrith's reign, he rode north and smashed them in battle. He was similarly successful against his other neighbours, winning back control of the lesser kingdom of Lindsey from Mercia at some point before 675, and taking land from the British kingdoms to the west.[41]

As far as Wilfrid was concerned, this naked aggression was wonderful news, for as the power of the king of Northumbria increased, so too did the power of its bishop. The *Life of Wilfrid* depicts a vivid scene in the early years of Ecgfrith's reign, when the two men were together for the rededication of the bishop's church at Ripon. Whatever buildings had originally been erected on the site by its Irish founders had evidently been torn down. Wilfrid, explains his biographer, 'started and completed from foundations to roof-beams a church built of dressed stone, supported by columns and complete with side aisles'. During the ceremony, the bishop stood before the altar and read out a list of the lands that previous kings had given him, and then proceeded to list 'the holy places in various parts of the country which the British clergy, fleeing from our own hostile sword, had deserted'. Ecgfrith had lately conquered a large part of what is now Lancashire, and had generously donated the churches within it to Wilfrid. 'God would be pleased with the gift of so much land', affirmed the bishop's biographer. After the sermon was finished, the assembled company celebrated with a three-day feast.[42]

This convivial relationship, alas, was not to last. At the start of his reign, Ecgfrith was married to a woman named Æthelthryth, who reportedly refused to sleep with him. At the king's request, Wilfrid intervened, with the result that Æthelthryth became a nun. Because this outcome was apparently what the queen wanted, and because she rewarded Wilfrid by granting him the land on which to build his church at Hexham, it has often been assumed that it was the cause of Ecgfrith's subsequent animosity. It seems more likely, however, that the bishop had obliged the king by finding a way to end his unhappy and childless marriage. Indeed, it may be that this was another of Wilfrid's actions that drew condemnation from his episcopal colleagues. The Synod of Hertford, which met soon afterwards, declared that 'if anyone puts away his wife, joined to him by lawful matrimony, he may not take another if he wishes to be a true Christian. He must either remain as he is, or be reconciled to his wife.'[43]

As on other matters, neither Wilfrid nor Ecgfrith paid any attention to the criticism. Æthelthryth remained in her monastery, and Ecgfrith soon remarried, this time to a woman named Iurminburh. It was at this point, according to Stephen of Ripon, that Wilfrid's problems began. The new queen, he says, poisoned her husband's heart against the bishop with malicious stories, using all her powers of persuasion to describe his acquisitions – 'his possessions, the number of his monasteries, the vastness of his buildings, [and] his countless followers arrayed like a king's retinue'.

Although Stephen, with typical monkish misogyny, calls Iurminburh a she-wolf and jezebel, other passages in the *Life of Wilfrid* suggest that she was merely pointing out the obvious, and that the bishop was indeed conducting himself like a second king. He and his followers, for example, clearly enjoyed a good feast. The fact that his biographer insists Wilfrid never drank a full glass on such occasions, and that there were plenty of witnesses who would vouch for this, merely tells us that there must have been plenty of people at the time who remembered it rather differently. It seems unlikely that his household was any more abstemious. Noblemen, we are told, sent their sons to be raised there, 'so they might have the choice of giving themselves to God, or of returning as grown men, with Wilfrid's recommendation, to enter the king's service as warriors'.[44]

The kind of power that the bishop could exercise as a result of his enormous wealth is well illustrated by an episode that occurred in the mid-670s, when he helped a Frankish prince named Dagobert. As a young man, Dagobert had been driven into exile, and had spent almost twenty years living as a monk in Ireland. Around 675, however, his relatives in Francia sought to bring him home, and asked Wilfrid to assist them. 'This the holy bishop did', says Stephen of Ripon. 'He made him welcome on his arrival from Ireland, provided him with arms, and sent him back in great state with a troop of his companions to support him.'

A bishop who could spare sufficient warriors from his entourage to sponsor a successful foreign coup – Dagobert, thanks to Wilfrid, went on to become king of the Franks – was clearly something that would have given any sensible secular ruler cause for concern. The obvious way to bring an overmighty bishop down to size was to endorse the archbishop of Canterbury's plan for the division of existing dioceses. Theodore may have been generally rebuffed on this issue at the Synod of Hertford in 672, but he had since scored several individual successes. Shortly after the synod the bishop of East Anglia had fallen seriously ill, enabling the archbishop to appoint two new bishops in his place. The East Anglian diocese was thus split in two, with new sees based at Dunwich (in Suffolk) and Elmham (in Norfolk). A little while later, Theodore had become displeased with the bishop of Mercia for some undisclosed offence and deprived him of office. It may be that the bishop had simply refused to comply with a fresh demand to share his power, for once he was gone, his diocese was also divided: the originally bishopric, based at Lichfield, was reduced by the creation of new ones in the west, based at Hereford and Worcester.[45]

The writing was therefore very much on the wall for Wilfrid when Ecgfrith and Iurminburh asked the archbishop to convene a synod in Northumbria in 678. We do not know what charges were brought against him, for Bede does not discuss it, and Stephen of Ripon merely asserts that his hero was completely blameless, while alleging, improbably, that Theodore had been bribed. The result was that Wilfrid was deposed, and his huge diocese was divided between three new appointees: Deira would have a bishop based in York, Bernicia a bishop based at Lindisfarne, and the newly conquered province of Lindsey would have a bishop of its own, probably based at Lincoln.[46]

Wilfrid did not go quietly. He protested to the bishops of other kingdoms about his treatment, and it seems possible (again based on his biographer's later denials) that he may even have attempted to stir up some sort of armed opposition. When these efforts came to nothing, however, he decided that his only remaining option was to take his case to Rome.

This was a far more perilous proposition than it had been on his first visit, twenty-five years earlier, when he had been a teenager of no consequence. Now, thanks to his recent backing of King Dagobert, he was a marked man. Dagobert's enemies greatly resented Wilfrid's interference in Frankish politics, and, having been tipped off about his journey, were ready to take their revenge. As soon as the English bishop stepped off the boat he was seized, assaulted and robbed, and many of his companions were killed. Luckily, says Stephen of Ripon, the English bishop in question was not Wilfrid, but his near namesake, Bishop Winfrid of Mercia, who was making the same journey and mistaken for the true target. Wilfrid, meanwhile, had taken a more northerly route and sailed to Frisia, a pagan country, where he remained throughout the winter of 678, preaching and converting with the permission of its king. In the spring he headed south, passing through the realm of his friend, Dagobert, who offered to make him bishop of Strasbourg if he would stay. But Wilfrid was not to be deterred from his mission, and pushed on to Rome.[47]

He arrived to discover that Pope Agatho and his advisers were already aware of his case. News of the quarrel had been brought by pilgrims from Britain, and also by an envoy from Archbishop Theodore, who had come with written letters. It would be extremely interesting to know what allegations against Wilfrid these letters contained, but once again all we have is the partisan account of Stephen of Ripon. Wilfrid's accusers, says his biographer, raised 'many dubious points' which were not credited by the papal council assembled to consider the matter. 'We are of the opinion', they apparently declared, 'that he refrained from implicating himself in seditious quarrelling on account of his modesty.' The only revealing part of Stephen's obviously biased account comes when he describes Wilfrid's petition to the assembly. After arguing that he had been deposed illegally, and denying any wrongdoing, the bishop asked one favour: if they decided that Theodore's partition of his diocese should stand, could the new appointees at least be drawn from among Wilfrid's own clergy? This went to the heart of the matter. The three men appointed the previous year all represented the traditional Irish party within the Northumbrian Church, being disciples of either Bishop Aidan or Abbess Hild. Although they had accepted the Roman victory at Whitby in 664, they evidently harboured a lasting resentment against Wilfrid himself, and a strong desire to exclude him from Northumbria altogether. Wilfrid, for his part, clearly repaid their resentment in kind, and depicted them as dangerous malcontents – 'strangers and outsiders' was how he described them in his address to the papal council: men who threatened to reintroduce the irregular practices he had worked so assiduously to eradicate.[48]

In the end, the council's decision was to adopt just such a compromise. They declared they could find no evidence of wrongdoing on Wilfrid's part, and that he should therefore be reinstated as bishop of Northumbria. At the same time, they ruled that the division of the northern diocese must stand – to have decided any differently would have been to undermine the authority of Archbishop Theodore. As per Wilfrid's recommendation, the three new Northumbrian bishops were to be expelled and replaced with alternative candidates chosen by a council that Wilfrid himself would convene. Anyone who failed to obey this ruling was threatened with deposition and excommunication.[49]

Armed with this decision, and pausing only to purchase lots of saintly relics, Wilfrid made his way back to Britain in 680, after an absence of almost two years. Once back in Northumbria, he was permitted to summon an assembly at which he read out the pope's verdict. Unsurprisingly, it did not go down well. Some simply rejected it outright. Others maintained it must have been obtained by bribery. King Ecgfrith became enraged, and ordered that Wilfrid be thrown into prison. All the bishop's possessions were seized, including his reliquary, which Queen Iurminburh took for herself and wore as a necklace.[50]

After several months of imprisonment, Wilfrid was eventually released and expelled from Northumbria. He went at first to Mercia, but was soon obliged to move on by its new king, Æthelred, who was married to Ecgfrith's sister. From Mercia he went to Wessex, but there too he found no welcome, for the king of Wessex was married to the sister of Queen Iurminburh. Everywhere the bishop travelled, complains his biographer, Ecgfrith somehow managed to stir up persecution against him.[51]

So it was that Wilfrid ended up in Sussex, a pagan land that lay beyond Northumbria's reach. Dense forests and a rocky coast, explains Stephen of Ripon, had saved it from conquest by other kingdoms. Wilfrid, of course, already knew something of the Sussex coast, having accidentally landed there fifteen years earlier and fought on the beaches with the locals. Happily, by the time of his second visit in 681, the South Saxons were no longer quite so inhospitable. Their king, Æthelwealh, had converted at least six years earlier, and taken a wife, Eafe, who had been raised as a Christian in the kingdom of the Hwicce. Stephen of Ripon is wrong, therefore, when he claims that the royal couple were converted by Wilfrid after his arrival, but there is no doubt that, having been welcomed at Æthelwealh's court, the vagabond bishop did much to advance the cause of Christianity. In the months that followed he reportedly baptized many thousands – 'some freely', says Stephen, in a moment of greater candour, 'and some at the king's command'. So pleased was Æthelwealh with this campaign of forced conversion that he gave Wilfrid an extensive royal estate at Selsey on which to found a monastery. It became the seat of the South Saxon bishopric, and Wilfrid was its first incumbent.[52]

Although his biographer presents Wilfrid's time in Sussex as a great success, to others it must have seemed more like the Apocalypse, with each of the Four Horsemen stalking the land in turn. Bede tells us that before the bishop's arrival there had been a three-year drought, and that as a result 'a most terrible famine assailed the populace and piteously destroyed them'. Happily, at the time of Wilfrid's arrival, the rain miraculously returned. But a few years into his stay, there came a dreadful pestilence. In truth, the plague had never entirely disappeared from Britain since its catastrophic return in 664, and in the intervening twenty years there had been many localized outbreaks. At some point after 666, for example, it had devastated the double monastery at Barking in Essex; in 672 it had carried off that reluctant equestrian, Bishop Chad, and many of his monks at Lichfield; and in 680 it had claimed the life of Æthelthryth, the former queen of Northumbria, and latterly abbess of Ely. But the disease that erupted in 684 was a true pandemic, and spread all the way across Britain and Ireland. Since some of its victims died during the winter, it seems likely it was pneumonic plague, and thus all the more contagious. Among the hundreds of communities it ravaged was Wilfrid's new monastery at Selsey. 'Many of those who had come with the bishop,' says Bede, 'as well as those who had been recently called to the faith from the South Saxon kingdom, were indiscriminately snatched away from this world.'[53]

More still were killed by war, which was carried into Sussex by Cædwalla, a vicious warrior with whom Wilfrid collaborated around the same time. This was arguably the most disgraceful episode in the bishop's chequered career, despite the attempts of his biographer to apply thick layers of whitewash. In Stephen of Ripon's version of events Cædwalla was merely a wandering exile of noble birth who sought Wilfrid's guidance, an obedient son in search of a spiritual father. With the bishop's help he successfully overcame adversity to become king of Wessex, and afterwards appointed Wilfrid as his chief adviser, rewarding him with extensive lands 'because of his love of God'.

It falls to Bede to supply the unsavoury details that Stephen conveniently omits. Cædwalla, he explains, was a young and warlike exile from Wessex, who burst on to the political scene around 685 by leading an army into Sussex, wasting the kingdom 'with fierce slaughter', and killing its king, Æthelwealh. Driven out by the king's leading nobles, he turned his violent attentions to Wessex, persuading its king, Centwine, to relinquish his throne and pursue a new career as a monk. Once established in his homeland Cædwalla returned to Sussex, killed one of its new rulers, and reduced the kingdom, in Bede's words, 'to a worse state of slavery'.[54]

Presumably by this point, if not before, the young warrior must have struck up his friendship with Wilfrid, for his next conquest was carried out with the bishop's blessing. In 686 Cædwalla invaded the Isle of Wight, intending 'to wipe out all the natives with merciless slaughter, and to replace them with people from his own kingdom'. This genocidal scheme was evidently justified by Wilfrid on the grounds that the island's inhabitants were pagan, just as the people of Sussex had been until his own arrival a few years earlier.

What Bede additionally reveals, however – and what Stephen of Ripon conceals completely – is that Cædwalla was a pagan himself. His pact with Wilfrid appears to have been a spiritual test-drive of the kind described in the case of other heathen rulers – an undertaking to consider the merits of Christianity if God granted him victory over his enemies. The bishop's incentive for lending his spiritual support to Cædwalla's bloody enterprise was a quarter of the profits: after the conquest he received 300 of the island's 1,200 hides for the use of the Church. (He gave them to his nephew, a cleric named Beornwine.)

Wilfrid's influence over his 'obedient son' did not, alas, extend to persuading him to spare his defeated opponents. The king of Wight, Arwald, appears to have been killed in the course of the invasion, but his two young brothers had fled to the mainland before the fighting began. Hopeful of remaining hidden, they were soon betrayed and sentenced to die on Cædwalla's orders. The conqueror's only concession was to allow them to be baptized in their final days, an act of clemency suggested and carried out by the abbot of Redbridge. Cædwalla's chief adviser and spiritual father, to judge from Bede's account, had no involvement in obtaining even this small mercy. Endeavouring to put the best possible spin on the story, Bede consoled his readers that the two boys had gone gladly to their deaths, 'assured of their entry into the eternal kingdom'. The conquest of the Isle of Wight, he concluded positively, meant that all the Anglo-Saxon kingdoms had now accepted the faith of Christ.[55]

Northumbria, meanwhile, had fared no better in Wilfrid's absence. There are, admittedly, no reports of famine affecting northern Britain as it had done Sussex, but otherwise the north had experienced its full measure of biblical disasters. The plague had ripped across the landscape, depopulating villages and monasteries, and war and death had reduced the kingdom to confusion.[56]

To begin with, there had been more ecclesiastical controversy. Soon after Wilfrid's expulsion, Archbishop Theodore had further divided his diocese, creating two more bishoprics. One was located in the far north, on the banks of the River Forth at Abercorn, with the aim of converting the pagan Picts. The other was based at Wilfrid's splendid church at Hexham, but for unknown reasons its bishop had proved to be a disappointment. And so, in the autumn of 684, Theodore — now in his early eighties — had been obliged to make his way laboriously northwards from Canterbury, across a plague-ridden country, to arrange for a replacement. Everyone agreed that the best man for the job would be Cuthbert.[57]

Cuthbert was a native Northumbrian, born at almost exactly the same moment as Wilfrid, and destined for a career in the Church, but beyond that their careers and characters could not have been more different. Whereas Wilfrid had travelled widely and was a man of great ambition, Cuthbert had stayed at home, and was content with his role as the prior of Melrose Abbey. Wilfrid was quite prepared to carry out mass conversions at sword-point, but Cuthbert's methods were more gently persuasive, and he would often head off (on foot, naturally) for weeks on end to preach to people in remote places, deep in the hills and mountains. The bishop revelled in his power and authority, and never tired of the controversy that came with it. Cuthbert, however, eventually grew weary of the world, and went to live as a hermit on Farne, an island off the Northumbrian coast, not far from Bamburgh. He had been there for nearly a decade by 684, when the synod assembled by Theodore nominated him to become a bishop, and consequently proved difficult to dislodge. It was not until a delegation of the most important people in Northumbria, led by King Ecgfrith himself, sailed out to Farne and begged him on their knees to take up the vacant post that he reluctantly agreed to do so. The following Easter, in the presence of the king, the archbishop and a host of others, Cuthbert was consecrated in York as Hexham's new bishop.[58]

This controversy over, Ecgfrith was free to concentrate on his main secular priority, which was the continued expansion of his kingdom. The previous year he had sent an army to Ireland, led by one of his chief nobles. The operation had apparently been a success, but at the same time it had not obtained the same benediction as his earlier campaigns. When Ecgfrith had gone to war at the start of his reign, Wilfrid had been there to egg him on, ready to condemn the king's Celtic enemies as heretics because of their reckoning of Easter, and reassuring him that their extermination was pleasing to God. Now, by contrast, the churchmen at his court offered nothing but criticism, and had urged him not to attack the Irish. Bede, writing fifty years later, echoed their complaint, accusing the king of 'wretchedly devastating a harmless race' and destroying churches and monasteries. What followed, thought Bede, was divine retribution.

In the spring of 685, a month or so after Cuthbert's consecration in York, Ecgfrith went to war against the Picts. Once again he was urged not to do so by his clerical followers, the new bishop being one of the chief prophets of doom. But the king would not be dissuaded, and led his army into the north, far beyond the confines of his kingdom. The Picts, says Bede, feigned flight, and lured Ecgfrith into 'narrow passes in the midst of inaccessible mountains'. At a place later named as Nechtansmere, they fell upon the invaders, putting them to the sword, so that only a few escaped. Ecgfrith and his bodyguard were among the slaughtered.

The king's death in battle dealt a heavy blow to his extensive northern empire. Northumbria had been expanding for over a century at the expense of its British, Irish and Pictish neighbours. Now all these peoples seized the opportunity to reverse the tide of conquest. The British rulers to the west, says Bede, recovered some of their former independence, while the Picts and the Irish of Dal Riata drove the Angles back as far as the Forth. Among those who fled from their destructive wrath was the bishop of Abercorn, whose diocese had been established only four years earlier. The Battle of Nechtansmere, from Bede's later perspective, seemed to be a crucial turning point in Northumbria's history. After this defeat, he said, the hopes and strength of the kingdom began to ebb and fall away.[59]

In the space of a single year, therefore, the fortunes of the northern and southern Anglo-Saxon kingdoms had been radically transformed. Northumbria had been thrown into chaos, and greatly reduced in size, as the result of the death of its king in battle, a disaster foretold and opposed by its leading churchmen. In the south, meanwhile, Cædwalla was carrying all before him, his violent victories cheered and encouraged by his chief adviser, Wilfrid. Already the conqueror of Wessex, Sussex and the Isle of Wight, by the end of 686 the young warrior had further extended his power into Kent, Surrey and Essex. In Kent he had appointed his brother as the new ruler, having apparently killed its previous king.[60]

One is bound to wonder if the death of a king whose chief residence was in Canterbury helped focus the mind of Archbishop Theodore on ending his feud with Cædwalla's spiritual father. It was at this point that Theodore made overtures of peace towards Wilfrid, inviting him to a conference in London. As related by Stephen of Ripon, this meeting consisted mostly of the archbishop apologizing for his former conduct, and Wilfrid magnanimously granting his forgiveness. However the conversation went in reality, the certainty is that both men realized that Ecgfrith's death had created an opportunity for Wilfrid to return to Northumbria, an outcome that by this point they each probably saw as desirable.[61]

In 686, therefore, Theodore sought to make peace between Wilfrid and Northumbria's new ruler, Aldfrith. Precisely how Aldfrith had come to be king is a mystery. Genealogically speaking, it was straightforward enough, for he was the only surviving brother of Ecgfrith, who had produced no children of his own. But Aldfrith's claim was complicated by his bastardy – he was the fruit of an early relationship between his father, Oswiu, and an Irish princess. As such he seems to have been deliberately sidelined by Oswiu's legitimate descendants, and had lived a quiet and uncontroversial life in Ireland for several decades. But as Ecgfrith's reign had worn on, and it had become obvious that he had no heir apparent, Aldfrith's claim must have been discussed and promoted in some circles among the Irish, and perhaps also among the Picts. How a peace between the Picts, the Irish and the Northumbrians was patched up in the wake of Nechtansmere is unknown, but a key player seems to have been Ecgfrith's and Aldfrith's sister, Ælfflæd, who had succeeded Hild as the abbess of Whitby five years earlier. Experienced and respected, Ælfflæd looks to have been the principal peace-weaver in negotiating Aldfrith's succession, and she remained a powerful figure during his reign. When Archbishop Theodore sent letters to Northumbria seeking a reconciliation on Wilfrid's behalf, he addressed them to both the new king and his half-sister.[62]

The result was that, at some point in the second year of Aldfrith's reign, Wilfrid was readmitted to the land of his birth and his position as Northumbria's most prominent churchman. Initially he was given the dioceses of Hexham and Lindisfarne, which had conveniently fallen vacant with the deaths of Bishop Eata in October 686 and the saintly Cuthbert in March the following year. But soon Wilfrid, still brandishing the papal judgement he had received in 680, had engineered the expulsion of the sitting bishops of York and Ripon, allowing him to resume his power in those places as well. Almost a decade since his humiliating deposition in 678, his ecclesiastical empire had been restored.[63]

By the time of Wilfrid's return, the pestilence that had swept across Britain and Ireland for the past three years had almost run its course, but the damage it had done to the population had been catastrophic. In Northumbria, largely thanks to Bede, we know about the heavy toll it had taken on the monasteries. At Lindisfarne, it had wiped out almost the whole community, and some smaller and less celebrated houses must have disappeared completely, their survivors disbanding to join institutions that had fared better, or were more richly endowed.[64]

In one instance the devastation led to a famous merger. In 681 or 682 King Ecgfrith had founded a new monastery on the banks of the River Tyne at Jarrow. (It was dedicated in his presence on 23 April 685, just four weeks before his death at Nechtansmere, and, remarkably, its original dedication stone is still set in the wall of the church.) Soon afterwards the plague had struck the community, killing everyone except for one young boy and the abbot, Ceolfrith. Meanwhile, the disease had also ravaged a more established monastery that stood seven miles to the south, near the mouth of the River Wear. Founded around a dozen years earlier, Wearmouth was the creation of Biscop Baducing, the Northumbrian noble who had accompanied Wilfrid on his first trip to Rome. Since that youthful experience Biscop had become a monk, changed his first name to Benedict, and studied at a wide variety of monasteries across Europe. Returning from his sixth trip to Rome in 686, he found that the plague had ripped through his beloved community, killing many of the brothers. A short time later Biscop himself was seized with a fatal paralysis, and implored Ceolfrith, the surviving abbot of Jarrow, to fill the same position at Wearmouth. In this way, the two neighbouring monasteries were brought under the same management, and combined to become one of the most influential institutions in Britain.[65]

10. The original dedication stone of the church (*basilica*) of St Paul's at Jarrow. It is dated the 9 kalends of May (23 April), in the fifteenth year of the reign of King Ecgfrith, and the fourth year of the rule of its founder (*conditor*), Abbot Ceolfrith (685).

Thanks to Biscop's generosity, Wearmouth–Jarrow was fantastically wealthy, and boasted perhaps the finest library in Britain. It was this unrivalled collection of imported books that enabled Bede, who was placed in the community in 680 as a boy of seven, to become one of the greatest historians of the Middle Ages. It also enabled the other monks to study the skills of book production, so that in the years that followed their scriptorium became famous for its illustrated manuscripts. It helped that Northumbria was outstandingly rich in cattle: to produce the three great Bibles known to have been completed under the direction of Abbot Ceolfrith would have required the skins of over 1,500 calves.[66] Nor was Ceolfrith's monastery alone in its literary and artistic endeavours: the monks of

Lindisfarne also began creating books of outstanding beauty, most famously the Lindisfarne Gospels, produced to adorn the tomb of St Cuthbert (colour picture 10). One of the principal sponsors of this 'Northumbrian Renaissance' was the new king, Aldfrith, who during his long exile in Ireland had become exceedingly learned. He gave Wearmouth–Jarrow eight hides of land in return for what Bede describes as 'a codex of the cosmographers of miraculous workmanship', and when the abbot of Iona gave him a book about the Holy Land, the king had it copied 'for lesser folk to read'. Even Stephen of Ripon, writing the *Life of Wilfrid*, allowed that Aldfrith 'proved to be a wise ruler'.[67]

Nevertheless, the new king and Wilfrid soon fell out. The cause, as before, was the scope of the bishop's authority. Wilfrid seems to have assumed that on his return to Northumbria he would be allowed to resume the dominant position he had enjoyed at the start of his career, before Archbishop Theodore had divided his original diocese. One of his main complaints, according to Stephen of Ripon, was that Aldfrith insisted on adhering to the decisions Theodore had made 'when all the trouble started'. It must therefore have come as a disappointment to discover that his custody of Hexham and Lindisfarne had been intended only as a temporary measure – by 688 both dioceses had new bishops. Wilfrid also complained that lands and rights had been removed from his church at Ripon during his exile, when it had been an episcopal seat. Although these disputes sound as though they rumbled on from one year to the next, they probably became worse after the death of Theodore, who died in September 690 at the advanced age of eighty-eight. Wilfrid doubtless hoped that, with his old adversary gone, the division of Northumbria could be more easily reversed. He may even have plotted to become Theodore's replacement, to judge from Stephen of Ripon's implausible suggestion that this had been the old archbishop's wish. It was a year or two after Theodore's death, and just five years after Wilfrid's return to Northumbria, that Aldfrith grew tired of the constant arguments and banished the troublesome bishop from his kingdom for a second time.[68]

Frustratingly, Wilfrid then disappears for over a decade. We know, thanks to his biographer, that he went to Mercia, where he was welcomed by King Æthelred and apparently made bishop of Leicester, but what he did during these unchronicled years is a mystery. He evidently made another appeal to Rome by sending proctors to the pope, and probably tried to stir up support else-where in Britain to undermine his opponents in Northumbria. When his story resumes, tempers were already at boiling point.[69]

The occasion was a council summoned by the new archbishop of Canterbury, Berhtwald, who had taken office almost two years after the death of Theodore. It met in 702 or 703 at Austerfield, a settlement about nine miles south-east of Doncaster, which might plausibly have been selected as neutral ground because it was located near the border of Mercia and Northumbria. According to Stephen of Ripon, who provides the only account of the meeting, nearly all the other bishops were present, and so too was King Aldfrith. As soon as Wilfrid arrived, says his biographer, 'tremendous disputes and altercations broke out'. We are not told the nature of the allegations that were brought against him, only that they were false. It emerged that the other bishops intended to strip Wilfrid of his episcopal status and seize all his possessions, 'so that he would not be able to call the smallest cottage his own in either Mercia or Northumbria'. In response, Stephen of Ripon puts a self-justificatory speech into his hero's mouth. Had he not been the first to root out the 'foul weeds' planted by the Irish? Had he not converted all of Northumbria to the correct reckoning of Easter, and the correct form of tonsure? Was it not he who had introduced the proper method of chanting to Britain, and the rule of St Benedict? Wilfrid concluded his retrospective by declaring that he was going to appeal to the Holy See, at which point the meeting broke up in acrimony.[70]

And so Wilfrid set out once more for Rome. It was the third time he had made the 1,500-mile journey, and he was now almost seventy years old. He arrived at the same time as the representatives of the archbishop of Canterbury, who had come to counter his complaint with written ones of their own. Deducing exactly what happened during the many months of argument that followed is impossible, for the only account we have is that of Stephen of Ripon. We may infer, however, from Stephen's almost hysterical tone, and his shameless attempts to distort and misdirect, that the outcome was not strongly in Wilfrid's favour.

In Stephen's account, Wilfrid, 'bent under the weight of honourable old age', complains that he has been forced to return to Rome because his opponents have ignored the papal ruling he received in 680, and have once again robbed him of his bishopric, lands and property. Against this, the archbishop's envoys make 'many and serious allegations', which are dismissed as 'a pack of lies'. When the verdict is eventually delivered, Stephen prefaces it with a long speech by 'the wise citizens of Rome' who were present, and who apparently remembered Wilfrid from his previous visit almost a quarter of a century earlier. 'This Bishop Wilfrid', they declare, 'is the same one whom blessed Agatho sent home cleared of every charge ... but now, alas, the malice of troublemakers has sent him wandering from his own see.' The citizens go on to say how shameful it is that Wilfrid's false accusers have presumed to have 'the venerable old man' arraigned before the Holy See, and have even forged documents against him. 'They deserve the harshest punishment', concludes the wise crowd. 'Let them be thrown into the deepest dungeons to waste away until death.' Clearly, this is what the pope *ought* to have said, but for some reason did not.[71]

The pope's actual verdict, when it came, was inconclusive. Wilfrid's principal antagonists in Northumbria are named as Bosa, who had replaced him as bishop of York, and John of Beverley, who had become bishop of Hexham. Both were former pupils of Abbess Hild of Whitby, and had evidently inherited all her disdain that dated back to the synod of 664. But because neither had been present in Rome, the pope announced that he could not make a ruling, and simply referred the whole matter back to the archbishop of Canterbury. It was a measure of how dissatisfied Wilfrid must have been with this outcome that he tried to remain in Rome, and had to be ordered by the pope to return to Britain.[72]

In the end, as on previous occasions, a series of deaths accomplished what the pope could not. At first it seemed that Wilfrid himself would be the one to oblige: on his return journey he fell so sick he had to be carried on a litter and lost consciousness for several days, leading his companions to fear the worst. But eventually he recovered, crossed the Channel, and sent messengers to Northumbria, announcing the papal command for a further council. King Aldfrith listened politely, but explained that he was not for turning. 'As long as I live,' he reportedly declared, 'no documents you produce from the Holy See will make me change my mind.' The king, who was a similar age to Wilfrid, then promptly died, triggering a succession crisis. He was replaced in the first instance by an unknown contender named Eadwulf, who threatened Wilfrid and his associates with death if they did not depart immediately from Northumbria, only to be expelled himself a few weeks later by a rival faction championing the cause of Aldfrith's young son, Osred.[73]

One of the leading members of this faction was Abbess Ælfflæd, half-sister of the late king, who once again stepped forward to play the role of peacemaker. It was evidently on her initiative that Wilfrid was welcomed back into Northumbria and accorded a role in royal government, leading Stephen of Ripon to praise her as 'the best of advisers and a constant source of strength to the whole province'. A short time later the archbishop of Canterbury journeyed north, in accordance with the pope's command, to convene a new church council to decide Wilfrid's case. It took place in southern Northumbria, somewhere along the River Nidd. The archbishop explained that all parties to the dispute would have to find some way of making peace, or else all of them would have to travel to Rome so that a judgement could be made there. Wilfrid's opponents still refused to budge, pointing out that they had already arrived at a unanimous decision a few years earlier at Austerfield.[74]

At this point Ælfflæd intervened, announcing to the assembly that King Aldfrith, when seized with his final illness, had repented of his treatment of Wilfrid, and that his dying wish had been for his successor to make amends with the bishop. It was clearly a carefully orchestrated moment, contrived to allow those nobles who had stood behind Aldfrith during the dispute to save face. Eventually the abbess and the archbishop were able to talk the Northumbrian clergy into a compromise. It must have helped considerably that one of Wilfrid's principal opponents, Bosa, the bishop of York, died around the time of the council. His place at York did not go to Wilfrid, but to Wilfrid's other main antagonist, John of Beverley. But this meant John had to vacate the bishopric of Hexham, enabling it to pass to Wilfrid. At the same time, the council restored to Wilfrid his original church at Ripon, along with all its revenues. Although his biographer presents it as a total victory, Wilfrid had settled for considerably less than he had hoped his final appeal to the papacy would deliver. In the end he seems to have decided to be content with the material advantages of possessing 'his two best monasteries', as Stephen of Ripon calls them, and ready to forego the prestige and seniority that went with being bishop of York.[75]

Perhaps his declining health persuaded him to settle. Soon after the council, as he was en route to Hexham, his earlier illness returned with even greater severity, and for a time deprived him of the power of speech. He recovered, but decided it was time to put his affairs in order. A short time later he summoned his dependants in Northumbria to Ripon, and divided up his treasure in the manner of a mortally wounded warrior king. On his instructions, all his gold, silver and precious stones were set into four separate piles. The first, he explained, was to go to Rome, adding that he had hoped to carry it there himself, but now others would have to do so on his behalf. Another pile was to go to the poor, and a third to the abbots of Ripon and Hexham, to enable them 'to secure the favour of kings and bishops'. The last pile was reserved for those who had followed him into exile, but had not been rewarded with land. 'Share it out between them according to their needs,' he commanded, 'so that they will be able to maintain themselves after I am gone.'[76]

Wilfrid died a short time later, while making a tour of Mercia to dispose of his property there. By this point seventy-five years old, he was staying at his abbey in Oundle, near Peterborough, when his sickness returned, and he took to his bed, surrounded by his tearful disciples. 'He talked a little while and blessed them,' says Stephen of Ripon, 'then, quietly, without any fuss or complaint, leaned back on his pillow and rested.' On 24 April 710, as the monks softly sang psalms around his bedside, the bishop breathed his last.[77]

In the days that followed, abbots and monks from across his empire assembled at Oundle to pay their last respects. His body was solemnly conveyed back to Northumbria, and his beloved church at Ripon, where it was reverentially laid to rest next to the altar. The inscription on his tomb, preserved by Bede, commended him for building the church and clothing it in purple and gold. It also lauded him for driving out error in the reckoning of Easter, and for firmly establishing the Benedictine Rule in Britain. The epitaph names him as *Wilfridus magnus* – Wilfrid the Great.[78]

Although this was intended as unqualified praise, 'great' is for modern purposes an appropriately ambiguous description. Any assessment of Wilfrid has to acknowledge the enormous impact of his extraordinary life. Arguably no other person, not even Augustine or Theodore, did more to shape the course of Christianity in Britain during its first century. He was born into a world that was still overwhelmingly pagan, at a time when the Roman mission was in crisis and the Celtic mission was barely underway. Raised in the Irish tradition, he rebelled against it and became Rome's most determined champion, seeking to eradicate what he came to regard as Celtic heresy. In a career that spanned more than half a century, he held bishoprics in

Northumbria, Sussex and Mercia, and, if we believe his biographer, had been offered the sees of Lyon, Strasbourg and Canterbury. His influence was wide and pervasive. 'Who can tell how many bishops, priests and deacons he had consecrated and ordained,' asked Stephen of Ripon, 'or count the churches he had dedicated in all those years?' The modern reader of Stephen's work, however, is left to contemplate other questions: how many thousands died as a result of the wars of conquest that were unleashed with Wilfrid's blessing, or resisting his campaigns of forced conversion? How many careers of pious men and women did he ruin in pursuit of doctrinal purity and personal vendettas? Wilfrid's impact was undoubtedly great, but to achieve it he committed many terrible deeds.[79]

A lasting part of his legacy was an increased division between Northumbria and the other Anglo-Saxon kingdoms. When Theodore had arrived in Canterbury in 669, Gregory the Great's plan for Britain to have two metropolitans was long dead, and Theodore was soon confidently styling himself 'archbishop of Britain'. Wilfrid seems to have accepted this state of affairs while Theodore lived, but showed notably less deference towards Canterbury thereafter. His biographer dismissively refers to Theodore's successor, Berhtwald, as 'archbishop of the Kentish Church', while claiming that Wilfrid had been recognized in Rome as 'bishop of all the northern part of Britain and Ireland, and the islands inhabited by the Angles, Britons, Picts and Scots'. This was a flat-out falsehood, disproved by papal records, but by the time of Wilfrid's death, the idea that there ought to be a prelate in the north with such wide-ranging power was evidently popular among his followers and the wider Northumbrian Church. Twenty-five years later, York was at last elevated to the status of an archbishopric.[80]

By this time there were other reasons for Northumbrians to seek independence from their neighbours in the south. Concluding his great *Ecclesiastical History* in 731, and emphasizing how far the Church had come in the past hundred years, Bede listed with satisfaction the names of all the bishops who were ministering to the various kingdoms below the Humber. Wessex, Essex and Sussex, along with East Anglia, Lindsey, the Isle of Wight, and the people of the Hwicce, now had a dozen prelates between them – almost precisely the number that Gregory the Great had originally planned. But all these kingdoms, Bede noted ominously, were now subject to the authority of a single secular ruler: the king of Mercia.[81]

0	10 20 30 40 50 miles
0	25 50 75 kilometres

Mersey

Basingwerk

Chester

Treuddyn

Pillar of Eliseg

Dee

Trent

P O W Y S

Shrewsbury

Lichfield

Tamworth

Severn

M E R C I A

Teme

Knighton

Lugg

Worcester

Wye

Hereford

Severn

Wye

G W E N T

H W I C C E

Thames

Chepstow

Offa's Dyke
Wat's Dyke
Wansdyke

W E S S E X

4

AN ENGLISH EMPIRE?

King Offa and the Domination of the South

The town of Knighton lies in Wales, but only just. Travel there by train and you alight at a station which is in England: to reach Wales you must cross a small bridge over the River Teme, which has defined this part of the Anglo-Welsh border since 1536, when its line was permanently fixed by Henry VIII.[1]

Knighton's status as a border town, however, had been established well before this, for it also sits on a boundary created eight centuries earlier by another imperious king. Its Welsh name, Tref-y-Clawdd, provides a substantial clue, for it translates as 'the town on the dyke', and the tourist information signs reveal all by directing you to the Offa's Dyke Centre. The ancient earthwork known by that name since at least the thirteenth century runs through Knighton from north to south. A few miles to the north, at Llanfair Hill, it reaches its highest point above sea level, and one of its best-preserved and most monumental sections (colour picture 11). Along its whole length the dyke has an average height of about twelve feet – a ditch about six feet deep and a bank about six feet high – but here in places it increases to almost four times that total.[2]

Those wishing to walk the dyke from one end to the other should be advised that this is not a trivial landmark. From Knighton it extends northwards for a further sixty-four miles, a continuous groove across the countryside broken only by a five-mile gap near the middle, where it intersects with the River Severn. Not until it approaches the town of Treuddyn, nine miles from the sea, does it finally come to a halt. To the south of Knighton, meanwhile, the route is similarly daunting, but the line of the dyke is more debatable, with larger and more frequent interruptions. Arriving at accurate totals is therefore difficult, but the overall distance from one Welsh coast to another, following the path of the dyke, is roughly 150 miles, and along this line more than eighty miles of embankment has survived. This makes Offa's Dyke the longest linear earthwork in Britain, exceeding even Hadrian's Wall.[3]

There are no reasonable grounds for doubting that the dyke was created at the command of King Offa, who ruled Mercia for almost forty years in the second half of the eighth century. 'There was in fairly recent times a certain warlike king called Offa, who terrified all the neighbouring kings and provinces around him, and who had a great dyke built between Wales and Mercia, from sea to sea.' So wrote Asser, the contemporary biographer of King Alfred, about a hundred years after Offa's death. Asser was himself Welsh and must have crossed the line of the dyke several times in the course of his career. Some historians have worried about his use of the phrase 'from sea to sea', given that Offa's Dyke stops about nine miles short of Wales' north coast, but this is not particularly problematic. The northern part of the dyke runs parallel with another earthwork, Wat's Dyke, apparently commissioned by one of Offa's immediate successors, and this does run all the way to the estuary of the River Dee. Later medieval writers often conflated the two near-contemporary ditches and the likelihood is that Asser had done the same.[4]

The difficult question to answer is not who built the dyke, but why. People had been building dykes in Britain since the Bronze Age, and there seems to have been a particular enthusiasm for constructing them in the centuries immediately after the collapse of Roman rule: examples from this period probably include the Devil's Dyke in Cambridgeshire and Tor Dyke in

Yorkshire. We can be no more precise than this because dating them is almost impossible. Archaeologists can usually assume that the earth they dig will be layered chronologically, but an earth-moving exercise such as building a dyke upends that assumption. Nor are dykes likely to yield the kind of datable objects that are routinely found on sites with high amounts of human traffic, such as monasteries, markets or towns – they are by their nature peripheral and seldom visited after their creation. Their purpose is therefore also largely conjectural. Most are fairly short, extending for only a few miles, and in some cases only a few hundred metres. Judging from their locations, the intention of their creators seems to have been to block established route ways, presumably in the hope of frustrating raiders or rustlers. The nearest rival to Offa's Dyke – though smaller by a very long margin – is the Wansdyke, which runs through Wiltshire and Somerset in two sections, east and west, both approximately eleven miles in length. Attempts to date it accurately have so far proved fruitless, so we can only guess from its position that it might have been built against Mercia by the rulers of Wessex at some point during the early history of those two kingdoms. Offa's Dyke was evidently conceived in similar terms, as a boundary between the Mercians and the Britons to their west. But was it a political boundary, or a strategic one? A military installation, or a check against sporadic raids? A negotiated frontier, or an imposed one? As we shall see, historians have come up with a wide variety of answers.[5]

It would be far easier to say what Offa's Dyke was for if we had more information about the king himself, but, alas, no narrative account of his life has come down to us. Mercia was either poorly served by contemporary writers, or extremely unlucky that none of their works have survived. Bede, who would doubtless have furnished us with a detailed explanation of such a massive engineering project, died in 735, a generation before Offa's accession. The works of other eighth-century chroniclers are pitifully thin compared to those written by Bede, and furnish us with only a few bare scraps of information about Offa's reign.

By way of slight compensation, we have some new sources, such as charters, coins and collections of letters, but a comprehensive account of Offa's career lies frustratingly beyond our grasp.

One thing which we can say for certain about Offa, which the scale of his dyke makes abundantly clear, is that he was an extremely powerful ruler. Asser is quite correct to say that he 'terrified all the neighbouring kings and provinces around him'. Mercia, of course, had been a dominant player in the struggle between the various Anglo-Saxon kingdoms since the mid-seventh century, when the pagan warlord Penda had violently compelled the other rulers of southern Britain to march under his banner. But power such as this, based on personal charisma and continuous military success, would always be volatile, and liable to challenge. Towards the end of the seventh century, as we have seen, Mercia's dominance in the south was contested by Cædwalla of Wessex, whose brief but bloodstained career saw him extend his authority into Sussex, Surrey, Kent and Essex. Yet by the time Offa came to power in the mid-eighth century, there was no question that Mercia had not only regained the initiative, but cemented its power on firmer foundations. One of those foundations – arguably the most important – was London.[6]

London, the great city established by the Romans, had become a ghost town after the Romans' departure. Its wooden buildings had rotted and collapsed, and its grander stone structures had crumbled into ruins. With no one to maintain its sewers and conduits, large areas within its walls had flooded and returned to marsh. There is no archaeological evidence to suggest that any of the earliest Anglo-Saxons settled in this urban wasteland. It was only with the arrival of St Augustine's mission at the close of the sixth century that London acquired its first inhabitants in almost two centuries, when Mellitus, the newly appointed bishop of the East Saxons, established himself in the deserted city with a small band of companions. Roman missionaries were drawn to imperial ruins because of their association with Rome's ancient authority, and because the old masonry could be reused to build new churches – in London's case, the new cathedral church of St Paul's. Everyone else, however, tended to shun such strange and empty places. To the Anglo-Saxons themselves, the cities established by the Romans were places of mystery, wondrous but useless, the haunted relics of a vanished civilization. The phrase used in more than one Old English poem to describe their massive ruins was *enta geweorc* – 'the work of the giants'.[7]

But around the time that Mellitus and his followers were erecting their new church in the old, disused London, a new settlement was being established to the west of the city, about half a mile further along the Thames. At first it amounted to very little – a huddle of traders who found the strand of beach on the river's northern shore was a convenient spot to unload their boats. Such informal settlements that sprang up outside the walls of old cities were commonly referred to as *wics*, from the Latin word *vicus* ('group of dwellings') and so this particular settlement became known as Lundenwic.[8]

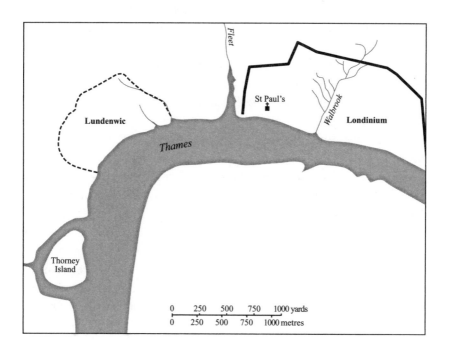

Shortly after the middle of the seventh century, Lundenwic exploded. Part of the reason for its sudden expansion must have been the relatively peaceful conditions that prevailed in southern Britain after decades of destructive war between the newly emerged Anglo-Saxon kingdoms, the boundaries of which were now starting to stabilize. But the economic revival that fuelled this growth was not merely a British phenomenon. All around the coast of northern Europe, there was a similarly sudden take-off in international trade. It was facilitated by the reintroduction of a silver coinage, the like of which had not been seen since the collapse of the empire. Anglo-Saxon and Frankish kings had issued gold coins, but largely for reasons of prestige. The reappearance of silver coins, suitable for lower-value transactions, seems to have been the initiative of the traders themselves, and the vast numbers in the archaeological record attest to its phenomenal success.[9]

This economic renewal turned the little community to the west of London into a boom-town. At some point in the 670s a new wharf was built along the Strand, and new arterial roads were laid out with wooden gutters. From these main thoroughfares a jumble of lesser lanes and alleys spread in all directions. It was not a classical urban environment, and certainly not an urbane one – there were no forums, churches or monuments, never mind theatres, baths or royal residences. All the buildings were single-storey affairs, with dirt floors and walls of wattle and daub.[10]

But in spite of its rude appearance, there were rich profits to be had. We know from anecdotal evidence that traders came to London from overseas in order to buy slaves, but they must also have come to snap up the surpluses being produced by enterprising landlords in the surrounding countryside. At the forefront of this trend were the monasteries that had been founded in large numbers during the second half of the seventh century. A religious community that had been generously endowed with land would have extensive herds and flocks, generating volumes of produce far beyond its own material needs.

In some cases markets and fairs were held at the monastery's gates to turn the hides and fleeces into ready cash. But such events must also have been held at other locations across the country by the end of the seventh century, to judge from the number of so-called 'productive sites' that have been discovered by metal-detectorists in recent decades.[11]

No other market or *wic*, however, was on a par with the one outside of London. Like its Roman predecessor, Lundenwic was perfectly located to capitalize on the industry of its agricultural hinterlands, fed by the Thames and its tributaries, and open to the Continent beyond. It was also ideally situated between the southern Anglo-Saxon kingdoms, lying conveniently between Kent, Mercia, Wessex, Essex and East Anglia. Bede, writing around 731, described London as 'an emporium for many nations, who come to it by land and sea'. At its peak, the new settlement covered about sixty hectares, and extended the whole length of the Strand, from what is now Trafalgar Square to the Aldwych – a street which takes its name from 'the old *wic*'. Its population of artisans, traders, beggars and prostitutes was probably somewhere in the region of 7,000 people.[12]

At least some of these people were making a fortune, so much so that even kings began to sit up and take notice. At the start of the seventh century London lay within the kingdom of Essex, which originally extended far beyond the boundaries of the present county. But in the course of the decades that followed, the medium-sized kingdom was squeezed and carved up by its bigger, more powerful neighbours, and by the second half of the century it seems clear that these rival rulers were contending with each other for control of Lundenwic. Such evidence as we have suggests that Mercia may have gained the upper hand in the 660s, before losing out to the kings of Kent in the 670s, who in turn forfeited to Wessex in the 680s, when Cædwalla was carrying all before him. But by the early eighth century, if not before, the struggle for London had been decided, and Mercia had emerged as the victor.[13]

11. An artist's impression of Lundenwic at its greatest extent.

We can see this thanks to a series of charters issued by King Æthelbald, who ruled Mercia from 716 to 757 – a reign even longer than that of Offa himself, and indeed longer than that of any other Anglo-Saxon king for whom we have reliable dates. Charters – sometimes called diplomas – were written records of grants of property or privileges made by the king. They were introduced to the previously illiterate Anglo-Saxons in the seventh century by Roman churchmen, who were anxious to have guarantees of the extensive lands and rights they had received from royal benefactors. In Æthelbald's case, half a dozen charters have survived in which he granted to various religious institutions an exemption from having to pay tolls in London. This not only proves that the king was in possession of the city by 733 at the latest, but also illustrates the principal way in which he was able to turn that possession into profit. Tolls were a straightforward way for whoever controlled London to cream off a percentage. Unlike a land tax, they did not require a horde of officials to tour the countryside for collection and assessment, but could easily be levied by a few royal officers at the point where goods arrived, either by demanding cash or a portion of the cargo. The fact that bishops and minsters were going to the trouble of obtaining exemptions indicates that the size of these tolls cannot have been negligible.[14]

By the middle of his reign, therefore (and probably from the start), Æthelbald had gained the golden goose that would apparently never stop laying. From a geographical point of view, one can see why he and his predecessors had fought hard to obtain it. All the other Anglo-Saxon kingdoms had coastlines where traders could land if they wished. Mercia, by contrast, was virtually landlocked, and for a long time had been denied the direct links to the Continent that had underpinned the early prosperity of kingdoms like Kent and East Anglia. Other rulers responded to Mercia's victory in the struggle for London by developing existing *wics* or even founding new ones: Wessex had Hamwic, the forerunner of modern Southampton, East Anglia had Ipswich, and Northumbria had Eoforwic, a development outside the walls of York. But none of these was as large or as lucrative as London. Æthelbald was not wholly reliant on its profits. Like his predecessors, he was a warrior king, and the annals of Wessex and Northumbria, thin as they are, reveal that he invaded each kingdom on more than one occasion. But unlike his predecessors, he was not dependent on the flow of tribute and plunder from military campaigns. The profits of London and its international trade boosted his existing power, and gave him the competitive edge.[15]

This edge made Æthelbald supremely powerful in southern Britain. His charters reveal that he was not only granting economic privileges to religious communities in other kingdoms – in some cases he was actively interfering in the government of other kings, granting lands within their territories as if they were his own. The formerly independent rulers of the Hwicce, whose power was centred on Worcester, found they were more or less relegated to rubber-stamping decisions that had already been made by the Mercian king. If this was an extreme case, the rulers of other southern kingdoms must have in some way acknowledged Æthelbald's superiority, perhaps through the payment of tribute. In one of his charters, issued in 736, he is described as 'king not only of the Mercians, but also of all the provinces which are known as the south Angles', and in witnessing the same grant he went even further, referring to himself as 'king of Britain'. We might be tempted to dismiss such titles as little more than vainglorious posturing, but the first receives substantial endorsement from Bede, who stated in 731 that all the kings south of the Humber were subject to Æthelbald's authority.[16]

Sadly, this is the only thing Bede has to say about Æthelbald. (He must have known a great deal more, but was prudently tight-lipped about contemporary rulers.) But some additional light – and, indeed, shade – is thrown on the king by the letters of contemporary churchmen – in particular, churchmen who were working as missionaries on the Continent. Since the end of the seventh century, numerous Anglo-Saxon monks and priests, infused with the evangelical fervour that had recently spread across Britain, had begun travelling to the European mainland with the aim of converting the peoples on the fringes of Francia who were still pagan. The most celebrated of all these missionaries was Boniface.[17]

Boniface had begun his career as Winfrith, a West Saxon monk, born in the early 670s – he was given his new name almost forty years later by the pope, who granted him permission to preach in Frisia. As St Boniface, he has long been regarded as the apostle of Germany, not least because he eventually died a martyr's death, but in truth his own missionary endeavours were fairly limited. He did, however, enjoy great success as a reformer of existing churches across Europe, and rose to a position of great eminence, becoming archbishop of Mainz in 746. As such he was frequently in correspondence with other leaders, both secular and religious, and many of his letters were collected together after his death.[18]

Very soon after his appointment as archbishop, Boniface wrote a letter to Æthelbald, co-signed by eight other European bishops, many of them Anglo-Saxon émigrés like himself. He began by praising the good things he had heard about the king: that he was a generous giver of alms, a defender of widows and the poor, and a ruler who maintained peace throughout his realm. But this was little more than a polite preamble. Boniface soon revealed his real purpose, which was to berate Æthelbald for his lascivious lifestyle. Reports had reached the archbishop's ears that the king had never taken a lawful wife because he was 'governed by lust' – a notorious adulterer who compounded his sin by cavorting 'with holy nuns and virgins consecrated to God'.[19]

Interesting as this is as a character note for Æthelbald, the letter's arguably more intriguing criticism comes towards its conclusion, when Boniface says he had also heard that the king had stolen revenues from churches and monasteries, and violated their privileges. Mercian noblemen are accused of doing the same, afflicting monks and priests with unprecedented violence and oppression.[20]

What was going on? One possibility is that the king and his companions were cracking down on 'fake monasteries', a problem that had evidently become rife in recent decades. 'There are innumerable places, as we all know, allowed the name of "monasteries" by a foolish manner of speaking, but have nothing at all of a monastic way of life.' So wrote Bede towards the end of his life in a letter to the bishop of York. The root cause was that, since the introduction of charters, the Church had enjoyed security of landownership in a way that the laity had not. Once a religious institution acquired a charter (or *boc*) from the king, its estates became 'book-land', free of royal demands forever. By the early eighth century, certainly in Northumbria, envious laymen had come up with the ruse of claiming their households were monasteries in order to enjoy the same privileges. Apart from perpetual tenure of land, being a monastic community meant never having to provide the king with military service. Bede regarded this as outrageous on two scores. First, it meant there were countless so-called minsters where men were leading wanton and gluttonous lives, cohabiting openly with women and fathering children. Second, it meant that there were not enough estates left for the king's military followers, leaving the kingdom undefended against its enemies.[21]

If such bogus monasteries were as common in Mercia as they were in Northumbria, this could explain why Æthelbald had been, in Boniface's words, 'violating their privileges'. The king might quite rightly have regarded his actions as a necessary overhaul of a system that was being abused, denying him the customary services to which he was entitled. Another of the archbishop's letters, however, reveals that Æthelbald's demands went further than this. Writing to the archbishop of Canterbury in 747, Boniface encouraged him to speak out against 'the forced labour of monks upon royal buildings and other works', adding that this was 'an evil unknown in earlier times'.[22]

The fact that Æthelbald was compelling monks – or, more probably, the labourers who toiled on monastic estates – to work on unspecified royal building projects has proved irresistibly tempting to historians in search of answers about dykes. Starved of other evidence, they have suggested that this might mean the king was the creator of Wat's Dyke – the earthwork which runs slightly to the east of, and some miles beyond, the northern part of the more celebrated dyke built by Offa. This theory, however, has lately been discredited by scientific dating methods, which suggest that Wat's Dyke was built in the early ninth century.[23]

The construction projects that were of greatest concern to Æthelbald are revealed in a charter he issued two years later, in response to his censure by Boniface and the other bishops. In 749 the king held a council at Gumley, a royal estate near Leicester, during which he promised that in future neither he nor his men would oppress churches or monasteries with any unjust impositions. But – and it was a significant qualification – these institutions were forewarned that they would nevertheless be expected to contribute to two things: 'the building of bridges and the defence of fortresses against enemies when necessary'. These, the king insisted, were duties incumbent upon everybody, secular and religious, and were 'not to be refused'.[24]

1. The Hoxne Hoard (pp. 9–11). The transparent display case replicates the wooden chest and caskets in which the treasure was originally packed.

2. Hadrian's Wall (p. 14). The famous frontier-marker, extending seventy-three miles from coast to coast, reflects the scale of Roman military might.

3. Two artists' impressions of Durovernum (Canterbury), showing the city at the height of its Roman splendour, and its ruinous condition after the end of imperial rule.

. The Kingston Down brooch (p. 60).

. The belt buckle from Sutton Hoo (p. 66).

6. Items from the Staffordshire Hoard (pp. 82–3).

7. The pectoral cross once worn by St Cuthbert (p. 248).

8. The crypt at Hexham Abbey, built by St Wilfrid (pp. 85–7).

9. The church at Bradwell-on-Sea in Essex, built by St Cedd (p. 95).

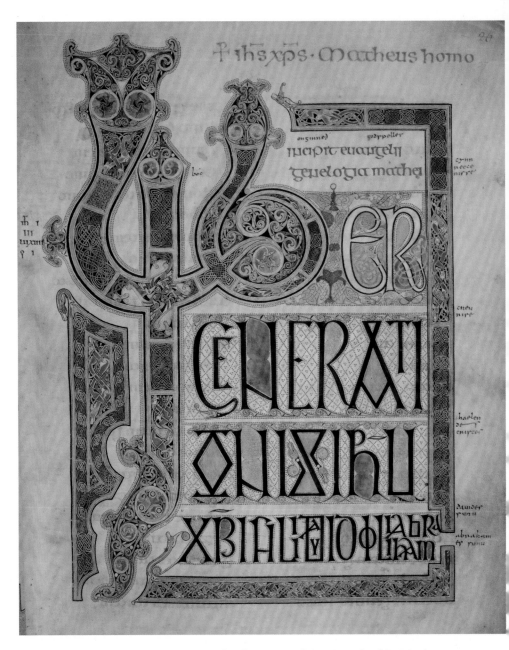

10. The Lindisfarne Gospels (p. 123). The first page of the Gospel of St Matthew.

11. Offa's Dyke crossing Llanfair Hill (p. 133).

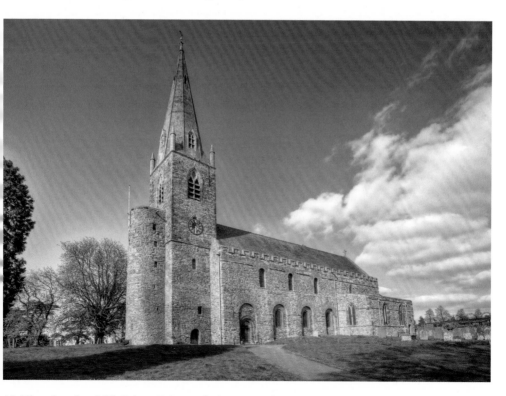

12. The church of All Saints, Brixworth (p. 164). The tower and spire were added in the eleventh and thirteenth centuries, but most of the nave dates to the late eighth or early ninth centuries, and was probably commissioned by King Offa.

13. A gold coin issued by King Offa, in imitation of a Middle-Eastern dinar (p. 158). Now in the British Museum, it was first recorded in Rome, suggesting it may have been one of the 365 gold coins a year that Offa promised to pay the pope.

14. A carved animal head – one of five – found in the ninth-century Oseberg ship-burial (p. 182).

This clearly indicates that, when it came to building projects, bridges and fortresses were Æthelbald's top priority. The broad wooden bridges that had carried Roman roads across the otherwise impassable rivers must have been long gone, either swept away by severe weather, or destroyed by a lack of routine maintenance during centuries when people lacked the engineering skills to repair or rebuild them. When early Anglo-Saxons wished to create a permanent river crossing they had to settle for the low-tech solution of dumping stones in the water to construct a causeway. For a king and a country that were becoming increasingly reliant on long-distance travel and international trade, bridges were thus essential – they were the missing links that would render the Roman network fully operational again. There is even some surviving fabric from a bridge that might have been built at Æthelbald's command. At Cromwell Lock in Nottinghamshire, a few miles along the River Trent from Newark, timbers of a crossing have been recovered and dendro-dated to the early eighth century.[25]

When it comes to Æthelbald's other priority – 'the defence of fortresses against enemies' – we are on less certain ground. Some historians have argued that the king was expecting his subjects to contribute their labour to the repair or rebuilding of forts, but 'defence' might simply mean the duty of manning the walls in the event of an attack. Nor is it clear what these fortresses were. With one or two celebrated exceptions – Bamburgh in Northumbria being one – early Anglo-Saxon kings seem not to have invested in fortifications: their wooden halls were seldom surrounded by anything more than a timber stockade. The most reasonable explanation, therefore, is that Æthelbald was reusing old fortifications, most likely Iron Age hill forts. But so far the archaeological evidence that would support such a theory has not been found.[26]

An alternative approach, therefore, is to ask: who were the 'enemies' these fortresses were being held against? We know from the scanty annals compiled in Wessex and Northumbria that Æthelbald had on occasion gone to war against both these kingdoms, but in each case he is named as the aggressor. It seems unlikely that he needed his people to be forever on guard against invasion from his neighbours to the north or the south.[27]

But what of the people to the west? One of the few narrative sources that relates to Æthelbald's reign is the *Life of St Guthlac*, written at some point before 749. Guthlac was a holy man, a hermit who lived in the fens of eastern Mercia, and had been a spiritual adviser to Æthelbald before the king's accession. Earlier in his career, however, when he was a young man, Guthlac had been a warrior, engaged in the bloody business of wasting towns and villages with fire and sword. His war-band, we are told, was assembled from people of various different races, and at one time he had lived as an exile among the Britons – so much so that he could understand their speech. Yet when Guthlac, as a hermit, had a vision one night that his island in the Fens was being attacked by a horde of angry demons, he imagined that they were speaking British. As his biographer explains, the Britons were at that time oppressing the Mercians 'with war, pillage and devastation'.[28]

Æthelbald's desire to have defensible fortresses was thus most likely a result of his kingdom's extended frontier with what is now Wales. He may have clashed with Wessex and Northumbria on occasion, but his relations with these other Anglo-Saxon kingdoms were for the most part reasonably stable.[29] To judge from the *Life of St Guthlac*, Æthelbald clearly could not count on that same stability when it came to his British neighbours. Just as the economic fortunes of the Anglo-Saxon kingdoms had risen in the seventh century because of the burgeoning international trade around the North Sea, so those of the British kingdoms to the west had rapidly declined. The Britons of the fifth and sixth centuries had imported wine, oil and other luxuries from the Mediterranean, maintaining the vestiges of a Roman existence. But by the start of the seventh century that trade was gone, and the elite centres at Tintagel and Cadbury Congresbury had been abandoned. Henceforth, the most straight-forward way for Britons to obtain high-value goods would have been to lead raids into the more prosperous lands to their east.[30]

As it turns out, the enemies that Æthelbald ought to have worried about were not foreign but domestic. In 757, having ruled for forty-one years, he was killed by his own bodyguard – 'wretchedly and treacherously', in the opinion of the anonymous scribe who added a few brief entries to Bede's *Ecclesiastical History.* The murder triggered a protracted and vicious struggle for power. Æthelbald was succeeded in the first instance by a man named Beornred, who was presumably a participant in the original coup. But within a few months this new king had also been toppled. 'In that same year,' explains Bede's continuator, 'Offa put Beornred to flight, and attempted to conquer the Mercian kingdom with sword and bloodshed.'[31]

So began the rule of the greatest king of eighth-century Britain, in a bloody civil war with rival contenders for the Mercian throne. Like so much of his life, the story of Offa's rise to power is frustratingly obscure. He *claimed* to be a descendant of Eowa, brother of the mighty King Penda, but this may have been just a fiction to boost his credentials: the same claim had been made by his predecessor, Æthelbald. The essential problem was that Æthelbald's notorious failure to marry and father children within wedlock had left the question of who would succeed him wide open, and thus likely to be resolved by violence. Given that he would go on to reign for almost forty years, Offa must have been a young man in 757, warlike and ambitious, with an existing following of other warriors ready to champion his claim. In this respect his story is no different to that of any number of kings, such as Cædwalla of Wessex or Oswiu of Northumbria: a dissatisfied pretender, vigorous and hungry for power, able to persuade others that their fortunes would improve under his leadership. During the last years of Æthelbald's reign, Mercia seems to have suffered military reverses against Wessex and perhaps Northumbria as well, so Offa might perhaps have presented himself to potential supporters as the candidate who would restore the kingdom to its former greatness.[32]

But if Offa at first cut a familiar figure, once in power he soon embarked upon a plan far more ambitious than that of any of his predecessors. Penda and his descendants, and after them Æthelbald, had exercised a wide authority over the other kingdoms of southern Britain, but in each case this had been exercised as a loose hegemony, with lesser rulers acknowledging Mercian superiority through the payment of tribute. Offa, by contrast, set out to build something more permanent. In his scheme, Mercia would not simply dominate neighbouring kingdoms; it would annex them, absorb them, and relegate them to the status of mere provinces within an expanded Mercian empire.

The first kingdom to experience this treatment was Kent, which was seemingly brought under direct control within just a few years of Offa's accession. In 764 the king was in Canterbury, issuing a charter, surrounded by a crowd of Mercian nobles, who are listed as witnesses. The charter shows him disposing of land in Kent as if it was his own, much as Æthelbald had done in the case of the kingdom of the Hwicce. The land in question was a large estate on the River Medway that had already been given to the bishop of Rochester two years earlier by Sigered, one of the several kings who shared the rule of Kent between them. Offa had decided that this grant had been invalid because it had been made without his say-so, and was charging the bishop for its re-approval. Among the witnesses to the charter, besides the Mercian entourage, was another Kentish king named Heahbert, who meekly added his consent. The kings of Kent, who had once been regarded as the most powerful rulers south of the Humber, had apparently been reduced to the status of puppets.[33]

But they were at least allowed to retain the fig leaf of royal status. When Offa turned his attention to the rulers of Sussex a few years later, no such niceties were involved. It looks as if the Mercian king brought the South Saxon kingdom under his direct control by outright military conquest – a northern annalist records that in 771 he 'subdued the *Hastingas* by force of arms' – and the following year another of his charters shows him making a grant of land in Sussex with the same proprietorial self-assurance he had previously displayed in Kent. This grant, to the bishop of Sussex, was made at a particularly august assembly. After Offa himself, the subscribers to the charter include the kings of Kent and Wessex, the archbishop of Canterbury, and the bishops of London, Leicester and Rochester. They also include, at the end of the list, four men who were individually designated as *dux* – the Latin word for 'leader', later translated as 'duke', for which the Anglo-Saxon equivalent was 'ealdorman'. This was a prestigious title, but at least three of these men had previously been pleased to describe themselves as kings of Sussex. Offa had demoted them to the rank of provincial governors.[34]

This kind of high-handed reordering of power was bound to generate resistance – that much is suggested by the fact that Offa had led armies into Sussex in order to bend it to his will. There was also a fightback in Kent. Under the year 776 the *Anglo-Saxon Chronicle* drily reports a battle between Mercian and Kentish armies. The outcome of this clash is not recorded, but it was almost certainly a defeat for Offa – after that date, the kings of Kent began issuing charters independently again, without any reference to their supposed Mercian overlord. It is hard to imagine that Offa would have taken this rejection of his authority lying down, but at that point his ability to retaliate may have been restricted. Other sources suggest that around the same time he was experiencing similar difficulties with the peoples to his west.[35]

The abbey of Valle Crucis lies in the Welsh county of Denbighshire, a few miles north of the small town of Llangollen. It was founded at the start of the thirteenth century, and named after a stone cross that stood nearby in the same valley. The cross, which still survives in part, was already very ancient by this date. It had been erected at some point in the early part of the ninth century by Cyngen ap Cadell, ruler of the British kingdom of Powys. We know this because the surviving pillar of the cross once had an inscription telling us as much. It is now, alas, too faded to read, but it was transcribed in the seventeenth century when it was still partially legible. Cyngen, it informs us,

12. The Pillar of Eliseg.

had erected the cross to celebrate the memory of his great-grandfather, Eliseg – a king who had 'united the inheritance of Powys', and had apparently done so by taking land from 'the power of the Angles'.

The dates of the events recorded on the Pillar of Eliseg (as it is now known), and indeed the dates of the rulers of eighth-century Powys, are impossible to recover with any precision. We know that Cyngen, who commissioned the pillar, had come to power in 808 and died in 854 – a usefully long reign that suggests he was probably born at some point in the 780s.[36] If we allow an average generation gap of twenty years, his father would have been born in the 760s, his grandfather in the 740s, and his great-grandfather, Eliseg, in the 720s. Thus Eliseg's reign is likely to have fallen at some point in the middle decades of the eighth-century, and must have overlapped with either the later years of Æthelbald or the early years of Offa. His achievements as celebrated on the Pillar of Eliseg – the unification of Powys and the apparent recovery of territory from his eastern enemies – must have occurred during the reign of one or other of these two kings. Perhaps it happened in the chaotic period between Æthelbald's death and Offa's accession, when the Mercians were fighting among themselves. Perhaps it happened around 760, when a later Welsh chronicle recorded 'a battle between the Britons and the Saxons' at Hereford. Or perhaps it happened later in Offa's reign, for the same chronicle records that the king devastated the Britons on two occasions, first in 778 and again in the summer of 784. Precision is impossible, but what the Pillar of Eliseg and the later chronicle undoubtedly show is a situation on Mercia's western frontier that was increasingly hostile, with the Britons at one point recovering territory, and at other times suffering the force of Offa's retribution.[37]

Is this ongoing war of attrition enough to explain the creation of Offa's Dyke? An extensive investigation of the earthwork that ran from the 1970s to the early 2000s, known as the Offa's Dyke Project, eventually concluded it was not nearly as long as had always been assumed. Its apparently incomplete southern sections were dismissed as unrelated ditches and embankments from earlier or later periods. Far from running from sea to sea, as Asser had insisted, the dyke had extended for only sixty-four miles along the frontier between Mercia and Powys. From this the project's leaders argued that it had been built by Offa as a military installation to thwart any future raids or reconquests by Eliseg or his successors.[38]

This interpretation, however, has lately been called into question. In the first place, it has been observed that the boundaries of eighth-century Powys are impossible to determine, and largely adduced from the dyke itself, so the argument is a circular one. More problematic still, some of the southern sections of the dyke that had been dismissed as unrelated earthworks have now been shown to be built in exactly the same way as the central section attributed to Offa. It seems, therefore, that Asser's assessment was correct. The dyke may be incomplete in places, but there is no reason to doubt that it was originally intended to run for the whole length of the Anglo-Welsh frontier, and not merely the border with Powys.[39]

Moreover, the notion that Offa's Dyke was intended to function as a military barrier against the Britons is also open to doubt. Some historians, underwhelmed by the earthwork's current appearance, have suggested it must have originally had a host of additional features to increase its military effectiveness – a wooden fence running along its ridge, garrison forts for soldiers, a path for riding patrols to follow, and so on. Such features would have made it a genuine defensible line, akin to Hadrian's Wall, which had many forts along its length, garrisoned by thousands of soldiers. But no evidence for such features on Offa's Dyke has ever been found, and it is unlikely that all trace of them would have completely disappeared, had they actually existed. Nor is it likely that the local communities along the length of the dyke, or even Mercia more generally, could have spared the manpower necessary to patrol and guard such an extensive frontier. The obvious conclusion is that Offa's Dyke was not really intended to function in this way.[40]

Those historians who accept the dyke on its own terms have therefore tended to conclude it was built not so much to guard against some anticipated British invasion, but as an obstacle to frustrate raids across the border. A ditch and embankment with an average height of around twelve feet would certainly have made the rustling of sheep and cattle a good deal more difficult. But the construction of the dyke represented a massive deployment of manpower. Just to build its sixty-four-mile central section, it is reckoned, would have required 5,000 men to work relentlessly for twenty weeks.[41] Would Offa, or indeed any king, really go to all this trouble simply to deter cattle-rustlers?

Soon after his devastation of the Britons in 784, Offa must have returned his attention to Kent. In that year King Egbert of Kent was still issuing charters without reference to his unwanted Mercian overlord. But in the following year, Offa was once again treating the smaller kingdom as his own, granting lands there just as if it was a part of Mercia. The conclusion must be that Offa had reimposed his power, probably with violence. The kings of Kent, who had been permitted to retain their position during Offa's previous takeover, now disappear altogether from the historical record. The year 785 was the effective end date for Kent as an independent kingdom.⁴²

It was perhaps to celebrate this successful takeover that Offa embarked on a major reform of his coinage. The vast number of silver pennies that had spread all around the North Sea coastal zone since the 670s, facilitating trade and boosting the fortunes of London and other new *wics*, had all but disappeared in the middle decades of the eighth century, apparently because of a European-wide shortage of silver. By the start of Offa's reign, there was hardly any money at all in circulation. In response to this crisis, kings had taken over production, adding their names to coins for the first time. The pioneers were the kings of Northumbria, who reformed their coinage in the 740s, and by the 760s the practice had been adopted by their Southumbrian counterparts. But none of these rulers seem to have had much silver to work with. Although Offa was issuing personalized pennies within a few years of his accession, they were still extremely few in number.⁴³

All this changed in 785, at which point Offa began issuing coins in much greater quantities. His takeover of Kent must have been a major contributing factor, for it handed him control of the mint at Canterbury. At the start of the eighth century, when the old silver monetary economy had been booming, coins had been struck in around twenty locations across southern Britain, but by the start of Offa's reign this had dropped to only three: London, Ipswich and Canterbury. The first two were already under Offa's control, but the addition of the Kentish mint must have given him access to a new team of moneyers and perhaps greater supplies of silver. Certainly from this point on his coinage suddenly becomes far more voluminous.⁴⁴

It also becomes far more impressive. After 785 not only did Offa's pennies bear his name, they also in some cases featured his portrait. The king's face appears in profile, and he is depicted wearing a diadem, like a Roman emperor (though his curly hair might be an allusion to the biblical King David). This became the standard design for Anglo-Saxon and then English coins until the thirteenth century, but none of these later coins would match the quality of those issued in Offa's reign after 785. (Indeed, Offa's own moneyers were unable to sustain it, and by the end of his reign it had been discontinued in favour of a simpler design, *sans* portrait.) The brief appearance of a coinage of exceptional quality suggests a concerted effort at image-making carried out at the instance of the king himself. At the same time, he must have forbidden the circulation of foreign coins within his kingdom: ninety-nine per cent of all the pennies in use after this date had Offa's name on them.[45]

In a few cases, they had the name and face of his queen, Cynethryth. This too was a unique experiment in Britain – no other Anglo-Saxon queen, so far as we know, was ever accorded such a distinction, nor was it known in Europe outside of Byzantium. Sadly, little else is known about Cynethryth – we know nothing of her background or how she came to be married to Offa. But the fact that they were married, and that Offa honoured her in such a public way, is surely significant. His two predecessors, Æthelbald and Ceolred, had been condemned by contemporary churchmen for their licentious and adulterous behaviour. Cynethryth, by contrast, was apparently Offa's only wife, and had borne him several children. At least three were daughters, but only one of them was a son.[46]

The boy's name was Ecgfrith, and it was upon him that his father's plans for the future depended. Offa, as we've seen, had fought his way to power with a bloody sword, and the same had probably been true in the case of Æthelbald, who had been sent into exile by the king he eventually succeeded. There was, of course, nothing unusual in this. In the age of *Beowulf*, it was expected that a king's death would bring chaos and dissolution, as contenders piled in to demand either the whole kingdom of some parcel of it for themselves. Offa, however, evidently wished

13. A silver penny depicting King Offa.

14. A silver penny depicting Queen Cynethryth. 'Eoba' is the
name of the moneyer.

to avoid this scenario, and wanted Ecgfrith to succeed him as the ruler of the greatly enlarged Mercia he had fought so hard to create. This might explain the decision to mint coins with the queen's face on them. It certainly explains the king's decision to emulate his neighbours on the Continent, and have the boy consecrated.[47]

The neighbours in question were the new kings of Francia, a dynasty known as the Carolingians. They took their name from Charles Martel, who had been 'mayor of the palace' in Francia during the early eighth century. By the middle of the century the old Frankish kings had become so enfeebled that Charles' son and successor, Pippin, sought and received permission from the pope to replace them. Offa's contemporary in 785 was Pippin's son, named Charles after his illustrious grandfather, but eventually and more memorably known as Charles the Great, or Charlemagne.

By that date Charlemagne was well on the way to earning his famous soubriquet: he had already annexed northern Italy, and was completing a long and bloody conquest of the Saxons. Even so, for all their success, both he and his predecessors were acutely conscious that they had come to power as usurpers, and craved legitimation. On assuming power with papal permission in 751, Pippin had been anointed. This was a new departure. Biblical kings – most famously, King David – had been consecrated in this way, but never before had such a procedure been performed to create a king of Francia. It involved the new ruler having holy oil, or chrism, poured on his head, which was seen as imbuing him to some degree with divine power. (The word 'Christ' means 'anointed one'.) Charlemagne had been similarly anointed as a young boy, and arranged an identical ceremony for his own sons in 781, performed by Pope Hadrian I.[48]

By seeking to have his own son consecrated, therefore, Offa was clearly taking a leaf out of the Carolingian playbook, and hoping to buttress the legitimacy of his own newly established dynasty. But this plan immediately ran up against an unfortunate fact of ecclesiastical geopolitics. In order to carry out the ceremony, the king would need to secure the services of the archbishop of Canterbury, whose cathedral city was also the capital of Kent. Since Offa had spent most of his reign attempting to bludgeon Kent into submission, and had recently disappeared or otherwise retired its long-established rulers, his expectation of willing co-operation from Canterbury cannot have been high. And so it predictably proved: when the request to anoint Ecgfrith was put to Archbishop Jænberht, he evidently made it clear that he was not going to oblige.[49]

Offa therefore came up with an audacious workaround. If the archbishop of Canterbury would not assist the king of Mercia, it was obvious that Mercia needed an archbishop of its own. Shortly after his annexation of Kent, Offa must have sent messengers to Pope Hadrian, requesting his intervention: in 786, papal legates arrived in Britain for the first time since St Augustine had landed in Kent almost 200 years before. The official reason for their visit was to review the progress that the Christian mission had made in the meantime, and to correct any abuses – 'to uproot anything harmful', as they put it in their written report to the pope, 'and to secure the most wholesome fruit'. But while the legates did hold two reforming councils, one in Mercia, the other in Northumbria, and propounded decrees against pagan practices, the tacit reason for their visit was obviously Offa's overriding concern to expedite the consecration of his son. It sounds from their report as though they gave fairly short shrift to Archbishop Jænberht, advising him 'of those things that were necessary' before proceeding to 'the court of Offa, king of the Mercians', who received them with 'immense honour and joy'. One of the decrees they read out in Offa's presence, surely designed to meet with his approval, reminded all those present that men 'begotten in adultery or incest' could not become kings. 'Let no one dare to kill a king,' it added, 'for he is the Lord's anointed.' Anyone who committed such a sacrilegious act would burn in hell for all eternity.[50]

The following year Offa's plan came to fruition. The *Anglo-Saxon Chronicle* records that a Church council was held at Chelsea, and that it was 'contentious', which must have been putting it mildly. 'Archbishop Jænberht lost certain parts of his province', continues the *Chronicle*, and we can deduce from later evidence that this loss amounted to more than half the bishoprics in the southern archdiocese. In future, the bishops of Rochester, Selsey, Sherborne, Winchester and London – in other words, the ones with sees south of the Thames – would answer to Canterbury, as before. But the bishops of Leicester, Lindsey, Hereford, Worcester, Dunwich and Elmham – all those between the Thames and the Humber – would be ruled by the new archbishop of Lichfield. The pope signalled his approval of this division by sending a pallium, or stole of office, to the existing bishop of Lichfield, Hygeberht, just as he did when confirming the appointment of the archbishops of Canterbury and York – a decision perhaps not entirely unconnected to Offa's promise to make an annual payment to the papacy of 365 gold coins, one for every day of the year (colour picture 13). From Offa's point of view this was money well spent. As soon as Hygeberht had been elevated as archbishop, notes the *Chronicle*, 'Ecgfrith was consecrated as king.'[51]

Even as Offa was redrawing the ecclesiastical map of Britain to smooth the path for his son's succession, Wessex was thrown into chaos by exactly the sort of vicious politics that the Mercian king was anxious to avoid. The king of Wessex, Cynewulf, had come to power in 757, the same year as Offa, and after a similarly bitter struggle. Just as the Mercian ruler had driven out his rival, Beornred, so too had Cynewulf expelled his short-lived predecessor, Sigeberht, who soon died in exile, stabbed to death by a swineherd. Since that time Cynewulf had enjoyed a long and reasonably successful reign, fighting against the British to his west while simultaneously resisting domination by Mercia. Offa, it is true, had defeated him in battle on their shared border in 779, and appropriated lands along the upper Thames Valley. But unlike the other southern kingdoms, Wessex had retained its independence. When the papal legates had visited in 786, Cynewulf had been treated as a ruler in his own right.[52]

Later that year, however, Cynewulf's past finally caught up with him. Almost three decades after the death of his rival, Sigeberht, the dead man's brother, Cyneheard, came looking for revenge. What followed clearly became a legendary story, for a lengthy account of it was entered into the *Anglo-Saxon Chronicle* over a century later. In brief, Cyneheard learned that the king was staying in a particular location, visiting his mistress, and had taken with him only a small number of followers. Seizing his chance, the would-be avenger rode there with his own large retinue and slaughtered everyone who was present – the king first, who charged from the doorway at his attackers, and then the men who had rushed to his aid.

But the following morning, the tables were turned. When the rest of the king's men discovered what had happened, they rode to the place and found Cyneheard and his eighty or so followers holed up inside. He offered them rewards of money and land if they would recognize him as their new ruler, but to no avail. They would never serve the slayer of their late master, they declared, and proceeded to break into the enclosure, killing Cyneheard and his accomplices.[53]

This famous episode obviously emphasized the virtue of Offa's recent efforts to elevate his dynasty – it was exactly the kind of carnage he hoped the consecration of his son would discourage. At the same time, the bloodbath provided the Mercian ruler with an unmissable opportunity. With both Cynewulf and Cyneheard dead, and many of their men with them, the kingship of Wessex passed to a man called Beorhtric, whose connection with his predecessors is unknown, and whose position must have been much weaker than his long-lived predecessor. Offa, it seems, decided to lend his support to his new royal neighbour. Three years later his daughter Eadburh was married to Beorhtric, and around the same time he helped the new king of Wessex drive out a dynastic rival. But it is unlikely that this kind of backing came without a price. On the surface Beorhtric seems to have retained his independence, but it seems very probable that he admitted some degree of subservience to his Mercian father-in-law.

Whereas his predecessors had proudly used the title 'king of the West Saxons' in their charters, Beorhtric on one occasion timidly styled himself 'king of this province'.[54]

The downside to Offa's intervention in Wessex is that it may have led to a falling-out with Charlemagne. The two kings clashed at the start of 790, but the reason for their rift was unclear, even to contemporaries. At that moment, another expatriate Anglo-Saxon churchman, Alcuin of York, who had been part of the circle of scholars at Charlemagne's court for the past four years, wrote to a friend in his native Northumbria. 'A certain dissension, fomented by the Devil, has lately arisen between King Charles and King Offa,' he confided, 'so that on both sides the passage of ships has been forbidden to merchants.' Alcuin's other letters, however, make it clear that he had no clue as to what the non-diabolical causes of the disagreement might have been. Half a century later, the chronicler at the Frankish abbey of St Wandrille, near Rouen, stated that the row had arisen as a result of marriage negotiations between the two kings. Charlemagne had apparently suggested that his son, Charles, should marry one of Offa's daughters, but Offa had responded by saying he would agree to this match only if one of Charlemagne's daughters married his son, Ecgfrith. At this, says the chronicle, the Frankish king had become 'somewhat enraged' and ordered a trade embargo – presumably the one mentioned by Alcuin.[55]

While the argument about royal weddings may have some mileage, it seems unlikely it was the root cause of the problem. A more fundamental factor might have been the fact that Charlemagne was in the habit of harbouring Offa's enemies – 'exiles who, in fear of death, have taken refuge under the wings of our protection', as the Frankish king described them in a letter written later in the 790s. The particular exile who may have upset relations at the start of the decade was Egbert, a scion of the royal house of Wessex, and the rival to Beorhtric whom Offa had helped to banish in 789. In a later resume of his career, the *Anglo-Saxon Chronicle* reveals that Egbert had spent his years of exile 'in Francia'.[56]

The fact that Egbert was being sheltered in Francia would seem the likeliest cause of the sudden cooling in relations between Charlemagne and Offa. If Offa protested about it, as well he might, nothing would have been more natural than for the Frankish king to have tried to mend fences by proposing a marriage alliance. But if Offa was already suspicious of Charlemagne's intentions, he would have balked at the prospect of sending one of his daughters to the Carolingian court, where she would effectively become another pawn who might be used against him. To allay his own fears, Offa could well have insisted that the exchange of brides be reciprocal, and demanded that Charlemagne dispatch one of his own daughters to be married in Mercia. In these (admittedly conjectural) circumstances, it is easy to imagine how the Frankish king could have been 'somewhat enraged': he had proposed his daughter as a peace offering, but Offa tried to turn it into an exchange of hostages.

How long their contretemps lasted is unclear, but relations had evidently been repaired by the first half of 796, when Charlemagne sent Offa a letter written in the warmest of tones. Addressing the Mercian king as 'his dearest brother', he expressed his desire to 'untie the knots of enmity' for their mutual profit of their two peoples. As this implies, much of the letter was concerned with the restoration and regulation of commerce. Charlemagne renewed an earlier dispensation that permitted pilgrims travelling from Britain to Rome to pass through Francia without having to pay tolls, provided they were genuine in their pious intent and not merchants who were simply seeking to avoid payment. As for bona fide merchants, the Frankish king granted them his protection and allowed them to appeal to his judges if they were afflicted or oppressed. He also asked Offa to ensure that the cloaks being exported from his realm to Francia were the same size as they used to be. This was apparently a concern close to Charlemagne's own heart, to judge from a story told by a later Carolingian chronicler. 'What's the use of these little bits of cloth,' he said, testily, when presented with imported cloaks that were cut too short; 'I can't cover myself with them when I'm in bed, I can't protect myself when against the wind and rain when I'm riding, and when I get down to answer a call of nature, I suffer because my legs are frozen.'[57]

Interesting as all these details are, the letter is no less important for what it tells us about Offa's power. Charlemagne was no doubt flattering the Mercian king by describing him as a brother, with the implication that the two of them were equals, for in territorial terms his own dominion was at least ten times greater. Nevertheless, Charlemagne elsewhere acknowledges the reality of Offa's authority in southern Britain. Towards the end of the letter he mentions that he has sent several gifts – a belt, a 'Hunnish' sword, and two silk cloaks for Offa himself, and similar cloaks and vestments for all the Anglo-Saxon bishops. Some of these vestments, he explained, were for the bishops of Northumbria, but the rest were for the ones in 'your kingdom'; in other words, he regarded the Mercian king as the ruler of all Britain below the Humber, which by this point was a perfectly reasonable assessment. Offa, as we've seen, had already annexed both Kent and Sussex, and enjoyed indirect authority in Wessex thanks to his compliant son-in-law. Indeed, he could hardly have imposed an effective trade embargo had he not been able to close all the ports on the south coast. Whether he was able to do the same on the east coast is more debatable, because we know virtually nothing about East Anglia in the eighth century. The fact that some of the coins issued by Offa in the early part of his reign were minted in Ipswich implies he must have exercised a degree of political dominance there, but later coins issued in the name of King Æthelberht of East Anglia suggest that this control may have been lost in the 780s. If so, it had been reinstated not long before Charlemagne sent his letter. 'In this year,' says the *Anglo-Saxon Chronicle* for 794, 'Offa, king of the Mercians, had Æthelberht beheaded.'[58]

The other revelation in Charlemagne's letter comes when he allusively mentions the 'black stones' that Offa had requested.

This had previously mystified scholars, who for a long time assumed it must be a reference to quern stones, used to grind corn, made from black volcanic rock – such querns were sometimes brought from Francia to Britain. But Charlemagne's additional comments make it clear that the stones under discussion were a good deal more special than this. He asks Offa to send a messenger to explain exactly what sort of stones the king has in mind, and in particular how long they needed to be, after which he promises to help locate them and arrange for their transport. Clearly, these were no ordinary stones. They were hard to find and shift without royal assistance, and their precise length was a matter of crucial importance.

The most convincing explanation is that these stones were columns of black porphyry, a commodity that had recently become highly desirable on account of Charlemagne's own enthusiasm. From his own correspondence we can see that the Frankish king was in the habit of sourcing the most valuable materials from ancient Roman buildings in Italy, transporting them hundreds of miles beyond the Alps, and then reusing them in his own building projects in Francia. His famous chapel at Aachen, begun around the time of his letter to Offa, had just such black columns. Porphyry was particularly prized because of its rarity – the black variety was originally quarried in Egypt – and because of its connection with the imperial past. In his quest for respectability, Charlemagne drew heavily on Roman precedent. His coins, his legislation, and the manuscripts produced at his court, all attest to this determination to revive trappings of empire, so much so that since the nineteenth century historians have spoken of a 'Carolingian Renaissance'. Writing to Offa in 796 Charlemagne styled himself not only 'king of the Franks and Lombards', but also 'patrician of the Romans', a title bestowed on him by the pope after his conquest of Italy. Just four years later, he would acquire a new title when the pope raised him to the rank of emperor, crowning and anointing him in Rome on Christmas Day 800.[59]

Offa had witnessed this revival of *Romanitas* and wanted the same. His coins, and the consecration of his son, show that he was already consciously imitating Carolingian practices that looked to Roman models. So too, probably, does the great church at Brixworth in Northamptonshire, dated stylistically to the late eighth or early ninth centuries, but almost certainly a product of Offa's reign (colour picture 12). The tiles, bricks and stones that were used to construct it were Roman, laboriously lugged from the ruins of Leicester, some twenty-five miles away. If columns of black porphyry were a must-have symbol of imperial power, Offa presumably wanted them for some similar but now vanished building project. Of course, we have no idea whether he ever received them, or where he might have installed them had they been delivered. Possible contenders are Tamworth, where the king seems to have been developing a permanent royal residence late in his reign, or Bath, where his son Ecgfrith held an assembly later in 796. Either location could have been intended as the Mercian answer to Aachen.[60]

The undoubted fact that Offa craved the same imperial trappings as Charlemagne may, in the final analysis, be the clue to unlocking his famous dyke. Even today, the earthwork that still bears his name invites automatic comparison with the two great walls built in northern Britain at the behest of Roman emperors, and that alone may have been inspiration enough for a king who wanted to present himself in similar terms. But great ditches were also enjoying something of a renaissance across Europe in the eighth century, with rulers building or renewing them in places as far apart as Denmark and Bulgaria. In 793 Charlemagne attempted to construct a canal between the Main and the Danube, a project which saw the king assemble a workforce of 5,000 or 6,000 men who collectively shifted around 1 million cubic metres of earth. And perhaps this, some have speculated, was at least part of the point. Since none of these ditches were particularly effective as military barriers, the motivation for their construction may have been ideological rather than practical. They were large, impressive, and redolent of imperial power: a highly visible demonstration of a ruler's authority. It is, therefore, quite possible that Offa's Dyke was yet another exercise in projecting power in an imperial fashion, its purpose more political than pragmatic.[61]

But why was it built against the Britons, and not the Northumbrians, the East Anglians, or the West Saxons? The answer was almost certainly because, despite their very real and occasionally violent differences, by this date the people in these Anglo-Saxon kingdoms regarded themselves as a single ethnic group – a group that we can reasonably start to describe as 'English'. The word, of course, derives from *Angli*, or Angles, which had earlier signified the settler peoples to the north of the Thames – the East Angles, the Mercians, and the Northumbrians. But increasingly during the eighth century people were using *Angli* as a general term to describe *all* the Germanic-speaking peoples in Britain, including those who at other times were referred to as Saxons and Jutes. Bede, for example, sometimes uses *Angli* in a narrow sense, in reference to the people of Northumbria. But he more frequently employs the phrase *gens Anglorum* to mean something like 'the English people', not least in the title of his most famous work, the *Ecclesiastical History of the English People*, completed in 731.

The lexical trend was not all one way. Bede may have favoured *Angli* because it was the generic term used by Gregory the Great, both in his legendary encounter in the slave market and in his letters, but there is evidence to suggest that at the start of the eighth century even the archbishops of Canterbury occasionally used the term 'Saxon' to mean the same thing. To some extent the two words had become interchangeable. Nevertheless, there is a clear sense that *Angli* was pulling ahead. In his famous charter of 736, Æthelbald of Mercia described himself as ruler of the 'south Angles' (*sutangli*), a phrase apparently intended to cover not only the peoples of Mercia and East Anglia, but also those of Sussex, Wessex, Essex and Kent. In a letter of 738, Boniface, born a West Saxon, acknowledged his ancestral links with the continental Saxons he was hoping to convert, saying they were 'one and the same blood and bone'. Yet when he wrote home to ask fellow churchmen to pray for his success, he addressed them as 'the race of the English', and described himself as 'a native of that same race'. Penning his celebrated rebuke to Æthelbald nine years later, the bishop described the king as 'wielding the glorious sceptre of imperial rule over the English'.[62]

If Mercians, Saxons and Northumbrians were feeling an increasing sense of kinship with each other, they were simultaneously growing less and less well disposed towards the Britons. As we saw in the first chapter, the barbarian settlers who came to Britain in the migration period appear to have found little in Romano-British culture that they considered worthy of emulation. If they lived alongside Romano-British people, they regarded them as low-status, and did not adopt either their language or their customs. Across Europe, wherever Germanic-speaking peoples encountered Roman communities, they called them *walas*, meaning 'foreigners' or 'strangers'. In French it is the source of the words 'Gaul' and 'Walloon' (as in the French part of Belgium). In English it is the root of the words 'Wales' and 'Welsh', though it did not acquire the geographically specific meaning that those words now convey until the twelfth century. In Old English, *wealas* meant all Britons, whether they dwelt in Wales, Cornwall or Cumbria. It was also applied to British enclaves within Anglo-Saxon areas, giving rise to the place name 'Walton', and came to be a synonym for slave (*walh*). Its earliest use in an Anglo-Saxon text occurs in the laws of King Ine of Wessex, compiled in the late seventh century, which repeatedly distinguish between those who are *englisc* and those who are *wilisc*. In every instance, to be *wilisc* meant to be worse off.[63]

Whereas in Francia the hostility between Frank and Gaul disappeared over time, in Britain it grew only deeper. One reason, it seems clear, was the language divide. The Anglo-Saxons, despite the diversity of their roots, could comprehend each other, but they were baffled by the British tongue. Another reason was the bitter religious rift that developed between them. The Britons had, of course, retained the Christianity of the late Roman Empire, and preserved it while the Anglo-Saxons were still pagan. But once the newcomers had converted, relations between the two parties, far from improving, had grown even worse. Bede condemned the Britons because 'they never preached the faith to the Saxons or Angles who inhabited Britain with them'. This was almost certainly unfair and untrue, for there is good reason to believe that the Britons must have converted some of the new settlers. But the principal reason for mutual enmity was, yet again, the disagreement over the dating of Easter. According to Bede, the leaders of the British Church rejected the authority of St Augustine over this issue, an error for which neither the saint nor the historian would ever forgive them. When Æthelfrith, the pagan king of Northumbria, subsequently slaughtered hundreds of British monks and priests during a battle at Chester, Bede's attitude was essentially *serves them right*. Concluding his *Ecclesiastical History* in 731, he felt able to say positive things about the other Celtic peoples. The Irish had his respect for their role in the conversion of Northumbria, and even the Picts were praised for having recently seen the light. But the Britons, sighed Bede, 'oppose the English through their inbred hatred, and the whole state of the catholic Church through their incorrect Easter and their evil customs'. This hatred was indeed so ingrained that when the Britons finally adopted the Roman Easter in 768 it made hardly any difference. They were, opined the author of the *Life of St Guthlac*, 'the dangerous enemies of the Saxon race'.[64]

Against this background, it becomes easy to see why Offa, in deciding to build a dyke, would do so on his western frontier. At one time that frontier had been a more permeable affair, a zone where Germanic settlers and native Britons had overlapped. (The word 'Mercians' itself, it is pertinent to recall, meant 'the borderers'.) But during the eighth century the ethnic identities of the English and the Britons had sharpened, and with it the hostility between them. Scholars have noted that Shropshire, a county which shares its western border with Wales, has considerably fewer British place names than Staffordshire, the county that lies to its east. A plausible explanation for this peculiar state of affairs would be that during the eighth century, the communities on the western fringe of Mercia became more anglicized than those closer to its centre, in order to distinguish themselves from the Britons to their west. People in this zone who might have formerly identified as British must have adopted English customs, learned to speak English, and given new English names to their settlements.[65]

Offa's career shows a determined attempt to bring all the Anglo-Saxon kingdoms south of the Humber under his rule, and the principal means by which he did this was by applying brute force – making war on Kent, Sussex and Wessex, and beheading the king of East Anglia. But even brutal empire builders need ideological props for the power they win by the sword. In Offa's case, we can see how he consciously copied the imperial symbolism used by Charlemagne, who was in turn imitating the imagery of the Roman Empire. To this same end, it is possible that Offa also tried to capitalize on the growing sense of ethnic unity among the various peoples he ruled. In some of his charters from the 770s he adopts the style 'king of the English' (*rex Anglorum*). Unfortunately none of these charters has survived as an original, and some experts have dismissed 'king of the English' as an anachronism introduced by later copyists. If Offa did use it, he ceased to do so after the 770s, after which he is only ever styled 'king of the Mercians'.[66] But another way to encourage unity among disparate peoples is to identify a common enemy – an ethnic 'other', against whom they can define themselves. The obvious 'other' for the English of the eighth century were the *wilisc* – the 'strangers' to their west. By deciding to build a barrier against them, Offa was isolating them, frustrating travel and trade, and perhaps even improving the security of his subjects who lived close to the frontier. But over and above this he was emphasizing, in the most visible way possible for an early medieval ruler, the differences between the Britons on one side, and the English on the other.

Offa died on 29 July 796, not long after receiving his letter from Charlemagne. The circumstances and the location of his death are unknown. It seems most likely that he died of natural causes associated with his age, since no chronicler or letter-writer mentions any foul play. His place of burial is also unknown, though a much later tradition claimed it was Bedford.[67]

There is little doubt that he was the most powerful Anglo-Saxon ruler up to this date – a man who had bent the other kingdoms south of the Humber to his will, and varying degrees of dependency, in some cases eliminating their kingships altogether. 'You are the glory of Britain,' Alcuin of York told him in a letter written at some point in the decade before his death, 'the trumpet of proclamation, the sword against foes, the shield against enemies.' Alcuin was aiming to flatter, and being discreet, for he knew well that Offa's methods, which are for the most part invisible to us, could be vicious. Even as Offa was trying to instil the fear that those who killed anointed kings would burn in eternal hellfire, he had been happy to have the presumably unanointed king of East Anglia beheaded. It seems likely that, as well as removing the rulers of other kingdoms, he may have dispatched potential rivals within Mercia with similar ruthlessness, to ensure the smooth succession of his son, Ecgfrith. Commenting on Ecgfrith in a later letter, safe in the knowledge that Offa was gone, Alcuin recalled 'how much blood his father shed to secure the kingdom for his son'. And, sure enough, Ecgfrith, consecrated nine years earlier, succeeded as king of Mercia that same summer.[68]

But Offa's dynastic plans, over which so much effort had been expended, and so much blood spilled, ultimately came to nothing. Just a few months later, his son followed him to the grave, dying on 17 December. Alcuin, now blessed with the wisdom of hindsight, saw the young man's early departure as divine vengeance for his father's sins. All the blood Offa had spilled, he averred, 'was not the strengthening of his kingdom, but its ruin'.[69]

Death, sin, divine retribution, and ruin – these themes were much on Alcuin's mind during these years, and echo through all his correspondence. 'Times are dangerous in Britain,' he told the archbishop of York, 'and the death of kings is a sign of misery.' But there were other signs too. In a letter to the people of Kent, written in 797, he even referred to the *The Ruin of Britain*, written by Gildas almost three centuries earlier. The Britons, he reminded his readers, had once enjoyed God's favour, but lost it through sinfulness and fighting among themselves. As a result they had been punished by the invasion of the Anglo-Saxons. Alcuin saw this happening again, for God was now scourging the English in exactly the same way.

'Behold, a thing never heard of before,' he warned, 'a pagan people habitually makes pirate raids on our shores.'[70]

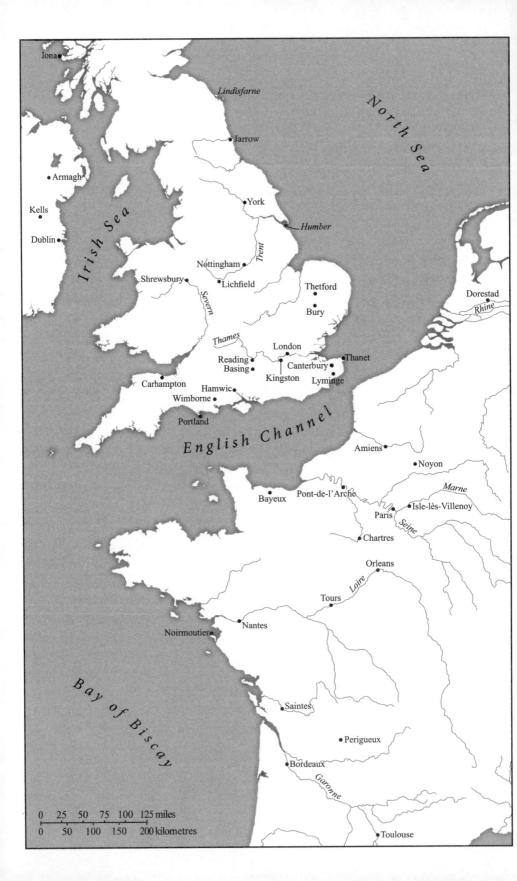

5

STORM FROM THE NORTH

The Viking Assault on Britain and Francia

I n the early months of 793, the people of Northumbria were terrified by a series of evil omens. According to the *Anglo-Saxon Chronicle*, drawing on an earlier set of northern annals that are now lost, there were great gales, flashes of lightning, 'and fiery dragons were seen flying in the air' – an illusion perhaps created by the Northern Lights, which can sometimes be seen in the Northumbrian sky. In a letter written that same year, Alcuin of York reported that, during Lent, the cathedral in his home city had been showered with rain the colour of blood. These signs in the heavens were seen as a warning of dire things to come, and sure enough, in the spring the kingdom was afflicted by a terrible famine.

But that was only the beginning. On 8 June, a band of what the *Chronicle* calls 'heathen men' landed their ships on the island of Lindisfarne, plundered the monastery there, and slaughtered many of the monks. Alcuin described in horror how the altar of the church was spattered with blood and the tombs of the saints were trampled underfoot. He also reveals that, as well as stealing the abbey's precious ornaments, the visitors seized some of the younger members of the community and led them off into captivity, presumably to be sold as slaves.

The 'heathen men' who attacked Lindisfarne in the summer of 793 are better known today as the vikings, and what the *Chronicle* and Alcuin were describing was the earliest datable viking raid on Britain. There had evidently been other attacks in the years immediately beforehand: the earliest reference occurs in a charter issued by King Offa in 792, which mentions 'seaborne pagans with migrating fleets'. But the assault on Lindisfarne was a seismic moment that sent shockwaves right across Europe. 'Never before has such an atrocity been seen in Britain at the hands of a pagan people,' said Alcuin, writing at the Carolingian court, in a letter to the king of Northumbria. Lindisfarne, he reminded him, was the cradle of Christianity in the north, and the place where the bones of the holy Cuthbert were buried. On the very site 'where the Christian religion in our nation took its rise', he lamented, 'there misery and calamity have begun'.[1]

15. A ninth-century commemorative stone from Lindisfarne, showing an attack by armed men.

Who were the vikings? The popular image of them as Scandinavian seafarers with horned helmets, shaggy beards, and dragon-prowed ships, raiding and pillaging the coasts of early medieval Europe, is a good place to begin. Its two most obvious anachronisms are the horned helmets – sadly, an invention of the nineteenth century, made popular by designers of theatrical costume – and the word 'viking' itself. This, too, only became popular in the nineteenth century, when people were gripped with a fascination for Norse sagas and legends, in which the word 'viking' does indeed occur. But these sagas were written in the twelfth and thirteenth centuries, long after the events they purport to describe. Back in the ninth century, the word 'viking' can be found in only a handful of instances, and only in Old English texts. Its origins are therefore debated, with at least half a dozen theories advanced. It might derive from Viken, an area of southern Norway, or from *vik*, the Old Norse word for 'bay', or from *wic*, the Old English word for the kind of commercial settlements that vikings would often target. Whatever its roots, it clearly meant something like 'pirate' or 'raider'. But the vikings were almost always referred to by their victims in Britain and Francia using other terms – 'Danes', 'pagans', 'heathens' or 'northmen'.[2]

The main problem, as the above suggests, is that we have almost no idea of how the vikings saw themselves, because as pagans they were illiterate, and the sagas they eventually wrote down centuries later are an unreliable guide to their original motives. It used to be argued, for example, on the strength of an eleventh-century source, that they were spurred on their travels because their homelands were overpopulated. But it was only after several decades of raiding that that vikings showed any desire to acquire land and settle outside of Scandinavia. What they sought in the first instance was moveable wealth – gold, silver and slaves. This has led to a more recent argument that they wanted this wealth in order to participate in the politics of their homelands, which were becoming increasingly competitive, resembling the kind of race for status and power that had characterized the formation of Anglo-Saxon kingdoms almost two centuries earlier.

A more straightforward explanation is that Scandinavians started seizing this wealth because they realized it was theirs for the taking. There had been plenty of prior contact between the Christian peoples of Britain and Francia and the pagan peoples to the north. The trade networks that had developed and flourished in the seventh and eighth centuries extended across the North Sea and into the Baltic. As a result there had been cultural interaction as well. Writing to the king of Northumbria in the wake of the attack on Lindisfarne, Alcuin had criticized him for copying the fashion of pagans in the way he cut his hair and beard.

Although the Scandinavians traded with their Christian neighbours, they were operating on the periphery. The *wics* of Francia and Britain were booming, and the kings and monasteries grew rich on the profits, but little of this wealth found its way to the men who trapped animals in the cold north so that their skins could be bought and sold in London or Aachen. The enormous economic growth of the preceding century had created huge disparities between the haves and the have-nots. The Scandinavians knew all about the rich coastal communities of the kingdoms to the south, and they also knew that they were undefended.[3]

There also appears to have been an advance in naval technology shortly before the raids began. Scandinavian peoples had experience of ships that went back several millennia, and were expert at building sleek vessels to travel short distances from one bay or island to another. But these ships were powered by oars, and the evidence, such as it is, suggests that they may have been late adopters of sails, which had long been in use further south. The combination of fast-moving ships with sails may have been the crucial development that enabled vikings to travel directly across the North Sea to Britain, giving them the ability to appear on the horizon without warning, rather than having to tack around the coast. Alcuin, certainly, was surprised that Scandinavian raiders had been able to reach Lindisfarne. 'Such a voyage was not thought possible', he told the Northumbrian king.[4]

Lastly, it is possible that there was an ideological element to the viking attacks. So far as we can tell, there was nothing inherent in paganism that compelled its practitioners to attack and kill non-believers. With eighth-century Christians, however, the reverse was true. English missionaries like Boniface may have hoped to convert the continental Saxons by preaching, on the grounds that they were of the same blood and bone, but the approach of his successors was to introduce Christianity at sword-point. When Charlemagne began his long campaign against the Saxons in 772, he destroyed their sacred tree, Irminsul, and when they rebelled a decade later, the king had 4,500 of them beheaded on the banks of the River Weser. This holy war must have made the pagan peoples further north feel that their religion, and their way of life, was under threat, and perhaps persuaded some of them that it was time to strike back. If they preyed on monasteries like Lindisfarne, it was undoubtedly because they were soft, isolated targets, located conveniently on the coast, almost begging to be relieved of their rich possessions; but it was also because attacking them was a way of striking an ideological blow against Christian oppression.[5]

The fact that vikings were prepared to violate sacred Christian sites was what, in the eyes of Christians, made them so appalling. Although they have a posthumous reputation for exceptional fierceness, in truth they were no more violent than warriors in either Britain or Francia. But the Christian rulers of these regions would rarely, if ever, target churches, for fear of social opprobrium and divine retribution. Both Christian and Arab writers also give gruesome descriptions of vikings making human sacrifices – slave girls who were drugged and raped before being stabbed, strangled and cremated; men hanged with dogs and horses in sacred groves. Archaeological excavation of such sites has also revealed evidence of cannibalism. What made such practices all the more terrifying was that, not so long ago, the Anglo-Saxons must have performed such rituals themselves. The Woden from whom their kings claimed descent was ancestrally no different to the Odin worshipped by their attackers. For the

English, the coming of the vikings meant a confrontation with the demons of their own pagan past.[6]

The raid on Lindisfarne in 793 was soon followed by other attacks, as the vikings rapidly extended the scope of their operations. In 794 they returned to Northumbria and sacked the monastery of Jarrow, founded a century earlier by King Ecgfrith. By 795 they had found their way to the western seaboard of Scotland, probably via the Great Glen, attacking Iona and other monasteries in the Irish Sea zone. And it was not just monasteries. At some point before 802 a group of vikings landed on the coast of Wessex, at Portland in Dorset, and killed the royal reeve who came to greet them in the mistaken belief that they were merchants.[7]

In Francia, the response to these raids was robust. In 799 the vikings made their first recorded raid on a Frankish monastery, attacking the monks on the island of Noirmoutier, near Nantes. The following year, Charlemagne travelled to the Channel coast in person, ordered the building of a fleet, and appointed watchmen to guard the shore. But in Britain, signs of similar initiatives are lacking. The rulers of Northumbria were probably too preoccupied with fighting among themselves, to judge from the cycle of feuds reported in northern annals. In the south, King Offa had insisted that the churches of Kent must provide military service to help defend against pagan raids, but his death in 796 put paid to any grander schemes. His successors had bigger problems to contend with.[8]

As we've seen, Offa's carefully laid plans for a smooth succession had come to nothing, and his only son had swiftly followed him to the grave. Power in Mercia passed to a new king named Coenwulf, whose claim to be descended from the same royal dynasty was probably just a convenient fiction. From the start of his reign, Coenwulf had to deal with multiple rebellions, as the peoples Offa had terrorized into submission attempted to throw off the yoke of Mercian overlordship. In Kent, a member of the old royal house, Eadberht Præn, returned from exile, and in East Anglia, a new king called Eadwald began issuing coins in his own name.

Coenwulf dealt briskly with these challenges to his rule. Much of the hostility in Kent, he realized, was due to Offa's dismembering of the archbishopric of Canterbury to create a new archbishop of Lichfield, so he quickly reversed the decision: Lichfield was returned to its former ordinary status, and the primacy of Canterbury was restored. With papal permission, Coenwulf then invaded Kent, seized Eadberht Præn, and packed him off to a monastery in Mercia, where he was deprived of his hands and eyes. Something similar may have happened in East Anglia, since the coins of its new king, Eadwald, ceased after just a few years. In some directions, Coenwulf extended Mercian power even further than it had reached under Offa. He reduced the kings of Essex to the status of ealdormen, and he led repeated military expeditions into Wales, advancing as far as Snowdonia. His preoccupation with Wales in his final years makes it plausible that Coenwulf was responsible for the construction of Wat's Dyke, a more defensible successor to the earthwork commissioned by Offa.[9]

The only region in which Coenwulf failed to maintain his predecessor's authority was Wessex. At the start of his reign the West Saxons were still being ruled by Beorhtric, who had received Offa's help in banishing his rival, Egbert. But in 802 Egbert had returned from his long exile on the Continent and triggered an anti-Mercian revolution. A great battle took place, says the *Anglo-Saxon Chronicle*: Egbert became king and Beorhtric died. (Whether in the battle, or by some other means, we are not told.)[10]

It was Egbert who was the chief beneficiary of the chaos that followed Coenwulf's death in 821. After the Mercian king's departure, says a contemporary source, 'many disagreements and innumerable disputes arose among leading persons of every kind – kings, bishops, and ministers of the churches of God'. Coenwulf was succeeded by his brother, Ceolwulf, but after only two years the new king was ousted by a rival named Beornwulf. Perhaps to prove his worth, Beornwulf went to war against Wessex, but was defeated in battle by Egbert, and died the following year. Egbert, meanwhile, was carrying all before him. In the immediate wake of his victory he sent a large army into Kent, driving out its Mercian puppet ruler, and in the two years that followed he obtained the submission of Sussex, Surrey, Essex and even East Anglia.[11]

Buoyed by a tide of long-nurtured resentments against Mercian rule, Egbert led the combined armies of his new dominions northwards in 829 and conquered the confused Midlands kingdom, proclaiming himself its new ruler. Later that year he advanced even further, receiving the submission of Northumbria, and the following year he invaded Wales and reduced all its leaders to similar obedience. The *Anglo-Saxon Chronicle*, looking back from the end of the century, recited the list of seven overlords of Britain recorded by Bede, and proudly added Egbert to their ranks. The victorious king of Wessex, the author declared, was the eighth *bretwalda*.

Egbert's overlordship was not destined to last. His direct rule of Mercia ended after only a year, at which point Wiglaf, the king he had deposed, was restored to power.[12] The 820s were not witness to the birth of a new superpower so much as the collapse of an old one whose time had come. Mercian kings had held sway south of the Humber for almost a century, but within a decade of Coenwulf's death their empire had evaporated. Henceforth there were four Anglo-Saxon kingdoms: Mercia, Northumbria, East Anglia and a greatly enlarged Wessex.

Throughout the first three decades of the ninth century, the vikings must have continued to make raids on these Anglo-Saxon kingdoms. Several of the charters granted by Coenwulf to recipients in Kent, for example, repeat the demand for defensive measures against pagan attacks, including the building and destruction of fortresses. In one charter, the king granted the nuns of Lyminge a small plot of land in Canterbury as 'a refuge in necessity', presumably in the event of a viking landing. Lyminge lies five miles from the sea, on the other side of the North Downs, suggesting that some Scandinavian pirates were becoming more audacious, but the corollary is that Canterbury was still considered safe. Although the raids continued in this period, none was reckoned consequential enough to be remembered in the *Anglo-Saxon Chronicle*. Such attacks that did take place must have been small-scale and opportunistic.[13]

But in the 830s, the scale of Scandinavian operations was greatly enlarged. On the Continent, this was encouraged by a bitter feud between Charlemagne's successor, Louis the Pious, and his sons. The eldest, Lothar, collaborated with the vikings and gave them licence to raid along the Frisian coast. In 834 they attacked Dorestad, the greatest *wic* in Francia, comparable in size to the major *wics* in southern Britain. According to a contemporary source known as the *Annals of St Bertin*, this viking fleet destroyed everything in Dorestad. 'They slaughtered some people, took others away captive, and burnt the surrounding region.' This was an ominous development. Although sited on the confluence of two major rivers, the *wic* lay some way inland, more than thirty miles from the nearest coast.[14]

At the same time, the vikings in the Irish Sea zone were growing in power and confidence. Iona, the most venerable of all the Gaelic monasteries, was raided for a second time in 802, and a third in 806, on which occasion sixty-eight members of the community were killed. When the raiders returned for a fourth time the following year, most of the survivors decided that enough was enough, and that the isolated site selected by St Columba in the sixth century was simply too vulnerable in the new conditions of the ninth. At that point they relocated to Ireland, re-founding a monastery at Kells that was located on the site of an ancient hill fort, over twenty miles from the sea.

But while this seems to have worked well enough for the monks of Kells, others in Ireland were not so fortunate. By this point the vikings were already raiding all the way around the Irish coast, and in the decades that followed their attacks on the interior became ever more daring. Although local rulers sometimes fought back, they were for the most part too busy fighting each other, or insufficiently powerful to resist. By the 830s, Scandinavians were venturing far inland, plundering with impunity, seizing great numbers of slaves, and even capturing bishops and kings for ransom. In 832 the abbey of Armagh, which lies twenty-five miles from the sea, was raided three times in the space of a single month.[15]

It was almost certainly vikings operating in Ireland who attacked Wessex in 836, landing on the Somerset coast. They came, says the *Anglo-Saxon Chronicle*, in thirty-five ships – a number presumably considered noteworthy because it was unusually large. Extrapolating numbers of warriors from numbers of ships is an inexact science, because ships varied in size, but the two best-preserved vessels from the ninth century, the Oseberg Ship (colour picture 14) and the Gokstad Ship, had fifteen and sixteen pairs of oar-holes respectively, indicating thirty and thirty-two rowers each. A fleet of thirty-five ships could therefore have carried 1,000 men – a force that could hardly be regarded as a raiding party, and must have more closely resembled an invading army. Their tactics on this occasion were not hit-and-run, and they probably intended to stay for some time, establishing a base camp and pillaging the surrounding countryside. That much is suggested by the fact that King Egbert of Wessex had time enough to raise an army of his own and ride to confront them in battle. The clash, which took place at Carhampton, did not go as the all-conquering king had hoped. 'A great slaughter was made there,' says the *Chronicle*, 'and the Danes had possession of the battlefield.'[16]

Although Egbert was able to escape from this encounter with his life, defeat at the hands of the vikings must have dealt a serious blow to his reputation as a *bretwalda*. The king was able to undo some of the damage two years later, beating a viking army that landed in Cornwall and made common cause with the Cornish, but after this he decided that it was time to hang up his sword. It was almost fifty years since Offa had driven him into exile. Even if Egbert had been a teenager at that time, he

16. The Gokstad Ship, built in the ninth century, rediscovered in 1880, on display in the Viking Ship Museum in Oslo.

would have been in his sixties by 838. That year the king summoned a great council to Kingston-upon-Thames, in which he set out his plans for the future. It seems likely that during this meeting he arranged for the consecration of his son, Æthelwulf, much as Offa had done with Ecgfrith, hopeful that this would lead to an undisputed succession.[17]

Egbert's own intention was to go to Rome, where he probably intended to live out his remaining days. This was partly family tradition: two of his illustrious predecessors, Cædwalla and Ine, had made the same journey at the end of their reigns and were buried in the Holy City. But Egbert also felt a particularly urgent spiritual compulsion to make the same pilgrimage. In the spring of 839, the king sent envoys to Louis the Pious, seeking permission to travel through his lands. According to the *Annals of St Bertin*, they warned the emperor to devote himself to the souls of his subjects. The English, we are told, had recently been terrified by a vision experienced by a priest, which the annalist went on to relate.

The priest had dreamed that a stranger had led him to an unfamiliar land with many wonderful buildings. On entering a church, he saw a lot of boys reading books which, on closer inspection, were written in alternating lines of black ink and blood. The bloody lines, explained the stranger, were the sins of the Christian people, and the boys were the souls of the saints who grieved for them. If the people did not atone and repent, the priest was warned, a great disaster would befall them. 'For three days and three nights a dense fog will descend, and then, all of a sudden, pagan men will lay waste with fire and sword most of the people and land of the Christians, along with all they possess.'[18]

We are not told who this priest was. He could have been a member of Egbert's household, or a wandering soothsayer whose story came to reach the royal ears by some less obvious route. But the king's readiness to act on the story, and indeed to communicate it via envoys to the Frankish emperor, reveals the disturbing effect that repeated viking attacks were having on his psyche and those of his subjects. The fear of the sudden arrival of heathen men bringing fire and death had become very real, and haunted their dreams.

Egbert, alas, never got to make his planned pilgrimage, and died later in the same year. Nor did Louis the Pious have much time to take heed of the English envoys' admonitions, for he died in the summer of the year that followed. But whereas Egbert was succeeded peacefully by his son, Æthelwulf, as he had planned, Louis died campaigning against his son, Lothar, who was once more in rebellion against him. With their father gone, the emperor's three surviving sons fell to fighting among themselves over the division of his inheritance.

Such division gave ample opportunities to the vikings. In 840 Lothar once again sought them out as allies, this time granting one of their leaders part of Frisia in return for his military support. ('An utterly detestable crime', fumed the author of the *Annals of*

St Bertin, because it meant that 'Christian folk have to serve men who worshipped demons'.) Other Scandinavian pirates, meanwhile, simply seized the chance to profit from the chaos of the disputed succession. In the same year, a group of them sailed along the Channel and attacked Rouen. According to the *Annals of St Bertin*, 'they plundered the town with pillage, fire and sword, slaughtered or took captive the monks and the rest of the population, and laid waste all the monasteries and other places along the banks of the Seine'.[19]

This escalation in Francia brought large viking armies to the coasts of southern Britain, where they engaged in an existential struggle with the ealdormen of Wessex. Like their namesakes in Mercia, these ealdormen were the king's most powerful deputies, but rather than ruling former kingdoms, they were responsible for administrative subdivisions of Wessex known as 'shires'. Both terms were in use in Wessex as early as the seventh century, but it is only at this moment that they come more fully into focus, with the *Anglo-Saxon Chronicle* mentioning certain ealdormen who led the armed levies of their shires against viking invasions. Thus in 840, when a fleet of thirty-three ships attacked Hamwic, Wessex's principal port, the *Chronicle* reports that their crews were slaughtered by forces led by Wulfheard, the ealdorman of Hampshire.[20]

Wulfheard's victory, however, was the sole ray of light in an otherwise dismal period. When Ealdorman Æthelhelm led the people of Dorset against the Danes who had landed at Portland that same year, he was defeated and killed, and so too was Ealdorman Hereberht and many of his men in Kent when they marched to confront the vikings who invaded Romney Marsh in 841. Later that year, says the *Anglo-Saxon Chronicle*, many people were 'killed by the enemy' all the way along the east coast, in Kent, East Anglia and Mercia, while in 842 there was 'great slaughter' in Rochester and London. Finally, in 843, King Æthelwulf himself was stirred to action when a large viking fleet, presumably from Ireland, landed on the Somerset coast near Carhampton, just as they had seven years earlier in the reign of his father, and with an identical outcome: Æthelwulf was defeated, and the Danes had possession of the field.[21]

It was understandable, after such a run of defeats, that the king and his subjects started to think seriously about improving their defences. As we've seen, as early as 804 the nuns of Lyminge had obtained a place of refuge in Canterbury, presumably because it was not only further inland but also boasted a serviceable circuit of Roman walls. Similar thoughts must have occurred to the citizens of London after the attack of 842. The *wic* to the west of the abandoned Roman city had grown up on the Strand because it offered better access by water, but now it was vulnerable for precisely that same reason. It had already decreased in size from its mid-eighth-century peak, perhaps due to a series of fires towards the century's end. But anxiety about viking raids must have discouraged tradesmen from staying put thereafter, and the defensive ditch which was created at some point in the early ninth century apparently did little to reassure them. By the middle of the century Lundenwic had effectively been abandoned, and its inhabitants had begun to relocate within the walls of the old Roman capital.[22]

Something similar probably happened in Wessex in the wake of the attack on Hamwic in 840. Hamwic, unlike Lundenwic, was not adjacent to an old Roman city. But twelve miles inland, along the navigable River Itchen, was the former Roman town of Venta Belgarum, known to the Saxons as Winchester. Since the middle of the seventh century Winchester had been the seat of the bishop of Wessex, but apart from that it had attracted few other settlers. After the viking assault on Hamwic, however, its walls must have taken on a new appeal to merchants and manufacturers in search of greater security. King Æthelwulf may have encouraged this development. The earliest mention of the royal right to fortress-work in Wessex comes in a charter he issued in 842. His father, Egbert, had been buried in Winchester Cathedral, and he himself held a major council in the city in 844.[23]

★

After 843 the vikings operating on the southern and eastern coasts of Britain returned their attention to Francia. In the summer of that year the sons of Louis the Pious had finally stopped fighting and agreed to divide the huge Carolingian Empire between them, splitting it into three so each had a roughly equal share. But disagreements between them continued, leaving ample scope for vikings invaders to run amok. That year Norse pirates attacked the city of Nantes and killed many people, including the local bishop. They then proceeded to make their way along the western seaboard of Aquitaine, plundering as they went. In 844 they sailed up the River Garonne, one of the great arteries of Francia, 'wreaking destruction everywhere and meeting no opposition', according to the *Annals of St Bertin*, and not stopping until they reached the city of Toulouse, almost 150 miles from the sea. The following year they repeated this exercise in the north, sailing 240 miles along the winding River Seine to Paris, laying waste the countryside and encountering no resistance. Paris escaped destruction only because the new king of west Francia, Charles the Bald, paid off the raiders with 7,000 pounds of silver. This, of course, was not a measure to deter predators in anything but the short term. The late 840s saw further attacks along the Channel and Atlantic coasts, and the destruction of cities far inland. Saintes fell in 845, Bordeaux was sacked after a long siege in 848, and Perigueux burned in 849.[24]

During this same period, the English did rather better, with no recorded attacks on the southern or eastern coasts. This must have been largely due to the fact that the vikings had moved on to new and more profitable hunting grounds in Francia – there would have been little point in them returning to Britain having already plundered it so thoroughly during the opening years of the decade. But there were still raids from the direction of Ireland, and here the English acquitted themselves better than before. In 845 the ealdormen of Somerset and Dorset combined their forces and defeated a viking army at the mouth of the River Parrett. A few years later, in 851, the men of Devon were victorious against a heathen army that landed on their stretch of the coast.[25]

That same year, however, the vikings who had been ravaging Francia returned, landing on the Isle of Thanet off the coast of Kent, and remaining there throughout the winter. It was a worrying innovation. Norsemen had been overwintering in Ireland since the 830s, building bases for their ships that the Irish called *longphorts* – the most famous being the one they established at the mouth of the River Liffey, named 'Black Pool', or *Duiblinn*. In Francia they had done this for the first time during the winter of 843, following their attack on Nantes, setting up camp on the nearby island of Noirmoutier. But the occupation of Thanet during the winter of 850–1 was, as the *Anglo-Saxon Chronicle* noted, the first time a heathen army had spent the winter in an English kingdom.[26]

This overwintering heralded a massive escalation: according to the *Chronicle* the viking fleet consisted of 350 ships. This figure strains credibility, but Frankish chronicles suggest that the size of fleets had been increasing steadily throughout the 840s, with reports of sixty-seven ships attacking Nantes in 843 and 120 ships descending on Paris in 845. If a fleet of comparable size had assembled in 851, it would have represented a twofold or four-fold increase on the numbers recorded for earlier attacks – 2,000, or even 4,000 men.[27]

A force this size was all but irresistible. In 851 it stormed Canterbury, demonstrating that Roman walls were no longer a guarantee of safe refuge. The fleet then moved to the mouth of the Thames and proceeded to take London – presumably the ancient walled city and not just the abandoned *wic*. London was still a Mercian possession, and the king of Mercia, Berhtwulf, evidently attempted to defend it, but without success, for the *Anglo-Saxon Chronicle* notes that the vikings caused him and his army to flee. The great pagan horde then crossed the Thames and entered Surrey, a province of Wessex for the past twenty-five years, ever since King Egbert had wrested it from Mercian rule. Now Egbert's son, Æthelwulf, advanced to meet the invaders, hoping to fare better than both he and his father had done on previous occasions at Carhampton. Against all odds, the king and his companions won the day and inflicted a heavy defeat. It was, says the *Chronicle*, 'the greatest slaughter of a heathen army that we have ever heard of'. Given the size of the enemy host, Æthelwulf's achievement must have seemed nothing short of miraculous. The *Annals of St Bertin* concluded that the king had clearly won 'with the aid of our Lord Jesus Christ'.[28]

In the wake of his providential victory, Æthelwulf decided it was time to bolster his kingdom's spiritual defences, and revived his father's plan of a royal pilgrimage to Rome. In 853 he sent a high-powered embassy to the Holy City to prepare the ground in advance of his own coming. Then, at Easter the following year, he held a great assembly, in which he granted away a tenth of the royal estate, giving book-land to both laymen and clergy. This was partly to secure the prayers of the churchmen for his safety, but it was also to ensure the continued loyalty of both groups – their 'humble obedience and fidelity', as the king put it in a charter. Æthelwulf did not plan to remain in Rome for eternity, like Cædwalla or Ine; he fully intended to return to Wessex and continue his reign.[29]

Fortunately the king and his wife, Osburh, had been blessed with many sons who could rule during his absence. Unfortunately for modern readers, they had given all but one of them names beginning with Æthel- (meaning 'noble'), making it difficult for us to distinguish between them. The eldest, Æthelstan, had ruled the formerly independent kingdoms of Kent, Surrey, Sussex and Essex since the time of his father's accession, but had died at some point after 851. The king therefore entrusted royal authority to his two eldest surviving sons: Æthelbald, who would rule the ancient heartlands of Wessex, and Æthelberht, who would rule the newly acquired provinces to the east.[30]

Having made these arrangements, Æthelwulf set out in the spring of 855. According to the *Anglo-Saxon Chronicle*, he travelled 'in great state', and the *Annals of St Bertin* describe how he was honourably received in West Francia by Charles the Bald, who escorted him across his dominions. The whole journey must have taken around two months, so Æthelwulf and his entourage would have arrived in Rome at the height of summer.[31]

The city had changed considerably since the days when Cædwalla and Wilfrid had visited over 150 years before. During the eighth century its population had continued to shrink and, by the time of Æthelwulf's arrival, probably stood at no more than 30,000 people. This still made it many times greater than anything the king or his English followers would have previously experienced. As one modern historian has nicely observed, Hamwic, the largest settlement in Wessex, could have comfortably fitted inside the Baths of Caracalla in Rome. The city was also less decayed than it had been around the year 700. In the intervening period, successive popes had refurbished many of its ancient public buildings, and added new ones of their own, aided by generous donations from rulers like Charlemagne and Offa. The most recent of these additions was a brand-new circuit of walls, two miles long, commissioned by Pope Leo IV in the wake of an attack by Saracens in 846.

Unfortunately, although his walls were very much in evidence, Pope Leo was gone by the time Æthelwulf arrived, having died just a few weeks earlier on 17 July. It was several months before his successor was consecrated, by which time it was probably too late for the king and his companions to contemplate recrossing the Alps. They therefore remained in Rome for the winter, presumably praying in the city's many churches, visiting the tombs of Cædwalla and Ine, and bestowing expensive offerings and gifts. Papal records show that these included a gold crown, a gilded candleholder and an ornamental sword.[32]

In the summer of 856, over a year since his departure from Wessex, Æthelwulf set off in the direction of home. As on his outward journey, he travelled through the lands of Charles the Bald, who welcomed him for several weeks, during which two extraordinary things happened. Firstly, Æthelwulf decided to marry Charles' daughter, Judith. His previous wife, Osburh, had probably died by this point, meaning there was no obvious impediment to this new match, though the age difference –

Æthelwulf was about fifty years old, Judith only twelve – may have raised eyebrows. Secondly, shocking news arrived from across the Channel. The king's eldest son, Æthelbald, who had been entrusted with the rule of Wessex, had decided he would rather not relinquish his position, and was plotting to prevent his father's return.[33]

Unfortunately, there is no way of knowing from our sources which of these events happened first, so determining cause and effect is impossible. Æthelwulf may have learned about his son's revolt, and married Judith in order to secure Frankish support in reclaiming his throne. Equally, it could be that the king decided to marry Judith for some other reason (diplomacy, prestige, lust), and it was news of the surprise match that triggered the rebellion. Recent kings of Wessex had minimized the political role of their wives, even to the extent of denying them the title of queen. Charles the Bald, however, insisted that his daughter should receive the full royal honours. As the author of the *Annals of St Bertin* explains, when Judith was finally married to Æthelwulf on 1 October 856, she was crowned and consecrated, and her new husband 'formally conferred on her the title of queen, which was something not customary before then to him or to his people'. Æthelwulf's sons might well have worried that their new twelve-year-old stepmother would in due course produce stepbrothers with stronger claims of royal descent.[34]

Whatever the case, immediately after his marriage, Æthelwulf crossed the Channel with his new bride to confront his rebellious son. Our only account of what happened next is given in Asser's biography of Alfred the Great, written around forty years later, which describes it as 'a disgraceful episode ... unheard of in all previous ages'. Æthelbald had decided to resist his father's return with the connivance and encouragement of certain churchmen and nobles. And, from Asser's account, it seems he was successful. On his return, Æthelwulf resumed the rule of the eastern part of his kingdom, formed by Kent, Sussex, Surrey and Essex, and previously delegated to his son, Æthelberht. But he was evidently unable to dislodge Æthelbald from the old part of

Wessex. Asser charitably ascribed this to 'great forbearance' on Æthelwulf's part, and insisted that his loyal subjects would have been ready to eject his 'arrogant' and 'grasping' son, had the old king been willing to allow it. The likelier explanation, however, is that Æthelwulf had no choice but to accept what had happened as a fait accompli.[35]

The situation after the king's return must therefore have been very fraught, and reminiscent of the ongoing state of affairs in Francia, where disagreements within the royal family had resulted in division and civil war, weakening their ability to resist viking attacks. Æthelwulf was determined to avoid this, and strove to restore harmony. According to Asser, he had a will drawn up, 'so that his sons should not quarrel unnecessarily among themselves' after his death. The plan was that, once he was gone, the kingdom should remain divided: Æthelbald would rule the western heartlands of Wessex, and Æthelberht the lands to the east. And this is exactly what happened when the old king died not long afterwards in January 858. The elder son retained the position he had usurped, and the younger one stepped into the position vacated by their father.[36]

The fact that the enlarged kingdom was divided was hardly very surprising, for this was effectively the way matters had been arranged ever since King Egbert had annexed the south-eastern kingdoms more than thirty years earlier. Æthelwulf had ruled these newly acquired lands as a sub-king during his father's reign, and his own son, Æthelstan, had done the same before his premature death in the early 850s. For the king's will to have stood a chance of succeeding, it must have received the assent of the leading men in both regions, who felt division was a sensible way to proceed.[37]

It was altogether more surprising that, barely two years after Æthelwulf's death, the two halves of his realm were reunited. This was in spite of the best efforts of his eldest son, Æthelbald, who wasted no time in getting married, raising the prospect that he would produce children of his own to succeed him. Unfortunately, he chose as his bride his father's fourteen-year-old widow, Judith, a move which scandalized the more law-abiding and God-fearing members of society. For a son to take over his father's marriage bed, said Asser, was 'against God's prohibition, and Christian dignity, and also contrary to the practices of pagans'. Presumably the new king calculated that the 'great disgrace', as Asser called it, would be offset by the prestige of having a Frankish princess for a queen, and reckoned that their children would have a better right to rule than any of his younger brothers.[38]

But in the early months of 860, before any children had been produced, Æthelbald died of unknown causes. The expectation had apparently been that the throne of old Wessex should pass to Æthelwulf's fourth son, Æthelred, but the nobles of the kingdom decided against it, probably because Æthelred was deemed too young to rule in his own right. Instead they turned to his older brother, Æthelberht, who was already ruling as king of Kent, Sussex, Surrey and Essex, and elected him to become the ruler of Wessex as well. Against expectations, and in disregard of the old king's will, the expanded kingdom had been restored.[39]

The nobles of Wessex had probably preferred an adult ruler in view of the ongoing viking threat. As far as we can tell, the kingdom had done remarkably well during its period of dynastic discord and escaped any major attacks. The only one recorded in the *Anglo-Saxon Chronicle* in the wake of Æthelwulf's departure on pilgrimage occurred in the spring of 860, around the time of the kingdom's reunification, when 'a great naval force came inland and stormed Winchester'. This sacking of yet another walled city, previously considered safe, must have been disturbing, but the West Saxons subsequently acquitted themselves well. As Asser explains, when the raiders were returning to their ships, laden with booty, they were attacked by levies led by the ealdormen of Hampshire and Berkshire. 'The heathens were cut down on every side,' enthused Asser, 'and when they could resist no longer, they took to flight like women, and the Christians were masters of the battlefield.'[40]

This party of vikings had come from across the Channel, where the story of the previous five years had been very different. In Francia, as the *Annals of St Bertin* make grimly apparent, Scandinavian fleets had enjoyed free rein along the coasts and major rivers, sacking and burning cities such as Orleans, Tours, Noyon, Amiens, Chartres and Paris. The list of high-ranking casualties was long. The bishops of Bayeux and Noyon had been killed, while the bishop of Chartres had drowned when he tried to escape by swimming across the River Eure. But increasingly the Norsemen realized that they could obtain massive amounts of money by seizing hostages for ransom, or simply by demanding it in exchange for not unleashing death and destruction. In 858, for example, they captured the abbot of Saint-Denis, and demanded a ransom so huge that every church treasury, and those of the nobles too, had to be drained in order to raise it.[41]

In 862, however, there came a significant turning point in Frankish fortunes, when Charles the Bald defeated a group of vikings who were raiding along the River Marne, a tributary of the Seine to the east of Paris. As they sailed up the river the vikings had destroyed all its bridges, but Charles and his counsellors had the idea of rapidly rebuilding the bridge at Isles-lès-Villenoy and lining the banks on either side with troops (presumably armed with bows and arrows or other projectile weapons). When the Norsemen tried to sail back downstream, they found their way was blocked, and they were at the mercy of their enemies. So effective was the king's ploy that the raiders were forced to give hostages, surrender all their captives, and swear to leave his realm. They even promised to persuade other vikings on the Seine to do the same, and to fight them if they refused.

The success of his spontaneous strategy on the Marne encouraged Charles to plan something bigger – a fortification on the Seine to thwart further viking attacks. Later that same year, as the *Annals of St Bertin* explain, the king 'caused all the leading men of his realm to assemble about 1 June, with many workmen and carts, at the place called Pîtres, where the Andelle from the one side and the Eure from the other flow into the Seine'. This confluence was also the location of Pont-de-l'Arche, the first bridge across the Seine that any ships sailing up the river from the coast would encounter. Charles set about militarizing the bridge by building fortifications on both its banks. It was evidently a massive undertaking: the king was still demanding labour services for its construction two years later, and work continued throughout the rest of the decade. It was not entirely successful, for there was a further raid up the Seine in 865, but it rendered such raids more difficult, and signalled a new determination on Charles' part to defend his kingdom. As a consequence, some Norsemen began to return their attention to the other side of the Channel.[42]

King Æthelberht, says the *Anglo-Saxon Chronicle*, had ruled Wessex 'in good harmony and in good peace' since reuniting the kingdom in 860. The first signs that this state of tranquillity was about to be shattered came towards the end of 864, when a viking army occupied the Isle of Thanet and demanded money with menaces from the people of Kent. The locals, says the *Chronicle*, consented to this for the sake of peace, but it turned out to be a ruse: having agreed terms, the invaders made their way inland under cover of darkness and ravaged the eastern part of the former kingdom. Such an outrage demanded a robust royal response, but any retaliation that was planned must have been overtaken by Æthelberht's death in 865. The king was succeeded by his younger brother, Æthelred, who had been passed over five years earlier, and now inherited the whole kingdom.[43]

Æthelred had barely had time to take up the reins of power when a much greater threat materialized. In the autumn of 865, says the *Chronicle*, 'the land of the English' was invaded by 'a great heathen army'. Precisely where it had come from is unclear. Some of its number were no doubt drawn from the force that had camped on Thanet the previous year – in retrospect, that occupation may have seemed a preliminary to the main campaign. Other warriors must have come from West Francia, now that Charles the Bald had stepped up his defences on the Seine. And there were also, of course, vikings who came directly from Scandinavia. A tenth-century Latin translation of the *Anglo-Saxon Chronicle* asserts that the army was led by a certain tyrant called Ivar, who 'came from the north'. Later tradition identifies him as 'Ivar the Boneless', a son of the legendary Ragnar Lothbrok. He may be the same Ivar who was operating in Ireland in the mid-ninth century, but who disappears from the Irish chronicles at this point.[44]

Beyond describing the heathen army as 'great' (*micel*), the *Anglo-Saxon Chronicle* gives us no idea of its size. Its extraordinary magnitude, however, is implied by its tactics and its ambition. The invaders, we are told, made their winter camp in East Anglia, and made peace with the East Angles. In other words, they accepted money and treasure from the people of the eastern kingdom in return for not ravaging the land and taking it for themselves. But on this occasion their demands were not limited to gold and silver. The *Chronicle* adds that they were also supplied with horses, an indication that their strategy and their aims were new. This was no mere raiding party, nor even an occupying force that intended to stay for a season or two until the wealth of the land was exhausted. It was an army of conquest, planning to take over entire kingdoms.[45]

After a year in East Anglia amassing supplies and marshalling its full strength, the great army set out in the autumn of 866 towards Northumbria. Their primary target was York, which fell to them on 1 November. Virtually nothing is known of either Northumbria or East Anglia in the ninth century – whatever charters or annals were produced in these kingdoms were lost through viking destruction – but the *Anglo-Saxon Chronicle* informs us that Northumbria was already in disarray even before the great army's arrival. King Osbert, we are told, had been deposed by Ælle, 'a king with no hereditary right', and as a result 'there was great civil strife'. Such divisions were grist to the mill of the vikings, and it may even be that this internal discord was what had drawn the invaders to Northumbria in the first place.

By the spring of the new year, the two rival kings had sunk their differences in order to tackle the viking menace. In March 867 their combined forces advanced on York, causing the Norsemen to flee inside its walls. Driving home their advantage, the Northumbrians proceeded to break into the city, only to be cut to pieces by those trapped within. Both the kings were killed. According to much later sagas, composed in the thirteenth and fourteenth centuries, Ælle was subjected to the horrific 'blood eagle', in which the victim's lungs were removed from his broken ribcage and draped around his neck, so they resembled an eagle's folded wings. Those who like such grisly history will be disappointed to learn that there is no contemporary evidence for the practice. It seems to be a flight of imagination based on a debatable line of eleventh-century verse, which might have meant nothing more than Ælle's body was left to be eaten by eagles.[46]

Having occupied East Anglia and conquered Northumbria, the viking leaders turned their attention towards Mercia. In the autumn of 867 the great heathen army made its way south, along the River Trent, into the heart of the Midlands realm, and established its winter camp at Nottingham. The sandstone outcrop in the centre of the modern town, later the site of Nottingham Castle, was already home to a fortress at this date, which the vikings must have taken over, just as they had done at York. Once again, the scale of the menace they posed is suggested by the reaction of the king of Mercia, Burghred, and his counsellors, who collectively decided that they could not defeat the invaders on their own, and appealed for aid to Wessex.[47]

This might seem surprising, given the long history of antagonism between the two kingdoms. Egbert of Wessex had invaded and conquered Mercia as recently as 829. But during the intervening decades the relationship had improved as the viking threat had grown. Mercia fared somewhat better than Northumbria or East Anglia when it comes to the preservation of documents, so the silence is not quite absolute. We know from the *Chronicle* that the east coast of Mercia (the former kingdom of Lindsey) was ravaged in 841, and one of Burghred's charters says it was issued 'when the pagans were in the province of the Wrekin', indicating that the vikings had penetrated inland as far as Shrewsbury, presumably by sailing up the River Severn. Under this common pressure, Mercia and Wessex had begun to collaborate. In 853 Burghred had asked Æthelwulf to join him in an expedition against the Welsh, and later that year the Mercian king had married Æthelwulf's daughter, Æthelswith.[48]

Burghred's appeal for help in 867 was therefore directed to his brother-in-law, Æthelred, who responded positively, and led his troops into Mercia. Together the two kings marched their combined forces to Nottingham and laid siege to the viking camp – but without success. 'The pagans,' explains Asser, 'defended by the protection of the fortress, refused to give battle, and the Christians could not break the wall.' The result was an inconclusive peace between the two sides. Æthelred led his forces back to Wessex, and the vikings withdrew to York, where they remained for the next year.[49]

It was towards the end of 869 that the great heathen army resumed its campaign south of the Humber, riding through Mercia and into East Anglia, where they made a winter camp at Thetford. This time there was no talk of peace, and the East Angles must have realized, in the wake of Northumbria's fall, that the fate of their own kingdom was now at stake. Their king, Edmund, led his forces into battle against the invaders and fought fiercely against them. 'But alas,' says Asser, 'he was killed there with a large number of his men, and the heathen rejoiced triumphantly.' As with Ælle of Northumbria, stories that Edmund was singled out for a sacrificial pagan death – in this case, tied to a tree and used for target practice – arose only later, and can be safely disregarded. But Edmund was revered as a Christian martyr soon after his death, and by the mid-tenth century his remains had been translated to the royal estate that eventually became known as Bury St Edmunds. Whatever the nature of his death, it spelt the end for the kingdom of East Anglia. After their victory, says the *Chronicle*, the vikings 'conquered all the land'.[50]

The following year they finally turned their attention to Wessex. Their first move was to cross the River Thames at Reading where, as usual, they established a winter camp. Reading lies in a neck of land between the Thames and a tributary, the Kennet, and the vikings made it defensible by rapidly constructing a rampart between the two rivers – an earthwork that must have extended more than a third of a mile. While some of them were engaged in this labour, the remainder rode out to plunder the surrounding countryside. At Englefield, six miles to the west of Reading, they were confronted by the local ealdorman and his followers, who defeated them in battle. A great number of Norsemen were killed, including one of their leaders, causing the rest to flee.

Four days later, no doubt encouraged by this early success, King Æthelred led his forces to Reading and attacked the viking camp. He and his men fought right up to the newly dug rampart, cutting down all the invaders they found outside. But the king and his men had not reckoned for the fury of those still inside the fortress. 'Like wolves,' says Asser, 'they burst out of all the gates and joined battle with all their might.' Both sides fought fiercely, continues the chronicler, but it was the heathens who were eventually victorious.[51]

Grieving and ashamed at their defeat, says Asser, Æthelred and his army tried again four days later, attacking the vikings at a place called *Æscedun*, or Ashdown, probably somewhere in the hills to the west of Reading. Asser describes it as a set-piece battle, with both sides drawing up their divisions into shield-walls. The heathens, he says, had the advantage of the higher ground, but the Christians were fighting for their lives, their loved ones, and their land. The two armies clashed with a deafening roar, and fought violently for a long time. By God's will, says Asser, it was the invaders who weakened first, and when the greater part of their force had been killed, the rest 'took to ignominious flight'.[52]

By now it was probably January 871, and the West Saxons must have felt that they had the invaders on the ropes. The heathen horde that had crossed into the kingdom a few weeks earlier was probably not quite so great as the one that had destroyed Northumbria three years earlier, or East Anglia the previous winter. Some vikings must have remained in those regions to prevent the resurgence of native resistance, and Ivar, the most important of their original leaders, appears to have returned to Ireland. The host that had come into Wessex was led by two pagan kings, one named Bacgsecg, the other named Halfdan, who was a brother of Ivar. Bacgsecg had been killed in the recent battle at Ashdown, along with five of his lieutenants, or 'jarls'. And in the rout that followed, many others had been cut down as they ran, the Christians pursuing them and killing them until nightfall. When the sun rose the next morning, there were 'many thousands' of viking dead, says Asser, 'scattered everywhere over the broad expanse of Ashdown, far and wide'.[53]

When Æthelred and his army engaged with the survivors a fortnight later, therefore, it must have seemed more like a mopping-up exercise than another existential struggle. The two hosts clashed at Basing, about fifteen miles south of Reading, in what Asser describes as a long and violent battle. But surprisingly, given the reported scale of their recent losses, it was the Norsemen who 'gained the victory and were masters of the battlefield'.

Two months passed, says the *Anglo-Saxon Chronicle*, before the two sides met again, at an unknown location called *Mæredun*. The fighting went on late into the day, and there was great slaughter on both sides, but once again the heathens held their ground and the Christians were forced to retreat. A great many important West Saxons, says the *Chronicle*, were lost in the encounter.

It must have been apparent by this point that the vikings were not going to be dislodged from Wessex as easily as their defeat at Ashdown had suggested. Both sides had now suffered significant losses, and the depletion of the West Saxons ranks may have been starting to tell. Then came two blows that must have caused the Christians to despair. First, around Easter 871, a new fleet of vikings came from overseas and sailed up the Thames, where it joined the existing forces at Reading. It was evidently large, for the *Anglo-Saxon Chronicle* calls it 'a great summer army'. Then, shortly after Easter, King Æthelred died, his reign cut short by unknown causes after just five troubled years.[54]

The dead king's body was carried west to Dorset, to be buried in the minster at Wimborne. Further west in the same shire, his older brothers Æthelbald and Æthelberht lay alongside each other in their tombs at Sherborne, their reigns having ended after similarly short periods. Four of the sons of King Æthelwulf now lay in the ground and, despite his pilgrimage to Rome for the souls of his subjects, the terrifying vision reported thirty years earlier had finally come to pass. Pagan men were laying waste to the land with fire and sword, mercilessly slaughtering the Christian people.[55]

What little hope was left was now vested in Æthelwulf's last surviving son, Alfred.

6

RESURRECTION

Alfred the Great and the Forging of Englishness

I t is a pleasing fact that the oldest memorial to Alfred the Great in Wessex – and very nearly the oldest in the world – is a pub. Alfred was born in Wantage, where the school was renamed in his honour in 1850, and a statue of him was erected in the marketplace in 1876. But it was decades before these Victorian commemorations, all the way back in 1763, that John and Elizabeth Stevens proudly announced in the local press that they had 'lately opened a New INN, in Wantage aforesaid, known by the Sign of ALFRED'S HEAD'. The couple reassured readers that their new establishment was 'genteely fitted up', and promised that potential customers 'may depend on civil Treatment'. On Saturday 17 September the opening of the King Alfred's Head Inn was celebrated with a concert, followed by a ball for ladies. And the pub is still there today, a Grade II listed building, trading under the same name, though now with quiz nights and open-mike evenings.[1]

The Stevenses were among the first adopters – or exploiters – of an enthusiasm for Alfred that was gradually sweeping the country in the mid-eighteenth century. On 1 August 1740, to cite an early and influential example, Frederick, prince of Wales, celebrated the third birthday of his daughter by staging a masque at Cliveden, his country seat in Buckinghamshire. Entitled simply *Alfred*, this musical extravaganza concluded with a newly composed number in praise of its subject's legendary naval victories, known as 'Rule, Britannia!' Around the same time, Allen Bathurst, an English lord, decided to rename the sham castle he had constructed some years earlier in his park at Cirencester, changing it from 'King Arthur's Castle' to 'Alfred's Hall'. (This building, now very dilapidated, appears to be the oldest standing monument to King Alfred, bar none.) In the decades that followed, other follies dedicated to Alfred's memory started to appear. By the end of the eighteenth century, he was also the subject of plays, novels, paintings, songs and poems, and in the nineteenth century such productions multiplied almost beyond counting. When, in 1901, the earl of Rosebery unveiled a new statue of Alfred in Winchester, to mark what was then assumed to be the 1,000th anniversary of the king's death, he described him as 'Alfred the good, Alfred the truth-teller, Alfred the father of his country, and of ours'.[2]

And yet, as the appearance of Alfred-mania in the eighteenth century suggests, much of this was modern invention: attitudes that were deemed praiseworthy and patriotic in the Georgian and Victorian eras were being projected back onto a distant ninth-century king. Unlike Charlemagne, who was dubbed 'Charles the Great' by his contemporaries, Alfred was not called *magnus* in his own lifetime. The first recorded instance of that word being applied to him occurs in the thirteenth-century chronicle of Matthew Paris and, despite the author's assurance that it was a common appellation, there is no record of it being used again during the next three centuries. It was not, indeed, until the publication of a biography of the king entitled *Alfred the Great* in 1709 that his now famous soubriquet became truly popular.[3]

The unadulterated modern praise for Alfred, to be fair, was not without foundation. It was the king's good fortune to be the subject of a contemporary biography, the *Life of King Alfred*, written by Asser, a Welsh bishop, already referred to in previous chapters. Asser resided for long periods at Alfred's court, and so is able to furnish us a fascinating and close-up view of the king, of a kind unavailable for any other Anglo-Saxon ruler. At the

17. The statue of King Alfred in Wantage.

same time, his work is not without its problems. Most obviously, as an official biographer, Asser heaps praise upon his subject and presents him in an almost entirely positive light. Like all such panegyrics, his treatment of Alfred demands a close and sceptical analysis. But the difficulty here is that no original version of the bishop's book has come down to us. A copy made in the early eleventh century survived for 700 years, but was destroyed when the Cottonian Library caught fire in 1731. (Just at the moment when enthusiasm for Alfred was starting to skyrocket.) This loss of the only known medieval manuscript leaves us reliant on imperfect early-modern copies which have been 'improved' by the addition of non-authentic material. The famous story about Alfred burning the cakes, for example, became popular partly because it was thought to have been written by Asser, but was in reality a later legend inserted in the sixteenth century. The lack of an original manuscript has even encouraged claims that the *Life of King Alfred* is not a contemporary composition at all, but a late tenth-century forgery.[4]

The forgery argument was always regarded by most scholars as flawed, and most would now accept that it has been settled decisively in Asser's favour.[5] Yet debate about Alfred continues. The king was long credited, for example, as the translator of several books, putting him centuries ahead of the next royal author in Britain, James I.[6] But lately this too has been called into question, with one Oxford professor publishing a paper entitled 'Did King Alfred Write Anything?'.[7] Similarly, it was argued in the 1970s that Alfred was responsible for laying out the streets of Winchester, but more recent archaeological investigation suggests this was more likely to have been the work of his predecessors.[8] Asser praises his patron's generosity to the Church, but the monks of Abingdon remembered the king as a despoiler of their lands, and branded him a 'Judas'.[9] All of which begs an obvious but crucial question: was Alfred really that great?

★

It is clear that one of the main proponents of Alfred's greatness was the king himself. Born in 848, or perhaps a year either side of that date, Alfred was the last of the five sons of King Æthelwulf of Wessex, but determined to convince others that he was not the least. According to Asser, as a boy Alfred 'surpassed all his brothers, both in wisdom and in all good habits'. He was apparently better-looking, better spoken, better behaved, a better huntsman and a better warrior. As a result, insists the king's own biographer, he was 'greatly loved, more than all his brothers, by his mother and father – indeed, by everybody – with a universal and profound love'.[10]

One factor that caused Alfred to feel he had been favoured above his older brothers was that, as a child, he had been to Rome on two separate occasions. In 855, at the age of six or seven, he had travelled there in the company of his father, who was making his celebrated pilgrimage. But Alfred had also made the same journey two years earlier, when he was no more than five, as part of the embassy that Æthelwulf had sent to the Holy City in advance of his own arrival. Why he was sent at so young an age is something of a puzzle. It may have been an attempt on his father's part to obtain papal recognition of the child's royal rights, in order to guard against Alfred being forced into a clerical career by his older brothers at a later date. In a letter to Æthelwulf, Pope Leo IV informed the king that he had honoured Alfred by belting him with the sword and robes of a Roman consul. Later in life, once he had outlived all his older brothers and succeeded to the throne, Alfred evidently came to see this papal investiture as a kind of predestination, telling Asser that the pope had anointed him as a future king.[11]

The other attribute that marked Alfred out as special were his illnesses. Asser explains that, as a young man, Alfred found himself 'unable to abstain from carnal desire', and feared this would lead to God's displeasure. So he would often get up at dawn to visit churches in order to pray, asking to be afflicted with a disease that would suppress his lusts but be tolerable enough to bear. God obliged Alfred by giving him haemorrhoids, a condition with which the future king struggled for 'many bitter years'. Eventually, when he found them too much to endure, he asked for a new illness, something that would not show outwardly, and found himself cured. But, alas for Alfred, this was only a temporarily lull in his suffering. When he was nineteen, he was struck by another more mysterious ailment. It first occurred on the occasion of his marriage in 868 to Ealhswith, the daughter of a Mercian nobleman. After a wedding feast that lasted day and night, says Asser, Alfred was afflicted by a severe pain, quite unknown to the doctors who were present. Some thought it was the return of his earlier piles, but others suspected it was something more sinister – a mystery fever, or witchcraft, or the Devil. One modern commentator has suggested it may have been Crohn's disease, but accurate diagnosis is of course impossible at such a distance. The fact that his new illness first flared up on the night of his wedding suggests it might even have been psychological, linked to the same anxieties about sex he had experienced earlier in his teens. Whatever it was, it lasted a long time, periodically plaguing him until the final years of his life, and the king interpreted it as a burden sent by God to test him. On more than one occasion, Asser links the 'savage attacks' of Alfred's illness with the relentless attacks of his enemies, the vikings.[12]

Alfred had become king in 871 at a moment of profound crisis. The great heathen army that had invaded Britain six years earlier had proved all but unstoppable. Mercia, with the assistance of Wessex, had managed to hold back the horde and negotiate a truce, but Northumbria and East Anglia had fallen, and the fate of their kings had served as a terrible warning to other rulers. When the Danes had finally moved into Wessex in the winter of 870, therefore, its leaders had fought back with desperate fury – Asser describes Alfred fighting at Ashdown 'like a wild boar'. That battle had been a victory for the West Saxons, and a moment of exultation, after which it seemed that the vikings would have to retire. But more clashes had followed, in which the defenders had been defeated, and then a new viking fleet had sailed up the Thames to Reading, replenishing the ranks of the heathen host. It was at this critical moment, in the spring of 871, that King Æthelred had died.[13]

The problem was not just the loss of another king of Wessex – the fourth in thirteen years – but the fact that the other ranks of the kingdom's warrior class had also been greatly depleted. Only one ealdorman, it is true, is named in the *Chronicle* as having been killed during the invasion, though the deaths of others may have gone unrecorded. But there were other important men – warriors who held extensive lands and were the leaders of local society – who must have perished in great numbers. The catch-all word for such men was 'thegns', a word that originally meant 'servant', but had latterly acquired connotations of nobility. Thegns were essentially the Anglo-Saxon equivalent of later medieval knights, and those who served the king were comparable to the later knights of the royal household. As young men they would reside permanently at the king's court, acting as his bodyguard and dining in his hall. After they had served for several years, they would be rewarded with land and assume the role of country gentlemen, helping to govern the provinces, but still expected to spend a third of their time attending to the king in person.[14]

Asser is full of praise for these elite warriors of Wessex, and the valour they had shown in the course of the viking invasion of 870–1. 'The individual ealdormen of that race,' he says, 'with their men, and also very many king's thegns, had fought ceaselessly and intently against the pagans.' But there had been so many battles and skirmishes, he explains, that these warriors had been 'virtually annihilated'. Alfred, says his biographer, 'had already sustained great losses of many men while his brothers were still alive'. All of which may have been true, but it was essential for Asser to emphasize the extent of these losses, to explain the fact that Alfred's reign began with yet another defeat. A month after his accession, the new king, 'victorious in virtually all battles', engaged the viking host at Wilton, the royal administrative centre that gave its name to Wiltshire. He did so, says his biographer, 'almost unwillingly', because his numbers were so few. He and his men fought vigorously, and seemed to be about to vanquish the much larger heathen host, who had turned and started to flee. But the Danes regrouped, attacked again, and became masters of the battlefield.

Having spent so much effort trying to square the circle of Alfred's defeat, Asser wasted few words on its consequences, saying simply that 'the Saxons made peace with the heathens, on condition that they would leave them; and this they did'. But peace after being beaten in battle must have come at a price, meaning the defeated must have paid a massive tribute. It is highly unlikely that the vikings would have accepted payment in coin. Decades of raids had devastated the economy of southern Britain, causing international trade to collapse, and as a result the coinages of both Mercia and Wessex, which had once been close to pure silver, had been greatly debased: at the start of Alfred's reign, the silver content of his coins stood at a pitiful sixteen per cent. The tribute must therefore have been made up of more valuable items – rings, torques, sword pommels, chalices, candlesticks and crosses – collected in vast quantities. Having extracted the most they could, the army withdrew from Wessex, as agreed, and occupied London, making their camp there for the winter.[15]

Whatever terms were agreed in 871, it would have been naive of Alfred and his advisers to expect that paying the vikings to go away would offer anything other than a temporary reprieve. Fortunately for them, however, the attention of the heathen army was diverted by a rebellion in Northumbria. After conquering the northern kingdom in 867 and killing both its competing kings, the Danish host had returned to East Anglia in search of further spoils, leaving Northumbria in the care of a native Anglo-Saxon named Egbert. But in 872 the Northumbrians ejected this client king and replaced him with a ruler of their own choosing named Ricsige.[16]

This revolt drew the vikings back north. That autumn they left London and established a new camp at Torksey, about ten miles north-west of Lincoln. The site, then an island in the River Trent, has been identified and excavated in recent decades. It spread over fifty-five hectares, reinforcing the impression that the great army must have numbered several thousands. The quantity of the finds – over 350 coins, and almost 300 gaming pieces – pointed to the same conclusion. Over a third of the coins were dirhams from the Middle East, indicating the extent of their trade networks. The Scandinavians were also minting their own money on site and making other metal objects such as arm-rings. It is worth emphasizing that this was not a hoard, deliberately left in the ground, but an accumulation of items that had been accidentally dropped and lost. As the excavators concluded, these losses imply that 'plunder was being processed on a massive scale'.[17]

Some of the coins at Torksey were Northumbrian, so perhaps the army raided the northern kingdom in the winter of 872. The following year, however, they turned their attention to Mercia, moving up the Trent to Repton. The minster there was probably built by the great eighth-century king, Æthelbald, whose bones lay in the crypt, along with those of his ninth-century successor, Wiglaf. The vikings occupied the church and incorporated its tower into the circuit of their new defensive enclosure. They also used the churchyard for burying their own dead: excavations in the garden of the modern vicarage uncovered a mass grave of at least 264 people who had died in the early 870s. Most were male, aged between eighteen and forty-five, but just under a fifth were female – possibly spouses from Scandinavia, or else local women who had been seized.[18]

The occupation of Repton heralded Mercia's fall. 'They conquered all that land', says the *Anglo-Saxon Chronicle*. King Burghred, who had ruled for twenty-two years, fled into exile, along with his queen, Æthelswith, Alfred's older sister. Together they made their way to Rome, presumably in search of divine assistance, but neither would return, both dying in Italy at a later date. In Burghred's place, the victorious vikings installed a new king, Ceolwulf. The *Chronicle* dismisses him as 'a foolish king's thegn' and, despite modern attempts to explain this as retrospective vitriol, it is hard to see how he could have been anything other than a viking stooge. 'He swore oaths to them and gave hostages', says the *Chronicle*, promising that Mercia would be theirs whenever they wanted it, 'and that he and his followers would be ready at the enemy's service'.[19]

The fall of another Anglo–Saxon kingdom, and the presence of a viking army on his own northern frontier, boded extremely ill for Alfred – Burghred had 'made peace' with the vikings just five years before they decided to topple him. Once again, however, Wessex was lucky. It seems likely that in the course of the fight for Mercia the Danes had lost some of their leaders. The burials at Repton were arranged as if to honour some great fallen warrior, and other nearby burial mounds point to the same conclusion. Perhaps for this reason, differences broke out among the survivors, and the great heathen army divided. One of its original leaders, Halfdan, took his forces and went to Northumbria, establishing a camp on the River Tyne from where they harried and plundered the Picts and the Britons of Strathclyde. The other leaders, named as Guthrum, Oscetel and Anwend by the *Chronicle*, decided to remain in the south. In 874 they left Repton with the remainder of the army and moved east, establishing a new camp at Cambridge.[20]

But Alfred's luck could not last forever, and in 875 the viking attack on Wessex was resumed. In the summer of that year, says the *Chronicle*, the king set out to sea with a naval force to fight against the crews of seven Scandinavian ships, one of which he succeeded in capturing. It is not clear whether these ships were connected to the remnant of the great heathen army that had remained in the south, but what followed makes it seem highly probable. At some point later in the same year, or early in the next, the army camped at Cambridge advanced into Wessex. They evidently moved quickly, for the *Chronicle* says they evaded the West Saxon levies sent against them, and rode right the way across the kingdom to seize Wareham in Dorset – a distance of almost 200 miles. This must have been ominously reminiscent of the events that led to Mercia's fall – Wareham, like Repton, was an important royal estate, developed at the end of the eighth century by King Beorhtric, who was buried in the church there. According to Asser it was a fortified site, protected on both sides by rivers. More importantly, Wareham was located on the coast, making it likely that the viking ships that Alfred had engaged a short time earlier had been a preliminary attempt to open up this new front, so the kingdom could be invaded by sea. At some point after the viking army had seized Wareham they were joined by a large fleet, reportedly in excess of 120 ships.

Alfred, in response, assembled an army and went to confront the invaders, though whether or not any military action took place is unclear: all that Asser and the *Chronicle* tell us is that the two sides once again 'made peace'. The fact that the vikings were obliged to surrender high-ranking hostages, however, suggests that Alfred had the upper hand in the negotiations, as does the *Chronicle*'s comment that the vikings swore on a 'holy ring' that they would leave his kingdom immediately. But once the peace had been agreed, the vikings immediately disregarded it, departing from Wareham under cover of darkness and riding west into Devon, where they seized the old Roman city of Exeter. Alfred rode after them, says the *Chronicle*, but was unable to overtake them before they reached the safety of Exeter's walls. Again there was a stand-off. The good news for Alfred and the Saxons was that, when the viking fleet went west from Wareham, intending to join the army at Exeter, they sailed into a great storm that sank many of their ships. But despite these losses the Danish occupation of Exeter appears to have lasted for several months. Eventually, in the summer of 877, the vikings once again agreed to terms, swearing oaths and surrendering hostages, and in August they withdrew to Mercia.[21]

While the southern vikings had been attempting to conquer Wessex, there had been a significant development in the north.

The vikings who had based themselves on the Tyne to raid the Picts and the Britons had decided it was time to settle. For some of them, including their leader Halfdan, it had been a decade since their arrival in Britain, and in that time they had ravaged and plundered almost all of its most profitable areas. They now wished to transform themselves from rootless raiders into permanent residents, dispossessing Anglo-Saxon landowners and appropriating their estates. In 876, says the *Chronicle*, 'Halfdan shared out the land of the Northumbrians, and they proceeded to plough and support themselves.' According to one report, this takeover caused the Northumbrian king, Ricsige, to die of grief. One year on, the southern vikings decided to follow the example of their friends in the north. Having retreated into Mercia, says the *Chronicle*, they shared out some of the kingdom amongst themselves, and gave some to their client ruler, Ceolwulf.[22]

If Alfred or his advisers interpreted this as a sign that their enemies were ready to hang up their swords, however, they were soon seriously disappointed. A few months later, in early January 878, the Danish army launched another attack on Wessex. This time their target was Chippenham, an important royal estate in northern Wiltshire – the wedding of Burghred of Mercia and Alfred's sister, Æthelswith, had been celebrated there in 854. It is possible that festivities were also being held there at the time of the attack in 878, which the *Chronicle* says was carried out 'in midwinter, after twelfth night'. Vikings would frequently attack on feast days, when they knew that Christians would be congregating and celebrating. The fact that the *Chronicle* adds that on this occasion the attackers approached 'stealthily' is similarly suggestive, evoking the possibility that Alfred and his court were carousing at Chippenham on the last day of Christmas and caught off-guard.[23]

What is certain is that this new assault was catastrophic. The vikings, says the *Chronicle*, 'occupied the land of the West Saxons and settled there', just as they had recently done in Northumbria and Mercia. This, of course, implies a terrible military defeat had been inflicted on the leaders of Wessex, leaving them utterly at the mercy of the invaders. 'By strength of arms,' says Asser, 'they forced many men of that race to sail overseas, through both poverty and fear, and very nearly all the inhabitants of that region submitted to their authority.'

But not Alfred. The king disappeared into the woods and fens of Somerset, accompanied by a small band of nobles, soldiers and thegns.[24]

In this way, Alfred joined the ranks of famous royal fugitives, such as King David, Robert Bruce or Charles II, forced to flee for their lives, later to return in triumph. As in other cases, Alfred's flight into the wilderness became a fertile source of legend. It was during this period that the episode involving the king and the cakes was supposed to have occurred. Alfred, the story goes, was obliged to take refuge in the cottage of a swineherd, where he rested for several days. One day, when the swineherd was out herding swine, his wife placed some loaves in the oven, apparently anticipating that her royal house-guest would keep a watchful eye on them while she attended to other tasks. But Alfred was too busy reflecting on his greatly reduced circumstances, wondering how he could regain God's favour, to notice when the bread began to burn, and as a result was subjected to a tongue-lashing from his exasperated hostess. 'Look here, man!' she said. 'You hesitate to turn the loaves which you see to be burning, yet you're quite happy to eat them when they come warm from the oven!'

Such at least was the tale as originally told. It first appears in the *Life of St Neot*, a source written a hundred years after Alfred's adventures in the fens, and was almost certainly an invention by its anonymous author. But, as already noted, in the sixteenth century the story was inserted into the earliest printed editions of Asser's biography, lending it an undeserved legitimacy. By the time it was identified as an interpolation in the nineteenth century, it was too late – Alfred had been established in the popular imagination as the king who burned the cakes.[25]

Asser certainly gives the impression that Alfred and his small band of followers had a miserable time, 'leading a restless life in great distress amid the woody and marshy places of Somerset', with nothing to live on besides what they could steal, either from vikings, or from those English who had submitted to viking authority. There are other indications, however, that the king's situation was perhaps not quite as lonely as legend made out. A tenth-century Latin translation of the *Anglo-Saxon Chronicle* mentions that Æthelnoth, the ealdorman of Somerset, had also escaped into the woods with a small force of men. Asser, meanwhile, mentions that a group of king's thegns and their followers in Devon had shut themselves up in a fortress he names as *Cynuit* – possibly Countisbury, an Iron Age hill fort close to the sea. In the early months of 878, these men were confronted by a viking army that had been ravaging south Wales, led by an unnamed brother of Ivar and Halfdan. The vikings surrounded the fortress, but made no attempt to storm it, confident that those inside would be forced to surrender through lack of food and water. But, says Asser, 'judging it far better to gain either death or victory', the thegns and their followers burst out and attacked their besiegers, killing the viking leader and many others, and forcing the rest to flee to their ships. The *Chronicle* adds that the victorious Saxons also captured the enemy's banner, 'which they called "Raven"'.[26]

Perhaps inspired by this success, Alfred and his followers established a fortress of their own soon after Easter at a place called Athelney. Now the site of a farm in the middle of the Somerset Levels, which were drained in later centuries, Athelney was then an island. 'Surrounded on every side by swampy, impassable and extensive marshland and groundwater,' says Asser, 'it cannot be reached in any way except by punts.' From this isolated fastness, the king and his followers 'struck out relentlessly and tirelessly against the pagans'.[27]

During this time Alfred must have been secretly communicating with other ealdormen and thegns who had gone into hiding or submitted to the dominion of the Danes. In early May, the king

and his followers left Athelney and rode east to a place called
Egbert's Stone – now sadly unlocatable, but situated somewhere
'in the eastern part of Selwood Forest', on the border of Somerset
and Wiltshire. It was a prearranged rallying point. There, says
the *Chronicle*, the king was joined by all the people of those two
shires, as well as the people from the western part of Hampshire.
The timing of Alfred's return appears to have been deliberately
symbolic, for he left Athelney 'in the seventh week after Easter',
meaning his public reappearance coincided with Whitsun, the
festival which commemorated the descent of the Holy Spirit on
the disciples in the wake of Christ's resurrection. Asser certainly
appreciated the symbolism, saying that the assembled people were
filled with joy when they saw the king, 'as if one restored to
life after suffering such great tribulations'.

Alfred had returned with one purpose – to confront and destroy
the Danes who were occupying his kingdom. On the morning
after the muster at Egbert's Stone he marched his forces
northwards in the direction of the viking camp at Chippenham.
The following day they encountered the entire viking army at a
place called Edington, and a fierce battle ensued. Typically, our
sources tell us almost nothing about the battle itself. All we learn
is that the fighting lasted a long time, but eventually – thanks to
God's will – Alfred was victorious. 'He destroyed the pagans with
great slaughter,' says Asser, 'and pursued those who fled as far as
the stronghold' – presumably the camp at Chippenham, twenty
miles to the north of the battlefield. There the king and his army
killed all the Danes they caught outside the compound and seized
all the horses and cattle, putting immense pressure on those holed
up within. After a fortnight's siege, says Asser, hunger and fear
drove those inside the fortress to despair, and they sought terms
of surrender.[28]

The magnitude of Alfred's victory at Edington is demonstrated
by the conditions he was able to impose. In the first place, the
king was in a position to demand as many hostages as he wanted,
without having to hand over any of his own men in return.
This, according to Asser, was a novelty: never before had the

vikings made peace on such terms with anyone (a statement that implies Alfred's earlier negotiations with the vikings had involved the *exchange* of hostages). Secondly, and more momentously, the viking leaders agreed to convert to Christianity, and to be baptized at Alfred's court. This had happened on earlier occasions in Francia, but it is the first recorded instance of it happening in Britain.[29]

And so, three weeks after the siege had ended, thirty of the highest-ranking warriors in the viking army came to meet Alfred at an estate called Aller, about three miles east of Athelney, in order to be ritually converted. Their leader was Guthrum, last mentioned in our sources in 874 as part of a triumvirate of viking kings. What had become in the meantime of his erstwhile colleagues, Oscetel and Anwend, we are not told. Guthrum, says Asser, was raised from the font by Alfred himself, becoming the king's godson, and the *Chronicle* reveals that he received the baptismal name of Æthelstan, evoking the memory of Alfred's eldest brother who had died over two decades earlier. As part of the ceremony the converts were clothed in white robes, and their heads anointed with holy oil, held in place by white bandages. These had to be worn for a week, during which Guthrum and his men remained in Alfred's company. After eight days the robes and bandages were ceremoniously removed, and after a further four days the Danish visitors finally departed. Alfred, says Asser, bestowed on them 'many excellent treasures'.[30]

The baptism of Guthrum and his leading men conjures a remarkable scene – the vikings placidly submitting to what they must have considered a bizarre and bemusing ritual, not least because it was orchestrated by a king who only a few weeks earlier had slaughtered many of their comrades, and Alfred conferring blessings and presents on men who until recently had been trying to hunt and kill him. Yet it would be a mistake to interpret Alfred's actions as naive, or arising from a misplaced belief in the virtue of Christian forgiveness. The conversion of Guthrum and his followers in fact indicates a major but logical shift in Alfred's strategy.

At the start of his reign, the king had been obliged to make peace with the vikings on highly unfavourable terms, almost certainly paying them a large tribute in order to go away. Other Anglo-Saxon rulers and communities had done the same, no doubt harbouring the desperate hope that the vikings, once sated, would depart from Britain, either returning to the Continent or retiring to Scandinavia. But by the late 870s, it was apparent that the invaders were not going anywhere. In Northumbria they had toppled the native kings and begun, in the *Chronicle*'s words, 'to plough and support themselves'. The same was probably true in East Anglia, where King Edmund had been martyred back in 869. And at least part of Mercia had been appropriated and settled by Guthrum and his men as recently as 877. Alfred, after his decisive victory, could insist the vikings leave his kingdom, but they were going to remain his neighbours, with whom he or his successors would inevitably have to interact in the months and years to come. Part of the problem of dealing with vikings had always been their refusal to play by Christian rules – not only in their contemptuous desecration of holy sites, but also when it came to swearing sacred oaths. Inducing the Danes to swear on a pagan ring at Wareham in 875 had been a bold attempt on Alfred's part to square the circle, but a fruitless one – as soon as the vikings had sworn, they sloped off and seized Exeter.

By requiring his defeated enemies to receive baptism, therefore, Alfred was aiming to normalize relations with the new rulers beyond his own borders. Heartfelt or token, the vikings' submission and conversion indicated a willingness on their part to abide by Christian rules. By recognizing Alfred as a godfather, Guthrum acknowledged some degree of subordination. By adopting Guthrum as his spiritual son, Alfred conferred legitimacy on him as a ruler.

It seems likely that, during the twelve days that Alfred and Guthrum spent in each other's company, they must have discussed the fate of Mercia. The vikings had already appropriated part of

Mercia for themselves the previous year – presumably the eastern part, leaving the western part of the kingdom to their client ruler, Ceolwulf. It is hard to imagine there was much love lost between Ceolwulf and Alfred. It has been suggested that the two rulers may have collaborated on the strength of their coinages. Remarkably, from around the middle of the 870s, the debased currencies of both Mercia and Wessex were restored, their silver content multiplying by a factor of five or six. But this could equally well have been an initiative driven by the moneyers. Ceolwulf had been the beneficiary of the deposition and exile of Alfred's sister and brother-in-law. He may even have connived in their downfall. In Wessex he was probably never regarded as anything other than a viking puppet.[31]

Alfred's ambition was evidently that he should replace Ceolwulf, and that the western part of Mercia should be annexed to Wessex, for that is exactly what happened in the months that followed. Shortly after Guthrum and his men left Alfred's court, they departed from his kingdom, as promised. But they did not withdraw very far. Abandoning their camp at Chippenham, they moved twenty miles north to Cirencester, which lay in the part of Mercia that notionally belonged to Ceolwulf. Guthrum and his army remained there for the next year, during which time Ceolwulf's reign came to a mysterious end. We do not know whether he was driven out or died. If the latter was the case, the timing was certainly very convenient.[32]

It was probably in this period that Alfred and Guthrum negotiated a treaty partitioning Mercia between them, the text of which has survived. Its first clause drew a line between their territories. Crucially, Alfred was to retain London – the first part of the new border was the line of the River Lea, which runs to the east of the city. The border then went 'in a straight line to Bedford, then up the Ouse to Watling Street'. Presumably Watling Street itself, the ancient routeway that ran right through the heart of Mercia, formed the remainder of the new frontier – it may, perhaps, have been the line already agreed when the kingdom had been divided between Guthrum and Ceolwulf two years earlier.[33]

This annexation may have been welcomed in some quarters of Mercia – the triumphant Christian leader liberating at least some of the Midlands kingdom from viking overlordship. Alfred himself had built on the good relations developed by his predecessors in recent decades by his marriage to his Mercian wife, Ealhswith, in 868. But there must have been plenty of people who objected to the dismemberment of Mercia – a proud, independent kingdom which within living memory had been the most powerful in southern Britain. One such person may have been Æthelred, a Mercian nobleman who by 883 was ruling the western rump of Mercia on Alfred's behalf. We know nothing about his background, so we cannot say whether Æthelred's expectations had been thwarted, but in different circumstances he and his supporters might have expected him to take on the mantle of royalty. In his charters he is described in quasi-regal terms, on one occasion styled 'by the gift of divine grace raised to the rule and lordship of the Mercians'. But Æthelred never went as far as styling himself 'king' in any official documents, nor were any coins minted in his name. Instead he adopted the title 'ealdorman', in deference to the superior authority of Alfred.[34]

But if he insisted on his superiority in western Mercia, Alfred also took steps to assuage the feelings of his new Mercian subjects. At no point did the king claim that Mercia was being absorbed into Wessex, in the way that Kent, Sussex, Surrey and Cornwall had been subsumed in earlier decades. Instead, Alfred began to promote the idea that the peoples of Wessex and Mercia were united by a common ethnicity. In his treaty with Guthrum, for example, the king is stated to have acted in conjunction with 'all the counsellors of the English race' (*ealles Angelcynnes witan*). The word *Angelcynn* was not a brand-new coinage – it occurs once before, in a Mercian charter of 855 – but from this point onwards its usage becomes much more frequent, as Alfred and his advisers began to push the idea that he was not merely the king of Wessex, but a king for all the English peoples. Alfred may have been experimenting with this notion for a few years: one of his coins from the mid-870s bears the legend 'REX ANGLO[RUM]'. But after his takeover of western Mercia, such proclamations begin to multiply. From 882, for example, Asser consistently styles Alfred 'king of the Anglo-Saxons' (*Angulsaxonum rex*), and the same designation was also used in some royal charters. The long-established idea that the people of Mercia and Wessex, and for that matter those of East Anglia and Northumbria, were all in some sense 'English', was being used for overtly political ends: to convince the people of Mercia that they had not been annexed, but were an integral part of a new, larger, political entity, 'the kingdom of the Anglo-Saxons'.[35]

No sooner had this new kingdom been created than its viability was put to the test. Late in 878, while Guthrum and his army were at Cirencester, a new force of vikings arrived from overseas and sailed up the Thames. According to Asser they established a winter camp at Fulham, a convenient bend in the river five miles west of London, and made contact with Guthrum. This was an acid test of the viking leader's recent professions of faith and fidelity. Was he going to remain loyal to Alfred, his godfather, and respect the terms of their peace, or would he join forces with the newcomers in the hope of conquering Wessex?

Guthrum chose to maintain his pact with Alfred. The following year, he and his army left Cirencester and withdrew to East Anglia, where, says the *Chronicle*, they settled and shared out the land. This must have disappointed the new force of vikings at Fulham, and perhaps dissuaded them from attacking Wessex, but it is unlikely to have persuaded them to leave. The task of convincing them to depart probably fell to Alfred – a later reference in the *Chronicle* recalled a time when the king's prayers were answered 'when the English were encamped against the enemy army at London'. Whatever pressure was brought to bear, the new viking army left Fulham at some point in 879 and returned to Francia.[36]

The threat was thereby averted, and the peace with Guthrum held. But how long before the viking force on the Continent returned, boosted by new recruits, hungry to feast on English riches? Scandinavians had been attacking Britain and Francia for almost a century, and despite Alfred's recent victory, the tide had unquestionably been in their favour. The Anglo-Saxons and the Franks were no slouches when it came to warfare, as the triumphant histories of both peoples prior to 800 proves, nor had they somehow grown soft in the meantime. Yet time and again they had been outwitted and defeated by armies of Norsemen.

We know disappointingly little about early medieval warfare. Detailed accounts of battles are virtually non-existent, even if penned by those who participated in them. Tactics and strategies are not described in our sources, and have to be inferred by modern historians. But despite the huge holes in our evidence, a couple of things seem reasonably certain. Firstly, being a warrior in this period was an elite occupation. The old notion that Germanic societies had folk-based armies formed by the participation of all freeborn men is at odds with sources that suggest warfare was primarily an aristocratic pursuit. Kings raised armies by looking to the support of other powerful men – their ealdormen and their thegns, who in turn called upon the services of their own followings of well-equipped warriors. A considerable amount of evidence suggests these men were mounted, not only for transport but also in battle, if occasion demanded.

Secondly, the kind of warfare that these warriors practised was primarily offensive. They carried destruction into the territory of their enemies, burning and ravaging, and occasionally clashed with their opponents face to face. They went to war because of the opportunities it afforded for plunder. A few may have served out of obligation, for land they had already been given, but most of them probably participated on a campaign-by-campaign basis, riding to war because they were willing to gamble that war would make them richer. Such is the impression we get from poems like *Beowulf*, and finds like the Staffordshire Hoard.[37]

This type of warfare was utterly unsuited to dealing with vikings. If they came as hit-and-run raiders, they would be long gone before any mounted warriors arrived. If they came in larger armies, by the time the king had mustered a host large enough to confront them, they would already be ensconced behind the banks and palisades of a temporary camp. Siege craft in early medieval Britain was virtually non-existent, with none of the sophisticated machines and devices used in the ancient world or the later Middle Ages. Laying siege to a fortress typically involved trying to storm the gates, or else surrounding it and waiting for those inside to starve. If the besieged were well supplied, there was little that could be done to dislodge them, as the combined forces of Wessex and Mercia found to their frustration at Nottingham in 868.[38]

Since the first appearance of the vikings, both Anglo-Saxon and Frankish kings had endeavoured to come up with effective countermeasures, but both ran up against the same fundamental problem – it is much more difficult to persuade people to participate in a defensive war than an offensive one, because there are far fewer opportunities for profit, and still a good chance of death. Accordingly, kings began to insist that military service was a duty that fell on a much wider cross-section of society, not just a warrior elite. From the start of the ninth century, Charlemagne and his successors demanded that quite minor landowners participate in defending the Carolingian Empire. Similarly, King Offa made clear in a charter to all the churches of Kent in 792 that he expected them to provide men to fight against pagan raiders, even if it meant venturing into neighbouring Sussex. These royal demands must have met with some compliance, as well as some resistance, but the increasing success of viking raids as the ninth century progressed suggests that such new initiatives were not terribly effective.[39]

Alfred is widely credited with turning the situation around for the Anglo-Saxons, largely thanks to his creation of an extensive network of fortifications across his kingdom. The Old English word for such fortresses was *burh*, from which we get the word 'borough'. In the minds of many, the *burh* was a revolutionary concept introduced by Alfred himself: a fortified town, created from scratch, with a precisely laid out grid of streets, combining urban and military functions, and capable of accommodating hundreds, even thousands, of soldiers and citizens.[40] As with other aspects of his rule, however, here too the extent of Alfred's originality has been called into question. Was the king a genuine innovator, or has he been unfairly credited with the achievements of his predecessors?

Any discussion of Alfred's *burhs* has to begin with a document known as the Burghal Hidage, so-called by historians because it contains a list of thirty-one *burhs*, along with the number of hides of land allocated to each in order to support it. In its present form the Burghal Hidage is generally reckoned to have been drawn up after 914, because it includes one *burh* (Buckingham) which, according to the *Anglo-Saxon Chronicle*, was not established until that year. But most historians believe that the other thirty *burhs* had been founded well before this date. Traditionally, most if not all of them were attributed to Alfred. In an extended chapter of praise, Asser says that the king not only rebuilt cities and towns, but built others 'where previously there were none'. Later in the same section, he also refers to Alfred ordering the construction of fortresses.[41]

There is, however, no good reason to assume that *all* the *burhs* listed in the Burghal Hidage were created by Alfred, or even renovated at his command. As we've already seen, the kings of Mercia were insisting that their subjects contribute to the construction and defence of royal fortresses as early as the middle of the eighth century, and the kings of Wessex were doing the same by the middle of the ninth. Presumably neither would have done so unless they had been building *burhs*. The defences at Wareham, which can still be seen today, may date back as far as King Beorhtric's development of the site in the later eighth century. They were certainly in existence by the time Wareham was occupied by the vikings in 875, a date rather too early in

Alfred's reign to make it likely that he was responsible for their addition.[42]

Wareham was laid out on an impressive scale, covering between eighty and ninety acres, and the streets of the modern town still adhere to the rectilinear plan of its original designers. It would, however, be a mistake to imagine all *burhs* were similarly large and regular. In the Burghal Hidage, Wareham is allocated 1,600 hides for its maintenance, but only three other *burhs* have more than this, and most considerably fewer. Over half are assigned under 1,000 hides each, and in some cases – Southampton, for example – the figure is less than a tenth of Wareham's size. Most were not new creations, but ancient defensive sites that had been pressed back into use: Iron Age hill forts, Roman shore forts, and Roman walled towns. Even among the *burhs* that were established in the Anglo-Saxon period, only three – Wallingford, Oxford and Cricklade – had the same extensive, grid-planned layout as Wareham. All three were located on the Thames. While they *could* have been the work of Alfred, or perhaps his Mercian deputy, Ealdorman Æthelred, they could equally have been established by any of the kings of Mercia before 879.[43]

Alfred undoubtedly created *some* new *burhs*. Asser describes the king's island refuge at Athelney, founded in 878, as 'a formidable fortress of elegant workmanship', and adds that it was linked to another fort (Lyng) by a causeway 'built by protracted labour'. At Shaftesbury in Dorset there was once an inscribed stone, mentioned by the twelfth-century chronicler William of Malmesbury, which proclaimed that the town had been founded by Alfred in 880. We know from the *Anglo-Saxon Chronicle* that the *burhs* at Exeter and Chichester were in existence by the end of the king's reign, and there must have been many others that were at least begun at his command. Asser relates how Alfred's determination to build fortifications 'to the general advantage of the whole realm' met with a dilatory response, and even disobedience, from some of his greater subjects, so that some *burhs* were still unfinished at the time the biographer was writing in 893.[44]

18. The layout of the *burh* at Wallingford is still clearly visible
within the modern town. The later Norman castle occupies the bottom
right-hand corner.

While it is important to realize that Alfred was not the inventor
of *burhs*, nor exclusively responsible for their construction, the
fact that these fortresses had diverse origins did not detract from
their effectiveness. What mattered is that they functioned as a
network, and here the king's reputation as an innovator seems
well deserved. The *burhs* listed in the Burghal Hidage seem to
have been chosen logically with regard to their location, so as
to control major roads and rivers, and spaced so that none of
the king's subjects was more than twenty miles from the safety
of their defences. But the crucial part of Alfred's plan was that
his defences were not simply intended to be refuges behind which
civilians could cower, but strongholds that would be permanently
garrisoned with soldiers. As the above survey shows, the Anglo-
Saxons were not without fortifications in the decades before
Alfred, but they were clearly not well defended: time and again
viking armies had descended rapidly on places like York,

Nottingham and Wareham, and seized existing fortifications to their own advantage.[45]

In Alfred's reign this problem was rectified. The most remarkable part of the Burghal Hidage is its second half, which reveals the king's scheme for keeping his fortresses fully manned. After the list of *burhs* comes the formula by which their allocations of hides were calculated, based on the number of men needed to man the walls. 'For the maintenance and defence of an acre's breadth of wall,' it states, 'sixteen hides are required. If every hide is represented by one man, then every pole [5½ yards] can be manned by four men.' Put more simply, one man was expected to defend just over four feet of wall. Because we have the output data of this equation – the number of hides allocated to each *burh* – we can work out the wall-lengths the author had used as the basis of his calculations. And, remarkably, there is a fairly close correspondence between the figures he used and the dimensions of surviving *burhs*. Wareham's allocation of 1,600 hides, for example, implies it had 2,200 yards of wall to defend, and the surviving circuit of defences extends for about 2,180 yards. There is a similar close correlation at Winchester. The city's assessment of 2,400 hides was based on a perimeter reckoned at 3,300 yards, and the length of Winchester's Roman walls as measured today is 3,318 yards.[46]

This inspires confidence that the Burghal Hidage was a genuine working document, not merely a theoretical exercise, which is important with regard to a final point. Adding up all the hides for all the *burhs* in the list produces a grand total of just over 27,000. So, in the words of the document itself, 'If every hide is represented by one man', Alfred was expecting his kingdom to supply him with 27,000 men to defend his network of fortresses.[47]

That is a truly remarkable figure. Alfred is often credited with the additional achievement of creating a standing army, though in truth the evidence he did so is exceedingly thin, amounting to little more than a single line in the *Anglo-Saxon Chronicle*.[48] But even if the king had affected such an overhaul, the size of his host is unlikely to have been much larger than the early medieval norm, which was at best a few thousand men. The Burghal Hidage, on the other hand, points to something altogether more impressive. Alfred had succeeded in widening the participation in warfare beyond the military elite who traditionally rode into battle with the king. In order to man the walls of his *burhs* he needed to find thousands upon thousands of lesser men, and convince them (or their lords) that it was their duty to contribute to the kingdom's defence. Precisely how he achieved this mobilization of a much greater proportion of the population than any of his predecessors is a mystery. Asser says that Alfred bent people to his will 'by gently instructing, cajoling, urging, commanding, and (in the end, when his patience was exhausted), by sharply chastising those who were disobedient'. Coercion, then, was one way in which the king persuaded people to do their civic duty, and he did not hesitate to deprive individuals, or even churches, of their lands and goods if he felt they were not contributing enough. It was for this reason that the monks of Abingdon remembered him as a 'Judas'.[49]

But the benefits of Alfred's forcible persuasion were soon demonstrated. In 885, the viking army that had left Fulham for Francia six years earlier split in two. One part went further east, but the others decided to try their luck for a second time in Britain. As Asser explains, these vikings sailed to Kent and laid siege to the old Roman city of Rochester, establishing a fortified camp of their own outside the walls. But, says Asser, they were unable on this occasion to capture the city 'because the citizens defended themselves courageously until King Alfred arrived, bringing them relief with a large army'. Rochester is not listed in the Burghal Hidage – Kent, as a separate subkingdom, is not covered in the document – but this was exactly the way the new network of *burhs* was supposed to work. Rochester was clearly garrisoned with sufficient strength to hold off a substantial force of raiders until the cavalry arrived. When Alfred and his army suddenly descended, the invaders fled to their ships, abandoning their camp, their horses, and most of the prisoners they had seized. In this way, says Asser, they were forced to depart that same summer and return to Francia.[50]

The fact that some *burhs*, like Rochester, were located in old Roman cities, should not mislead us into thinking that Alfred was consciously trying to sponsor an urban renaissance. His overriding concern was the defence of the kingdom that he had come within a whisker of losing, and the *burhs* he built or renovated were intended to serve as fortresses to keep his subjects safe. Although they are often described by historians as 'fortified towns', many of them never developed into commercial centres, and those that did so became urban only many decades after the king's death.[51] There were one or two exceptions. Winchester, as we've noted, may have become home to the merchants and manufacturers of Hamwic after the viking raids of 840: at some stage during the next four decades the city was laid out with a grid of cobbled streets, traditionally ascribed to Alfred, but more likely to have been commissioned by his father or brothers.[52]

The other main exception was London, and here Alfred's involvement is not open to doubt. In 886, the year after his successful routing of the vikings at Rochester, the king went to London and, in Asser's words, 'restored it splendidly'. Exactly what this entailed is unclear. Asser claims that this action made the city habitable again, but it is evident from the archaeological record that people had already been relocating within the old Roman walls of London for several decades, ever since the more accessible but undefended *wic* to the west of the city had come under viking attack. From the middle of the ninth century our sources stop referring to Lundenwic and start speaking of Lundenburh.[53]

It seems more likely that the king's 'restoration' of London in 886 involved fixing its defences, improving its appearance, and perhaps laying out a rough grid of streets, effecting the kind of transformation that his predecessors had carried out in Winchester. There was also a political purpose to the king's visit, for the *Anglo-Saxon Chronicle* reports that 'all the English people [*Angelcynn*] that were not under the subjection of the Danes submitted to him'. We might therefore picture a large gathering of the king's leading subjects from both Wessex and western Mercia, culminating in a ceremony in which all swore allegiance to him as their lord. At this point, we are told, the king entrusted London to Ealdorman Æthelred, an act of accommodation that acknowledged Mercia's long-standing claim to the city. Around the same time, Alfred bound Æthelred closer to him by making him his son-in-law: by 887 the ealdorman was married to the king's daughter, Æthelflæd.[54]

Alfred's restoration of London in 886, says Asser, came 'after so many towns had been burned, and so many people slaughtered'. It had been half a century since the vikings had begun invading Britain with large armies, and twenty years since the arrival of the great heathen army that had destroyed three of the four Anglo-Saxon kingdoms. Wessex alone had survived, and Alfred had done his best to repair the damage it had suffered. Asser speaks of the marvellous new halls of wood and stone commissioned by the king, and other royal residences that were moved at his command and reconstructed in new locations. But we may imagine, after decades of destructive warfare, that much of the kingdom remained wasted and in ruins.[55]

The devastation brought by the vikings had taken a particularly heavy toll on the Church. Monasteries had been targeted by raiders from the very first because they were easy prey, undefended and often extremely rich. Their ornaments of gold and silver had been seized, as had monks and nuns who could be sold as slaves or held for ransom. Occasionally, too, the vikings would see if they could extract ransoms for the safe return of valuable books. The *Codex Aureus*, an exceptionally rich gospel book, probably produced in eighth-century Canterbury, has a later inscription by an ealdorman named Alfred, explaining how he and his wife bought it back from a viking army with a payment of gold, 'because we did not want it to remain any longer in heathen hands' (colour picture 15). But for the most part, the libraries of minsters and cathedrals were worthless in the eyes of pagan raiders, and their contents were put to the torch.[56]

Alfred lamented this state of affairs in a remarkable letter that he sent to all his bishops at some point in the 890s. Once, he said, the English had enjoyed happy times. They were ruled by wise kings, who were successful in war and maintained peace at home, and the land had been full of holy men, so learned that their knowledge was sought by the people of other nations. But now, sighed Alfred, those days were gone. Learning had deteriorated to such an extent that there were few who could understand divine services, or translate a letter from Latin in English. The king's estimation is borne out by the dramatic drop in standards at Canterbury in the 850s and 860s, when a single scribe was producing charters in abysmal Latin, full of mistakes and corrections.

The likeliest cause of this deterioration was viking violence. It is probably no coincidence that Canterbury's decline followed the fall of the city to the Norsemen in 851. Alfred partially endorsed this explanation in his letter, referring in passing to the time when 'everything was sacked and burned'. But he was also convinced that the rot had set in well before the advent of torch-wielding pagans. Even when the libraries had been full of books, the king insisted, there was nobody able to read them, such had been the decline in literacy.

Although this has been seized upon by some modern historians as a way of downplaying the destructive impact of the Danes, we should be wary of accepting it at face value. Alfred was here simply doing what all Christian writers did in order to rationalize viking attacks. If God was in charge of human destiny, and events were unfolding accord to His preordained plan, it logically followed that He had sent the heathens, and they were merely His chosen instrument to chastise the English for their sins. 'Remember what punishments befell us in this world when we ourselves did not cherish learning', the king reminded his bishops. 'We were Christians in name alone, and very few of us possessed Christian virtues.'[57]

Christian writers had adopted this victim-blaming position ever since the vikings had made their first appearance. After the attack on Lindisfarne in 793 that had seen many of the island's monks slaughtered, the abbot received a letter from Alcuin of York, writing from Charlemagne's court, reminding him and the other survivors to correct any vanity in their dress and to avoid drunkenness. When the Danes had begun to invade Wessex in the 830s, people were reportedly terrified by the vision of the priest that emphasized it was all their own fault. Such fears had prompted King Egbert to prepare for a pilgrimage to Rome in 839, which was frustrated by his own death that same year, but eventually undertaken by his son Æthelwulf sixteen years later, with the young Alfred in tow.[58]

Raised in this self-lambasting, penitential tradition, Alfred as an adult did all he could to placate a wrathful God in the hope of recovering divine favour. The desperate struggle for survival during the first decade of his reign prevented him from contemplating a return visit to Rome, but he nevertheless endeavoured to maintain strong relations with the papacy. When his prayers for success against the viking army that camped near London in 879 were favourably answered, he signalled his thanks by sending alms to Rome on a regular basis. Surviving coins in the king's name with the inscription '*elimosina*' (alms) were probably struck especially for the purpose of making these payments, and in the 880s the *Chronicle* repeatedly notes the names of the ealdormen who carried them to the Holy City on Alfred's behalf. The king also founded two new religious houses for the good of his soul. One, at Shaftesbury, was a nunnery, and his daughter Æthelgifu became its first abbess. The other, for monks, was at Athelney, the island that had been his refuge during his darkest hour. But the monks, explains Asser, had to be imported from overseas, because there were not enough natives willing to commit to a genuine monastic life. Attempting to explain this shortfall, Asser hedged his bets: it was either because of the 'frequent and savage' attacks of foreign enemies, or else because Englishmen had lost the enthusiasm for properly regulated monasticism.[59]

It was this perceived decline in religion and learning that Alfred determined to correct. He wanted not merely to re-found the ruined monasteries and churches, but to restore their lost libraries, and to improve the literacy of all his subjects, laymen and clergymen alike. To this end, he began by recruiting learned men to his own court. According to the king himself, there was no one worthy of that description in Wessex at the start of his reign, so he sought them from elsewhere. In the first instance he turned to Mercia, presumably after his annexation of the western half of the kingdom around 880. Asser names four luminaries who hailed from this direction: Werferth, the bishop of Worcester; Plegmund, who later became archbishop of Canterbury; and two priests, Æthelstan and Wærwulf, who served as royal chaplains. Alfred, says his biographer, showered these men with honours, and they in return read to him whenever he wished, day or night. But this quartet of scholars, clever as they were, proved insufficient for the task the king had in mind, so he sought others from further afield. Around the time of his restoration of London in 886, he recruited two more experts from overseas: Grimbald, a priest from the monastery of St Bertin, 'extremely learned in every kind of ecclesiastical doctrine', and John the Old Saxon, 'immensely learned in all fields of literary endeavour'. It was also around this time that Asser himself joined Alfred's circle, agreeing to divide his time between the king's court and his monastery at St David's.[60]

As a boy, the king was evidently not very bookish. When he was no more than seven years old, his mother had given him a volume of English poetry as a reward for having memorized one of its passages before any of his older brothers. But although Alfred remembered this episode fondly, to judge from Asser's account, it was a tacit admission that at that time he was unable to read. In a preceding paragraph, Asser blamed the king's parents and tutors for the fact that Alfred remained illiterate until he was into his teens, and, on another occasion, we are told that as an adult the king would often complain to his closest advisers about his lack of formal education.

But despite his early disadvantages (or, more likely, disinclination), Alfred was determined to make good this intellectual deficit. The first task of the scholars he gathered at his court in the 880s was to improve the king's own comprehension of books written in Latin. Asser, who was one of these tutors, describes a breakthrough moment that occurred on 11 November 887, when Alfred asked him to copy out a particular passage, and then immediately began to translate it into English. After this, says the biographer, there was no stopping him. The king was constantly asking for copies of particular texts, which he put together to form a little book that he kept with him at all times.[61]

Alfred's additional reason for assembling his A-list of intellectuals was to assist him in producing books in English. This was a highly unusual initiative. English had been used since the start of the seventh century to draft administrative documents, such as charters and law codes, but never employed for great works of literature, theology or philosophy, which were composed exclusively in Latin or Greek. As the king explained in his later letter to the bishops, the revival of Latin literacy was his ultimate goal, but it had occurred to him that in the first place it would be beneficial to have great works ('books which are most necessary for all men to know') translated into English – 'the language we can all understand', as Alfred described it.[62]

At least seven books have been identified as products of this translation programme. Two were works of Gregory the Great, revered by the English for having dispatched the mission that led to their conversion. Two more were historical – Bede's *Ecclesiastical History* was an obvious choice, and Orosius' *Histories against the Pagans* was a popular text that covered the period from Creation to the early fifth century. Only one book – an English rendering of the first fifty psalms – was biblical. The remaining two were philosophical works: the *Soliloquies* of St Augustine, composed in the fourth century, and the *Consolation of Philosophy* by the sixth-century Roman nobleman, Boethius.[63]

Traditionally, all but one of these translations were believed to be the work of Alfred himself. Asser informs us that Gregory the Great's *Dialogues* had been translated by Bishop Werferth, but the remaining six books were credited to the king, albeit with the aid of his team of experts. Then, during the twentieth century, this Alfredian canon was reduced to four, when scholars concluded that the English versions of Bede and Orosius were too dissimilar to the other works to have been carried out by the same person. Latterly, however, it has been suggested that Alfred probably had no direct involvement in the translations of any of these books. The idea that he did so, it is argued, was merely a literary convention, and the reality was that the king would have lacked both the time and the depth of understanding to have done any of the intellectual heavy lifting that such complex texts required.[64]

On the strength of Asser's testimony, however, there seems to be no good reason to doubt that Alfred could have done at least *some* translating, backed up by his team of internationally renowned experts. In particular, it is hard to discredit the idea that he worked on Gregory the Great's *Pastoral Care*, because he proudly boasts of having done so in the celebrated letter he sent to all his bishops. (The letter survives because it forms the book's preface.) 'I began to translate the book which in Latin is called *Pastoralis*, in English "Shepherd Book", sometimes word for word, sometimes sense for sense,' says the king, 'as I learned it from Plegmund, my archbishop, and from Asser, my bishop, and from Grimbald, my Mass-priest, and from John, my Mass-priest.' Alfred was, indeed, so pleased with his achievement that he decided to have a copy of the book made for every bishopric in his kingdom. 'And in each copy', he enthused, 'there will be an *æstel* worth fifty mancuses.' An *æstel* was apparently a pointer, intended as a reading aid, and a mancus was gold coin worth thirty silver pennies. These particular pointers must therefore have been highly ornate, and it has been plausibly suggested that the famous 'Alfred Jewel', discovered in 1693, was the decorative handle that once belonged to one of them (colour picture 16). Wrought from fine gold, it bears the legend 'AELFRED MEC HEHT GEWYRCAN' (Alfred ordered me to be made), and has a socket that could have held a small rod, perhaps made of ivory.[65]

19. A page from Alfred's translation of Gregory the Great's *Pastoral Care*.

Whether or not Alfred had a hand in the translation of any of the other books attributed to him by later chroniclers and copyists is impossible to say for certain. The arguments for and against his involvement, which turn on forensic analysis of the language of individual texts, are ultimately incapable of conclusive proof either way.[66] But unless we are attempting to divine the king's inner thoughts from these translations, this hardly matters. The important and incontrovertible point remains that the scheme to turn Latin works into English was Alfred's own initiative. He selected the texts he thought were 'most necessary for all men to know', and discussed their contents with the scholars he had recruited to assist in this endeavour. Without Alfred directing their labours, none of this would have happened. The king's determination to spread literacy was very much a personal mission. At his court he established a school which, according to Asser, was attended by both noble and non-noble boys. He also, says Asser, compelled his ealdormen and thegns to learn to read, on pain of being deprived of their positions. The aim, as Alfred explained in his letter, was to ensure that all freeborn young men among the English should be literate in their own language. In pursuing it, he promoted that language, previously used only for administrative purposes, to a language of literature. And, at the same time, he promoted the idea that the English themselves were one people. In the translation of Bede's *Ecclesiastical History*, '*gens Anglorum*' is rendered as '*Angelcynn*' – the same word that Alfred used in his administrative documents to describe his subjects in both Wessex and Mercia. Despite their past differences, the king was determined to show that the inhabitants of the two kingdoms shared a common identity. It was perhaps for this reason that he commissioned his own work of history, the *Anglo-Saxon Chronicle*. In its original form, the *Chronicle* appears to have concluded in 890, with Alfred ruling his people in peace.[67]

Unfortunately, the *Chronicle* was soon in need of a continuation, because in the years that followed Alfred's kingdom once again came under sustained viking attack. In 892 a crop failure in northern Francia led to widespread famine, and the large Danish army that had been raiding and pillaging there for the previous decade decided it would be better off in Britain. Towards the end of the year, two separate fleets sailed from Boulogne. The first, consisting of 250 ships, headed for the south coast of Kent and made its way up the estuary of the River Rother, establishing a fortified camp at Appledore. The second, numbering eighty ships, landed a short time later on the northern Kentish coast and made their camp at Milton, near Sittingbourne. The larger southern army had announced its arrival at Appledore by storming a nearby *burh* which was only half built and garrisoned by only a handful of peasants. This appears to have provoked a furious rant from Asser, writing his biography of Alfred the following year, about those who had scorned the king's commands and neglected their duty to construct such fortresses. These same people, he said, were now left bewailing the loss of their possessions and their loved ones, who had either been slaughtered or led off into Danish captivity.[68]

Alfred responded to the invasion by summoning an army and taking up a position in the middle of Kent between the two forces – 'so he could reach either host', explains the *Anglo-Saxon Chronicle*, 'if they chose to come out into the open country'. In this way, the king set the tone for his conduct during these years, which was extremely cautious. No doubt he recalled the days, more than two decades earlier, when the men of Wessex had hurled themselves heroically into battle against the invaders, only to be worn down by repeated losses and eventually defeated. Now in his mid-forties, Alfred had learned to be more prudent, and placed his trust in the defensive system he had patiently constructed. Whenever the vikings from either camp rode out in small bands to go raiding, says the *Chronicle*, they were kept at bay by mounted companies from the king's army or from the surrounding *burhs*.[69]

By the spring of 893, the larger viking force in southern Kent had grown impatient at their confinement and lack of progress. At Easter they abandoned their camp at Appledore and moved west through the forest of the Weald, harrying their way through Hampshire and Berkshire and seizing lots of plunder. Before leaving Kent they had sent their ships eastwards around the coast to Essex, intending to rejoin them there once their raid was over. But as they were retiring from Wessex, laden with booty, they were confronted by an army led by Alfred's eldest son, Edward. The young prince, who was then around twenty years old, acquitted himself well, beating the invaders in battle at Farnham, pursuing them across the Thames, and besieging them when, in desperation and exhaustion, they took refuge on an island in the River Colne. Total victory was denied him, however, when his own men declared that the term of their military service had expired, and departed before their replacements had arrived. Edward was therefore forced to negotiate a truce, and allow his enemies to depart.[70]

Alfred, meanwhile, had tried to neutralize the vikings in north Kent by negotiation, bestowing money on their leader, Hastein, in the hope of ending hostilities. This was obviously an attempt to replicate his successful dealings with his previous Danish opponent, Guthrum, who had been baptized in 878 and apparently maintained peaceful relations down to his death in 890. In return for the king's generosity, Hastein swore oaths and surrendered hostages, and his two sons accepted baptism. He presumably also promised to withdraw from Alfred's kingdom, for once the negotiations were over he and his followers sailed across the Thames Estuary and established a new camp on the coast of Essex at Benfleet.

Any hopes that this was the end of the matter, however, were quickly dispelled. No sooner had Hastein and his army departed than new attacks were reported on the south coast of Wessex, led by those Danes who had already settled in East Anglia and Northumbria. The previous year, as soon as the vikings from Francia had landed in Kent, Alfred had sought assurances of neutrality from the new Scandinavian rulers of these former English kingdoms, but in the event the temptation to join in the attack on Wessex had proved impossible to resist. A fleet of a hundred ships, apparently led by a Northumbrian king named Sigeferth, sailed down the east coast, along the Channel, and began attacking the coast of Devon. Meanwhile, the two viking forces that had withdrawn from Kent, having both retired to Essex, now united under Hastein's leadership and began launching raids into Mercia.[71]

Alfred decided to deal with the vikings in Devon himself, but on arrival he discovered that the enemy fleet had split in two. Forty of their hundred ships had sailed around the tip of Cornwall, and were attacking a fortress on the north Devonshire coast. The remaining sixty ships had stopped in Exeter, and their crews were laying siege to the city. News of the king's coming caused them to break off the siege and return to their boats, but once again Alfred found himself caught between two camps, engaged in a containment exercise.

With Alfred pinned down in the south-west, the defence of Mercia fell to others – his thegns and ealdormen, and the thousands of ordinary soldiers manning the *burhs*. They began strongly, assembling an army in London and advancing into Essex to attack Hastein's camp at Benfleet. At the time of their arrival the viking leader was out raiding with some of his forces, and so the English were able to storm the fortress, seizing all the goods within it, as well as the women and children – Hastein's wife and sons were among those taken captive. The attackers rounded off their successful mission by destroying the viking fleet, smashing up or burning some of the ships, sailing others across the estuary to Rochester, and taking the rest with them back to London, along with their plunder and prisoners.[72]

Hastein, however, was not deterred by this defeat. He was soon joined by lots of warriors from East Anglia and Northumbria, and, in the months that followed, these combined forces launched two major raids right across Mercia. On the first occasion, they rode all the way to the Welsh border and made a camp on an island in the River Severn at Buttington. In response, the ruler of Mercia, Ealdorman Æthelred, assembled a great army, drawn from all the surrounding *burhs*, and laid siege to the temporary fortress for several weeks, until its starving defenders broke out and engaged them in battle. Many Danes were killed, says the *Chronicle*, but also many king's thegns, meaning that most of the surviving vikings managed to escape back to Essex. Later in the year, having recruited more East Anglian and Northumbrian allies, they launched a second raid, this time riding rapidly across the country to seize the deserted Roman ruins of Chester. Once again the English besieged them and forced them to flee, and after a brief foray into Wales they again made their way back to Essex, taking a circuitous route through Northumbria and East Anglia to avoid having to pass through Mercia itself.

A year had now passed since the arrival of the vikings from Francia, and it must have been becoming frustratingly clear to them that, in spite of their best efforts, and apparently limitless supply of new recruits, the tried-and-tested tactics that had served them so well in the past were no longer working. Of old they had been able to burst unopposed into a kingdom and ensconce themselves in one of its existing centres of power, such as

Canterbury, York or Repton. But on this occasion they found they could not break into Wessex because of its well-defended *burhs*, and their attempts to create new bases on the western periphery of Mercia had come to nothing. In Devon, the *Chronicle* found nothing exciting to report about Alfred's activities, but that merely proved that his overall strategy had been successful. The *burh*-men of Exeter had successfully prevented the Danes from seizing control of the city, and the presence of the king and his army had deterred them from plundering the countryside. By the autumn of 893 the attackers had concluded that there was no point in staying put and headed home towards Northumbria. As they sailed along the south coast, they decided to try to compensate for their disappointing result in Devon by raiding into Sussex, only to be attacked by the garrison of the *burh* at Chichester. Many hundreds of vikings were killed, says the *Chronicle*, and some of their ships were captured, while the rest were put to flight. It was a striking vindication of Alfred's onerous but effective defensive measures.[73]

After almost a whole year without recorded incident, the viking army in Essex tried a new tactic. Towards the end of 894, explains the *Chronicle*, they left their base on Mersea Island and sailed up the Thames Estuary, then up the River Lea, establishing a new camp 'twenty miles above London' – perhaps somewhere in the vicinity of Hertford. Since the Lea had been the boundary agreed between Alfred and Guthrum, this did not constitute an invasion, assuming the vikings were camped on the river's northern bank. It did, however, constitute a serious threat, as the people of London and its rural hinterland keenly appreciated. Having spent the winter waiting and watching this dragon on their doorstep, the Londoners set out to vanquish it themselves in the summer of 895. But the battle did not go as they hoped, and after four of the king's thegns in their company were killed they were forced to flee.

The failure of this assault and the death of his own men caused Alfred himself to arrive with an army. As on previous occasions, his actions were more pragmatic than conventionally heroic.

Rather than risk another direct assault on the Danish fortress, he ordered his troops to protect the peasants while they gathered in the harvest, thus denying the enemy the opportunity of stealing it for themselves. The king then devised a cunning strategy for dislodging his unwanted neighbours altogether, riding along the Lea until he identified a suitable place to plant two new *burhs*, one on either bank. As soon as the construction of these fortifications commenced, the vikings perceived his plan was to prevent them from sailing their ships back along the river. Alfred may have drawn inspiration from Charles the Bald, who had done something similar on the Seine more than thirty years earlier, but this was apparently the first time such a tactic has been tried in Britain. The Danes, realizing they were trapped, abandoned their boats and took to their horses. Reverting to their earlier ambition of establishing themselves in western Mercia, they rode all the way back to the River Severn and created a new camp at Bridgnorth, where they remained throughout the following winter.[74]

Not all of Alfred's schemes were quite so successful. When the vikings of Northumbria and East Anglia resumed their assault on Wessex in 896, the *Chronicle* noted that their ability to maraud at will along the south coast was due to their naval superiority – 'the warships which they had built many years before'. Alfred responded by ordering the construction of a fleet of his own to counter this threat – vessels built to his personal design, 'as it seemed to him that they would be most useful'. It is, of course, from this initiative that the king's later reputation as the father of the Royal Navy derives. But Alfred's ships were vaingloriously large affairs, some with more than sixty oars apiece, and hence less effective than they might otherwise have been. When they were sent out to confront a small Danish fleet that same summer, all the king's new vessels ran aground. Their crews still managed to engage the enemy by disembarking and fighting on the beaches, but when the tide came back the surviving Danes were able to get away first. Some of the escapees were subsequently forced to land in Sussex, and brought to Winchester, where Alfred ordered them to be hanged.

Nevertheless, it was in the summer of 896 that the renewed viking attack on Wessex that had begun four years earlier finally subsided. The loss of at least twenty ships along the south coast seems to have persuaded the seaborne raiders to depart, and around the same time the Danes who were camped on the Severn at Bridgnorth also decided to leave. They must presumably have experienced some military pressure from Ealdorman Æthelred and the English forces in Mercia, but the *Chronicle* has nothing to say on the matter, noting merely that during the summer the army at Bridgnorth divided, with some going to East Anglia, others to Northumbria, and those who were moneyless taking ship back to Francia.[75]

The *Chronicle* is similarly silent about the last three years of Alfred's life, down to his death in 899, and accords him only the briefest of obituary notices. Asser, who would undoubtedly have penned something far more fulsome, finished his biography in 893, while the king was still alive. All that the *Chronicle* tells us is that Alfred died on 26 October, after a reign of twenty-eight years, and that he was king over the whole English people, 'except the part that was under Danish rule'. That last clause is a quite considerable caveat, and needs to be set against the misleading claims of later medieval chroniclers, who wrongly asserted that Alfred was the first king to rule over all of England. The reality was that he had defended Wessex and annexed about half of Mercia. Everything to the north and east of Watling Street lay beyond his power, and there were probably more English people living under Danish rule than his own.[76]

But to have saved his own kingdom from destruction, and wrested part of a neighbouring one from Danish conquest – these were still very considerable achievements. Every other Anglo-Saxon ruler had been toppled by the viking storm that had struck Britain in 865: Alfred alone had withstood it. His survival, and his eventual triumph, were not merely a result of his skills as a warrior. They owed as much to his strategic vision, and his more subtle political talents. The king had understood the necessity of reorganizing the manpower of Wessex, and bolstering its defences, in order to save it from the fate of the other English kingdoms, and successfully persuaded people to implement his schemes. Nor is his achievement to be measured solely in territorial terms. Alfred, in his determined efforts to undo the cultural destruction that decades of viking attacks had caused, was also responsible for a remarkable renaissance in learning, and the elevation of English to a language of literature. He was clearly not the superhero of Georgian and Victorian myth, the founder of the Royal Navy, let alone 'the most perfect character in history', as one nineteenth-century scholar hyperbolically insisted.[77] But he was courageous, clever, innovative, pious, resolute, and far-sighted: qualities which, taken together, more than justify the later decision to honour him with the word 'great'.

After his death the king's body was taken for burial in the royal *burh* at Winchester. Apparently in the last months of his life Alfred had formed the idea of founding a new monastery there, and had purchased a suitable plot of land, but died before construction could begin. It was therefore in the small seventh-century church that still served as the city's cathedral that the king was laid to rest. The task of building something bigger and more impressive would fall to his heirs.[78]

KINGDOM
OF THE
SCOTS

STRATHCLYDE

Tweed

Norham •

Lindisfarne

Bamburgh •

North Sea

Chester-le-Street •
Durham •

Wear

Eamont •

Ouse

KINGDOM

OF YORK

• York

Humber

LAND OF

THELWALL • Manchester

THE

Mersey

Bakewell •

• Lincoln

Brunanburh

• Chester

FIVE BOROUGHS

Farndon •

Nottingham •

Derby • *Trent*

Stafford •

Welland

EAST

ANGLIA

Wednesfield •

Tamworth •

Leicester • Stamford

Severn

KINGDOM

Great Ouse

Worcester •

• Cambridge

Hereford •

Towcester •

Tempsford

OF

Buckingham •

Hertford • Witham

Gloucester •

• Oxford

Cirencester •

London

Lea

Malmesbury •

• Cricklade

Thames

• Kingston

THE ANGLO-SAXONS

• Winchester

Wimborne •

Tamar

Exeter •

English Channel

0   25   50   75   100 miles
0   50   100   150 kilometres

— · — · — Line of the Alfred-Guthrum treaty

7

IMPERIAL OVERSTRETCH?
King Æthelstan and the Conquest of the North

The terrible attack on their community by 'heathen men' in 793 must have long haunted the monks of Lindisfarne, and left them feeling vulnerable and unsettled. At some point in the first half of the ninth century, with viking activity increasing everywhere, they abandoned the island that St Aidan had selected for them two centuries earlier and moved to the mainland, bringing with them the bones of their most celebrated and powerful predecessor, St Cuthbert. For a time they resided on the banks of the Tweed at Norham, but in the mid-870s, as Northumbria was being carved up by Scandinavian warlords, they set off again, apparently wandering from place to place for seven years. Eventually, around 883, they settled at Chester-le-Street, an old Roman fort about sixty miles to the south, situated on the River Wear. They were still there half a century later, when they were visited by King Æthelstan.[1]

The year was 934, and Æthelstan was leading an army from Wessex through Northumbria in order to fight the Scots. He decided to pause at Chester-le-Street to venerate the remains of St Cuthbert, and to shower the monks with gifts. These were described in a charter issued by the king at the time of his visit and copied into a history of the community composed a century or so later. They included many items of richly embroidered fabric: ecclesiastical vestments, altar coverings, curtains, tapestries, and 'a royal headdress woven with gold'. There were also numerous other treasures worked from or decorated with both gold and silver: cups, candlesticks, armlets, bells, drinking horns, and a cross 'finished with gold and ivory'. Æthelstan in addition gave the monks an extensive royal estate on the south bank of the Wear, and also several books: three ornate sets of gospels, a missal, and 'a life of St Cuthbert written in verse and prose'.[2]

Remarkably, some parts of this generous donation have survived. Six decades after the king's visit, and more than a century after their arrival at Chester-le-Street, the monks decided to move again, and relocated seven miles further south, establishing a new church in a loop of the Wear which became Durham Cathedral. The shrine that was constructed in the cathedral for Cuthbert's body after the Norman Conquest was destroyed during the Reformation, but his coffin was secreted in a wall space and survived. When it was rediscovered and opened in 1827, it was found to contain not only the saint's complete skeleton, but fragments of the elaborately carved wooden casket in which he had originally been buried, his gold pectoral cross (colour picture 7), and a gospel book written not long after his death. It also contained some scraps of the embroidered items donated by Æthelstan in 934 – probably the stole and the maniple mentioned in the king's charter (colour picture 19). All these items are now on display in the cathedral's treasury.[3]

No less miraculously, one of the books donated by Æthelstan is still with us. Many items from the cathedral's library were dispersed during the sixteenth century, including the Lindisfarne Gospels, which ultimately ended up in the British Library. In the case of Æthelstan's books, we do not know what happened to the missal, and two of the three gospel books are also unaccounted for. The third survived until the eighteenth century, but perished in the fire of 1731 that also consumed Asser's *Life of Alfred* and singed the pages of *Beowulf*. But the volume donated by the king that contained a life of St Cuthbert is still in existence, having found its way to Corpus Christi College in Cambridge. It is a copy of the two lives of Cuthbert written by Bede, and has at the beginning a full-page picture of the saint being presented with the book by Æthelstan himself (colour picture 18). It is the earliest manuscript image of an English king.[4]

This image, and the royal visit that inspired it, tell us several important things about Æthelstan. In the first place, he was notably pious. 'The most pious King Æthelstan' is how he was described on the first page of the gospel book that was destroyed by fire in 1731. The scale of his donation indicates that he was also abundantly rich: a ruler who could afford to reward his favourite subjects with almost embarrassing quantities of precious artefacts, as well as land and money. And, as his pronounced wealth implies, he was extremely powerful – arguably the most powerful of all the English kings before the Norman Conquest. Æthelstan was in Northumbria in 934 not as a foreign visitor but as its self-appointed ruler, having forcibly annexed the formerly independent kingdom seven years earlier. The army he was leading against the Scots was composed of men drawn from every region in southern Britain – not only English warriors from Wessex and Mercia, but also Danes who had settled in the eastern parts of the island, and Britons from the west. As the ruler of all these regions, Æthelstan has good claim to be considered the first king of England (although the word 'England' had yet to be invented) and even grander titles were touted at his court, where he was sometimes styled 'king of all Britain'.[5]

According to the same chronicle that preserved his charter, before Æthelstan continued on his expedition against the Scots, he gave instructions that 'if anything sinister should befall him', his body was to be returned to Chester-le-Street for burial near St Cuthbert, who would be able to present him before God on the Day of Judgement. As it turned out, this precaution proved unnecessary: the king's campaign was a success, and he returned south to reign for a further five years. When he eventually died in 939, he was buried in Malmesbury, an ancient monastery in Wessex, founded in the late seventh century. The abbey church, now the parish church, still contains a tomb chest built for his remains in the late Middle Ages, topped with a life-sized effigy of its sometime royal occupant. But Æthelstan was less fortunate in death than Cuthbert, and during the Reformation his remains were destroyed. All we have now is a description of his body, written in the early twelfth century by William of Malmesbury, one of the greatest English historians. William was a monk at Malmesbury and had evidently seen inside the king's tomb. He describes Æthelstan as being slim, 'not beyond what is becoming in stature', and having blond hair, 'beautifully mingled with gold threads'.[6]

It is thanks to William that we know more about Æthelstan than most other tenth-century English kings, whose lives are on the whole very poorly chronicled. Writing his *Deeds of the Kings of the English*, William interrupts his section on Æthelstan to explain how he had recently discovered 'a certain obviously ancient volume' that contained an earlier account of the king's career, and goes on to incorporate some of this new material into his own narrative. Doubts have been raised in recent years about the authenticity of this information, chiefly because the sections that William appears to present as verbatim quotes can be shown on stylistic grounds to have been composed in his own day, rather than at some point in the more distant past. But this apparent obstacle is not insuperable, since William himself tells us that the original text in his 'ancient volume' was written in such a florid, bombastic style that he felt compelled to rewrite it using simpler and more comprehensible language. In addition, some of the information William reproduces from his lost source is so mundane in its detail that it seems unlikely to have been whimsically invented. Most modern historians are therefore prepared to admit this material as evidence, though perhaps with the caveat that it might not be wholly reliable.[7]

The most famous anecdote that William of Malmesbury relates from his ancient book sits on the cusp of plausible history and convenient legend. As a child, we are told, Æthelstan was good-looking and graceful, and these qualities endeared him to his grandfather, King Alfred, who publicly acknowledged the boy's suitability as a future ruler by investing him at a young age.

Æthelstan, who could have been no more than six, was given a scarlet cloak, a jewelled belt, and a Saxon sword with a golden scabbard. Since his accession, which eventually happened twenty-five years after Alfred's death, proved to be a very contentious affair, stories of him having been pre-approved by his illustrious grandfather might rightly be viewed with suspicion. But the tale draws some support from a poem dedicated to Æthelstan as a child that expresses similar sentiments, and from the fact that Alfred himself, at a comparable age, had been blessed and invested by the pope in a similar ceremony. Perhaps, then, the old king had indeed publicly bestowed honours on his grandson as his own reign drew to a close. The pity was he had not done more to quell the family feud among the generation immediately below him, which erupted in the days after his death.[8]

Alfred was succeeded in October 899 by his son, Edward – Æthelstan's father. An author writing about a century later dubbed him 'Edward the Elder' (*Edwardus senior*) to distinguish him from his short-lived descendant, Edward the Martyr, and the name stuck. It has the unfortunate effect of making him sound senior in years, when he was actually in his mid-twenties at the time of his accession. Although Edward reigned for a quarter of a century, very little is known about him as a person. Asser implied the new king was less bookish than his younger brother, Æthelweard, and William of Malmesbury concurred, asserting that Edward was 'much inferior to his father in the cultivation of letters – but incomparably more glorious in the power of his rule'.[9]

Edward's right to rule, however, was initially contested by his cousin, Æthelwold. The son of Alfred's older brother Æthelred, Æthelwold had been a young child at the time of his father's death in 871, and so the throne that might in different circumstances have passed to him had been given instead to the adult Alfred. A decade or so later Æthelwold and his older brother, Æthelhelm, had begun agitating for redress, complaining that their rights had been overlooked, and that their uncle had cheated them of their inheritance. Alfred had attempted to settle the matter, as can be seen from a will the king had drawn up in the 880s, but the measly compensation it granted to his nephews evidently left them feeling short-changed and embittered. Nothing more is heard of Æthelhelm, and the reasonable assumption is that he died before his uncle's reign had ended. But Æthelwold was still alive in 899, and bent on having his revenge.[10]

As soon as the news of Alfred's death broke, Æthelwold went into rebellion. His first act was apparently to break into a nunnery, seize one of its residents, and make her his wife. The *Anglo-Saxon Chronicle* refers to this event allusively, commenting that Æthelwold had acted 'without the king's permission, and contrary to the orders of the bishops'. The conclusion must be that he had wished to marry this unnamed woman at an earlier date, but had been denied by Alfred and his counsellors. She may have been too closely related to him or, perhaps more likely, a member of a powerful family whose lands and support would prove useful in pressing his claim. Whatever the case, the prohibition of this match and the cloistering of his prospective bride provided Æthelwold with an additional grievance. Having liberated her, he and his supporters rode to Wimborne in Dorset, seized the royal residence there and barricaded themselves inside. This location was deliberately chosen to emphasize his claim to the throne, for his father was buried in Wimborne Abbey. Holed up inside the royal lodgings, says the *Chronicle*, Æthelwold declared 'he would either live there or die there'.

In the event he did neither. The new king, Edward, responded quickly to his cousin's defiance, and rode with an army to Badbury Rings, an Iron Age hill fort four miles north-west of Wimborne. Faced with the prospect of a siege he was unlikely to survive, Æthelwold decided that desertion was the better part of valour, and rode off under cover of darkness, abandoning the woman he had abducted. Edward, when he heard the news, ordered a pursuit, but the king's men were unable to overtake the fugitive pretender before he reached the border of the kingdom, and crossed over into the territory of the Danes.

★

The territorial status quo between the English and the Danes at the end of Alfred's reign was much the same as it had been twenty years earlier. For all the later praise he attracted as the 'founder of England', the extent to which Alfred had expanded his kingdom had been relatively modest. He had maintained his rule in Wessex, and annexed the part of Mercia that lay to the west of Watling Street – the boundary agreed between the king and his erstwhile enemy, Guthrum, after the viking leader's submission in 878. Everything to the north and east of that line was ruled by men of Scandinavian descent.

The question of how many Scandinavians had settled in these areas cannot be answered decisively, but all the reliable evidence indicates that the number was substantial. As with the debate on Anglo-Saxon immigration to Britain in the fifth and sixth centuries, attempts to come up with an answer using DNA science produces inadequate data and highly debatable results. The linguistic and archaeological evidence, however, is both clear and compelling. Across large areas of northern and eastern England, we find many place names that end with either -by or -thorpe, both of which are elements imported from Old Norse. It was at this point, for example, that the monastery founded by St Hild at Streaneshalch became known as Whitby, and the settlement that had been Northworthig was renamed Derby. Almost half the place names in Yorkshire recorded in the Domesday Survey of 1086 had such Scandinavian origins. In addition, thousands of Norse loan-words appear in English sources written after the late ninth century. One notable grammatically borrowing was the words *they, their,* and *them.*[11]

The linguistic argument, which has stood for some time, has lately been boosted by the discovery of archaeological finds from the late ninth and early tenth centuries that are unmistakably Scandinavian: coins, clothes fittings, and amulets with pagan symbols. In recent decades metal-detectorists have uncovered around 500 such items in northern and eastern England, often in isolated rural areas. Most are non-elite objects and, in the case of the clothes fittings, made for both male and female owners, suggesting that Scandinavians of all ranks had settled in these areas, just as the testimony of the *Anglo-Saxon Chronicle* would lead us to suppose. Historians who have analysed all this evidence have cautiously suggested that the total number of newcomers might have been somewhere between 20,000 and 35,000.[12]

Modern historians often refer to the area of Scandinavian settlement as 'the Danelaw', although that term does not occur in our sources until the early eleventh century, and can give the misleading impression that these lands somehow constituted a single entity. The reality was that the area of Danish settlement was split into several distinct political zones, and governed by a galaxy of competing rulers – kings whose names are mostly unrecorded, and also jarls and holds, who were equivalent in status to ealdormen and king's thegns. The ancient English kingdom of East Anglia, governed by Guthrum down to his death in 890, was thereafter ruled by kings whose names are known only through their coins. The East Midlands, meanwhile, up as far as the River Humber, appear to have been ruled by a loose coalition of Danish warlords with bases at Leicester, Nottingham, Stamford, Lincoln and Derby, collectively referred to in later sources as the Five Boroughs. Lastly, Northumbria, carved up by Halfdan and his followers in 875, had been split in two. Its northern half, beyond the River Tees, was still held by an English dynasty with a base at the ancient fortress of Bamburgh, but its southern half had become a new Scandinavian kingdom centred on the city of York.[13]

The Danelaw and its various rulers posed a standing existential threat to the kingdom of the Anglo-Saxons created by Alfred. As we have seen, when a large viking army from Francia invaded Kent in 892, and made repeated attacks on Wessex and Mercia in the four years that followed, the Danes who had already settled in Northumbria and East Anglia became their willing allies. *We* know that Alfred and his heirs survived and ultimately triumphed, and so can easily fall into the trap of assuming this triumph was inevitable, especially given the praise that is lavished on Alfred for having turned the viking tide. The English at the time, however, enjoyed no such certainty, and knew that their neighbours to the north and east needed only the slightest encouragement to resume hostilities in the hope of bringing about the kingdom's destruction.[14]

That encouragement was provided at the start of Edward the Elder's reign by his fugitive cousin. Having arrived in Northumbria in 899, Æthelwold managed, by some unknown wizardry, to persuade the Scandinavian settlers there to accept him as their king. The news that a succession dispute had divided the royal house of Wessex must have been sweet music to those vikings who had settled in the north, and Æthelwold wasted little time in rekindling their hopes of conquest and fanning them to his own advantage. In the autumn of 901, barely two years after Alfred's death, he sailed down the east coast 'with all the fleet he could procure' and made his camp in Essex. Within a short time they had persuaded the Danes in East Anglia to join their enterprise, and in 902 their combined forces invaded Mercia, harrying right up to the Thames, and then crossing the river at Cricklade to plunder within Wessex itself.

By the time Edward had raised an army with which to repel this attack, the invaders had withdrawn with their loot and were already back in East Anglia. The king therefore took his retaliation in kind, leading his troops into the enemy's territory and letting them pillage the region around Cambridge and Ely. But the men of Kent, explains the *Anglo-Saxon Chronicle*, lingered too long, ignoring repeated orders from Edward to break off their ravaging and return home. As a result, they were attacked by the Danish army at a place called Holme, and a bloody battle took place. The *Chronicle* lists the high-status casualties on both sides, giving the names of the ealdormen, thegns and holds who perished in the fighting. It was technically a Danish victory, since they remained in possession of the field, but among the fallen were their two leaders: Eohric, the king of East Anglia, and Æthelwold, king of Northumbria, and would-be king of Wessex.

★

The death of his cousin was an extremely fortunate outcome for Edward, ending at a stroke the challenge to the legitimacy of his rule. In terms of protecting his kingdom from invasion, however, it may have made little difference. The *Chronicle* is silent for the next three years, during which time attacks from both East Anglia and Northumbria probably continued. Not until 906 does it state that Edward made peace with the new rulers of these regions, and even then one version of the text adds that he did so 'from necessity'. Those two words raise the possibility that the new English king, like his father, may have had to pay tribute to the Danes in return for a cease of hostilities.[15]

The first sign of Edward seizing the military initiative occurred in 909, when he dispatched a force of Mercian and West Saxon troops on a month-long raid into 'the territory of the northern army'. This was evidently the area around Lincoln, since besides slaves and cattle, they also brought back the bones of the Northumbrian king, St Oswald, from Bardney Abbey. The Danes sought retribution by invading Mercia the following year, confident in the knowledge that Edward was in Kent, supervising the assembly of a large fleet. But the king received news of his enemies' activities, and dispatched an army to intercept them as they were on their way home. On 5 August 910, at Wednesfield, just east of Wolverhampton, the invaders were ambushed as they were crossing a river. Thousands of them were killed, with heavy losses among their leaders: the *Chronicle* names five holds, two jarls and two kings in its list of the Danish dead.[16]

The *Chronicle* claims this as a victory for Edward but, as he was evidently not present, the laurels probably belonged to his sister, Æthelflæd. The eldest child of King Alfred, Æthelflæd had been married by her father to the de facto ruler of Mercia, Ealdorman Æthelred, at some point before 887, when she was still in her teens. By the time of the battle at Wednesfield she must have been about forty, and her husband was probably considerably older. According to Irish annals, by this point the ealdorman had already been ill for several years, and Mercia was being governed by his wife. The same annalist calls Æthelflæd 'queen of the Saxons', and describes how she had fought against the vikings who had settled near Chester after being driven out of Dublin. When the ailing Æthelred died the following year, therefore, very little changed. King Edward seized the chance to take direct control of London and Oxford, but beyond that he did not encroach on the authority of his older sister, who continued to rule in her own right as 'Lady of the Mercians'.[17]

Whoever truly deserves the credit for the victory at Wednesfield, the elimination of the northern viking elite afforded an opportunity to Alfred's children which they readily embraced. No longer would they confine themselves to sending armies across the frontier to seize cattle, slaves or relics – from now on they would take territory. Edward began by pressurizing the Danish kingdom of East Anglia, planting a new *burh* at Hertford in 911 and another at Witham in Essex the following year. Æthelflæd, having already secured north-western Mercia, began pushing against the frontier of Watling Street, building *burhs* at Stafford and Tamworth. The latter, which had been one of the most important royal residences in Mercia since at least the time of Offa, must have been seen as a particularly significant reconquest.[18]

If the inhabitants of these regions sometimes submitted willingly, their Danish rulers did not, and retaliated with raids into English territory. But they were not very successful, and local people responded by putting them to flight. The Scandinavians, having settled, lacked the cohesion they had possessed as a single great army. When the *Chronicle* describes their attacks, it speaks of forces from different Midlands towns – 'the army from Northampton and Leicester', for example. As Æthelflæd and Edward built more *burhs* along the frontier throughout 915 and 916, some Danish leaders appeared before the English king and accepted him as their lord.[19]

In 917, the dam burst. In the spring of that year Edward's forces advanced further into the Danelaw, building a *burh* at Towcester and storming the Danish camp at nearby Tempsford, slaughtering all those inside who refused to surrender, including two jarls and an unnamed king – most likely the king of East

Anglia. When Edward arrived on the frontier in person that autumn, he was met by a rush of Scandinavian lords from across the East Midlands, all anxious to submit, and when he moved into Essex, the story was the same, with Danes from all over East Anglia bowing before him in return for having his peace. His sister, meanwhile, had advanced into the territory of the Five Boroughs, and taken Derby after a bloody struggle.[20]

By this point the two English campaigns were close to converging. At the start of 918 Æthelflæd took Leicester without a fight, and in the spring Edward occupied Stamford. But on 12 June Æthelflæd died of unknown causes at Tamworth, causing her brother to break off his advance in order to take control of western Mercia. It seems quite likely he had attempted to do this at the time of Ealdorman Æthelred's death in 911, but had been thwarted by his strong-willed sister and a separatist tendency that remained resistant to direct rule from Wessex. If so, Edward was determined not to be denied a second time. Having occupied Tamworth, he received the submission of 'all the nation of the land of the Mercians'. Some no doubt submitted willingly, but others clearly hoped to preserve their independence by recognizing Æthelflæd's adult daughter, Ælfwynn, as their new ruler. Edward, when he later learned about this scheme, acted swiftly to scupper it. Ælfwynn, we are told, 'was deprived of all authority in Mercia and taken into Wessex'. There was to be no new Lady of the Mercians.

Having finally annexed English Mercia, Edward immediately resumed his advance into Danish-held territory and captured Nottingham, the fourth of the Five Boroughs to fall. By this stage, however, there are signs that his campaign was running out of momentum. The *Chronicle*, which strives to maximize the king's triumphs, claims that all the Danes in Mercia submitted to his will, but its failure to mention Lincoln strongly suggests that the last of the Five Boroughs remained defiant. Even Nottingham's submission to Edward appears to have been something of a compromise deal, for the *Chronicle* admits that it was subsequently garrisoned 'with both Englishmen and Danes'.

Nevertheless, the king's advances in 917 and 918 had been spectacular. At the start of that period, the area over which he exercised direct authority had been scarcely any greater than that ruled by his father. But by the end of 918 he was acknowledged, however grudgingly or tentatively, as master of all southern Britain beneath the Mersey and the Trent. The local leaders of Mercia, East Anglia, and all but one of the Five Boroughs had been compelled to recognize his superior lordship, as had the various rulers of Wales. In the two years that followed, Edward sought to shore up these conquests, constructing new *burhs* on the Mersey at Thelwall and Manchester, and reinforcing Nottingham with a fortified bridge across the Trent. In 920 he led his army up the Derwent, a tributary of the Trent, and planted a *burh* at Bakewell.[21]

This last flurry of fortifications marked the northernmost limit of the king's advance. Beyond them lay the territory of the vikings of York, who had withdrawn from the fray after their devastating defeat in battle a decade earlier. According to the *Chronicle*, it was also in 920 that these vikings acknowledged Edward as their 'father and lord', as did the more distant kings of the Scots and the Britons of Strathclyde. It seems highly unlikely that these rulers actually made any such admissions of subservience, though quite possible that Edward may have met them somewhere on the frontier to agree the terms of a peace.[22]

After that, the *Chronicle* has nothing more to tell us about Edward before his death, which occurred four years later, when he was in his early fifties. 'In this year,' says the annal for 924, 'King Edward died, and his son Æthelstan succeeded to the kingdom.' But it was in fact a good deal more complicated than that.[23]

The complications arose because of Edward's busy family life: he had been married three times, and had fathered at least thirteen children, five of whom were boys. Æthelstan was his eldest, and the only son the king had produced with his first wife, Ecgwynn. But by the time of Edward's succession in 899, Ecgwynn had either died or been discarded, leaving the king free to marry his second wife, Ælfflæd, who subsequently presented him with two new sons, as well as five daughters. Ælfflæd was understandably keen to promote the careers of her own offspring, and may have been responsible for disparaging the reputation of her predecessor, who is dismissed in some sources as a mere concubine. Certainly, around the time of her marriage to Edward, the king's firstborn son, Æthelstan, had been removed from his father's court and packed off to Mercia, to be raised in the household of his uncle and aunt, Æthelred and Æthelflæd.[24]

A quarter of a century later, this decision threatened to rip apart the kingdom of the Anglo-Saxons created by Alfred. As the failed attempt to promote the daughter of Lady Æthelflæd shows, there were still many people in Mercia in favour of regaining their former independence. According to William of Malmesbury, when Edward died in 924 he had been suppressing a Mercian revolt against his authority in Chester – a statement that draws support from contemporary sources that place the king at Farndon, ten miles south of Chester, at the time of his death. It was hardly surprising, therefore, that as soon as news of Edward's death broke, the Mercians agreed that Æthelstan, now aged thirty, and raised in Mercia since he was a small boy, should be his father's successor. It was also equally predictable that, among the powerful men of Wessex, the preference was for Ælfweard, the eldest son from the king's second marriage, who had been reared in their midst.

As it was, an immediate rift between Mercia and Wessex was averted when Ælfweard died barely a fortnight after his father. This was far from being the only time that Death made a conveniently well-timed intervention during an Anglo-Saxon succession dispute and, as in other, better-documented cases, we may reasonably suspect foul play. It is notable that Ælfweard died at Oxford, on the border between Wessex and Mercia, suggesting that he had gone there to negotiate and perhaps paid with his life. His departure, however, did not necessarily make it any more likely that Æthelstan would inherit the whole of their father's dominion. Among the nobles of Wessex, the news that their preferred candidate had inexplicably died on his first royal outing must surely have increased resistance and resentment. In Winchester, especially, the citizens must have been surprised to find themselves lining the streets for Ælfweard just days after the funeral of his father. Both were buried in the New Minster, the splendid church imagined by Alfred that had been realized during the reign of his son. We may well believe the story told by William of Malmesbury that during these days there was a plot among certain nobles in Winchester to seize Æthelstan and put out his eyes.[25]

For some time, it seems, there was uncertainty and division: when Æthelstan issued a charter early in 925, it had no West Saxon witnesses. Eventually, however, a deal was hammered out that satisfied the rival factions within the royal family. A key figure in whatever negotiations took place must have been Edward the Elder's third wife, Eadgifu, who had given the old king two more sons in the final years of his life. Speculatively, the agreement reached with Æthelstan may have required him to recognize these young half-brothers as his heirs, and not to prejudice their rights by fathering any children of his own. Procreation was the expected duty of medieval rulers, but one that Æthelstan conspicuously failed to fulfil. Despite living into middle age, he never married and produced no known offspring. Plausibly this was the price he paid for being accepted as the king of Wessex.[26]

These kinds of delicate negotiations would also explain the long delay between the deaths of Edward and Ælfweard in July 924 and Æthelstan's consecration, which did not take place until 4 September 925. The setting for the ceremony was Kingston, a royal estate on the Thames, about twelve miles upstream from London. This may not have been entirely novel, for we do not know where earlier West Saxon kings had been consecrated, and at least one major royal council had previously been held there. But Kingston was certainly an appropriate location for an investiture in 925, lying right on the ancient border of Mercia and Wessex. A new order of service had apparently been drawn up by the officiating archbishop of Canterbury especially for the occasion, and its prayers repeatedly stressed that Æthelstan was being blessed as the ruler of *two* peoples. It also introduced a genuine novelty in the shape of a new item of royal regalia. Previous Anglo-Saxon ceremonies had culminated with the bishops placing a helmet on the head of their new king, but in Æthelstan's case they used a crown. The practice of rulers wearing a circlet of gold originated with the Romans, but had recently been revived by contemporary emperors in Europe. This was the first time it had been used in Britain, making the ceremony at Kingston in 925 the first English coronation.[27]

Did his new imperial-style headgear hint at Æthelstan's larger ambitions? Having affirmed the unity of Wessex and Mercia, the new king sought to resume the negotiations his father had begun with Northumbria five years earlier. Back then the northern kingdom had been ruled by a viking named Ragnall, who had recently arrived from Ireland and conquered York. Links between Scandinavians in Northumbria and Ireland had been strong ever since the 860s, when Ivar the Boneless had raided on both sides of the Irish Sea, and after his day most of the rulers of York and Dublin were probably members of his dynasty. Their careers were typically turbulent and as a result their reigns were often short. Ragnall, for example, had barely had time to strike a deal with Edward the Elder in 920 before he was toppled and replaced by another of Ivar's descendants, Sihtric. It was in an effort to stabilize relations with this new Northumbrian ruler that Æthelstan proposed a marriage alliance. On 30 January 926, five months after his coronation, the king welcomed Sihtric to Tamworth and, in the *Chronicle's* words, 'gave him his sister in marriage'.

Barely a year elapsed, however, before the wheel of fortune turned again, with momentous consequences. In the early months of 927 Sihtric died, leaving the Northumbrian throne once again vacant. As the news spread, various men set out immediately to make themselves his replacement. One contender was his kinsman, Guthfrith, who set sail with a fleet from Ireland. Another, perhaps, was Ealdred, the English ruler based at Bamburgh. But both these hopefuls were beaten by Æthelstan, who rapidly intervened to make himself Northumbria's new master. The *Chronicle* says simply that he 'succeeded to the kingdom', but other sources make it plain that this was a military struggle: the king marched north with an army, drove out Guthfrith and Ealdred, and destroyed the viking stronghold in York. William of Malmesbury, writing much later, insisted that Æthelstan's men pursued Guthfrith all the way to the court of Constantine, the king of Scots, and demanded that the fugitive be handed over. True or not, Constantine was one of several northern rulers who were compelled by Æthelstan to attend a conference. On 12 July, at Eamont in Cumbria, the English king met with his Scottish counterpart, along with the king of the Strathclyde Britons and Ealdred of Bamburgh. In terms of its composition, the meeting resembled that arranged by Edward the Elder seven years earlier, but this was plainly not a discussion between equals. Æthelstan was no longer a distant shadow in the south but a power in their own midst: imposing, surrounded by soldiers, and demanding subservience.

Nor did his conquest stop in Cumbria. Having asserted himself in the north, Æthelstan turned his attention to the British communities in the west. According to William of Malmesbury, the king demanded similar subjection from the rulers of Wales, forcing them to meet him on the border at Hereford in order to make professions of obedience. From there he proceeded to deal with the Britons of the south-west, 'who are called the Corn-Welsh'. Æthelstan reportedly drove the Cornish from Exeter, compelling them to reside beyond the River Tamar, and then ordered the fortification of the city with walls of stone. The *Anglo-Saxon Chronicle* clearly regarded 927 as an auspicious year, noting that fiery lights had been seen in the northern skies, and that Æthelstan had 'brought under his rule all the kings who were in this island'.[28]

The massive expansion of his authority raised the question of what to call him. One clerk in his entourage composed a poem celebrating the king's military success in terms presumably calculated to please a courtly audience in Winchester: Æthelstan was referred to as 'king of the Saxons', his troops 'the army of the Saxons', and his enlarged kingdom 'this Saxon-land made whole' (*ista Saxonia perfecta*).[29] After 927, however, it was more common for talk of Saxons to be ditched. The king's earliest charters had styled him *Rex Angul-Saxonum*, the compound title employed by his grandfather and retained by his father, but after his annexation of Northumbria Æthelstan became simply *Rex Anglorum* – king of the English. Even then, there were clearly some who felt this did not adequately reflect the extent of his power. The single scribe who composed his charters between 928 and 934 frequently augmented 'king of the English' with extra accolades, such as 'ruler of the whole world of Britain'. Coins struck in Æthelstan's name after 927 bore the legend 'king of the whole of Britain', and those minted a few years later depicted him wearing the new symbol of his authority, his crown.[30]

It is worth considering how Æthelstan had managed to achieve such spectacular results in so short a time. Part of the answer must surely be his personal prowess as a warrior. According to William of Malmesbury, the king had subjugated his enemies 'by the terror of his name alone'. Although we have no record of his exploits before his accession, Æthelstan must have participated in the campaigns of his father's day, presumably fighting in, and possibly leading, the armies of his formidable aunt. Another factor, arguably even more essential, was his wealth. By the time of his birth around 893, the economic decline that had crippled Wessex and Mercia in the mid-ninth century had been arrested by his legendary grandfather. Alfred had restored the coinages of both kingdoms and increased the number of mints. The return of peace meant he was once again able to tap the profits of trade, and perhaps even able to exploit the natural resources of Wessex, such as silver and tin. As a result he had died a rich man, bequeathing his successors around £2,000 in silver – almost half a million pennies, though probably not all of it was in coin. His son, it is true, must have disgorged a great deal of this treasure during a reign that had demanded almost unbroken campaigning and heavy investment

20. A coin of Æthelstan, wearing his crown, proclaiming him 'king of all Britain' (*rex to[tius] Br[itanniae]*).

in military infrastructure. Yet Edward's investment would ultimately have paid large dividends. The Scandinavian rulers who submitted to him in the East Midlands and East Anglia must have paid handsomely in return for having his peace, just as he and his predecessors had once paid to prevent their depredations.[31]

Æthelstan, therefore, must also have started his reign with a strong financial advantage. Raising an army with which to conquer Northumbria would have presented no problem, and after the kingdom's fall the funds kept flowing. William of Malmesbury informs us that the viking fortress in York was found to be full of plunder, which Æthelstan generously divided among his men. When the king compelled the Welsh to submit to him a short time later, they were obliged to promise a vast annual tribute: twenty pounds of gold, 300 pounds of silver, 25,000 oxen, and as many hunting dogs and birds as he demanded. The detail supplied by Malmesbury may be invented, but the basic underlying truth seems undeniable: success bred success. Æthelstan's military superiority meant he was able to demand renders from those who bowed before him. If the Welsh paid him tribute, then the same must have been true of the Cornish, the Scots, and the Britons of Strathclyde.[32]

Rapid expansion made Æthelstan incomparably rich, but it also brought problems – the most obvious being how such a wide dominion could be effectively governed. His father had built *burhs* in Essex and across the East Midlands which served as outposts of royal authority in areas that had previously been part of the Danelaw. But beyond, in East Anglia and Northumbria, Æthelstan had no such permanent presence. The Scandinavian kings who had ruled these regions may have been toppled, but their jarls and holds had been left in place. These men had sworn allegiance to Æthelstan, and agreed to pay him tribute, but otherwise little had changed.

Earlier Anglo-Saxon kings had maintained their authority by itineration, riding around their kingdoms with their households, consuming food that had been rendered to royal estates, and generally making their presence felt. Æthelstan did this within Wessex, and spent more time in Mercia than other tenth-century kings, no doubt because he enjoyed revisiting the familiar places of his youth. But there was no question of him routinely travelling from Winchester to York in order to supervise his Northumbrian subjects, or making an annual tour to check all was well in East Anglia.[33]

The solution was to make his dependants do the travelling, by requiring them to attend royal assemblies. This was not in itself a new idea: earlier West Saxon and Mercian kings had regularly summoned their leading subjects for consultation, and the archbishops of Canterbury had convened synods that were attended by churchmen from multiple kingdoms. No king, however, had ever held assemblies as large as those summoned by Æthelstan. The charters the king issued on such occasions have very long lists of witnesses, sometimes numbering more than a hundred names. Among them we see not only English bishops, ealdormen and thegns, but also Scandinavian jarls drawn from the recently conquered Danelaw, as well as the various rulers of Wales, now reduced in status to 'little sub-kings' (*subreguli*) by Æthelstan's principal scribe.[34]

These men, and the others listed as witnesses, were the most important individuals present, but they would have travelled with their own entourages, meaning that Æthelstan's assemblies must have been attended by many hundreds of men, with total audience numbers probably reaching four figures. No building could have contained that many people, so they must have been held in the open air. Æthelstan followed the tradition of holding them on the great feasts of Christmas and Easter, but also introduced the practice of summoning an additional meeting seven weeks after Easter, on the feast of Pentecost, or Whitsun. They would have been occasions for gift-giving, dispute-settlement, law-making, and communicating royal decisions back to the furthest parts of the king's dominion. Perhaps above all, they were a means of demonstrating Æthelstan's majesty: acts of royal theatre, carefully stage-managed, through which the king, wearing his crown, was presented to his people as a divinely appointed figure of power.[35]

In the seven years after the conquest of Northumbria, two men were conspicuously absent from these councils. Constantine, the king of Scots, and Owain, king of the Strathclyde Britons, had both sworn oaths to Æthelstan at Eamont in 927, but neither had subsequently made the long journey south to attend his court. It seems unlikely that they were never invited: the third figure present at Eamont, Ealdred of Bamburgh, had dutifully attended several assemblies down to his death in 933. Was his death the cause, or the consequence, of some fresh contention in the north? Or had Æthelstan simply grown tired of the excuses of men who had promised to obey him, and decided to punish their contumacy? Whatever the reason, in 934, the king set out to discipline Constantine by invading his territory.[36] That spring he summoned an army, which mustered in Winchester at Pentecost. A charter drawn up on that occasion shows him surrounded by three Welsh sub-kings, five jarls, seven ealdormen, eleven king's thegns, and no fewer than eighteen bishops, including the archbishops of both Canterbury and York. Together with hundreds, probably thousands, of armed dependants, this great company rode north, covering about fifteen miles a day. On 7 June, at Nottingham, their leader issued another charter, describing himself as 'I, Æthelstan, king of the English, elevated by the right hand of the Almighty, which is Christ, to the throne of the whole of Britain'. A week or so later, having covered another 150 miles, he paused at Chester-le-Street to venerate St Cuthbert. After that he plunged his forces into Scotland, leading his army to lay waste as far north as Dunnottar, while his fleet ravaged the coast as far as Caithness.[37]

Constantine was an old man by 934, at least fifty-six years old, and had been king of Scots since the start of the century. During that time he had repeatedly fought against viking raiders from Ireland and defeated them in battle. But he quickly realized that the enemy that was now devastating his kingdom was irresistible. By early August at the latest, he must have sought out Æthelstan and made renewed professions of obedience. The English king, however, was not content to let the matter rest there. As he and his mighty entourage rode south, the compliant king of Scots rode with them. By September they were back in Mercia, and by the middle of the month they had reached the *burh* at Buckingham, where Æthelstan issued another charter. Constantine was accorded first place among the witnesses, but he was now styled *subregulus*, like the petty kings of Wales. Presumably thereafter he was allowed to return to Scotland, having perhaps made a public proclamation of loyalty for the benefit of a southern audience. But the following year he was once again in Mercia, this time witnessing a charter at Cirencester. As the scribe who drew up the document noted, Cirencester was 'a city at one time built by the Romans', and this was surely significant: the town's amphitheatre would have been a perfect setting for a great outdoor assembly. Besides Constantine the attendees included the three kings of Wales, as well as Owain, the king of Strathclyde, who had lately decided that one or two trips a year to Mercia or Wessex was preferable to having his territory torched by a wrathful English king. All five rulers were naturally styled *subreguli*; only Æthelstan himself, 'endowed with the rank of extraordinary prerogative', was accorded the title *rex*. We may picture him, seated in the amphitheatre at Cirencester, wearing his crown, surrounded by the British rulers he had bent to his will, the jarls and holds who had submitted to his father, and all the English bishops, ealdormen and thegns united by his grandfather – 'the whole class of nobles', in the words of the charter, 'rejoicing under the arms of royal generosity'.[38]

21. The remains of the Roman amphitheatre at Cirencester.

One is bound to wonder if the Celtic kings at this great council felt genuinely joyful, or whether, as seems more likely, they accepted Æthelstan's generosity smiling with gritted teeth. In the case of the three Welsh rulers, some indications of their feelings can be surmised from the literature produced in Wales during the ninth and tenth centuries. The Britons and the Saxons, of course, had a long history of antagonism that stretched all the way back to the fifth century, and there are reasons to think that their mutual hostility became more entrenched as time wore on. The great dyke built by King Offa, whatever other purposes it may have served, emphasized the divide that existed between the two ethnicities by the end of the eighth century. A generation or so after its construction, one Welsh author had responded to continuing Mercian pressure by writing a proud and assertive *History of the Britons*, which contains the first securely datable references to Arthur – not yet a king, but a heroic British warrior, battling victoriously against the Saxons at Badon Hill and many other places besides.[39] Some Welsh kings, it is true, had sought the protection of King Alfred against the depredations of their own countrymen, but others had chosen to side with his viking enemies, and by the time Alfred's grandson was in power, demanding punitive tributes and regular attendance at his court, those that had initially welcomed the embrace of an English king may have been wondering if they had made the wrong decision. It was probably in Æthelstan's reign that another Welshman composed the *Great Prophecy of Britain*, a long, poetic diatribe that looked forward eagerly to the total destruction of English power. The Britons, lamented the poet, had suffered at Saxon hands ever since the days of Hengist and Horsa, and had latterly been forced to pay tribute to 'the Great King' and his stewards at Cirencester. But those days, he continued, were about to come to an end, just as Merlin had foretold. Soon the Britons of Wales, Cornwall and Strathclyde would unite, joining forces with the Scots, the Irish and the vikings of Dublin, and together they would drive the English from Britain completely. 'There will be heads split open without brains', enthused the author. 'Women will be widowed, and horses riderless.' Corpses, he happily imagined, would stand supporting each other all the way to the coast of Kent, where the last surviving Saxons would take to their ships, leaving the island forever.[40]

The Welsh were evidently not alone in entertaining such ideas. The fact that the author of the *Great Prophecy* could envisage such a grand alliance of Celtic peoples suggests similar sentiments were being harboured by all those who had lately been forced to submit to English power. It is perhaps more surprising that the poet should include the vikings of Dublin in this imagined partnership, for on many occasions in the past they had been considered the enemy. But such had been the humiliation of the rulers of western and northern Britain at Æthelstan's hands, required to trot obediently south whenever he demanded, that they were now ready to contemplate an alliance with the vikings if it promised to rid them of their English tormentor.

While Æthelstan had been busy belittling these British rulers, a new king had come to power in Ireland. Olaf Guthfrithson, as his name implies, was the son of the viking Guthfrith, who had tried and failed to seize the kingdom of York in 927. Olaf had succeeded him as king of Dublin, and gone on to win victories over neighbouring Irish rulers, so that he was soon sufficiently confident to claim the prize his father had been denied a decade earlier. In the summer of 937 he sailed across the Irish Sea with a fleet of 600 ships, to join a coalition of the kind foretold in the *Great Prophecy*. The kings of Wales, no doubt to the poet's disgust, decided to remain at home. But Olaf was met by Constantine, the king of Scots, and Owain, the king of Strathclyde, and together the three of them exacted their revenge, laying waste to the lands of their oppressor. 'They despoiled everything with continuous ravages,' says William of Malmesbury, quoting lines from his ancient volume, 'driving out the people, setting fire to the fields.'[41]

Æthelstan, according to the same source, was surprised by this invasion, but responded rapidly when he heard the news, summoning an army and advancing north to confront his foes.

They met at a place called *Brunanburh*, the location of which has long been debated, but was most likely Bromborough, a settlement on the Wirral peninsula, separated from the later city of Liverpool by the estuary of the River Mersey. Vikings had been attempting to settle on the Wirral since the days of King Alfred. It was an obvious destination, directly across from Dublin, surrounded on all sides by the sea, and a convenient place at which to rendezvous with the armies marching from the north. Bromborough itself is spelt *Brunanburh* in a twelfth-century source, and is the only modern place name that can plausibly derive from that particular Old English spelling. Recent archaeological finds of tenth-century war-gear in the surrounding fields add extra weight to the argument that this was indeed the site where the armies of Æthelstan and his enemies clashed.[42]

Their confrontation was extremely bloody. An Irish source, the *Annals of Ulster*, calls it 'a great, lamentable and horrible battle', and says that thousands of vikings fell, as well as a large number of English. The *Anglo-Saxon Chronicle*, frustratingly reticent for the rest of Æthelstan's reign, describes the engagement in a poem of some length. Banners clashed, spears mingled, and warriors met, says the anonymous author, 'cleaving the shield-wall, hewing the linden boards with hammered swords'. From sunrise to sunset the battle raged, the earth growing dark with the blood of the fallen. Among the English dead, reports William of Malmesbury, were two of Æthelstan's cousins, whose bodies were recovered afterwards and taken to Malmesbury for burial.

But despite the loss of his kinsmen, and a great many of his other followers, this was the English king's victory, and the poet dwelt at length on the death and discomfort of his enemies. Seven of Olaf's jarls were slain, and also 'five young kings', presumably petty rulers he had recruited to his banner in Ireland. Constantine, meanwhile, described as 'the grey-haired warrior', was left lamenting the loss of countless Scottish soldiers, including one of his own sons. When it became clear that the English were going to win, the battle became a rout, the victors pursuing their fleeing adversaries 'with whetted swords'. Constantine fled back to

Scotland, while Olaf and his surviving men were chased back to their boats, escaping 'over the deep water' to Dublin with nothing to show for their efforts but shame. Æthelstan's army, by contrast, withdrew from the field rejoicing, leaving behind them a rich banquet of corpses for the ravens and wolves.[43]

Although its location was eventually forgotten, *Brunanburh* was long remembered as a great English victory. Half a century later, the chronicler Æthelweard wrote that the common people of his own day still referred to it as 'the Great Battle', and went on to wax lyrical about its happy consequences. 'The fields of Britain were consolidated into one, there was peace everywhere, and an abundance of all things', he enthused, adding that since that time 'no viking fleet has remained here ... except under treaty with the English'.[44]

But this was nonsense, as Æthelweard must have known from the subsequent entries in his principal source, the *Anglo-Saxon Chronicle*. He was most likely mythologizing *Brunanburh* because, in his own day, Britain was anything but united and peaceful, and was once again under sustained viking attack. In reality, the effects of the 'Great Battle' were extremely limited and far from permanent. The casualties on both sides may have been numerous, but the leading combatants on both sides survived unscathed: Constantine, Olaf, and apparently Owain of Strathclyde (not mentioned in the poem) all escaped and lived for several more years. The first to die, in fact, was Æthelstan himself. Two years after his victory, on 27 October 939, the king passed away peacefully at Gloucester, aged about forty-five. His body was carried from there to Malmesbury Abbey, where he was buried with great pomp beside the altar, near to his two cousins who had fallen in the battle.[45]

'His years, though few, were full of glory', said William of Malmesbury. 'All Europe proclaimed his praises, extolled his excellence to the skies.' In terms of the power he had projected within the British Isles, Æthelstan was certainly remarkable. Not until the reign of the equally imperious Edward I, three and

273

a half centuries later, would an English king lead armies so far north, or compel the rulers of both Wales and Scotland to attend assemblies in southern England.[46] It is also noteworthy that Æthelstan's reign witnessed a reaffirmation of the bond between the peoples of Wessex and Mercia. At the time of his accession they had been ready to go their separate ways, but in the *Brunanburh* poem preserved in the *Chronicle* the West Saxons and the Mercians are portrayed as brothers in arms, fighting side by side. The poem's final lines are a forceful restatement of their common identity as *Angelcynn*, and of a belief in their shared history, that served as a pointed retort to the sentiments expressed in the *Great Prophecy*:

Never yet in this island before this, by what books and our ancient sages tell us, was a greater slaughter of a host made by the edge of the sword, since the Angles and Saxons came hither from the east, invading Britain over the broad seas, and the proud assailants, warriors eager for glory, overcame the Britons and won a country.

One may suspect, however, that the poet was not rubbing salt into British wounds simply for the sake of it. He was evidently writing some time after the battle, during the reign of Æthelstan's successor, Edmund, who is accorded equal credit for the victory, even though he was only sixteen at the time.[47] At the start of Edmund's reign, there were urgent reasons for reminding men of their heroic feats of the recent past, as well as the distant triumphs of their ancestors. Northumbria had once again fallen to the vikings, and a pagan king of York ruled everything as far south as Watling Street. Within a vanishingly short space of time, all of Æthelstan's conquests had been undone.

8

ONE NATION UNDER GOD

St Dunstan and the Pursuit of Uniformity

Nowadays, if someone says they are looking forward to going to Glastonbury, it is generally safe to assume they mean the world-famous music festival that takes place at Worthy Farm in Somerset, and not the small market town situated eight miles further to the west. But in the Middle Ages, the town was a destination in its own right, for at its heart lay Glastonbury Abbey, one of the richest monasteries in England, which acted as a similarly powerful draw for devotees.

Like the promoters of the modern music festival, the monks of Glastonbury relied on big names to pull in the paying crowds. In the late twelfth century – coincidentally soon after the abbey had suffered a devastating fire – they 'discovered' the bones of King Arthur and his queen, Guinevere, and made their invention tally with the contemporary tales of Arthur by insisting that Glastonbury had originally been called 'Avalon'. By the fourteenth century, they were also claiming that it was the final resting place of Joseph of Arimathea, the man who had arranged Christ's burial, and the first keeper of the Holy Grail.[1]

For these later medieval myths to have been true, of course, the church at Glastonbury would have had to have been quite exceptionally old – far older than seventh-century Lindisfarne or sixth-century Canterbury – and indeed the monks had long maintained that this was the case: William of Malmesbury, writing in the early twelfth century, believed the abbey had been founded soon after the death of Christ by one of the Twelve Disciples. The reality was rather more mundane. It is not impossible that the first church on the site might have been built by a British ruler in the post-Roman period – artefacts have been found there dating from the fifth or sixth centuries – but the earliest written evidence suggests that the monastery was established in the decades either side of 700, during the reign of the West Saxon king, Ine.[2]

The person who transformed Glastonbury from a place of only local importance into an intellectual and political powerhouse that dominated the whole nation was Dunstan – or St Dunstan, as he later became. One of the most important figures in England during the second half of the tenth century, Dunstan was both a pioneering scholar and a persuasive politician whose ideas helped to give ideological cohesion to the new kingdom. Aided by family connections within the Church and at the royal court, he rose through the ecclesiastical ranks, becoming abbot of Glastonbury, and eventually archbishop of Canterbury, a position he held for almost thirty years. His rise was facilitated by his keen intelligence and forceful personality, but what really marked him out for preferment was his place at the forefront of a revolutionary movement that swept through the Church during his lifetime. Dunstan and his followers saw it their duty, even their destiny, to resurrect monasticism, which had declined everywhere in Europe during the disastrous ninth century, in many places to the point of extinction. They set out to re-found monastic houses and restore them to what they imagined was their original state of purity. Their ideals were taken up with enthusiasm by most of the secular elite, who endowed the new monasteries with vast estates, and handed great power to Dunstan and his allies, whose ideals they embraced and aspired to emulate. As a result reform came to comprehend not only the Church but the whole of Christian society.

Dunstan and his episcopal colleagues were thus far more important and influential than any of the kings they served. In the forty years after Æthelstan's death in 939, the united kingdom he had forged was ruled by five consecutive monarchs, none of whom made it past their early thirties, and two of whom perished while still in their teens. The leading reformers, by contrast, all lived to be old men, with political careers that extended over several decades; Dunstan's life coincided with the reigns of no fewer than eight English kings. In addition, the lives of the reformers are far better documented than those of their royal masters. No biographies exist for any of the mid-tenth century monarchs, and the *Anglo-Saxon Chronicle* preserves only a fragmentary and often confused record of their activities. Dunstan and his fellow bishops, on the other hand, left a rich written legacy. As intellectuals and patrons of learning, they produced books, charters, and other documents that help to illuminate their careers – some of Dunstan's writings in his own hand survive. Moreover, because several of them were regarded as saints after their death, they were the subject of posthumous biographies that chronicled their careers.

By far the most interesting of these saints' lives is the one about Dunstan. Written by an anonymous author who identifies himself only by his initial, 'B', the *Life of St Dunstan* differs from those of other tenth-century churchman by describing its subject's involvement in secular politics. 'B' had once been a member of Dunstan's household, and his book provides us with valuable glimpses of what was going on at the royal court. It also portrays the saint himself in a surprisingly candid and not always flattering light. Others remembered Dunstan as a venerable old man, serene and snowy-haired, but 'B' depicts him in his younger days as fanatical and almost half-crazed – a priest prone to visions and night-time wanderings, who would often perceive the presence of the Devil in various disguises and engage in erratic behaviour as a result. As such Dunstan excited wonder and admiration in some people, but provoked profound irritation in others, and frequently ended up in altercations that led to his expulsion. The first people to tire of his antics, we are told, were his own kinsmen, who drove him from his childhood home in Glastonbury.[3]

Dunstan was born in the neighbourhood of Glastonbury in the early tenth century, probably in its opening decade. His parents are named as Heorstan and Cynethryth, but unfortunately his biographer tells us little else about them. They were evidently well-connected local landowners, though perhaps not quite as eminent as we are led to suppose. Later references to Dunstan being the kinsman of various bishops and royals may simply be the author's attempt to exaggerate the nobility of his subject.[4]

What is established from the first is the centrality of Glaston-bury to Dunstan's existence. The settlement was located in the same marshy levels in Somerset that had once concealed King Alfred. Contemporaries often described it as an island, though it was in fact not entirely surrounded by water. Then, as now, its dominant geographical feature was Glastonbury Tor, the conical hill that rises 500 feet above the otherwise flat surrounding landscape, and which on a clear day can be seen from more than twenty miles away (colour picture 20). The abbey itself lay on lower ground to the west, and in Dunstan's day, says his biographer, 'all the faithful round about thronged to worship at this spot'. As a boy Dunstan was taken there on one occasion by his father to spend the night in prayer, and later, once he had demonstrated his aptitude for learning the Holy Scriptures at home, his parents arranged for him to join the abbey's community to continue his studies.[5]

Although the *Life of St Dunstan* describes Glastonbury as a monastery at the time of his arrival, there was probably little about it by this point that could be considered truly monastic – certainly not compared to the standards that Dunstan and his fellow reformers would eventually adopt. When the Anglo-Saxons had begun to convert to Christianity in the seventh century, they had used the word 'minster' to describe a wide variety of different religious communities. Some, like those founded by St Wilfrid, had proudly proclaimed their adherence to the Benedictine Rule, and in these houses the monks lived celibate and secluded lives, submitting themselves to a limited diet and a routine of prayer, study and contemplation. But although this was the ideal for some, it was in no sense the norm. Most abbots and abbesses simply invented their own rules, and often took a more relaxed attitude to earthly luxuries. Even in institutions where high standards of abstinence and devotion were observed, it was seldom the case that the entire community was monastic. Even famous minsters usually contained both celibates and secular priests. Early English monasticism had always been a very mixed bag.[6]

For all these monasteries, whatever their condition, the coming of the vikings had been a disaster. This was most obviously true in those areas that had fallen to Danish occupation. Famous houses such as Ripon, Whitby and Wearmouth–Jarrow had been destroyed and abandoned; their buildings stood in ruins, overgrown and neglected, and their wide estates had been seized and divided up among the heathen settlers. The only surviving communities in Northumbria were the monks of Lindisfarne, who had been forced to leave their island, and the monks of York Minster, who were left impoverished. Nor was it just the minsters in these areas that had been destroyed. In the same period the bishoprics of East Anglia at Elmham and Dunwich had disappeared, as had the Northumbrian sees at Hexham and Whithorn. Throughout the Danelaw, organized Christianity as a whole had collapsed.[7]

In Wessex and western Mercia, where Danish occupation had been swiftly reversed, the devastation had not been nearly so severe or comprehensive. In Wessex the number of bishoprics had actually increased, from two to five, with new sees created during the reign of Edward the Elder at Wells, Ramsbury and Crediton. But even in these regions, monasteries had still suffered as a result of decades of repeated Danish raiding. In Kent, for example, ancient coastal communities at places like Dover, Thanet and Folkestone had disappeared, and in other places they survived only in a much diminished state. Even in areas where

Christian rulers had prevailed, minsters had seen their estates appropriated by lay nobles, or by the rulers themselves, perhaps justifying their actions by pleading urgent military necessity. It was because he had deprived them of some of their lands that the monks of Abingdon remembered King Alfred as a 'Judas'. Places that had formerly been rich on account of their massive endowments found they were no longer able to support a contemplative existence in isolation from the world. Where minsters survived into the tenth century it was usually as houses of secular clerks, who might be married and have families.[8]

This was apparently the situation at Glastonbury in the early decades of the tenth century. Lying fifteen miles from the sea, and easily accessible by water, the 'island' is unlikely to have escaped the attentions of the Scandinavians who had repeatedly ravaged the Somerset coast during the previous hundred years. Its ancient church had survived and remained a place of worship, and its religious community seems to have had a continuous existence. The holy men who dwelt there, however, were no longer monks – at least, not by the standards of reformers. They were probably married, with local families, and perhaps as a result better integrated into secular society, welcoming visitors and pilgrims, and taking on the responsibility of teaching bright young boys like Dunstan.[9]

But from around the time of Dunstan's birth, elsewhere in Europe, ideas of reform were starting to germinate. In 909 or 910, the duke of Aquitaine, William I, founded a monastery at Cluny, about sixty miles south of Lyon. Unlike a typical aristocratic patron, the duke did not expect to have a say in the running of the new abbey, or assume that it would remain the property of his family: Cluny was created with the intention that it should be free from lay control, and was answerable only to the pope. Its monks were expected to follow the Benedictine Rule, having no private property, abstaining from meat, and above all abstaining from sex. Once established, the influence of Cluny started to spread. From 925, its second abbot, Odo, began to reform other monasteries in western Francia – most notably the one at Fleury on the River Loire. Meanwhile, in the eastern parts of the Carolingian Empire, similar initiatives were taking place at Gorze, near Metz, and in the Low Countries, at Brogne and Ghent.[10]

It was inevitable that these ideas would eventually find their way across the Channel, but their transmission was accelerated by international diplomacy during the reign of Æthelstan. The king had forged close connections with his continental counterparts, arranging for four of his many sisters to be married to Frankish kings and dukes. As a result, high-ranking men from his court had cause to travel widely across Europe, where they were able to witness the monastic revival at first hand. When Coenwald, bishop of Worcester, escorted two potential royal brides overseas in 929 so that the future duke of Saxony, Otto I, could choose between them, a contemporary writer noted that it gave the bishop the opportunity to visit 'all the monasteries throughout Germany'. Similarly, when Oda, bishop of Ramsbury, was sent on a diplomatic mission to western Francia in 936, he may have used the occasion to visit the newly reformed monastery at Fleury. Oda's spiritual journey had already been a remarkable one, for he was later said to have been the son of viking parents who had come to East Anglia with the great heathen army. Rejecting their paganism, he had joined the household of an English nobleman, and from there entered the service of the king. It was on his visit to Fleury that Oda decided to take his devotions to a higher level by becoming a monk. Coenwald, too, must have received a monastic tonsure at some point after his tour of Germany, for he witnesses some later royal charters as *monachus*.[11]

Around the time that these reformist ideas were starting to be discussed in English circles, Dunstan decided to leave Glastonbury – or perhaps was forcibly driven out. As his biographer explains, Glastonbury was a destination for Irish pilgrims on account of its claim to be the burial place of St Patrick, and Dunstan, a voracious and inquisitive reader, had made a careful study of the books these men brought with them. But to the rest of the island's inhabitants, such strange volumes seemed suspicious, and they accused the devout young man of learning heathen spells; some of his accusers, we are told, were his own kinsmen. Having obtained a judgement from the king that he should be banished, they seized Dunstan, bound his hands and feet, and threw him into a muddy marsh. Although his biography claims he was cleared of the charges against him, it also indicates that his tormentors tried to drive Dunstan from his position on more than one occasion, and it seems likely that they eventually succeeded. The next we hear of him he was in Winchester, living in the household of its bishop, Ælfheah.[12]

We are less well informed about Ælfheah than his episcopal colleagues, Coenwald and Oda, though it seems probable that, like them, he was also a monk – his contemporary nickname, 'the Bald', may have arisen on account of his adoption of a monastic tonsure, which was more severe than the modest crop that all clerics sported as a mark of their special status. Ælfheah was certainly a keen advocate of monasticism, for it was he who persuaded Dunstan to take the habit. Dunstan was apparently a relative of the bishop, but had yet to join his household. He was, however, by no means keen to comply with his kinsman's suggestion, for by this point, probably in his mid-twenties, he was engaged to be married. ('To a young woman', hissed his biographer, 'in whose blandishments he could luxuriate every day rather than clothe himself in woollen rags, like monks do.') Undeterred, Ælfheah asked for divine assistance, and God responded by causing blisters to break out all over Dunstan's body. Fearing he had contracted leprosy, and was about to die, the young man sent for the bishop and signalled that he had changed his mind, and wished to become a monk after all.[13]

Being sworn to celibacy did not mean avoiding the company of women. At some point in the late 930s, Dunstan left Ælfheah's household and returned to Glastonbury, where he entered the service of a rich widow named Æthelflæd. She too is described as a relative by his biographer, and had taken a similar decision to live chastely. Widows enjoyed far greater independence in Anglo-Saxon England than either married or unmarried women, and by vowing to celibacy they could avoid the prospect of being remarried against their will to men who were after their estates. For such women, the ideals of monastic reform may have had particular appeal. It must have been preferable for female communities to secure the services of holy men who were sworn to chastity rather than secular clerks who were not. Before departing from Winchester Dunstan had been ordained as a priest by Bishop Ælfheah, so was well qualified to minister to the religious needs of his new mistress. He was also able to share his artistic talents. 'He took much trouble cultivating writing, harp-playing, and painting, too', says his biographer. 'It is no exaggeration to say that he shone as a careful exponent of all the useful arts.' On one occasion, another noblewoman, knowing of Dunstan's needlework skills, commissioned him to make her an embroidered stole for religious services, decorated with gold and jewels.[14]

Dunstan was not long in Æthelflæd's service before she fell ill; he attended her throughout her sickness and buried her when she died. This might have left him without employment, but in the meantime he had attracted the attention of another widow – one with even greater power and influence. Eadgifu, the third and final wife of King Edward the Elder, had bidden her time since her husband's death in 924, disappearing from court after the highly contentious succession of her stepson, Æthelstan. As has been suggested above, she may perhaps have agreed to step aside having secured an agreement that her own offspring would be next in line, for that is exactly what happened: when Æthelstan died in October 939, the crown passed to Eadgifu's eldest son, Edmund, who was eighteen years old. The dowager queen, who was probably around forty, returned triumphantly to court, where she appears to have played a dominant role. It seems fairly certain that she was behind the decision to summon Dunstan to her side, intending that he should become one of her son's principal advisers.[15]

Edmund, alas, did not share his mother's high estimation of his new monastic counsellor, and nor did his aristocratic companions. Some of the king's thegns, says the *Life of St Dunstan*, admired the saint for his way of life, but many of them soon came to detest him, and eventually Edmund himself lost his temper. One day, when the royal household was at Cheddar, about twelve miles north of Glastonbury, the teenage king exploded in rage, and ordered Dunstan into exile. Distressed at this development, the holy man sought the protection of some foreign visitors who happened to be at court, and made ready to leave the kingdom.[16]

Happily, God soon intervened to redress the situation. Cheddar, which lies on the edge of the Mendip Hills, was a royal hunting lodge, and, a day or so after banishing Dunstan, Edmund and his men rode out to amuse themselves in the surrounding forests. When they came across a group of stags they chased them in different directions, the king charging off in pursuit of one particular animal, accompanied only by his braying pack of hounds. Caught up in the thrill of the chase, he was oblivious to a hidden hazard, described in the *Life of St Dunstan* as a cleft in the hill that 'drops to an astonishing depth'. This must have been the famous Cheddar Gorge, where the ground does indeed fall away vertically for over 400 feet (colour picture 21). The frightened stag ran headlong into this ravine, plummeting to its death, as did the excited dogs running close behind it. Edmund, suddenly real- izing the danger, tried to restrain his horse, but it stubbornly refused to slow. In what seemed to be his last few seconds, the king recalled his treatment of Dunstan, and vowed to make amends if his life was spared. 'At these words,' says the saint's biographer, 'the horse stopped on the very brink of the precipice, when its front feet were just about to plunge into the depths of the abyss.'[17]

It is a good story, not least because it gives us an early glimpse of an English king engaged in a favourite royal pastime. Naturally, we do not have to believe that it is true in every respect, or that it reveals 'some secret plan of God's', as Dunstan's biographer insists was the case. A more likely explanation for Edmund's change of heart would be an intervention on the part of his mother, or by another of Dunstan's supporters at court: it is shortly after this episode that we learn the saint had an older brother, Wulfric, who witnesses royal charters as a king's thegn. The essential point is that, whatever influences were brought to bear on him, divine or otherwise, the young king recalled Dunstan and proposed a new way of resolving their differences. As soon as the banished monk reappeared, Edmund commanded him to mount up, and together they rode the short distance to Glastonbury. After they had prayed in the church, the king went through a public performance of reconciliation with his unpopular counsellor, and then appointed him as Glastonbury's new abbot, promising to provide all the funds that were necessary to restore the monastery to its former glory.[18]

This was a shrewd move: at a stroke it removed Dunstan from court, where his presence was clearly divisive, and simultaneously set him up as an officially sanctioned exponent of reform, whose prayers and holiness would benefit the royal house. The new abbot, now probably in his early thirties, set about his task with

22. A reconstruction of the new abbey church at Glastonbury built by Dunstan.

gusto. His aim was the reintroduction of bona fide monasticism, following the Rule of St Benedict, and he began by rebuilding the abbey in stone, surrounding the whole site with a wall so that, in his biographer's words, 'he could pen in the sheep of the Lord'. One of St Benedict's key provisions was that monks should avoid contact with the outside world, and remain strictly cloistered. New recruits rushed to join his flock, and Dunstan began to instruct them in the principles of monastic life, as well as scripture, grammar and metrics. 'He shone forth', says his biographer, 'as the premier abbot of the English people.'[19]

It was probably not long after Dunstan was installed as abbot of Glastonbury that the whole kingdom was plunged into crisis. In December 940 a viking army from Dublin landed in Northumbria, led by Olaf 'Cuaran' – nicknamed, it would seem, after a distinctive type of shoe. This new Olaf was the son of Sihtric, the man who had made himself king of York twenty years earlier by similar means, but had been succeeded after his death in 927 by the all-conquering Æthelstan. Sihtric's son had arrived in 940 determined to reclaim his father's throne, and met with swift success. 'The Northumbrians were false to their pledge,' says the Anglo-Saxon Chronicle, 'and chose Olaf from Ireland as their king.'[20]

Nor was it just the Northumbrians. From the *Chronicle*'s scrappy record of these events, it seems that Olaf must have also gained the submission of the Five Boroughs – that extensive area of eastern Mercia settled by the Danes in the late ninth century, and laboriously retaken by Edward the Elder and his sister Æthelflæd in the second decade of the tenth. The year after Olaf's invasion, a contemporary English poet praised 'the son of Edward, King Edmund' for liberating the region from Danish rule. This in turn drew a response from Olaf, who in 943 marched his army south, all the way through the Five Boroughs, and laid siege to Northampton. The defenders there managed to hold out, but the viking leader succeeded in taking Tamworth by storm, and then occupied Leicester. Edmund arrived with an army, but decided against a direct confrontation. Instead, the two sides agreed to parley. Olaf's chief negotiator was Wulfstan, the archbishop of York, and a native Northumbrian. Edmund was represented by Oda, the former bishop of Ramsbury, who, despite his viking parentage, had recently been appointed as archbishop of Canterbury. In their own persons, the two primates showed the mutability of ethnic identities and political loyalties. The struggle for the north was not a simple struggle of heathen versus Christian, and owed more to Northumbria's determination not to be ruled by the kings of Wessex. The peace they concluded was devastating to the claim of those southern kings to be rulers of all the English. It was decided that the border between Edmund and Olaf should be the line of Watling Street, just as it had been in the days of Alfred and Guthrum. In a matter of months, the conquests of Æthelstan, Edward and Æthelflæd had been undone.[21]

This shameful setback for Alfred's dynasty was soon reversed. The details are extremely sketchy, but it seems that before the end of 943 Olaf had been joined in York by a relative named Ragnall and obliged to share power. Then, the following year, Edmund invaded Northumbria and drove out both its new viking rulers: Ragnall seems to have died and Olaf returned to Ireland. In 945 the English king completed the restoration of Æthelstan's authority by ravaging Strathclyde and handing it over to Malcolm, the new king of Scots. The Strathclyde Britons and the Scots had been allied against Æthelstan at *Brunanburh*, so setting them against each other was a canny move on Edmund's part. During these campaigns, the English king also took the opportunity to liberate the relics of several northern saints, exhuming the body of Abbess Hild from Whitby and the remaining bones of Aidan from Lindisfarne, and sending them south to be reinterred at Glastonbury.[22]

Unfortunately, the next body to be buried at Glastonbury was Edmund's own. In the spring of 946 the king was stabbed by a man named Leofa while staying at Pucklechurch, a royal estate about eight miles east of Bristol. The *Anglo-Saxon Chronicle* provides nothing else in the way of details, and the *Life of St*

Dunstan is more concerned to record the abbot's premonitions of the killing than its actual causes. Later sources suggest that Edmund was not the intended target, but had died trying to defend his steward. Deliberate or not, the attack proved fatal, and the king died on 26 May, aged about twenty-five. His body was conveyed to Glastonbury where Dunstan himself conducted the funeral.[23]

Edmund was succeeded by his younger brother, Eadred, who was in his early twenties, and perhaps more committed to the cause of monastic reform: one of his first acts was to recall Dunstan to court, and the saint's biographer claims that the king preferred him to almost all his other counsellors. Dunstan was certainly present in Eadred's entourage on many occasions, for he appears frequently as a witness to royal charters – in some cases he may even have drafted them himself. Apart from the reappearance of the controversial abbot, however, the composition of the new king's court remained much the same as it had under his predecessor. His mother, Eadgifu, was still a prominent royal witness, as were Archbishop Oda and Coenwald, the reformist bishop of Worcester. Among the lay nobility, meanwhile, the outstanding individual was Ealdorman Æthelstan. He had been appointed to govern East Anglia during the reign of his royal namesake, and since then his power had increased, to the extent that he was responsible for most of eastern England. According to a later writer, he was nicknamed Æthelstan Half-King, 'since he was a man of such authority that he was said to maintain the kingdom and its rule with his advice'.[24]

This degree of continuity and stability was crucial, for Eadred faced renewed opposition in the north. In 947, a few months after his coronation, he travelled to the southern border of Northumbria, meeting Archbishop Wulfstan and other northern leaders at Tanshelf (now Pontefract), and obliging them to swear oaths of obedience to him. But very soon afterwards these leaders broke their oaths and accepted as their new king a viking invader named Erik. (Perhaps not the Norwegian king, Erik Bloodaxe, as is often claimed.) Eadred responded ferociously,

ravaging all of Northumbria in 948 until the northerners agreed
to reaccept him. During the campaign his troops burned down
St Wilfrid's minster at Ripon, and Archbishop Oda seized the
opportunity to claim Wilfrid's bones for Canterbury, justifying
his actions by accusing the northerners of having neglected their
holy relics. Despite the severity of the king's harrying, however,
and the tribute he imposed, the settlement did not last. The
following year saw the return of Olaf Cuaran from Ireland, who
ruled Northumbria until 952, when he in turn was ousted by
Erik. The contest between the two rival vikings continued until
954, when the northerners expelled Erik and submitted once
again to Eadred. Although no one knew it at the time, this was
a decisive moment. The English king appointed the ruler of
Bamburgh, Oswulf, to govern the north, but as an ealdorman,
not a king. 'Here the kings of Northumbria came to an end',
wrote a later northern chronicler.[25]

Around the same time that Erik was persuaded to bow out, there
was also a highly significant departure from Glastonbury. Of all
the pupils that Dunstan had managed to attract to his monastery,
none was more important than Æthelwold. Like Dunstan, he
would become one of the leading lights of the Reform Movement,
and was the subject of a saint's life, which has happily survived.
At first a clerk at the court of King Æthelstan, Æthelwold had
moved in the mid-930s to the household of Bishop Ælfheah of
Winchester, like Dunstan, and it was probably there that the two
men first met: according to his biographer, the pair of them were
ordained as priests by Ælfheah on the same day, suggesting they
were much the same age. When Dunstan was promoted to become
abbot of Glastonbury, Æthelwold soon joined him, and was
tonsured as a monk. Dedicating himself to a rigorous routine of
discipline and study, he became Dunstan's most accomplished
disciple, and was appointed as his dean, or second in command.[26]

But after a decade or so at Glastonbury, Æthelwold began to
grow dissatisfied. He was by all accounts more zealous than
Dunstan, and may have been irked by the fact that their abbey

still contained a mix of monks and secular clerks. Eventually he decided he could no longer tolerate the situation, and resolved to go abroad 'to receive a more perfect grounding in a monk's religious life'. He was prevented, however, by the queen mother, Eadgifu, who once again revealed her attachment to reform, and persuaded her son to forbid the dean's departure. On his mother's advice, Eadred appeased Æthelwold in the same way that his older brother had dealt with Dunstan, by re-founding an old monastery and appointing him as abbot. The house in question was Abingdon, a former royal abbey a few miles south of Oxford, which was reportedly neglected and impoverished, partly thanks to the depredations of King Alfred. With Dunstan's blessing, Æthelwold left Glastonbury around 954, taking with him a number of clerks who wished to become monks under his more ascetic rule. Eadred and his mother showered them with land, money and presents, making the newly revived monastery extremely rich. The king, we are told, came to visit in person, and measured out the foundations of some of its buildings with his own hand. His entourage, says Æthelwold's biographer, contained quite a few Northumbrian thegns, who became riotously drunk over dinner.[27]

Perhaps they drank to distract themselves from Eadred's disgusting table manners. As the *Life of St Dunstan* explains, the king had developed the habit of sucking the juice out of his food, chewing it for a bit, and then spitting it out – 'a practice that often turned the stomachs of the thegns dining with him'. He did this on account of a mystery illness that had afflicted him since the start of his reign. As the years had worn on his condition had worsened, and by the autumn of 955 it had brought Eadred to his deathbed. He died on 23 November at Frome in Somerset, having struggled into his early thirties. His body was taken to Winchester and buried in the Old Minster, another institution that had benefitted from his largesse. The king, we are told, had presented the church with many precious ornaments, including a great gold cross and a golden altar, and had planned to decorate its eastern portico with gilded tiles.[28]

★

Whether it was because of his ill health, or his want of dining etiquette, Eadred had never found a wife, nor fathered any children. At his death, therefore, the succession reverted to the line of his late brother, Edmund, whose two sons had been passed over a decade earlier because they were infants at the time. It was the oldest of these boys who became the new king in November 955. His name was Eadwig, and he was by this date around fifteen years old. According to a sympathetic lay chronicler, writing a few decades later, Eadwig was a handsome young man, nicknamed 'All Fair' by the common folk, and 'deserved to be loved'. But most other commentators disagreed, and presented the king as a degenerate who brought about his own ruin after just four years. As these divergent opinions indicate, his reign was highly divisive, and very nearly disastrous.[29]

As depicted in the *Life of St Dunstan*, the problem was that Eadwig was addicted to debauchery. From the start of his reign, the teenage king was apparently pursued by a noblewoman called Æthelgifu, whose hope was to have him for herself, or else to persuade him to marry her daughter. Dunstan's biographer scurrilously alleges that Eadwig 'took it in turns to subject them to his lustful attentions'. Matters came to a head on the day of his coronation, which took place at Kingston on 25 January 956. During the banquet that followed the ceremony, Archbishop Oda noticed that the king had disappeared with the two ladies, and demanded that the other diners take action. None of the nobles was willing to do so, for fear of incurring Eadwig's displeasure, and in the end they decided to send Dunstan, accompanied by Cynesige, the bishop of Lichfield. The two delegates went in search of the absent king, and found him in flagrante with Æthelgifu and her daughter. The crown, 'brilliant with wonderful gold and silver, and variously sparkling jewels', had been tossed carelessly aside, and the man who should have been wearing it was 'disporting himself disgracefully between the two women, as if they were wallowing in some revolting pigsty'. Dunstan scolded the mother and her daughter, but Eadwig still refused to be parted from their company. Eventually the abbot pulled the adolescent king into an upright position, placed the crown on his head, and frogmarched him back to the coronation feast.[30]

It is another good story, well calculated to scandalize its celibate monastic audience, and may contain some elements of truth. Dunstan's biographer goes on to assert that, as a result of the above confrontation, Æthelgifu convinced Eadwig to banish the saintly abbot, and this was indeed what happened: after February 956 Dunstan disappears from the witness lists to royal charters, as does Bishop Cynesige, suggesting that he too had been expelled on account of his role in the coronation drama. The king's bailiffs came to Glastonbury to seize Dunstan's possessions, and the abbot was forced to make his way across the Channel to Flanders, where he found refuge in the reformed monastery at Ghent.[31]

But this story is merely part of a bigger picture, for the two churchmen were not the only ones to find themselves cast out. At the start of Eadwig's reign other senior figures who had dominated the counsels of his predecessors were also ejected. Perhaps the most notable was his grandmother, Eadgifu, who was not only driven from court but also deprived of all her estates. Another major casualty was Æthelstan Half-King, the most powerful nobleman during the previous two reigns, and perhaps, given Eadred's incapacity, the true author of the English reconquest of Northumbria. ('His warlike virtue', wrote a later eulogist, 'aroused great dread among the enemies of the country.') He too was now induced to leave, and to resign his position as ealdorman. A good friend of Dunstan, and a supporter of monastic reform, he retired to Glastonbury, where he lived out his remaining days as a monk. His son succeeded him, but did not enjoy the same extensive authority as his father.[32]

All these people, and many others too, had been toppled by the rise of a rival faction. Its most prominent member was a man called Ælfhere, who was immediately promoted to become ealdorman of Mercia, despite hardly featuring as a witness in earlier royal charters. He and his three brothers were related to the royal family, but their connection was seemingly recent, perhaps on the female side. Obviously at some point they had established a hold over the young Eadwig: it is possible that the king, who had been orphaned as an infant, had been raised in their circle. How they intended to maintain their influence is much clearer, for at the start of his reign Eadwig was married to Ælfgifu, the younger of the two women involved in the alleged coronation threesome. She and her mother, Æthelgifu, were descendants of Æthelwold, the rebellious cousin of Edward the Elder, who had been killed in battle back in 902. The people who seized power at Eadwig's accession had apparently been biding their time for over half a century.[33]

Quite probably, therefore, the sex scandal involving Ælfgifu and her mother was a story concocted much later by Dunstan's circle to justify their disapproval of Eadwig's marriage. Similarly, the later suggestion that the new king was an opponent of monastic reform appears to have been an attempt to blacken his name that had little basis in actual fact. Eadwig was initially backed by Abbot Æthelwold of Abingdon, Dunstan's former pupil, and the most zealous of all the reformers. Royal charters show that the king was one of Abingdon's benefactors, and in one of them Ælfgifu is explicitly recognized as his wife. Although his biographer attempts to disguise the fact, omitting Eadwig entirely from his account, Æthelwold was clearly a supporter of the new king, and may have been a member of the kin-group that had taken over his court.[34]

Although it was neither debauched nor anti-reform, Eadwig's regime was highly unstable. Some sixty royal charters have survived from the first year of his reign, a greater rate of issue than at any other time in Anglo-Saxon history. The new king and his advisers were evidently granting away massive of amounts of land in a desperate attempt to buy political support. But extravagant as this bonanza was, it was not enough. Their coup had left their opponents down but not out, and opposition began to crystallize around Eadwig's younger brother, Edgar, who had been raised in the household of Æthelstan Half-King. By the summer of 957, it must have seemed to many people that the dispute between the two factions would result in civil war.[35]

War was avoided by summoning a great council, in which it was decided that the country should be partitioned. 'With the whole people as witness,' says the *Life of St Dunstan*, 'the kingdoms were divided along lines laid down by the wise, the famous River Thames becoming the boundary between the two.' Eadwig retained control of Wessex, but Edgar became the new king of both Mercia and Northumbria. It is possible that Eadwig, as the older brother, retained some degree of overall sovereignty – the coinage in both realms continued to bear his name and face – but this development was clearly a serious blow to the notion that there was a single 'kingdom of the English', and raised the prospect that Wessex, Mercia and Northumbria might once again go their separate ways.[36]

With Edgar ruling north of the Thames, his supporters were swiftly restored to power. The dowager queen, Eadgifu, regained her confiscated estates, and the exiled churchmen were recalled. Dunstan, returning from Ghent, not only resumed his position as abbot of Glastonbury, but was also promoted to the rank of bishop, a responsibility he had previously refused. In the first instance he succeeded Coenwald, the monastic bishop of Worcester, but soon afterwards the bishop of London died, and Dunstan succeeded him as well, holding the two sees in plurality.[37]

Once reinstated, these people presumably plotted ways of ending the regime of their opponents. Before the summer of 958, they scored a major victory when Archbishop Oda dissolved the marriage of Eadwig and Ælfgifu, on the grounds that the couple were too closely related. (She was his third cousin, once removed.) This was crucial, because the young king and queen had not yet produced any children; had they done so, it would have increased the likelihood that the partition of 957 would become permanent. Before he was able to find a new wife and father an heir, Eadwig died on 1 October 959 of unknown causes. By fair means or foul, he joined the ranks of those unfortunate young royals who died in the middle of a succession dispute, conveniently resolving the situation by making way for a rival. His body was taken to Winchester for burial in the city's New Minster, and his younger brother replaced him as ruler of Wessex. 'Chosen by both peoples as the rightful heir', says Dunstan's biographer, Edgar 'united the divided kingdoms beneath him under one sceptre'.[38]

In Edgar, the reformers had at last found a suitable king to advance their long-cherished project. His father had veered between indifference and hostility; his uncle had been cursed with ill health; his brother, whether personally sinful or not, had plainly been backed by the wrong people. But Edgar had been fostered as a child by Æthelstan Half-King and his wife, Ælfwynn, both strong supporters of reform. Now sixteen years old, and apparently in robust physical condition, he was ready to give the holy men at his court the fullest royal backing.[39]

One of his first acts on acceding to the whole kingdom was to appoint a new archbishop of Canterbury. Old Archbishop Oda, born to heathen parents, had gone to join the saints in June 958, and the late King Eadwig had appointed two successors, both of whom the reformers regarded as unsuitable. The first had frozen to death in the Alps while en route to Rome to receive his pallium from the pope. The second was still in post at the time of Edgar's accession, but was swiftly deposed and returned to his former position as bishop of Wells. Into his place the new king appointed Dunstan. The foremost advocate of reform, now probably in his early fifties, once expelled by his own kinsmen, exiled by two previous kings, was thereby elevated to the most powerful position in the English Church.[40]

Dunstan wasted little time in formalizing his appointment. Having sensibly waited until the summer to negotiate the Alpine passes, he was invested by the pope in September 960 and back in Canterbury the following month for his ordination. By the end of the same year he had probably selected the candidates to fill the two bishoprics he had vacated in order to take up the metropolitan seat. To London he appointed an obscure figure named Ælfstan, who served in that role for over thirty years, apparently without accomplishing anything worthy of note. To Worcester, by contrast, he nominated Oswald, who immediately announced himself as a great champion of reform. A nephew of the late Archbishop Oda, Oswald, like his uncle, had been professed as a monk at Fleury, the renowned centre of reformed monasticism on the River Loire. After several years of study there, he had returned home in 958 and joined the household of the archbishop of York, who had in turn recommended him to Dunstan for the position at Worcester. Like Dunstan, Oswald was revered as a saint after his death, and his deeds were celebrated in a biography, which has survived.[41]

It is at this juncture, sadly, that Dunstan himself suddenly recedes from view. His own biographer, the mysterious 'B', parted company with the new archbishop on their return journey from Rome, and went to join the household of the archbishop of Liège. We can see from other sources that Dunstan continued to play a leading role in both ecclesiastical and secular politics – he appears in almost every one of Edgar's charters at the head of the list of witnesses – but with 'B's departure the up-close-and-personal account of his career comes to an end.[42]

Powerful as Dunstan was, however, his influence at court had already been partially eclipsed by that of his former pupil, Æthelwold. The abbot of Abingdon had apparently acted as tutor to Edgar at some point during his boyhood, perhaps during the reign of his brother. In an account he wrote himself, Æthelwold describes how the king had visited Abingdon as a child, and had promised the abbot he would glorify the abbey after his accession. Edgar now fulfilled this promise, endowing the monastery with large amounts of land and money, and commanding the construction of a great church that was completed in just three years. Æthelwold was clearly a charismatic master who must have exercised a compelling hold over his pupils, including the teenage king. But he also possessed a strong authoritarian streak. His biographer describes how, on one occasion, he punished a monk who had presumed to do *too much* work in the abbey's kitchen by ordering him to plunge his hand into a cauldron of boiling water.[43]

Before the new church at Abingdon was complete, Æthelwold was in a position to administer punishment on a much grander scale. In November 963 Edgar promoted him to become bishop of Winchester; Dunstan, in his capacity as archbishop of Canterbury, performed the consecration ceremony. This meant that the three richest sees in the kingdom – Canterbury, Worcester and Winchester – were now in the hands of ardent reformers. Æthelwold's ardour, however, was more intense than that of either Dunstan or Oswald. The archbishop, as we've seen, had tolerated the presence of secular clerks at Glastonbury, a decision that had prompted Æthelwold to depart and establish his own purely monastic house at Abingdon. Once installed as bishop of Winchester, therefore, Æthelwold was unwilling to accept a cathedral that was staffed by secular priests. According to his biographer, the canons at the Old Minster were wicked, proud and insolent men, and led such scandalous lives that they could not even correctly celebrate Mass. 'They married wives illicitly, divorced them, and took others; they were constantly given to gluttony and drunkenness.' As soon as he took up his post, Æthelwold asked Dunstan to obtain papal authority for their expulsion, and by February 964 he had received the necessary permission. He also sought the backing of the king, and Edgar obliged by sending some of his thegns to enforce the pope's order. They presented the offending priests with an ultimatum: take the habit, and lead chaste lives, or leave immediately. 'Stricken with terror', says Æthelwold's biographer, 'and detesting the monastic life', the priests departed. The bishop replaced them with monks from Abingdon.[44]

This was just the beginning of Æthelwold's house-cleaning exercise. The same year he drove the clerks from Winchester's New Minster, founded by Edward the Elder, and introduced the Benedictine Rule to the city's nunnery, the Nunnaminster, founded by Alfred's queen, Ealhswith. Nor were his efforts confined to Winchester. It was also in 964 that the bishop appointed new abbots to the minsters at Milton Abbas in Dorset and Chertsey in Surrey, who carried out similar reformations. The following spring, Edgar summoned a great assembly to coincide with Easter. The *Life of St Oswald* describes how the king was attended by the ealdormen and thegns from all his territories, his bishops, including Dunstan, Æthelwold and Oswald, and a great number of abbots and abbesses, along with their monks and nuns. In the midst of their company, Edgar 'ordered more than forty monasteries to be established with monks'. The king, says Oswald's biographer, loved monks like dear sons, and honoured them as brothers, but held clerics in contempt. This, he explained, was because Edgar had been tutored by Æthelwold, who was now his principal adviser. 'Æthelwold urged the king above all to expel the clerics from the monasteries and bestow them on our order.'[45]

The fact that Edgar is said to have ordered the establishment of *more than* forty monasteries suggests that this was not an arbitrary target, but that he had a list of specific houses in mind. Oswald, for example, in a personal interview with the king, was given the choice of several sites, including the ancient minsters at Ely and St Albans. His biographer describes Ely as 'the place of the beloved abbess, St Æthelthryth', in reference to the former Northumbrian queen who had founded it three centuries earlier. The reformers knew the early history of such houses because they had read about them in the pages of Bede's *Ecclesiastical History*. But they failed to appreciate that the monasticism in the age described by Bede had been a great deal more eclectic than it was in their own much narrower conception. In Bede's great work they saw a golden age in which every minster had once been a model Benedictine community, and they were determined to restore all of them to this imagined pristine state.[46]

In the years that followed, therefore, lots of monasteries were re-founded in accordance with the king's order. Oswald declined the royal offer of Ely and St Albans and chose instead to set up a new monastery at Ramsey in the East Midlands. In his own West Midlands diocese his biographer credits him with the re-establishment of seven older houses, and he was certainly responsible for those at Pershore, Evesham and Winchcombe. Dunstan's contribution seems to have been rather less spectacular: William of Malmesbury, writing in the twelfth century, claims that the archbishop re-founded Westminster and Malmesbury itself, and alleges he drove out the existing secular clerks in order to do so. But both Dunstan and Oswald may have shown greater restraint than Æthelwold in dealing with established clerical communities. In Oswald's case, he left the clerks in his cathedral at Worcester in place, and created a new house in the city for his fellow monks.[47]

The elemental force behind the re-establishment of the monasteries was Æthelwold. Besides his obvious passion for the project, the bishop also had the advantage of vast personal wealth, thanks to Edgar's earlier generosity. It was Æthelwold, in the end, who undertook the re-foundation of Ely, having purchased the site from the king at considerable expense. 'He renovated the place as it deserved,' says his biographer, 'giving it monastic buildings, and enriching it lavishly with possessions in land.' The restoration of Ely had been an ambition of Archbishop Oda, but his death in 958 had derailed the plan at an early stage. Perhaps because of his viking ancestry, Oda had been anxious to reintroduce Christian communities into the Danelaw, and this was a mission that Æthelwold shared. Besides Ely, he also re-established monasteries in East Anglia at Crowland, Thorney and St Neots. Another ruined minster in the same region, known in Bede's time as Medeshamstede, was bought by the bishop and rededicated to St Peter. He rebuilt it on such a scale that it resembled a royal *burh*, and so in time became known as Peterborough.[48]

As the number of monasteries began to multiply, Æthelwold took it upon himself to tour them all, laying down the standards of behaviour he expected. ('The obedient he encouraged by words to advance the good,' says his biographer, 'the foolish he corrected with lashes to make them depart from evil.') As he made his way around the country, praising and chastising, the bishop must have realized that there was a fundamental problem.

Although all the new abbots and abbesses were sworn to follow the Benedictine Rule to the letter, there were points of difference on how the rule ought to be interpreted. To Æthelwold's mind this was a dangerous state of affairs that threatened to bring the whole enterprise into disrepute. He must have conveyed his concerns to Edgar, who responded by commanding all the churchmen in his kingdom to come to Winchester, so that the problem could be resolved in a synod. After much deliberation, the assembly agreed on the customs they should adopt, aided by monks who had come especially from Fleury and Ghent to advise on the best practice. All present solemnly swore that in future there should be 'one uniform observance'. Æthelwold wrote up their conclusions in a document known as the *Regularis Concordia* (Agreement on the Rule), and had it distributed to all monasteries in the form of a small book.[49]

Despite the involvement of monks from the leading continental houses, the new agreement differed from the European norm in the central role it accorded to the king and his family. The Winchester assembly had repeated the fundamental tenet of reform that secular interference in monastic affairs was a deplorable evil, and forbidden abbots and abbesses on pain of anathema from acknowledging the overlordship of laymen – 'a thing which might lead to utter loss and ruin, as it did in times past'. But the assembled churchmen had immediately qualified this statement by adding that monasteries should actively place themselves under the protection of the king and queen. Five years into his reign, Edgar had married a noblewoman named Ælfthryth, a close confidante of Æthelwold, who had perhaps had a hand in arranging their match. As the prologue of the *Regularis Concordia* explains, while the king was to be the shepherd and defender of monks, he had wisely decided that Queen Ælfthryth 'should be the protectress and fearless guardian of the communities of nuns'.[50]

In return for their protection, the king and queen were to be constantly in the prayers of every monk and nun. The *Concordia* required that psalms and collects be said repeatedly, day and night,

23. An illustration from an eleventh-century copy of the *Regularis Concordia*, showing King Edgar flanked by St Dunstan and St Æthelwold.

for the well-being of the royal couple, 'and not chanted at excessive speed'. These prayers would be effective because they proceeded from the lips of the sexually pure. In 966 Edgar presented the monks of New Minster in Winchester with an elaborate charter of re-foundation, which survives in the original. Produced in the form of a book, it opens with a picture of the king, flanked by Mary and St Peter, presenting the charter to Christ (colour picture 22). Its text, written entirely in letters of gold, was doubtless drafted by Æthelwold, but purports to be the voice of Edgar himself. It justifies the decision to expel the secular clerks not only from New Minster but from other monasteries across his kingdom on the grounds of their worthlessness.

Because these men were sinful, says the king, their prayers availed him nothing.[51]

As the lavish portrait of Edgar in the New Minster charter suggests, Æthelwold sponsored an artistic revival at Winchester. The *Benedictional of St Æthelwold*, a book of blessings composed for the bishop's own use, is often described as the finest illustrated manuscript of the entire Anglo-Saxon era. He also encouraged the translation of Latin texts into English, just as King Alfred had done, with the aim of bringing greater religious knowledge to the laity. At Edgar's request he personally translated the Rule of St Benedict, explaining in his preface that he thought it a very sensible thing for unlearned laymen to understand its contents, 'that they may more zealously serve God, and have no excuse that they were driven to err by ignorance'.[52]

In all their endeavours, a key concept for Æthelwold and his fellow reformers was uniformity. That is most evident from their production of the *Regularis Concordia*, but it is also apparent in the texts that Æthelwold and his fellow scholars worked on at Winchester. The illustrations in his manuscripts became the basis for the so-called Winchester Style of illumination, which was taken up in other reformed monasteries. The handwriting they used was strictly controlled. For Latin texts they employed the pure 'Caroline' style developed by earlier reformers at the court of Charlemagne, whereas for English translations they used a different, insular script. Even the language itself was regulated and standardized, so that each Latin word had only one permissible English equivalent. A more varied vocabulary, which left choice to the individual translator, could lead only to confusion and error.[53]

It is very likely that the reformers' pursuit of uniformity had a profound impact on the structures of royal government – one which would endure for centuries. In the preface to his translation of the Benedictine Rule, Æthelwold criticized the king's older brother for partitioning the realm in 957: Eadwig, 'through the ignorance of childhood, had dispersed his kingdom and divided its unity'. It is probably no coincidence that during the period when men like Æthelwold and Dunstan were dominating royal counsels, there was a determined attempt to standardize the king's administration by exporting the ancient institutions of Wessex to more recently conquered areas. Shires, which had been a familiar feature of West Saxon government for centuries, were almost certainly introduced into the Midlands in this period. Focused on the *burhs* established by his ancestors half a century earlier, they were accorded names like Leicestershire, Staffordshire, Nottinghamshire and Northamptonshire. It is in Edgar's legislation that we hear for the first time of shire courts, presided over by the local ealdorman and the local bishop.[54]

It is also at this same moment that a standardized form of lower court appears. Since the start of the tenth century, English kings had been increasingly keen to involve themselves in the administration of local justice, but had not enjoyed much success, for the right to hold courts and collect fines had been given away whenever their predecessors had made grants of land. From the mid-tenth century, however, we start to see local courts whose head-men answered directly to the king. Sometimes the districts these courts served were ancient, but in other cases they were new creations, made up of precisely one hundred hides, and hence known as 'hundreds'. Edgar laid down that they had to assemble every four weeks.[55]

All this order and uniformity must have been pleasing to the king and his ecclesiastical advisers, and doubtless brought benefits to many of his lesser subjects. Others, though, must have had reason to lament the increasing royal emphasis on regulation and religious discipline. When a plague ravaged the kingdom in 962, Edgar and Dunstan interpreted it as an expression of divine displeasure, brought about by people withholding their dues to the Church, and together they commanded that in future all men, rich and poor, must render their tithes 'with all gladness and with all willingness'. Æthelwold, to enforce the strict seclusion of monks, nuns and laymen in Winchester, had the city divided into distinct zones, separated by walls or hedges, a scheme that involved the diversion of rivers, the demolition of houses, and the forcible relocation of some existing residents. When the zealous bishop decided in 971 to translate the bones of his ninth-century predecessor, St Swithun, to a new tomb in the cathedral, he made every citizen of Winchester, noble and slave alike, process barefoot for three miles to meet the body. As Edgar's reign wore on, Benedictine ideas were being extended beyond the walls of the cloisters and into the world at large.[56]

And who would refuse to participate, knowing that the godly men in charge could call upon the authority of the king? The *Anglo-Saxon Chronicle* has virtually nothing to say about the secular politics of Edgar's reign, so we have no specific knowledge of his military exploits. Bishop Oswald's biographer, however, describes the king as 'mighty in arms, exulting in sceptres and diadems, and regally protecting the laws of the kingdom with militant authority'. From the beginning of the eleventh century, if not before, Edgar was being accorded the Latin adjective *pacificus*, traditionally translated as 'peaceable', yet there was clearly nothing pacifist about him. The citizens of Winchester had witnessed the fate of the clerks who were forcibly ejected from the cathedral by royal agents in 964. When the people of Thanet displeased him in 969 (by robbing some merchants from York, according to a much later chronicler), the king responded by ordering the whole island to be ravaged. Edgar, says Oswald's biographer, 'trampled under his feet all the proud necks of his enemies' and the *Anglo-Saxon Chronicle* remembered him as a 'dispenser of treasure to warriors'. According to another contemporary author, writing in the 970s, the king ordered that thieves and robbers were to be punished by having their eyes put out, their ears ripped off, their nostrils carved open and their hands and feet removed, before being scalped and left in the open fields at night to be eaten by wild beasts and birds. With all this in mind, *pacificus* is probably better translated as 'peacemaker'. Like the nineteenth-century gun of the same name, Edgar kept the peace through the threat of deadly force.[57]

Fearsome as he was, there were limits to the king's power, and the extent to which uniformity could be imposed by royal fiat. The re-establishment of Benedictine monasticism was very much a southern phenomenon. Although several houses were re-founded in the Danelaw, they were clustered in the East Midlands near Peterborough and Ely. North of the River Welland, into the territory of the Five Boroughs, no religious houses were restored. When Oswald of Worcester, who was promoted to become archbishop of York in 971, attempted to revive St Wilfrid's decayed monastery at Ripon, the project ended in failure.[58] In terms of royal government, too, the geographical extent was similar. Local assemblies that were called 'hundreds' in parts of Mercia and East Anglia were known in the Five Boroughs and in Northumbria as '*wapentakes*', a Scandinavian word that apparently referred to the custom of attendees signalling their assent by brandishing their weapons. When it came to governing these northern areas, even an imperious king like Edgar had to show some discretion, and tolerate a degree of divergence in dealing with their inhabitants. 'It is my will', said the king in his final piece of legislation, 'that such good laws be in force among the Danes as they best prefer.'[59]

'Nevertheless', he added in his next utterance, measures for dealing with thieves were 'to be common to all the nation, whether Englishmen, Danes or Britons'. That uniformity remained the aspiration of Edgar and those around him is strongly indicated by his reform of the coinage. Before his accession, coins had been minted in the name of a single 'king of the English', but their design, weight and fineness had varied from region to region, according to the whim, skill or resources of individual moneyers. At some point towards the end of Edgar's reign, however, a comprehensive standardisation was imposed. From that moment on, all the coins struck within his realm, from the Channel coast to the River Tees, were the same size and purity, and bore an identical portrait of the king. The *Regularis Concordia* had spoken of 'one Rule and one country', and this was the numismatic equivalent: one kingdom, one coin.[60]

On his coins Edgar was always styled *Rex Anglorum*, but in his charters he was more ambitious, typically styled 'King of All

Britain'. His immediate predecessors, struggling to maintain their hold on Northumbria, appear to have been somewhat hesitant in their use of such grandiose titles, but soon into Edgar's reign his scribes were according him the full panoply of accolades that had been applied to Æthelstan forty years earlier, including *imperator augustus*.[61] This was hardly surprising, for the monastic reformers who dominated his counsels drew much of their inspiration from the Carolingian Empire. Many of their ideas about state-enforced uniformity were derived from the councils and legislation of Charlemagne's son and successor, Louis the Pious. They were also in regular contact with churchmen at the court of King Otto I, who had ruled the eastern part of the fragmented empire – Germany, as it would later be known – since 936. When Otto also became king of Italy in 961, it seemed appropriate to revive for him the title that had been defunct for several decades, and at the start of the following year he was crowned as emperor in Rome by the pope.[62]

Perhaps it was this that inspired Edgar's advisers to plan a similar coronation for him just over a decade later. The king must have been crowned and anointed by Dunstan at the start of his reign in 959. But if he, like Otto, was an emperor – the ruler of the whole island of Britain – why should he not also be given a second ceremony, which emphasized his imperial status? Such seems to have been the thinking behind the event the reformers organized in 973. It took place in Bath, probably because the hot springs and Roman baths that gave the town its Old English name made it comparable to Aachen, where Charlemagne had built his palace, and where both Louis the Pious and Otto I had been crowned. The date of the ceremony was fixed for the holy feast of Pentecost, and the year itself may also have had religious significance. By 973, as the *Anglo-Saxon Chronicle* noted, Edgar had reached his thirtieth year. Thirty was the age at which Christ had begun his ministry, and the reformers had been developing the idea that Edgar, as king, possessed priestly or even quasi-divine powers. In his charter to the New Minster at Winchester, he was described as 'the vicar of Christ'.[63]

Accordingly, in the spring of 973 the order went out for everyone to assemble in Bath for 11 May. The *Life of St Oswald* describes the 'splendid and glorious' gathering of archbishops, bishops, abbots and abbesses, ealdormen, reeves and judges – 'everyone whom it is fitting to describe as the nobility of this wide and spacious realm'. Dunstan, as the senior of the two archbishops, performed the ceremony, and reportedly wept when it dawned on him that they 'did not deserve to have a ruler so humble and so wise'. Oswald himself, recently installed as archbishop of York, assisted in the anointing and the investiture. The order of the ritual had been adapted especially for the occasion, probably by Bishop Æthelwold. Whereas previous coronation services had spoken of the king ruling two or three nations, Edgar was referred to simply as *rex*: a single king of a single people. At the feast after the ceremony, Edgar, crowned with laurel, sat on a lofty throne, with Dunstan and Oswald seated either side of him.[64]

There was a clear sense in all of this of a new beginning – a king on the threshold of great things. Immediately after the coronation in Bath, Edgar went north to Chester, another location redolent of the Roman past, taking with him what the *Anglo-Saxon Chronicle* called 'his whole naval force'. Six other rulers reportedly came to meet him there, including the king of the Scots and the king of the Strathclyde Britons, and swore to be his allies on land and sea. By the twelfth century, historians were describing how these under-kings had demonstrated their subservience by rowing Edgar along the River Dee, in a boat that the king himself steered. This may be a later improvement, but it was based on the reality of the domination within Britain that Edgar had achieved. 'Kings and earls willingly submitted to him, and were subjected to whatever he wished', said the *Chronicle*, adding that he had brought them under his sway without resorting to battle. Things had greatly improved in Edgar's day, the same author averred, because he had exalted God's name and loved God's law. And now he had been officially elevated to imperial rank, who knew what feats the thirty-year-old king would go on to achieve? As they had anointed and crowned him in Bath, Dunstan and Oswald had drawn near to Edgar and said, 'May the king live forever!'[65]

Edgar died on 8 July 975, barely two years after his imperial coronation. 'He was suddenly snatched from the world', says the *Life of St Oswald*, 'having with him only a few thegns and companions'. His body was carried to Glastonbury, where it was buried alongside that of his father, King Edmund. It was an appropriate place for Edgar's story to end, for it was in Glastonbury that the revolution had begun almost three decades earlier, around the time of his birth, when his father had granted the run-down minster at Glastonbury to Dunstan, perhaps as a means of keeping the exasperating monk away from court. Since that time, the kingdom had been expanded, partitioned, reunited and finally reborn as a godly realm in which Dunstan and his disciples had exercised almost unfettered power and influence. It seems likely that the former abbot of Glastonbury, now archbishop of Canterbury, would have officiated at Edgar's funeral. If so, he would have had ample cause to reflect in his eulogy on the transformation that he and his fellow reformers had wrought in the space of a single, truncated royal lifetime.[66]

But with Edgar gone, the reformers had lost their champion and protector – the Good Shepherd, as they called him in the *Regularis Concordia*, who would defend them from the savage maws of the wicked. 'At his death,' says Oswald's biographer, 'the entire kingdom was shaken. Bishops were disturbed, ealdormen were angry, monks were struck with fear, the people terrified.' Even as the Peacemaker was being lowered into the ground at Glastonbury, the country was collapsing into civil war.[67]

9

THE ILL-COUNSELLED
KING

Æthelred the Unready and the Fear
of Apocalypse

I t was apparently just days after his birth, on the occasion of
his baptism, that Æthelred the Unready revealed himself to
be a wrong'un. We do not know where or when the
ceremony took place, but William of Malmesbury informs us that
it was performed by Archbishop Dunstan, in the company of
other bishops, and presumably with the proud parents King Edgar
and Queen Ælfthryth also in attendance. At the moment that the
newest addition to the royal family was immersed in the font,
says Malmesbury, 'he interrupted the sacrament by opening his
bowels', much to Dunstan's dismay. 'By God and His Mother,'
the archbishop exclaimed, 'he will be an indolent man!'

This comical scene requires the immediate caveat that it
probably didn't happen. Malmesbury was writing more than a
hundred years after Æthelred's death, and appears to have borrowed
the idea of a ruler committing a baptismal faux pas from the
story of Constantine Copronymus, an eighth-century Byzantine
emperor who, as his byname suggests, was alleged to have done
exactly the same thing. But the tale, tall as it is, demonstrates
how wretched the memory of Æthelred had become by
Malmesbury's day. 'Indolent' is only one of several possible
translations of *ignavus*, the word allegedly used by Dunstan to

describe the infant king. It also conveys implications of cowardice and ignobility, and earlier in the same passage, Malmesbury attributes both these flaws to Æthelred. The king's life, we are told, was cruel, pitiable and disgraceful. He was an accomplice to murder, a coward who fled from danger, a wastrel who died a miserable death.[1]

Curiously, in this long litany of criticism, the one thing that Malmesbury does *not* accuse Æthelred of being is 'unready'. The king's famous nickname appears to have been a slightly later invention, first recorded in Latin in the late twelfth century, and not mentioned in English until the early 1200s, when it was written as *unræd*. In this original form it indicated not a lack of readiness, but a lack of good counsel (OE *rædas*). It was clearly a pun on Æthelred's own name, which meant 'noble counsel', and for some this is enough to suggest it may have been coined earlier, perhaps even during his own lifetime. There is certainly other evidence that some of the king's contemporaries considered him to have been poorly advised.[2]

Æthelred's exceedingly poor reputation was founded on the fact that during his reign the vikings had returned to England, and he had proved unequal to the task of resisting them. The country was subjected to repeated waves of devastation, leading to social upheaval and suffering on a scale to rival the tumults of the late ninth century. But whereas in that earlier period the situation had been retrieved by the heroic Alfred, his great-great-grandson failed to provide similar leadership. Under Æthelred, people feared the Apocalypse was close to hand, and felt that the king's own actions were making matters worse. His government was perceived to be not only incompetent, but onerous, intrusive and unjust. As his rule wore on, people began to contemplate removing him, even if it meant siding with his enemies, and his reign concluded with an outright Danish conquest.

Æthelred nevertheless ruled for thirty-eight years, making his reign one of the longest in Anglo-Saxon history, comparable to those of Æthelbald and Offa. And unlike the rules of those eighth-century kings, and indeed those of his tenth-century predecessors, Æthelred's reign is very well documented, with a comparative abundance of both administrative and narrative sources. As a consequence, England comes into focus as never before, and we can perceive its people and its institutions with greater clarity. Even its name appears for the first time, apparently as a new coinage. One of Æthelred's ealdormen, Æthelweard, who translated the *Anglo-Saxon Chronicle* into Latin, explained to his readers that the country he lived in had once been called *Britannia*, but was now called *Anglia*. The ealdorman's friend, Ælfric of Eynsham, a prolific composer of works in English, referred to it as 'Engla-Lande'.³

This plethora of evidence also means that Æthelred himself is well illuminated, more so than any previous king apart from Alfred the Great. By carefully scrutinizing his charters, it is argued, we can perceive something of his inner character. And just as in recent years Alfred's 'greatness' has been subject to reassessment, so too the extent of Æthelred's ineptitude has been questioned. Traditionally the main source for his reign has been the *Anglo-Saxon Chronicle*, which provides a very negative picture – it is the basis, for example, of William of Malmesbury's account. But the *Chronicle* for Æthelred's reign was written after its disastrous conclusion, and as such is shot through with hindsight. Its author frequently attributes English military failures to the treachery or cowardice of individual commanders, when the reality may have been more complicated. Historians have therefore taken to treating the *Chronicle's* account with greater scepticism, and endeavoured to use a wider range of sources to create a more subtle, nuanced and sympathetic picture of the king himself.⁴

But whatever explanations or apologies are lodged for Æthelred, there is no denying that his reign got off to a terrible start with the murder of his brother.

King Edgar had not been as sexually continent as his reputation for piety might suggest – at least, not during the opening years of his reign. His marriage to Queen Ælfthryth had been celebrated five years after his accession, when he was about twenty-one, and she had given him two sons: Æthelred, who was the second-born, and an older brother named Edmund. But before this, Edgar had been romantically involved with other women, two of whom had also presented him with children. One of these relationships, with a lady named Wulfthryth, was not particularly problematic, because she had given birth to a girl; both mother and daughter had been packed off to live with the nuns at Wilton Abbey in Wiltshire, where the daughter, Edith, later became the abbess. Edgar's other teenage liaison, however, was with a woman called Æthelflæd, and was altogether more awkward, because it had resulted in a son. Whether or not Æthelflæd had been married to Edgar is unclear, as is her subsequent fate – she does not feature in any of the witness lists to his early charters. But her son, Edward, does appear in those same lists, showing he was present at his father's court in the mid-960s, alongside his younger half-brothers.[5]

The situation in the latter part of Edgar's reign was therefore a familiar one: a king who had sons by more than one woman, leading to uncertainty about which of them would succeed him. After his marriage to Ælfthryth in 964 there was a determined effort in certain quarters to promote her offspring as the only acceptable candidates. Ælfthryth was a close ally of Bishop Æthelwold of Winchester, who did all he could to bolster her position. In royal documents she was consistently dignified with the title *regina*, and she may have been the first ever English queen to be consecrated, during Edgar's imperial coronation at Bath. Very tellingly, in the ornate charter that Æthelwold had drawn up in 966 for the re-foundation of the New Minster in Winchester, Ælfthryth witnesses as 'the legitimate wife of the king', and her son, the infant Edmund, is styled 'the legitimate son of the aforesaid king'. By contrast, her stepson, Edward, who was also present, is described merely as 'begotten by the same king' and accorded a lower position in the list, despite being the elder of the two boys. It must have been distressing for Ælfthryth that Edmund subsequently died in 972, aged around five or six, but it made little difference to her plans for the succession, for in the meantime, at some point between 966 and 969, she had given birth to Æthelred, who assumed the position as his father's legitimate heir.[6]

But when King Edgar suddenly died in the summer of 975, there was a strong showing of support for Edward. Some of the magnates may have felt that, as the eldest son, he had the better right, or they may have reasoned that older was simply better from the point of view of political stability. Edward must have been a teenager by this point, perhaps as old as sixteen; Æthelred, by contrast, was still only a child, possibly as young as five. There were evidently heated arguments among royal counsellors about how to proceed, but after several days of wrangling they elected Edward. A decisive voice in breaking the deadlock must have been that of Archbishop Dunstan, who signalled his support for Edward by crowning him a short time later.[7]

Æthelred's supporters, however, were not prepared to let the matter rest, and in the months that followed the dispute spilled over into violence. The final years of Edgar's reign had seen mounting tensions not only over the issue of the succession, but over the impact of monastic reform. The king's unqualified support for the restoration of dozens of monasteries, a cause of great celebration for the reformers themselves, had led to many of his other subjects losing out. The most obvious victims were the secular clerks who had been expelled from certain long-established religious communities, some of whom came from powerful aristocratic families that resented the assault on their kinsmen. But the expansion of monasticism had also adversely affected a much wider section of society. In order to endow houses like Ely and Peterborough with large amounts of land, it had been necessary to persuade other people to part with it. Lots of laymen had been obliged to surrender estates on the grounds that they had been usurped from these monasteries in the distant past. Sometimes they received compensation, but from their subsequent complaints it is clear that often they felt it was inadequate. Many of the bargains struck appear to have been forced, and sometimes the charters that the reformers produced to assert their claims were forged. Edgar, with his eyes fixed only on God, and his ears attentive only to the counsels of the reformers, had seen no injustice in this. And, given his reputation for keeping the peace with extreme prejudice, who would have the temerity to contradict him?[8]

But with Edgar now gone, and replaced by a boy in his early teens, these grievances erupted. In various parts of the country, monasteries came under attack, and their monks and abbots were driven out. According to the author of the *Life of St Oswald*, who provides the only detailed account of these years, they could be seen wandering the roads, penniless and barefoot. Meanwhile, says the same author, the secular clerks were delighted, because the wheel had come full circle, and in some cases they were brought back into the communities from which they had earlier been expelled, along with their wives.[9]

Although this 'anti-monastic reaction' was probably spontaneous, it provided a convenient excuse for the disappointed supporters of Æthelred to strike at those who had backed the accession of his half-brother, Edward. The ealdorman of Mercia, Ælfhere, led and encouraged the mob that targeted a number of monasteries in the West Midlands, including Winchcombe, Evesham, Pershore and Deerhurst. These houses had been founded or restored by St Oswald himself, and were presumably singled out for attention because the archbishop had refused to back Æthelred. Meanwhile, the ealdorman of East Anglia, Æthelwine – a supporter of Edward – raised an army to resist the anti-monastic attacks if they should spread eastwards into his own lands. Attempts to calm the situation by summoning a royal assembly failed. When Æthelwine spoke up in defence of the monks, the less exalted men present shouted him down. One of them verbally abused the ealdorman's brother, who responded by having his heckler killed. Everywhere, says the *Life of St Oswald*, there was 'dissension and trouble, which neither the bishops nor the leading men in ecclesiastical and secular affairs was able to assuage'. Sedition ('that detestable whore') had set province against province, people against people, ealdorman against ealdorman, and king against king.[10]

It was this factional fighting that eventually led to Edward's murder. In 978, by which time he must have been in his late teens, the king went to visit Æthelred, who was staying with his mother, Queen Ælfthryth, at Corfe in Dorset. He went, says Oswald's biographer, with only a small number of soldiers, arriving in the evening. The *Anglo-Saxon Chronicle* gives the date as 18 March. As he approached the royal residence, Edward was met by a number of magnates, whose names we are not told, then suddenly surrounded by armed men. They grabbed hold of the king, pulled him from his horse and killed him. His body was carried to nearby Wareham and buried without ceremony.[11]

Edward's martyrdom, as it quickly came to be regarded, is sometimes treated like a perplexing murder mystery, but it does not require the mind of a Holmes or a Poirot to come up with a list of likely suspects. The blow that killed the king may have been dealt by an anonymous armed retainer, but the authors of his death were almost certainly the people who had been plotting against him even since his accession. Ealdorman Ælfhere of Mercia, as the orchestrator of the assaults on the monasteries, must surely have been part of the conspiracy. So too, in all likelihood, was the dowager queen. Modern historians tend to give Ælfthryth the benefit of the doubt, reacting against later medieval legends that cast her as the wicked stepmother, but it is difficult to imagine she was not privy to the scheme and did not sanction its execution. We may even suspect her long-term collaborator, the saintly Bishop Æthelwold, had some role to play. What is certain is that these three people were the ones who bene-fitted most directly and immediately from Edward's downfall. With his half-brother hidden in an unmarked grave, young Æthelred was elevated to become king in his place, and Ælfhere, Ælfthryth and Æthelwold ruled the kingdom as his regents.[12]

Reconciliation with Edward's supporters evidently took some time. The first year of Æthelred's reign came and went without him being crowned, quite possibly because both archbishops, Dunstan and Oswald, refused to conduct the ceremony until the body of his murdered brother had been recovered and given a proper burial. At length, in the spring of 979, Ealdorman Ælfhere rode to Wareham with a great crowd of people and ordered Edward's grave to be opened. The king's corpse (or at least a corpse that looked plausibly like him) was unearthed and found to be miraculously uncorrupted. Reverentially washed and dressed in new clothes, it was placed in a coffin and carried to Shaftesbury Abbey, where it was honourably reinterred, and soon venerated as that of a saint.[13]

This public act, which may have involved some show of penance on the part of Ælfhere and others, served to resolve the impasse: a few weeks later, on 4 May 979, Æthelred was finally crowned. The ceremony took place, as had become traditional, at Kingston-upon-Thames, but contained a recent innovation that emphasized the new king's obligations to his subjects. Before he was anointed and crowned, Æthelred was required to swear a threefold oath, pledging to protect the Church, to punish theft and wickedness, and to be just and merciful in his judgements. Previously these sentiments had been expressed during the coronation only as a petition to the king by his people, but since Edgar's imperial ceremony in 973 they had been recast as a royal promise, sworn by the king himself. At Æthelred's coronation in 979 they were further reinforced by a homily, preached in the vernacular by Archbishop Dunstan, instructing the young king in his duties.[14]

In the immediate wake of his coronation, Æthelred's counsels continued to be dominated by his mother, Ealdorman Ælfhere and Bishop Æthelwold. The bishop, in particular, stands out in both the administrative and narrative sources as the power behind the throne, ensuring that his young charge pursued the pro-monastic policy of his father. His pre-eminence is apparent in his biographer's account of the rededication of Winchester's Old Minster. The cathedral had been modified several times since its foundation in the seventh century, but was not greatly enlarged until Æthelwold's day. After his translation of the body of St Swithun in 971, the bishop had commissioned a huge extension, doubling the size of the church by adding a towering 'west-work' of a type that was fashionable in Germany. By 980 the project was complete, and Æthelwold arranged a magnificent celebration. Eight other prelates were present, including Dunstan, as well as a host of abbots, thegns and ealdormen, and of course the young King Æthelred. In the course of two days of festivities, says the *Life of St Æthelwold*, 'all who had previously seemed his enemies, standing in God's path, were suddenly made, as it were, sheep instead of wolves: they revered him with extraordinary affection, and, lowering their necks to his knee and humbly kissing his hand, commended themselves in all things to the prayers of the man of God'.[15]

Besides emphasizing his power, Æthelwold's investment in architecture is a useful reminder that the peace of Edgar's reign had brought great prosperity. This was most obvious in the case of the splendid new stone churches built by the reformers themselves at re-founded monasteries, but it was also apparent in many other ways besides. Consider, for instance, what was happening in the *burhs*. When they had been laid out by King Alfred and his children, Edward the Elder and Æthelflæd, they had been intended to function as fortresses, and for the first half of the tenth century they had retained that aspect, with interiors divided into large military compounds belonging to a handful of different aristocratic commanders, within which the buildings were widely dispersed. But from the middle of the century, the appearance of the *burhs* began to alter, as merchants and manufacturers moved in from the countryside. In a written survey of Winchester produced in Æthelred's reign, we see Tanner Street, Shieldmaker Street and Fleshmonger (i.e. Butcher) Street. In archaeology, too, we see evidence in Winchester and elsewhere of the large aristocratic enclosures fragmenting, and the creation of regularly spaced plots that fronted onto the street, which were obviously the shops of merchants and artisans. York had such plots before the mid-tenth century; in Oxford they were in existence before the century's end. In many cases, suburbs were created outside the walls to accommodate the more noisy and noisome industries, or to facilitate the holding of regular markets. These *burhs* and cities still had a long way to go before they would become fully urban, but the late tenth century was the moment of urban take-off.[16]

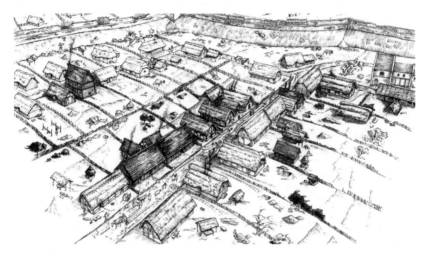

24. An illustration, based on excavations, of a corner of Winchester in the late tenth century, showing how the *burh* was being divided up into regular commercial plots.

Similar transformations were occurring in the countryside. For centuries the rural economy had remained essentially unchanged. Great lords – kings, ealdormen, bishops and abbots – held vast estates, extending over dozens or even hundreds of square miles. Within these wide areas, people lived in settlements that were spread out and scattered – isolated hamlets, or clusters consisting of a few adjacent farmsteads. The farmers owed renders of produce to their overlord, or sometimes rent, but beyond that their existence was essentially free and independent.

But by Æthelred's day, a new form of lordship was on the rise, and with it a new type of settlement. The great lords were splitting up their huge estates and granting much smaller ones to their dependants – compact lordships that might consist of only two or three square miles of land. As a result, farmers were persuaded or compelled to move closer together, forming communities that can reasonably be considered as villages. This offered greater opportunities for co-operation – closer-knit communities could club together to purchase plough-beasts, and lords might tempt them with new technology in the form of a watermill, so that corn did not have to be laboriously ground by hand. In many cases these new villages were named after the individual who had created them. Woolstone in Berkshire, for example, is a contraction of Wulfric's Tun ('the estate of Wulfric').[17]

The speed and extent of this transformation varied greatly from one region to another. In the central parts of Mercia and Wessex it was happening on some estates as early as the ninth century, while in Kent, East Anglia and the western parts of Wessex, there is no sign of it even in the eleventh. In overall terms, however, it is once again the mid-tenth century that seems to have witnessed a crucial period of acceleration. In documents, it can be seen in the spike in grants of land made by kings to their thegns, or in the leases recorded by Bishop Oswald, who rewarded his relatives and dependants with estates in the countryside around Worcester. In archaeology it can be seen in the sudden reappearance of domestic architecture. The dwellings built in the English countryside in the eighth and ninth centuries have left no discernible trace, but from the mid-tenth century we start to see the remains of substantial buildings that must have been the residences of prosperous landowners. Typically laid out as long ranges, they were internally divided to form halls, chambers and even indoor privies. In some cases they boasted an upstairs as well, which seems to have been a novelty. The *Anglo-Saxon Chronicle* reports how in 978 all the king's counsellors were injured, in some cases fatally, when the first floor of the building they were standing in collapsed. Only Dunstan, who happened to be providentially perched on a beam, escaped entirely unscathed.[18]

If a two-storey house with en-suite facilities was one aspiration for a member of England's newly emergent gentry, the other was his own personal church. Private churches suddenly appear in both the written and archaeological record from the 940s.

Almost always built of wood at this date, they were often sited next to the lord's residence, but also used by the other members of the local community. Previously the spiritual needs of ordinary people had been met by priests from the nearest minster, who travelled from place to place to perform church services. Now, increasingly, these needs were met by a priest who resided permanently in the village. A novel emphasis on the importance of being buried in sacred ground led to the simultaneous emergence of churchyards. As the minsters were reformed in the late tenth century and became more closed-up and cloistered, the foundations of the parish system were being laid.[19]

The causes of these social and economic transformations were multiple, and are therefore hard to pinpoint. Peace, as mentioned above, was an obvious precondition. There would have been little point in building ostentatious houses and churches during the viking raids and invasions of the ninth century, or during the long war of attrition between the English and the Danes in the opening decades of the tenth. But conditions in southern England were stable from the 940s onwards, and from 954 the same was true in Northumbria. As the kings of Wessex had extended their dominion across the country, there were huge opportunities for the powerful and ambitious to reorder the landscape to their own advantage.

Another factor, allied to the return of peace, was a rising population. In earlier centuries farming in England had been predominantly about the rearing of pigs, sheep and cattle, and only a small amount of land was used for the more arduous task of growing crops. But in places where villages had started to nucleate, more and more of the surrounding commons began to be converted to agriculture, a development that would eventually form the famous 'open fields' of the later Middle Ages. Whenever cereal production has risen in pre-industrial societies, it was because the population was increasing. More mouths to feed meant that the land had to be worked more intensively.[20]

A final, more specific spur to the economy during Edgar's reign was a sharp increase in the amount of coin in circulation, possibly as a result of new silver mines being opened up in Germany in the 960s. Although not as large as the massive spike that had triggered the boom of the late seventh century, its effects must have been broadly similar, and it implies that international trade was once again flourishing, with German silver being exchanged for exported English goods. Both periods had seen the rapid expansion of monasticism, and with it the development of more efficient and intelligent estate management. It was in the late tenth century that the Old English word *rice*, which had previously meant 'powerful', took on the new meaning of 'wealthy'. To be powerful in Æthelred's England was to be *rich*.[21]

Of course, even in an age of prosperity, there were plenty of people who remained poor. Slaves had been an integral part of Anglo-Saxon society from the very beginning, and may have accounted for as much as thirty per cent of the entire population. In contrast to the free farmers who kept them, such people had no rights at all, and could be punished by their masters with branding and castration. Ælfric of Eynsham, as well as supplying the earliest instance of the word 'England', also furnishes us with the first description of the life of an English slave. In a passage written from the imagined perspective of an unfree ploughman, he explains how he must rise at dawn and labour all day for fear of his master, however harsh the weather, until an acre or more has been ploughed. 'Oh, oh, the work is hard,' he laments, 'yes, the work is hard, because I am not free.'[22]

By the tenth century, there was also a growing class whose freedom was being steadily eroded. Geburs, as they were known, were originally the people who worked the intensively farmed estates of major landowners. Notionally free, they were nonetheless required to labour for their lord on several days each week, as well as supplying him with renders of food. Essentially they were the equivalent of later medieval serfs, performing services that we still tend to describe as 'feudal' – a fact that may surprise those who are accustomed to thinking of serfs and feudalism as bad things introduced only as a result of the Norman Conquest. The truth is they were present in late Anglo-Saxon England,

25. A ploughman, from an early eleventh-century English calendar.

and their incidence was growing, as ambitious new landlords sought to increase the profits from their estates. The number of geburs varied from place to place, with more in central parts of Wessex and Mercia, and no trace in East Anglia, but the overall trend was upwards. For every winner in the dynamic new economy, there were lots of people being made to work harder, with fewer rights, and less to show in the way of reward.[23]

At the time of his coronation in 979, Æthelred was no more than thirteen, and perhaps as young as nine – a child who could be trusted to do the bidding of his older and wiser counsellors. But as the king advanced into his teens he began, predictably, to rebel against the authority of his regents. Their grip on power was weakened in 983 with the death of Ealdorman Ælfhere, and then collapsed entirely in August the following year with the passing of the bishop of Winchester. 'Our dearest Bishop Æthelwold,' said Æthelred, 'whose industry and pastoral care ministered not only to my interest but that of everyone in the country.' This, however, was in a charter issued nine years later, after more mature reflection. At the time, in 984, the teenage king clearly relished his new-found freedom, and dispensed with the remaining members of the bishop's circle. His mother, Ælfthryth, immediately ceases to witness royal charters, indicating that she had been removed from court. A few months later, in early 985, the brother-in-law and successor of Ealdorman Ælfhere was sent into exile. It was probably in that same year that Æthelred celebrated his assumption of personal power by getting married. His wife, Ælfgifu, was the daughter of Thored, ealdorman of York.[24]

As his marriage implies, Æthelred was not only rejecting the control of his childhood mentors, but embracing the counsel of new ones. These men were part of a faction that had resented the regime of Bishop Æthelwold, and they wasted little time in seeking their revenge. As had been the case during the reign of Edward the Martyr, revenge was expressed by targeting the monasteries that were favoured by their rivals. When, for example, Æthelwold's beloved monastery at Abingdon lost its abbot in 984, the king sold the succession to the brother of the most prominent of his new advisers, Ealdorman Ælfric of Hampshire, who proceeded to reward his followers with the abbey's estates. There were similar expropriations at other houses associated with the bishop, including the Old Minster in Winchester, with both the king and his new associates enriching themselves at the expense of the monks. When the bishop of Rochester ejected a royal favourite who had been given one of the church's estates, Æthelred responded by sending an army to lay waste to the diocese. This reportedly drew condemnation from Dunstan, but the archbishop was very elderly and died in 988. From that point on, there was no one to resist the king's authority.[25]

At least, not within England. But around the coasts of the kingdom, people were once again becoming alarmed at the sight of viking sails. It had been the proud boast of the *Anglo-Saxon Chronicle* that during Edgar's reign there had been peace across what it poetically called 'the gannet's bath', and that no enemy fleet had been able to prey on the English while the old king had lived. Soon after Æthelred's accession, however, the raids had resumed: from 980 onwards the *Chronicle* reports attacks on various towns and monasteries around the south coast. The ones that struck the West Country and Cheshire most probably emanated from Ireland, but the vikings who targeted Kent and Hampshire are likely to have come directly from Scandinavia

– something that had not been heard of for almost a century. As in the earlier era, this was perhaps because of increasing political competition within Scandinavia itself, but a more compelling reason was probably the renewed prosperity of England. Ambitious opportunists were once again being drawn across the North Sea by the prospect of rich and easy pickings.[26]

At first these raids were evidently small-scale: Southampton was sacked in 980 by a fleet of seven ships, and two years later Portland was devastated by only three. Something more serious evidently occurred in 988, the year of Dunstan's death, when enough vikings landed at Watchet in Somerset to engage the English in battle. The *Chronicle* names one particular Devonshire thegn who died in the fighting, and says many others were slain alongside him. But according to the *Life of St Oswald*, the outcome of the clash was nevertheless a glorious victory for the home team. 'Many of our own men fell,' the saint's biographer admitted, 'but far more of theirs.' In spite of the escalation, there was as yet no sense of an impending crisis.[27]

Then, in the summer of 991, a much larger force arrived from Scandinavia. The *Chronicle* says it numbered ninety-three ships, and names its leader as Olaf Tryggvason, an adventurous viking warlord who would later become king of Norway. They first landed at Folkestone in Kent, ravaging the town and the surrounding countryside, then made their way around the south-east coast, inflicting similar terror on the citizens of Sandwich and Ipswich. Eventually they paused at Maldon in Essex, making their camp on an island in the Blackwater Estuary. There they were confronted on 11 August by an army led by the local ealdorman, Byrhtnoth. Despite his advanced years, Byrhtnoth refused the invaders' demand for tribute, and a fierce battle ensued, commemorated in a long poem written soon after the event. It presents the ealdorman as being confident of victory, so much so that he graciously allowed his enemies to cross the causeway that linked their island to the mainland and form a battle line. His confidence, alas, proved to be misplaced, and the English were roundly defeated. Byrhtnoth himself was cut down, surrounded by his devoted retainers, whose loyalty to their fallen lord is the poem's leitmotif.[28]

Defeat at Maldon was a devastating blow to the English, as much psychological as physical. Ever since the days of King Alfred, their identity had been defined by military success against the Danes. The *Anglo-Saxon Chronicle* was a celebration of over a century of victories by Æthelred's illustrious forebears, and the king had recently reminded everyone of these earlier glories by naming his firstborn son Æthelstan. The Church had been telling Englishmen that their success was due not to their prowess, but to their piety, especially when it was expressed in the support of monastic reform. Things had improved greatly in King Edgar's reign, according to the *Chronicle*, because 'he exalted God's praise far and wide, and loved God's law'. The slaughter at Maldon shattered that self-confidence, and raised the troubling question of why God had allowed it to happen.[29]

The immediate consequence of the catastrophe is that it forced Æthelred to do what Byrhtnoth had refused to countenance, and pay the vikings to cease their plundering. The *Anglo-Saxon Chronicle* says that £10,000 was handed over at once, adding that this was done on the advice of Sigeric, the new archbishop of Canterbury. The disapproval of the *Chronicle's* anonymous author, writing with hindsight, is palpable – Sigeric's counsel is implicitly understood to be bad. That was certainly how William of Malmesbury understood it. Paying the Danes to go away, he averred, was 'a disgraceful precedent, unworthy of true men', and countless other commentators over the centuries have echoed his damning verdict. But offering tribute to the vikings when all else failed was a time-honoured expedient. As Æthelred's modern defenders have long observed, even Alfred resorted to buying off the Danes at the start of his career when his military efforts had miscarried.[30]

A crucial difference between Æthelred and Alfred, however, is that Alfred fought against his enemies *in person*. His biographer, Asser, famously described him at the Battle of Ashdown as fighting 'like a wild boar'. Æthelred, by contrast, was notably absent from the Battle of Maldon and almost every military engagement that followed. When, for example, it was decided in the following year to assemble every serviceable ship in London in order to confront the viking menace, the king took no part in the expedition, and instead entrusted its command to others. The result was a total fiasco, allegedly because Ealdorman Ælfric secretly tipped off the enemy that an attack was imminent, allowing them to escape, and then to inflict another great defeat on the English. Of course, there is nothing to say that the outcome would have been any different had Æthelred been present, but in medieval societies, rulers were expected to lead from the front. As William of Malmesbury says quite correctly in his diatribe against Æthelred, 'there is great force in the presence of a general in battle, and his witnessed courage in such circumstances'. Personal participation exposed medieval kings to great risk, and many of them paid with their lives, but not to lead an army in person ran the opposite risk of being branded a coward. It seems likely that such accusations were being levelled at Æthelred in the 990s, for towards the end of the decade they were countered in a tract written by Ælfric of Eynsham. A king's life, Ælfric argued, was too precious to be exposed to the danger of battle, and he cited examples of biblical rulers and Roman emperors who had successfully delegated military command to others. But academic appeals to historical precedent are unlikely to have impressed a warrior elite who admired the kind of personal valour praised in the Maldon poem. The very existence of Ælfric's tract suggests that many of the Englishmen called upon to fight against the vikings were puzzled and angered by the absence of their king.[31]

The defeat at Maldon, and the failure of his deputies to avenge it, convinced Æthelred that he had been pursuing the wrong course. At Pentecost 993 he summoned an assembly to Winchester and announced that he had made a terrible error in departing from the wise policies of Bishop Æthelwold. Ever since the latter's death nine years earlier, he explained to his audience, the kingdom had been suffering calamities that were an obvious

sign of divine displeasure. The king set all this down a few weeks
later in a charter in favour of Æthelwold's abbey at Abingdon,
in which he blamed his bad behaviour on youthful ignorance,
and the greed of men who had misled him. In particular he
blamed Ealdorman Ælfric, who had personally profited from the
misappropriation of Abingdon's estates. According to the *Chronicle*,
Ælfric had been responsible for the military debacle the previous
year, and the Abingdon charter heralds his fall from grace. His
son, Ælfgar, was blinded on the king's orders, and a number of
other thegns who had been prominent in the late 980s suddenly
cease to witness royal documents.[32]

The Abingdon charter, in fact, reveals that a wholesale
revolution had taken place at Æthelred's court in the spring of
993. With the failure of his more recent advisers, those who had
been sidelined almost a decade earlier had seized the opportunity
to re-establish themselves in his good graces. Chief among them
was his mother, Ælfthryth, witnessing for the first time since her
exclusion from court almost nine years earlier. Besides the former
queen was her brother, Ordulf. Alongside the pair of them were
Ealdorman Æthelweard (later famous for his chronicle), his son,
Æthelmær, and a Mercian thegn named Ælfhelm who was
promoted to become ealdorman of Northumbria.[33]

What this new faction had in common was a commitment
to revive the policies of the late King Edgar – above all, a
commitment to monastic reform. In the Abingdon charter,
Æthelred promised to mend his ways, and restore the lands he
had taken from various monasteries. And over the next few years
he did just that, repeatedly stating in one charter after another
that he was sorry and wished to be purged of his sin. His tone,
in other words, was penitential, and this was very much the mood
of his court after 993. In the writings of intellectuals like Ælfric
of Eynsham, and also in charters and other documents, we find
repeated references to the end of the world being nigh, and the
urgent need for Christians to make amends. Such anxiety was
partly fuelled by the approaching millennium, for the Book of
Revelation had foretold that Satan would be unbound 1,000 years

after Christ's birth. The ravaging and burning of vikings suggested that the Apocalypse was indeed close to hand, and it was therefore felt to be essential for the king and his subjects to purify themselves, and to redouble their religious devotions. These years saw an almost frenzied enthusiasm in the production of religious texts, the building of new churches, and the translation of saints.[34]

They also witnessed a new approach to dealing with the vikings. After their victory at Maldon in 991 it seems that Olaf and his fleet had not returned to Scandinavia, but remained in England for the next three years, ravaging up and down the east coast. In September 994 they turned their attention to London, but met with unexpectedly stiff resistance. ('They suffered more harm and injury', says the *Anglo-Saxon Chronicle*, 'than they ever imagined any *burh*-dwellers would do to them.') Frustrated by their failure to take the city, the vikings switched to softer targets, and adopted a different strategy. Not only did they ravage the coasts of Kent, Essex, Hampshire and Sussex, says the *Chronicle*, but they also seized horses, 'and rode as widely as they wished', plundering, burning and killing.

The government, in response, appears to have offered no military resistance at all. Instead, Æthelred and his counsellors sought to negotiate with the invaders. They began, as before, by promising to pay them a large tribute, and to supply them with provisions, if they in return would cease their ravaging. The viking army accepted this offer and established a winter camp at Southampton, where the booty and supplies could be delivered to them as it was collected. But this was only the first part of the English plan. Once the army was settled, the king persuaded Olaf and the other viking leaders to visit him at the royal estate at Andover in Wiltshire – Ealdorman Æthelweard and the bishop of Winchester were sent to provide an escort, and left hostages with the viking fleet as a guarantee of good faith. When they arrived at Andover, says the *Chronicle*, the visitors were loaded with gifts and treated royally. Olaf, who had already been baptized as a Christian some years earlier, went through a confirmation ceremony, with Æthelred acting as his sponsor.[35]

The reason for this bonhomie and largesse was because, put simply, the English king wanted to purchase Olaf's army and keep it for himself. Rather than vainly trying to resist battle-hardened warriors whose main motivation was avarice, Æthelred and his counsellors had decided it would be better to retain some of them as a mercenary force, paying them the money that would otherwise have been obtained through violence, on the understanding that they would protect the kingdom from other predators. This attempt to turn poachers into gamekeepers was not entirely novel: Frankish kings had sometimes employed one viking army to fight against other, and it is even possible that the same approach had been tried on previous occasions in England. Although the *Anglo-Saxon Chronicle* lavishes praise on King Edgar, it contains one arresting criticism. 'He loved evil foreign customs,' it complains, 'and brought too firmly heathen manners within this land, and attracted hither foreigners, and enticed harmful people to this country.' Might this comment, which has long puzzled historians, indicate that Edgar too had been in the habit of recruiting Scandinavians to serve as mercenaries? If so, Æthelred's tactics in 994 would be another example of a reversion to the policies of his father's reign.[36]

The viking leaders at Andover accepted the king's proposal, and a treaty was drawn up, the text of which has survived. In return for £22,000 of gold and silver, Olaf and his associates, named as Jostein and Guthmund, promised to remain at peace with Æthelred, and to assist him against any hostile fleets that might attack his kingdom. Olaf, the *Chronicle* noted, was true to his word, and soon returned to Norway, where he successfully established himself as king, no doubt aided by his newly acquired riches. Most of his men, however, must have stayed behind in England. Under the terms of the treaty, Æthelred promised to keep them supplied with food as long as they remained in his service, and forgave them all the slaughter and destruction they had carried out before the peace had been agreed. No one, the king warned his English subjects, was to seek either compensation or revenge.[37]

By the start of 995, therefore, Æthelred was the employer of a Scandinavian fleet, perhaps still stationed at Southampton, and possibly numbering several thousand men. This was an unusual situation: in general, medieval kings did not attempt to maintain standing armies because to do so was prohibitively expensive. Æthelred had promised in the treaty to keep his new recruits supplied with food, and they doubtless made other demands on his pocket besides. It is worth considering, therefore, how the king raised the revenue and the provisions to keep his Scandinavian hirelings happy. What he had done, essentially, was to institutionalize plunder. By engaging Olaf's followers as mercenaries, he had stopped them seizing the goods of his subjects at sword-point, but undertaken to extract the same wealth himself by more peaceful means.[38]

To this end, the king built on the achievement of his tenth-century predecessors, who had created a uniform network of *burhs*, shires and hundreds, by introducing a new breed of royal official. The general term in Old English for a person with an administrative job was 'reeve', but it is only in Æthelred's reign that we first start to hear about reeves who were responsible for a whole shire: shire-reeves, or sheriffs. In later medieval literature – the tales of Robin Hood, for example – sheriffs are a byword for financial extortion, which is no surprise, because from the first a major part of their role appears to have been to extract money from people on the king's behalf. In Æthelred's reign, the evidence suggests that they were engaged in a protracted struggle with landowners over the profits of justice. When earlier kings had made grants of land, everyone involved had assumed that the right to hold courts and collect judicial fines would reside with the new owners. But Æthelred and his sheriffs were now arguing otherwise, and insisting that these revenues ought to be reserved to the king. The financial pressure on royal government, which must have been greatly exacerbated by the demands of the viking mercenaries, led Æthelred's new henchmen to demand money and supplies by any means they could devise.[39]

★

For a couple of years the agreement held and all was seemingly quiet. Probably in this time some of the vikings were dispersed, and billeted in towns and *burhs* across the country – the treaty of 994 anticipated that mercenaries would be mingling with and living alongside English communities. Others must have remained with their ships in Southampton. But, inevitably, these men eventually became bored and frustrated: a life of sitting around, living on subsidies, waiting for something to happen, hardly accords with their swashbuckling self-image. In 997 some of them rebelled, sailed around the coast of Devon and Cornwall, and went on the rampage. The following year they switched their attention to Dorset, raiding along the River Frome, and in 999 they went further east to Kent, sailing up the River Medway, seizing horses, and plundering wherever they pleased. According to the *Chronicle* the English response was characterized for the most part by cowardice and incompetence, though the king's efforts to assemble land and naval forces in Kent may have been more effective than the chronicler allows, for in the summer of the year 1000 the viking fleet withdrew from England and went to Normandy. But the next year they returned with greater fury, slaughtered lots of king's reeves and thegns in Hampshire, and then moved west to Devon, where they defeated an English army in battle.[40]

It must have been amply clear by this point that Æthelred's strategy of co-opting the vikings to defend his kingdom had failed. On their arrival in Devon in 1001, the attackers had been joined by a viking leader named Pallig, a mercenary who had evidently remained loyal to the king until this moment, and been richly rewarded with gold, silver and grants of land as a result. But now, says the *Anglo-Saxon Chronicle*, Pallig had also deserted the king, 'in spite of all the pledges he had given him', and taken as many ships as he could collect to team up with his compatriots. Together they ravaged Devon and then did the same to the Isle of Wight. Æthelred and his counsellors were left with no alternative but to seek another disadvantageous peace, agreeing to supply the plunderers with provisions and to pay them another massive tribute.[41]

With its mercenary policy in tatters, the government tried yet another new tack, and came up with a twofold plan. In the first place, they attempted to deal with Normandy. Normandy was, in effect, the cross-Channel Danelaw – a wide area of north-western Francia that had been invaded and settled by vikings since the late ninth century. Its name, Normannia, meant 'the land of the northmen'. Unlike the Danelaw, however, it had not been reconquered in the tenth century, and continued to be ruled by dukes of Scandinavian descent. When viking raids in the Channel had resumed, therefore, the duchy was not a target, but a friendly port of call, run by distant cousins – a place where ships could be repaired and refitted, and where plunder and slaves could be unloaded for profit. Æthelred had already attempted to prevent this by concluding a treaty with the Normans as early as 991, but it had not stopped the fleet that had recently ravaged his kingdom from being received in Normandy in the summer of 1000. The king's initial response was apparently to order a retaliatory raid on the Norman coast, but in 1002 a peace was agreed, and Æthelred forged an alliance with Duke Richard II by agreeing to marry his sister. The king's previous wife, Ælfgifu, had probably died at some point in the later 990s, leaving him free to pursue this diplomatic solution. In the spring of 1002 he was joined by his Norman bride, Emma, and she was consecrated as England's new queen.[42]

The second part of the government's plan was altogether less diplomatic. It was also in 1002, says the *Anglo-Saxon Chronicle*, that 'the king ordered all the Danish men who were in England to be killed'. This was done, the chronicler continues, on St Brice's Day (13 November) and hence it subsequently became known as the St Brice's Day Massacre. Later historians imagined it involved the elimination of everyone in the kingdom who was of Scandinavian descent, a scenario which, had it been the case, would have amounted to genocide in Northumbria, East Anglia and the East Midlands. The far likelier and more realistic assumption is that Æthelred had decided to do away with the remaining members of the mercenary force that had been in his employ since 994 – those vikings who had not deserted, and were still billeted in various *burhs*. Two years after the massacre, the king issued a new charter for the church of St Frideswide in Oxford, renewing its earlier privileges. The church's original documents, he explained, had been lost as a result of his decree that all the Danes dwelling in his kingdom should be killed. Those who had been living in Oxford had fled into St Frideswide's to escape death, and the townspeople, unable to dislodge them, had burned the building down. Just over 1,000 years later, in 2008, archaeologists working in the grounds of St John's College discovered the remains of at least thirty-four young men who had been unceremoniously dumped in what was the original town ditch. Some had been stabbed, others had been burned, and all had been stripped of their possessions. This made identification difficult, but the scientific analysis is consistent with their having come from Scandinavia during the reign of Æthelred.

26. The mass grave at Ridgeway Hill in Dorset. Note that the bodies have been decapitated.

Similar scenes must have played out across the country wherever mercenaries were stationed. At Ridgeway Hill in Dorset, between the towns of Weymouth and Dorchester, another mass grave was found in 2009, containing the skeletons of fifty young Scandinavian males, deposited carelessly in an Iron Age pit around the turn of the first millennium, and thus very likely victims of the massacre. Æthelred, though, would clearly not have regarded them as victims. In his charter for St Frideswide's, the king displayed no hint of remorse for having ordered the killing. The Danes, he declared, had sprung up in England 'like cockles amongst the wheat' – a reference to a parable in the Gospel of St Matthew, in which the poisonous weeds that had grown among the healthy crops were rooted out at harvest time and destroyed by burning. The massacre in Oxford, Æthelred insisted, had been 'a most just extermination'. The *Anglo-Saxon Chronicle* states that the king had feared that the Danes were about to rise up and kill him and his counsellors, and perhaps this was the line put out for public consumption to justify a policy of mass murder. But his English subjects, after suffering years of atrocities at Danish hands, would have needed no new reasons to stoke their existing hatred into homicidal rage. They were the king's willing collaborators in his attempt to purify the cornfield of his kingdom.[43]

If the St Brice's Day Massacre was meant to solve England's viking problem, however, it was a spectacular failure. It is unclear what effect it had on the enemy fleet that had been terrorizing the south coast in the years leading up to 1002. Perhaps some of the raiders, having agreed to peace that year, had been lured back into Æthelred's service, and were among those killed. But any who were not caught up in the carnage would surely have been provoked to take immediate revenge. Such sentiments, moreover, were not confined to those vikings camped on the Isle of Wight. Reports of the premeditated slaughter spread rapidly around the North Sea, where they reached the ears of King Swein of Denmark, and kindled similar thoughts of retribution.[44]

Swein, who in later centuries acquired the nickname 'Forkbeard', had been king of the Danes since the death of his father, Harold Bluetooth, in 986. Probably about forty years old, he had behind him a lifetime of successful plundering and warfare, some of which appears to have been practised along the coasts of England. Around the turn of the millennium he had increased his power in Scandinavia by defeating and killing Æthelred's earlier antagonist, Olaf Tryggvason, and annexing part of the kingdom of Norway. In 1003, he turned his attentions towards England, reportedly provoked by the events of the previous St Brice's Day.

The Danish king began his campaign in Devon, completely destroying the *burh* at Exeter, and then advancing his army inland. In Wiltshire they encountered an English army that had been gathered to oppose them, but it fled before any engagement could take place. The *Chronicle* blamed its commander, Ealdorman Ælfric of Hampshire, who was still in post despite Æthelred's blinding of his son a decade earlier. As soon as the two sides saw each other, we are told, Ælfric started retching, and claimed he was ill, leaving his troops in the lurch. Swein, seeing that he was unopposed, ravaged and burned the *burh* at Wilton, and then returned to his ships. The following year he sailed from Devon to East Anglia, and wreaked similar destruction in Norwich and Thetford. But there he met with more resolute resistance, thanks to a local magnate named Ulfketel, whom the *Chronicle* praises for his valour. Swein still emerged victorious from their clash, but we are led to understand that it was a close-run thing, and that even the vikings later admitted that it was the toughest fighting they had ever experienced in England.

Although the cowardice and courage of the two English commanders are implicitly contrasted, the common feature that unites both these stories is the absence of their king: Æthelred, as usual, had left the business of fighting to his deputies. It is often said in the king's defence that his kingdom was a great deal larger than that of Alfred the Great, and the 300-mile distance between Exeter and Norwich would on the face of things serve to underline that point. But Æthelred was not on this occasion trying to deal with the tactics of hit-and-run raiders, surreptitiously moving from one estuary to the next, elusive on account of their speed. Swein was a rival king, leading an army of invasion, advancing purposefully across the landscape, apparently spoiling for a fight. According to the *Chronicle*, almost three weeks elapsed between his destruction of Norwich and his subsequent attack on Thetford. Æthelred's failure to confront him in person, therefore, can hardly be read as the cool response of a commander anxious not to waste his energies in a fruitless pursuit, and is better regarded as further confirmation of the English king's lack of mettle. 'As the saying goes,' says the *Chronicle*, '"When the leader gives way, the whole army will be much hindered."' The chronicler was commenting on the craven behaviour of Ealdorman Ælfric, but his words were equally applicable to the stay-at-home king.[45]

Eventually, after two years of campaigning, Swein returned to Denmark in 1005, probably persuaded by the increasing difficulty of finding food. That year England and many other parts of Europe suffered an extremely severe famine. The *Anglo-Saxon Chronicle* called it 'the Great Hunger' (*micla hungor*), and said it was the cruellest anyone could remember, while later writers in Francia claimed that it led to incidents of cannibalism. The departure of the Danes was therefore hardly an occasion for much celebration. There was still death everywhere, only now it was not instant but slow and lingering. Crop failure and starvation were merely more evidence that God was still punishing His people, and that they must do more to purify themselves in order to recover His favour.[46]

Æthelred took it as a sign that he must conduct another purge of his court. The cabal that had dominated his counsels since the previous palace revolution in 993 had already been diminished by the passage of time. His mother, Ælfthryth, had died around the turn of the millennium, as had her kinsman, Ealdorman Æthelweard. In 1005 the king turned on its remaining members. Æthelweard's son, Æthelmær, was persuaded to leave court and retire to a new monastery he had established at Eynsham in Oxfordshire. Its abbot was to be his friend Ælfric, the famous homilist, but in its foundation charter, issued by the king, Æthelmær took the highly unusual step of promising that he too would dwell at the abbey for the rest of his days. It was also at this moment that the king's uncle, Ordulf, disappeared from court, perhaps to live a similarly secluded existence. The impression that these two counsellors had been rusticated against their will is strengthened by the fact that the other leading members of their circle were removed around the same time by more brutal means. Ælfhelm, appointed as ealdorman of Northumbria in 993, was murdered. His sons, Wulfheah and Ufegeat, who were among the most prominent witnesses to Æthelred's charters, were blinded, reportedly on the king's orders. It was perhaps in order to escape a similar fate that Ordulf and Æthelmær had agreed to remain in cloistered confinement.[47]

New advisers rose to take the place of the old, and two in particular were pre-eminent. The first was Wulfstan, the archbishop of York. Like Ælfric of Eynsham, Wulfstan was a celebrated man of letters, but his sermons and homilies were even more apocalyptic. Æthelred had appointed him as bishop of London in 996, and had promoted him to the northern archdiocese in 1002, but only after the purge of 1005 does he stand out as one of the king's principal advisers, witnessing that year's charter for Eynsham in first place after the royal family, and even taking precedence ahead of the archbishop of Canterbury. The second new figure who dominated Æthelred's counsels from 1005 was Eadric, a layman whose meteoric but unscrupulous rise earned him the contemporary nickname 'the Grabber' (*streona*). His first appearance as a witness occurs in 1002 as one of many king's thegns, but after the revolution of 1005 he is suddenly catapulted to the head of the pack, and the following year Æthelred raised him to the rank of ealdorman. Later chroniclers blamed Eadric for the murder of Ealdorman Ælfhelm and the blinding of his sons, an accusation that is extremely plausible, given their territorial rivalry in northern Mercia, and

Eadric's undoubted involvement in acts of assassination that came afterwards.[48]

If Archbishop Wulfstan was responsible for the increasingly doom-laden tone of royal pronouncements after 1005, it may be that Eadric the Grabber began urging a more robust military response against the vikings. It was around this time that the design of Æthelred's coinage was altered to depict him wearing a helmet rather than a crown, and when a large viking fleet landed at Sandwich the following summer, the *Chronicle* says that 'the whole nation of Wessex and Mercia' was summoned to fight against them. This massive English army, alas, did more harm than good, reportedly causing almost as much oppression as the Danes themselves before it disbanded in the autumn, leaving the invaders free to maraud through Wessex during the winter. In the end the king and his counsellors reluctantly concluded that the only solution was to pay another tribute, which was handed over in 1007.[49]

In 1008, however, their determination to pursue a military solution was reaffirmed, with Æthelred ordering a nationwide programme of rearmament. Decrees drafted by Archbishop Wulfstan at Pentecost not only required the whole kingdom to be more God-fearing and penitential; they also demanded the diligent repair of bridges and fortresses. The *Chronicle*, meanwhile, records that the king commanded every 300 hides of land to pay for the building of a new warship, and every eight hides to provide a helmet and mail-shirt – i.e. the equipment for one well-armed warrior. If these orders were obeyed to the letter across the whole of England, the result would have been over 8,000 sets of armour and over 200 ships. That something like this was indeed achieved is suggested by the *Chronicle*, which reports that when the new vessels were brought together at Sandwich in the spring of 1009, they constituted a greater armada than had ever been assembled by any previous English king.[50]

But it was at this point that the violent factional rivalries at Æthelred's court started to spin out of control. The rise of Eadric the Grabber had also led to the promotion of his many brothers, who soon came into conflict with the king's other counsellors. In the same spring of 1009, the *Chronicle* records that one of the brothers, Brihtric, accused a Sussex thegn named Wulfnoth of some unspecified offence before the king. Wulfnoth, who was evidently a man of some status, responded by persuading the crews of twenty of the ships stationed at Sandwich to support him, and led them on a destructive raid along the south coast, 'doing all manner of damage'. Brihtric, 'intending to make a big reputation for himself', took a further eighty ships and set off in pursuit, convinced it would be an easy matter for them to defeat the deserters and bring in Wulfnoth dead or alive. In their eagerness, however, the pursuers sailed into a terrible storm: those vessels that were not dashed to pieces by the waves were cast ashore, where they were subsequently burned by Wulfnoth. As a result, without so much as a single viking in sight, Æthelred lost more than half his newly constructed fleet. The king and his counsellors left Sandwich, and the remaining ships returned to London. 'The labour of the entire nation', lamented the *Chronicle*, 'thus lightly came to nothing.'[51]

With the deterrent gone, there was nothing to prevent the resumption of Scandinavian attacks. In August 1009, what the *Chronicle* calls 'an immense raiding army' landed at Sandwich, led by a viking chief named Thorkell the Tall. It immediately advanced on Canterbury, prompting the people of eastern Kent to sue for peace and pay a tribute of £3,000. The invaders then moved to the Isle of Wight, and from that familiar base they made raids into Sussex, Hampshire and Berkshire, ravaging and burning wherever they pleased.

Æthelred's initial response was to summon an assembly to Bath, a safe distance from the areas under attack. There he issued an edict, evidently drafted by Archbishop Wulfstan, requiring all his subjects to participate in a national act of penance. On the three days leading up to Michaelmas (29 September), everyone was to fast, eating nothing but bread and herbs and drinking only water. Then, on Michaelmas itself, they were to process barefoot to

27. Two coins of Æthelred the Unready. In 1005–6 the king is shown wearing a helmet (a), but a special coin of 1009 depicts the Lamb of God and the Dove of Peace (b).

church, accompanied by priests carrying holy relics and singing masses. All were to call earnestly on Christ, 'that we may be able, through his help, to withstand our enemies'. Slaves were to be excused from work in order to take part. Any that refused were to be flogged, while freemen who failed to do so were to face stiff fines. In addition, one penny was to be paid from every hide of land, so it could be distributed among the needy. It seems highly likely that a rare issue of coin from Æthelred's reign, depicting the Lamb of God on one side and the Dove of Peace on the other, was minted especially for this royally mandated act of almsgiving.[52]

There was also an attempt to combat the invasion by more conventional methods. As in 1006, Æthelred summoned a national army, and, to his credit, on this occasion he appears to have joined its ranks. But, as before, its leaders were allegedly reluctant to risk battle, refusing to engage when a suitable opportunity presented itself, and as a result the vikings continued to ravage with impunity. In November they established a winter camp on the Thames Estuary at Greenwich, a few miles east of London, from where they preyed on Kent and Essex. London itself withstood their assaults, but in the new year they advanced up the Thames and sacked Oxford. In the spring of 1010 they moved into East Anglia, sailing their fleet to Ipswich, and defeated an army raised against them in Cambridgeshire: the *Anglo-Saxon Chronicle* mournfully lists the names of the English nobles who perished in the battle. After that Thorkell's followers apparently faced no further resistance. They seized horses, and spent the next three months harrying all of eastern England, 'even into the wild fens'. The *Chronicle's* account is reminiscent of the arrival of the great heathen army destroying East Anglia in 866, and gives the impression that the vikings were now unstoppable. In the autumn they raided into Oxfordshire, Buckinghamshire, Bedfordshire and Northamptonshire, rounding off the year with a raid into Wessex before returning to their ships. Wherever they went, complains the *Chronicle*, the English army was somewhere else, and whatever plans the king and his counsellors devised

lasted no longer than a month. 'In the end,' laments the anonymous author, 'there was no leader who would collect an army,
but each fled as best he could, and in the end no shire would
even help the next.'

By 1011, therefore, Æthelred and his advisers were forced to
concede that the martial policy of the past years had failed, and
offered payment in return for peace. Even this time-honoured
expedient, however, did not bring an end to the violence. The
Chronicle implies that some form of tribute was handed over, and
that the vikings simply carried on raiding and killing regardless,
but it may be that Æthelred's crippled government found it
impossible to raise the vast amount of cash they had promised
during the peace negotiations. It was perhaps for this reason that
in September 1011 Thorkell's army returned to Kent and laid
siege to Canterbury. The city soon fell, apparently due to
treachery, and the victorious vikings seized everything of value
inside it, including its most important citizens. Among the crowd
of captive men and women they led back to their camp at
Greenwich were the king's reeve, Ælfweard, Bishop Godwine
of Rochester, and Ælfheah, the archbishop of Canterbury.[53]

If the abduction of England's most senior churchman from his
own cathedral city was a ploy to speed up payment of tribute,
it worked a treat: at Easter 1012 Eadric the Grabber and the
king's other counsellors came to London to supervise the handover of the collected cash, said by the *Chronicle* to have been a
monstrous £48,000. But the plan backfired somewhat when the
vikings tried to demand additional money for the safe return of
the archbishop. Ælfheah refused to be ransomed and forbade
anyone from paying anything on his behalf. Angry and frustrated,
and reportedly drunk on wine, his captors began pelting him
with animal bones and ox-heads, until one of their number
brought matters to a bloody conclusion by clouting the
archbishop on the head with the back of his axe.[54]

The death of a high-ranking churchman at viking hands might
not seem particularly surprising, given their long-standing
reputation as ungodly heathens. But that reputation had been

forged in the ninth century, when, as genuine pagans, they had indiscriminately slaughtered men and women of God and burned their churches to the ground. By the eleventh century, Scandinavians had started to embrace Christianity: the first Danish king to convert had been Swein Forkbeard's father, Harold Bluetooth, probably in the 960s. Thus, although the repeated invasions of England during Æthelred's reign had been hugely destructive, Christian sites had for the most part been spared. Ælfheah's martyrdom was therefore all the more shocking, as even the leaders of the viking army seemed to appreciate. The morning after the murder, they carried his body from Greenwich and handed it over to the bishop of London, who arranged for it to be reverentially buried at St Paul's.[55]

It is indeed conceivable that a degree of guilt about the archbishop's death caused some of the vikings at Greenwich to re-evaluate their priorities, if not their violent lifestyle. Immediately afterwards the long-awaited tribute was paid, oaths of peace were sworn, and the majority of the 'immense raiding army' departed for home. A great many of them, however, including Thorkell the Tall himself, remained behind in England, having agreed to fight for Æthelred. With few options remaining to him, the embattled king had decided to revive the strategy he had first adopted almost twenty years earlier, and retain the services of a mercenary Scandinavian fleet. The crews of forty-five ships – potentially almost 2,000 warriors – were added to the royal payroll, having promised to defend the country.[56]

Æthelred's new followers did not have to wait long to earn their keep. In the summer of the following year, yet another large viking force arrived, led once again by the king of Denmark, Swein Forkbeard. Historians have long recognized that Swein's intentions had altered since his previous assault on England in 1003. That earlier invasion appears to have been a punitive raid, perhaps inflicted in retaliation for the St Brice's Day Massacre. On this occasion, by contrast, the Danish king had clearly come to England intent on outright conquest. What caused this escalation in his ambitions is open to question, but a contributing factor must have been that Swein had come to realize that he could count on the support of some of Æthelred's own subjects, who had grown so heartily sick of their king that they were actively seeking his replacement.[57]

Their reasons are not hard to fathom. Over the last two decades Æthelred's government had grown more and more oppressive. Whether it was to fund gargantuan tributes to buy off invading armies, or to subsidise standing armies of mercenaries, or to build a fleet of new warships, or to provide armour for multiple thousands of men, the king had needed to extract vast sums of money from his subjects, and had used increasingly extortionate methods in order to do so. His sheriffs had borne down on ordinary people in their shires, compelling them to surrender their possessions for the king's use. At the same time, the king had demanded ever greater amounts from his nobles in the way of death duties. When an Anglo-Saxon warrior died, tradition decreed that his lord should receive some of his war-gear, but Æthelred had abused this custom, demanding excessive quantities of horses, weapons and gold from the families of the recently deceased. Finally, to fund his new force of mercenaries, the king had introduced a nationwide tax, known as the *heregeld* ('army money'), which the *Chronicle* later described as having 'oppressed all the English people'. None of this money-grabbing would have mattered quite so much had it produced anything practical or long-lasting in the way of results. But the huge sums that were raised had been repeatedly squandered through a combination of cowardice and incompetence on the part of the king and his counsellors. Many people may therefore have drawn the conclusion that rather than paying endless amounts to make the Danes go away, it might be preferable simply to let them take over.[58]

These were general grievances. There were also certain powerful individuals who harboured specific personal grudges against Æthelred and the leading members of his regime, and were thus ready and willing to collaborate with the Danish king. Swein's fleet first appeared at Sandwich, but it did not go on to attack conventional targets such as Canterbury, Winchester or London. Instead, his ships sailed rapidly up the east coast to the Humber, then down the River Trent, eventually landing at Gainsborough in Lincolnshire. The usual explanation for this is that the Danish king was hoping to exploit the cultural sympathies of the Danelaw, and there is no doubt some truth in this. But this was unlikely to have been a mere gamble on Swein's part, and he was almost certainly drawn to Gainsborough by specific offers of support. The strongest reason for supposing this is that, around this moment, probably soon after his arrival, the king's teenage son, Cnut, was married to an Englishwoman named Ælfgifu of Northampton. Ælfgifu was the daughter of Ælfhelm, the ealdorman of Northumbria murdered by Eadric the Grabber in 1005; her brothers, Wulfheah and Ufegeat, had been blinded that same year on Æthelred's orders. The marriage of this particular woman to Swein's son, therefore, represented an alliance between Æthelred's foreign and domestic enemies, likely to have been forged in the months or years leading up to 1013, and formally cemented upon the Danish king's arrival.[59]

The impression that Swein came to northern England by invitation is further bolstered by his peaceful reception. The Northumbrians and the people of Lincolnshire, says the *Chronicle*, submitted to him 'at once', and then so too did all the inhabitants of the Five Boroughs. The Danish king did not rely on promises of loyalty alone, and prudently took hostages from these leading families, but there was seemingly no fighting or harrying in any of these regions. Not until he reached Watling Street did Swein commence his military offensive. Leaving his son at Gainsborough to attend to the ships and hostages, and mounting the horses given to them by the locals, the king and his warriors crossed the ancient boundary line and, in the words of the *Chronicle*, 'did the greatest damage that any army could do'.

There was little resistance. Oxford surrendered immediately and handed over hostages, and a short while later Winchester did the same. Only London, where Æthelred himself was sheltering, put up more of a fight. The Danish army blundered on its approach to the city by trying to cross the Thames without the use of a bridge, losing many men in the process, and when they launched their assault they were repulsed by the citizens. The defence was probably also aided by the mercenaries of Thorkell the Tall, who is known to have been at Æthelred's side.[60]

For Swein, however, this was only a temporary setback. Withdrawing his troops from London, he went west to Bath, and there received the submission of the thegns of the western shires. Leading these men was Æthelred's former counsellor, Æthelmær, who had been banished from court in 1005 and obliged to live like a monk at Eynsham Abbey. A short time before the invasion the king had released him from his earlier promise and raised him to the rank of ealdorman, a role previously held by his father. But if this was an olive branch it was proffered far too late, and Æthelmær now pledged his support to Swein.[61]

The loss of the ancient heartlands of Wessex spelt the end for Æthelred's regime. From this moment, says the *Chronicle*, the whole nation regarded Swein as their undisputed king. With his western hostages in tow, the Danish leader returned to his ships at Gainsborough and demanded money and supplies for the coming winter. In the south Thorkell's army did the same. The citizens of London, fearing they would be destroyed by Swein in a second assault, submitted to him. With his strongest refuge lost, Æthelred moved to Thorkell's camp at Greenwich, and from there he sent his queen and her sons across the Channel to the court of her brother, the duke of Normandy. The king then sailed with his mercenaries to the Isle of Wight. After spending Christmas on the island, he finally conceded defeat, and fled to join his family in exile.[62]

It would have been reasonable for contemporaries to assume that Æthelred's reign had finally come to an end. Overcome by a foreign adversary, he had lost both his kingdom and the loyalty of his subjects. By this point he was in his mid-forties, and it must have seemed that he would play out his remaining days as a pensioner at the court of his brother-in-law in Normandy, eventually to pass away in obscurity. But fate decreed otherwise. A few weeks after his departure, Æthelred must have been surprised and delighted to learn that Swein had died. The Danish conqueror had breathed his last on 3 February 1014, and the *Chronicle* described his passing as 'a happy event'. The suddenness of his death might seem suspicious, but Swein was in his fifties, so it is a reasonable assumption that the causes were natural. Only at the end of the eleventh century was it reported that the king had died of supernatural causes, run through by a spear-wielding St Edmund, who thus obtained revenge for his own death at Danish hands almost 150 years earlier.[63]

Swein's body was taken for burial in York, which was starting to fill with English magnates who had travelled there in expectation of attending the new king's first national assembly. Instead, they found themselves as guests at his funeral, and wondering what would happen next. For the Danish army, still camped sixty miles away at Gainsborough, the solution was simple, and they promptly elected Cnut as his father's replacement. But the English nobles had no obvious reason to do the same. The oaths of loyalty they had sworn to Swein had expired on his death, and they were in no way obliged to renew them to his son. 'The people have the option to choose as king whomever they please', said Ælfric of Eynsham, who had died a few years earlier, in one of his famous homilies. 'But', the homilist continued, 'after he is consecrated as king, then he has dominion over the people, and they cannot shake his yoke from their necks.' For the English assembled at York, this maxim raised the worrying question of whether they had erred in abandoning Æthelred.[64]

It was a thought that Archbishop Wulfstan of York enlarged upon when he preached to these same magnates a few days later. Wulfstan must have accepted Swein's kingship and anticipated having to work with him. He had probably been planning to remind his audience of St Paul's insistence that the powers that be were appointed by God, and to recommend they all collaborate with their new Danish ruler. But the archbishop was nothing if not adaptable. Confronted with radically changed circumstances and no time for major revisions, he did what any sensible author would do, and dusted off an old classic. For several years he had been delivering an apocalyptic tirade entitled the *Sermon of the Wolf to the English* – 'Wolf' being a play on his own name. It began by reminding listeners that the end of the world was imminent, and dwelt at length on the evils that had been done to them by the vikings. Time and again, Wulfstan lamented, the invaders had brought devastation and bloodshed, raped the wives and daughters of noble thegns, and rounded up droves of Christians to sell into slavery. 'But all the insult which we often suffer, we repay by honouring those who insult us', said the archbishop. 'We pay them continually, and they humiliate us daily.' These were clearly not the words of a man who was about to endorse a viking candidate.

At the same time, Wulfstan impressed upon his congregation that this was all their own fault. God was punishing the English because they themselves were steeped in sin. There was too much murder, robbery, fornication and harlotry, infanticide and perjury, and too little praying, fasting and penance. 'And also here in the country,' he continued, in a section seemingly adapted for the occasion, 'there are many who are traitors.' It was an act of great treachery, said Wulfstan, for a man to betray his lord to death, 'or drive him in his lifetime from the land'. The first was a reference to the murder of Edward the Martyr which had inaugurated Æthelred's reign, the second to the recent exile that seemed to have ended it. Wulfstan's message, therefore, was clear: if the English magnates were to avoid further calamity and escape God's wrath, they needed to restore Æthelred as their rightful ruler.[65]

This suggestion must have filled many of those present, perhaps the majority, with great unease. If Æthelred was restored to unfettered power, he would surely seek revenge against those who had willingly sided with Swein. In addition, their many reasons for rejecting Æthelred in the first place still stood. If they were going to reinstate the banished king, they decided, they would need him to guarantee their safety and pledge to

15. A page (Matthew 1:18) from the Stockholm *Codex Aureus* (Golden Book), probably produced in Canterbury in the eighth century (p. 231). The minuscule text, added in the ninth century, describes how the book was retrieved from the vikings in return for a ransom.

16. The Alfred Jewel (p. 236).

17. The Gilling Sword. This well-preserved weapon dating from the late ninth or early tenth century was found in a stream in Gilling, Yorkshire, in 1976 by Garry Fridd, aged nine.

18. King Æthelstan presents a book to St Cuthbert (pp. 248–9). An image from a gospel book given by the king to the monastic community of St Cuthbert at Chester-le-Street in 934.

19. Fragments of a gold-embroidered stole and maniple given to the community of
St Cuthbert by King Æthelstan in 934, rediscovered in 1827 (p. 248). The image
on the left is Peter the Deacon; on the right, the Prophet Nahum.

20. Glastonbury Tor (p. 280).

21. Cheddar Gorge, Somerset (p. 286), where King Edmund (d. 946) had a near miss with death, prompting him to seek reconciliation with St Dunstan.

22. The frontispiece of the refoundation charter of New Minster, Winchester, issued in 966 (p. 303). King Edgar is depicted personally presenting the charter to Christ.

23. English ecclesiastical architecture on the eve of the Norman Conquest: the mid-eleventh century tower of Earls Barton, Northamptonshire (p. 389).

24. A folio from Domesday Book (p. 406). The entries for each county (in this case Bedfordshire) begin with a list of its major landholders. The first name here is King William (*Rex Willelmus*).

mend his ways. Accordingly, they sent messages to Normandy, indicating their willingness to take him back, but on conditional terms. 'They said that no lord was dearer to them than their natural lord,' explains the *Chronicle*, 'if he would govern them more justly than he did before.'[66]

Æthelred was in many ways remarkably similar to King John, and this was his Magna Carta moment. The notorious Plantagenet king who ruled two centuries later was criticized by his contemporaries for his cowardice and cruelty, his over-reliance on sheriffs and foreign mercenaries, and his harsh financial exactions – exactions that included exorbitant death duties, the forcible seizure of goods, and punitive levels of taxation. John's subjects had rebelled against him and plotted his removal, but then been persuaded to give him a second chance in return for a long and detailed promise to rule better – the celebrated 'great charter' of 1215.[67] The evidence suggests that Æthelred's subjects did the same in 1014, presenting him with a raft of grievances they wished to see redressed. With little room for manoeuvre, the exiled king agreed. Via messengers of his own, Æthelred 'said that he would be a gracious lord to them, and reform all the things that they hated'. At the same time, the king forgave his subjects all their trespasses against him, on condition they should receive him back without treachery. And so a rapprochement was affected, with pledges and oaths on both sides. At some point during Lent, says the *Chronicle*, 'King Æthelred came home to his own people, and was gladly received by them all.'[68]

Presumably these cross-Channel negotiations were kept secret from Cnut and the Danish army loitering at Gainsborough. It was apparently not until after Easter that the young viking leader realized that he was not in the running, prompting him to start preparing for a fresh military offensive. But by that point it was too late. Before leaving Normandy, Æthelred had recruited the services of Olaf Haraldson (a future king of Norway, but at the time a soldier of fortune) and on his return to England he was reunited with the mercenary army of Thorkell the Tall. These combined forces fell upon Cnut's army while it was still getting ready, killing as many as they could. Cnut himself and some of his troops managed to get to their ships and put to sea, taking with them the hostages his father had collected during the previous year's campaign. The English nobility had gambled that he would not kill their captive kinsmen, and so it proved. On his way back to Denmark, Cnut stopped off at Sandwich, and allowed the hostages to disembark. He did, however, signal his disappointment by depriving them of their hands, ears and noses.⁶⁹

In the immediate wake of his restoration, Æthelred endeavoured to appease his critics. To their disappointment, there was no reduction of the tax burden, and the *Chronicle* bewailed the king's demand for a huge *heregeld* to pay for Thorkell and his mercenary fleet. But the first royal assembly after Æthelred's return saw the enactment of several ordinances intended to improve his government. One of them, presumably, must have dealt with the material grievances he had promised to address at the start of the year. Another, drafted by Wulfstan, was concerned with spiritual and ecclesiastical matters. Its avowed intention was 'to cleanse the country', and it concluded with a plea for unity: 'Let us all loyally support one royal lord, and let each of our friends love the next with true fidelity.'⁷⁰

But this was wishful thinking, given the long-standing and unresolved tensions at Æthelred's court, revealed by a trio of deaths that occurred in the year after his return. The first was that of his eldest son, Æthelstan. Born soon after the king's first marriage in 985, Æthelstan was in his late twenties and in pole position to succeed his father, but around midsummer 1014 he became mortally ill and hurriedly drew up his will. A fascinating document, it survives as an original copy, and shows the dying prince distributing his treasure, money and lands to his friends and dependants. His foster mother, for example, was given an estate 'because of her great merits', while his younger brother, Edmund, received 'the sword that belonged to King Offa'. Another important beneficiary was a man named Sigeferth, who received lands in Bedfordshire, as well as a horse, a sword and a shield. He and his brother, Morcar (also named in the will), were prominent members of the king's court – the *Chronicle* describes them as the 'chief thegns' of the Five Boroughs. It was a position they had inherited by virtue of belonging to the same family as Ealdorman Ælfhelm, the man murdered in 1005 by Æthelred's notorious henchman, Eadric the Grabber.[71]

At the time of his death, therefore, Æthelstan had been aligned with the enemies of his father's chief adviser, indicating that this feud was now poisoning political relations at the very highest level. The situation exploded in the spring of 1015 at a royal assembly in Oxford, when Eadric had Sigeferth and Morcar assassinated. ('He enticed them into his chamber,' says the *Anglo-Saxon Chronicle*, 'and they were basely slain inside it.') As in 1005, this murderous act was apparently carried out with the complicity of the king: Æthelred, says the *Chronicle*, ordered the seizure of all the brothers' lands, and also Sigeferth's widow, Ealdgyth, who was brought to Malmesbury, evidently with the intention of forcing her into a nunnery.

She was saved from this fate, however, by Edmund, the eldest of Æthelred's surviving sons. Now in his mid-twenties, the new bearer of King Offa's sword had also assumed his late brother's mantle as the leader of anti-Eadric alliance. In defiance of his father, he rushed to Malmesbury, liberated Ealdgyth, and married her himself. Then, in August, he rode with her back to the Five Boroughs, and took possession of all the estates that had belonged to both of the murdered brothers. All the people of those parts, says the *Chronicle*, submitted to him.

It was at this moment, with impeccable timing, that Cnut returned to England. The young Danish prince came first to Sandwich, then sailed his army along the south coast to Dorset, where they began marauding deep into Wessex. Æthelred got as far as Portsmouth before falling sick and delegating the English military response to Eadric. This made a co-ordinated effort with the regions that had submitted to Edmund all but impossible. The two rivals raised separate armies which were briefly united, but rumours of treachery on the ealdorman's part caused them to split up almost immediately. And the rumours proved well founded: Eadric, sensing that Æthelred's dynasty was done for, deserted to the Danes. He took with him forty ships, most likely the mercenary fleet captained by Thorkell the Tall. The people of Wessex had no option but to surrender, and agreed to supply the invaders with horses. As the end of the year approached, Cnut led his massively reinforced and newly mounted host across the Thames, and began terrorizing the people of Mercia.[72]

Edmund attempted to rally an army of opposition, but with little success. The forces he raised before Christmas refused to fight unless they were joined by the king and the citizens of London. When he tried again after Christmas, having begged his father and the Londoners to turn out, the result was still a shambles, and Æthelred, fearing treachery, abandoned the muster. At the start of 1016, no doubt in some desperation, Edmund rode north, where he succeeded in persuading Earl Uhtred of Northumbria to join him, and together they ravaged Eadric's estates in north-west Mercia. But when Cnut moved through the Midlands and began to menace York, Uhtred also decided to desert to the Danish side, along with all the Northumbrians. In the earl's own case this defection did him no favours, and on Eadric's advice he was immediately executed and replaced with a Dane named Erik. With almost the whole kingdom now in his hands, Cnut returned to his ships on the south coast, arriving there before the start of April. Edmund, with no cards left to play, made his way to London, to join his ailing father.[73]

Æthelred died on 23 April – St George's Day, as the author of the *Anglo-Saxon Chronicle* noted. To modern readers, it might seem deeply ironic that a king who had proved so inadequate as a military leader should have expired on the feast of the most famously martial saint. But in 1016, the development of George into a chivalrous dragon-slayer was still some way off, at least in England, where he did not acquire the status of a national hero until the late Middle Ages. In the early eleventh century he was known only in his earlier guise as a Christian nobleman from the eastern Roman Empire – or, as Ælfric of Eynsham put it when he composed a passion of the saint, 'a rich ealdorman in the shire of Cappadocia'. This George had no military attributes, but had died a martyr's death at the hands of heathens. Perhaps, therefore, the author of the *Chronicle* did feel it was fitting that Æthelred had died on that particular day, suffering as the country was overrun by vikings. The *Chronicle's* only other comment on the king's passing was that 'he had held his kingdom with great toil and difficulties as long as his life lasted'.[74]

This was evidently the most charitable comment the author felt he could offer by way of an obituary. His overall opinion of Æthelred can be inferred from his account of the whole reign, which is portrayed as an unmitigated disaster. Although the king is never singled out for individual criticism, time and again he and his counsellors are collectively condemned for having acted unwisely. In 1011, when the 'immense raiding army' of Thorkell the Tall had been laying waste to the whole country for over a year, the *Chronicle* lambasted the English leaders, whom he says neither fought against the invaders nor offered tribute until it was too late, and everything had already been destroyed. 'All these disasters', he lamented, 'befell us through bad counsel [*unrædas*].'[75]

The use of *unrædas* in this context might strengthen the case for believing it was a contemporary nickname applied to the king himself, and one can see why people would have used it. Throughout his long reign, Æthelred was clearly dominated by the advice of others, and unable to control the factions at his court. His decision to advance a man like Eadric the Grabber suggests his judgement was poor. Contemporary writers like Ælfric and Wulfstan, who frequently stressed the need for kings to have good counsel, imply that this was precisely what their own king lacked. For all the recent attempts to rescue him from the exaggerated vilification of later writers like William of Malmesbury, Æthelred's reputation as an ill-counselled king still seems richly deserved.

Far from sealing the fate of his subjects, Æthelred's death was a liberation, allowing them to pledge loyalty to his more mettlesome son. Once they had lowered their late lord into his tomb in St Paul's, the citizens of London and the other counsellors who were present chose Edmund as their king, and he in turn defended them so staunchly that they gave him the nickname 'Ironside'. Throughout the spring and summer of 1016 he fought four battles against Cnut's forces, defeating them every time. Wessex submitted to him, the Danish siege of London was lifted, and the treacherous Eadric the Grabber renewed his allegiance.

But in October that year Edmund met with disaster, when he engaged in a final battle against the Danes at a place in Essex called *Assandun*. 'There Cnut had the victory', says the *Anglo-Saxon Chronicle*, noting that the outcome was determined by Eadric, who once again switched sides. Edmund escaped from the carnage, and agreed soon afterwards to divide his realm, ceding Mercia to Cnut while keeping Wessex for himself. But a few weeks later, on 30 November, the English king died, perhaps from wounds sustained at *Assandun*, enabling an outright Danish victory. Cnut, says the *Chronicle*, 'succeeded to all the kingdom of England'.[76]

10

TWILIGHT

The Rise of the House
of Godwine

I t is generally agreed that the Anglo-Saxon era ended on 14
October 1066, on a Saturday afternoon, about teatime. It was
on that day that an English army led by King Harold
Godwineson clashed with an invading army led by Duke
William of Normandy, on what until that moment had been an
unremarkable ridge some six miles north-west of Hastings. The
battle began around nine in the morning and lasted all day;
it was only as the sun was starting to set, according to contemporary
accounts, that the news flew around the field that Harold had
been killed, causing the surviving English troops to flee into the
descending autumn darkness. The king's death is famously
depicted on the Bayeux Tapestry, an extraordinary embroidered
cartoon, seventy metres long, sewn soon after the battle, and
miraculously still with us today. Harold is shown apparently
gripping the shaft of an arrow that has lodged in his eye, an
image that led later chroniclers to believe that this was how the
unfortunate king met his end.[1]

If this sounds a little too chronologically precise – historical
periods rarely divide up as neatly as historians pretend – there
are nevertheless good reasons for regarding 1066 as a momentous
turning point. The fact that Harold fell at Hastings meant that
his opponent went on to succeed him as king that Christmas,
and was later remembered as William the Conqueror, a king

whose reign witnessed astonishing levels of violence and social upheaval. The Norman Conquest saw the established ruling class of England almost entirely swept away, replaced by newcomers from across the Channel who had very different notions about the way a country should be governed. As a result, huge changes followed, affecting language, law, warfare, architecture and attitudes towards human life. There was a very real sense in which the Battle of Hastings heralded the dawn of a brave new world.[2]

Because 1066 was such a watershed moment, histories of the years leading up to it are often written as a prelude, and can give the impression that people at the time were expecting the Conquest, or could somehow have foreseen its cataclysmic effects. Yet there is no sense in the sources that contemporaries anticipated the storm before it broke. For most of the fifty-year period before 1066, the English were preoccupied, as they had been for centuries, with affairs in Scandinavia, and in particular with the fallout of the Danish Conquest of 1016, an experience that was far more traumatic than is generally recognized. For the first half of this period England was ruled by King Cnut and his sons, as part of a wider empire that stretched across the North Sea. In the second half there was a surprising reversal, which saw the restoration of the ancient house of Wessex, and the accession of Edward the Confessor, a son of Æthelred the Unready. These changes of dynasty made life for England's ruling elite extremely complicated: ancient loyalties were eroded, identities were called into question, and deep divisions were sown, with ultimately fatal consequences.

No one personifies these changes and conflicts better than Harold Godwineson, who ascended to the throne at the start of 1066. As his surname suggests, the doomed king was not a descendant of either Cnut or Æthelred, although he was indirectly related to both. His father, Godwine, was English, but his mother, Gytha, was Danish – a fact which explains why the couple gave their son the Scandinavian name 'Harold'. Their marriage had come about as a direct result of the Danish Conquest of 1016, and no Englishman had profited more from that hostile takeover than Godwine himself. In the course of the next half-century he and his family rose relentlessly, to the point where they could contemplate supplanting the rival dynasties that had promoted them. Their tumultuous story is the subject of this final chapter.[3]

According to Henry of Huntingdon, writing a century later, there were three particularly memorable facts about King Cnut. The first was that he married his daughter to the German emperor, and the second was that he had negotiated a reduction in tolls for English merchants travelling on the Continent. Unsurprisingly these achievements have long since faded from the collective memory, but Henry's third fact has proved truly unforgettable. When Cnut was at the height of his power, the chronicler claims, he ordered his throne to be set up on the seashore as the tide was coming in, and commanded the waves not to wet him. This makes the Danish king sound positively delusional, so much so that some later commentators decided it must have been a stunt, intended to demonstrate to sycophantic courtiers that royal power had its limits. Henry, however, makes no mention of courtiers, and offers no opinion as to whether it was a contrivance on the king's part.[4]

Leaving such legends to one side, historians have nevertheless arrived at the independent conclusion that Cnut was a canny politician, and a successful ruler who was respected by his subjects. Despite the violence of his conquest of England, there is little evidence that it led to any major structural changes. Naturally there were a few linguistic novelties – the king and his Danish followers, for example, called their military retainers 'housecarls', and referred to ealdormen as 'earls' – but beyond that not much appears to have altered. The traditional judgement has therefore been that Cnut brought peace and stability that were much needed after the tumultuous reign of Æthelred.[5]

The new king, moreover, seems to have made a determined effort to heal the divisions between his English and Danish subjects. In 1020, for example, he brought his whole court to *Assandun* in Essex, where he had defeated Edmund Ironside four years earlier, to attend the dedication of a new church he had commissioned to stand on the site of the battlefield. Sometime before this, on the anniversary of Edmund's death, Cnut had shown similar respect by visiting the tomb of his fallen adversary at Glastonbury, and presenting a cloak embroidered with pictures of peacocks. The king also sought to make amends for outrages that pre-dated his own invasion. In 1023 he arranged for the body of St Ælfheah, martyred eleven years earlier by a drunken viking army, to be reverentially removed from St Paul's Cathedral and translated with great solemnity to Canterbury. Such public acts of atonement advertised Cnut's credentials as a Christian ruler, an image he was clearly keen to cultivate. 'We were amazed at your knowledge, as well as your faith', said the bishop of Chartres in a letter to the king, after Cnut had sent him some richly decorated books. 'You, whom we had heard to be a pagan prince, we now know to be not only a Christian, but also a most generous donor to God's servants.'[6]

Cnut's most important measure to promote reconciliation between his peoples was his marriage to Emma, the widow of Æthelred the Unready: their wedding was celebrated just a few months into his reign, in the summer of 1017. Emma, who was probably at least a decade older than her new husband, would later insist how delighted she had been by this development, and how she had been wooed with promises and presents. The reality was almost certainly less romantic: the *Anglo-Saxon Chronicle* says that Cnut caused the queen 'to be fetched as his wife'. Apart from anything else, the king already had a wife in the shape of Ælfgifu of Northampton, whom he had married just a few years earlier, probably in 1013, and there is no indication he subsequently put her aside. The consolation for Emma was that she retained her royal title and was clearly Cnut's 'official' partner: the pair of them are depicted standing side by side in an illustrated manuscript produced at Winchester's New Minster, presenting a giant gold cross at the church's high altar. As well as emphasizing his partnership with Emma, this image again portrays Cnut as a model Christian king, gripping the cross with one hand and his sword with the other, while an angel places the crown on his head.[7]

28. King Cnut and Queen Emma (here styled with her English name, Ælfgifu) present a giant cross to the New Minster in Winchester.

We should be wary, however, of believing that Cnut was a benign ruler. Much of the evidence that has survived from his reign, like the above illustration, is essentially propaganda, produced at his behest by Christian churchmen trying to present him in the best possible light. Other evidence, less obvious and less copious, paints a quite different picture of the king and the regime over which he presided – one more in keeping with his background as a viking warlord.

In the first place, Cnut's conquest had been extremely savage. Even before his accession, in 1014, the king had demonstrated his capacity for brutality by ordering the mutilation of the numerous English hostages that had been handed over to his father the previous year. In the course of his own invasion campaign two years later, much blood had been spilled. At the climactic Battle of *Assandun*, the English dead included the bishop of Dorchester, the abbot of Ramsey, two ealdormen, and many others of aristocratic rank. 'All the nobility of England', lamented the *Chronicle*, 'was there destroyed.' And after his coronation, the killing continued, as Cnut set about murdering those Englishmen he mistrusted. In 1017 Eadric the Grabber was put to death, along with the sons of several ealdormen, and in the same year the king ordered the death of Eadwig, the only surviving son from Æthelred the Unready's first marriage. Around the same time, Cnut sent the infant sons of Edmund Ironside to Sweden, with a request to the Swedish king that they be quietly eliminated.[8]

As a consequence of all this killing, Cnut had lots of vacancies to fill, and unsurprisingly he chose to do so in the first instance by promoting Danes. At the start of his reign the new king divided the country into four major earldoms, based on the ancient Anglo-Saxon kingdoms. Northumbria had already been handed to his brother-in-law, Erik, in the course of the conquest. East Anglia was subsequently given to the mercenary viking leader, Thorkell the Tall, as a reward for his support. Mercia, initially given to Eadric the Grabber, was also soon in Danish hands, subdivided between several of Cnut's Scandinavian earls. Wessex the king kept for himself.[9]

The exception to this rule was Godwine, father of the future King Harold – an Englishman who not only escaped the purge of 1017, but was promoted to wield unrivalled power. About Godwine's own background we know next to nothing: possibly he was the son of Wulfnoth, the Sussex thegn who had commandeered part of the royal fleet in 1008 and gone on a piratical rampage along the south coast. About Godwine himself, however, we know a great deal, thanks to the book commissioned by his daughter to celebrate her family's rise. Today it goes by the name of the *Life of King Edward*, because midway through composition it was recast as a history of Edward the Confessor, but its original purpose, stated at the outset, was to sing the praises of Godwine and his children. According to the *Life*, Godwine prospered because of his talents as a statesman and a warrior, and his readiness to collaborate with Cnut. A clear turning point in his fortunes came in 1019, when Cnut returned to Denmark to claim the Danish throne following the death of his brother, Harold. Godwine went with him, and reportedly demonstrated both his courage and his wisdom, to the extent that the king determined to grant him major rewards. While they were still in Denmark Godwine was married to Cnut's sister-in-law, Gytha, and when they returned to England the following year, he was elevated to become earl of Wessex.[10]

Such was Cnut's confidence in Godwine, we learn, that the earl became England's most important nobleman. As the 1020s progressed, his Danish counterparts gradually disappeared. Thorkell was banished in 1021, Erik died in 1023, and towards the end of the decade the various earls of Mercia were redeployed to deal with affairs in Scandinavia. Cnut, too, spent most of the later 1020s outside of England, dealing with resistance to his expanding rule across the North Sea, and going on pilgrimage to Rome. All of which meant that he relied increasingly upon Godwine, his brother-in-law, to act as his regent in England. The *Life of King Edward* describes the earl as 'steward of almost all the kingdom', and assures us that he was extremely popular among the English, who regarded him not as a master, but revered him as a father.[11]

And yet there are reasons to suppose that everything was not quite so rosy as a tract commissioned by Godwine's daughter would have us believe, or as stable as historians have assumed from the near silence of contemporary English sources. (The *Anglo-Saxon Chronicle*, for example, has almost nothing to say about affairs in England during Cnut's reign.) Against the pious propaganda that was drafted on the king's behalf emphasizing the harmony between the conquerors and the conquered, we have to set the poetry that was composed in his praise, and almost certainly recited at his court. 'You smote the race of Edgar in that raid', crowed Ottar the Black in his *Knútsdrápa*, a skaldic celebration of the invasion of England. 'The deep dyke flowed over the bodies of the Northumbrians ... Edmund's noble offspring met with deadly wounds ... They could not defend their strongholds when you attacked.'[12]

Such sentiments, glorifying the Danes and the suffering they had inflicted, and at the same time rubbishing the military reputations of their vanquished opponents, would have played well with the Scandinavian members of Cnut's entourage, but must have left English listeners feeling uncomfortable to say the least. Many of the native nobles would have had living kinsmen who had been horribly disfigured and maimed on the king's orders. Clearly some of them, like Godwine, with his Danish wife, embraced the culture of the victors: archaeological finds suggest that the decorated horse-trappings of Cnut's Danish followers were widely imitated in England during his reign. Others, however, felt that to adopt such foreign fashions was a betrayal of their national identity. 'You do wrong in abandoning the English practices which your fathers followed', said an anonymous letter-writer to his brother, scolding him for wearing his hair in a Scandinavian manner, shaved up the back but with a long fringe. 'In loving the practices of heathen men', he added, 'you despise your race and your ancestors.'[13]

Anxiety about this culture clash ran deeper than horse-trappings and haircuts. Wulfstan, the archbishop of York and former adviser of King Æthelred, had quickly come to terms with Cnut and endeavoured to heal the rift between the English and the Danes. He was responsible for drafting legislation for the new king, and also a letter that Cnut sent from Denmark in 1019 or 1020 to his subjects in England, promising them he would be a faithful lord and a defender of Christianity. But before his death in or around 1023, the archbishop penned a homily, preserved in a gospel book in York, on the perils of heathenism. 'Here in the land', he said, 'there are enemies of the divine, and those who despise God's law, murderers and killers of kinsmen, those who hate the church and priest-killers, violators of holy orders and adulterers, prostitutes and murderers of children.' It was in most respects a rehearsal of the sins he had railed against in his earlier *Sermon of the Wolf to the English*, but written after the Danish victory, with a fear that heathen practices were on the increase.[14]

One practice that Wulfstan particularly abhorred was the overseas export of English slaves: he complained about it both in his homily on heathenism and in his famous sermon. With slavery itself the Church had no complaint – it was a condition that had existed since biblical times – but it was essential that both slaves and masters should be Christian. If English people were sold out of the country into the hands of heathens, then their souls would surely be lost. The international slave trade, however, was clearly big business in the early eleventh century. The fortunes of Bristol were founded on the export of English slaves, centuries before the town's better-known involvement in the trading of Africans across the Atlantic. Large numbers of slaves were sold to Scandinavia. According to William of Malmesbury, one of the people who profited from their misery was the Danish wife of Earl Godwine, who was 'said to buy parties of slaves in England and ship them back to Denmark'.

Some of these slaves may have been wanted for hard labour, of the kind performed by the ploughman in Ælfric's soliloquy, but others were rounded up and sold for sexual purposes. In Bristol, according to Malmesbury, you could see young people 'of both sexes' roped together in lines, and the merchants would sell their own maidservants after making them pregnant. Wulfstan, in his *Sermon of the Wolf*, asserted that it was common practice for men to club together to buy a woman for their pleasure, and then sell her 'out of the land, into the power of strangers'. Godwine's wife allegedly specialized in the export of young girls, 'whose beauty and youth would enhance their price'. Churchmen, particularly reformed churchmen, might condemn this vociferously, and advocate the virtues of celibacy and monogamous marriage, but there was clearly a competing notion in Cnut's England that a man's power could be measured by the number of concubines he possessed. The king, for all his pious posturing, had done little to dispel this notion by having two wives.[15]

The suspicion that England was not as stable and harmonious during Cnut's reign as is traditionally supposed is further reinforced by events after his death. The king fell ill in the autumn of 1035 and died on 12 November. (Since the poets commented on his youth at the time of his accession, he was probably no more than forty at the time of his passing.) In his final years he had tried to turn his polygamy to his political advantage. His first wife, Ælfgifu, had been sent to rule Norway with her eldest son, Swein, and his second wife, Emma, had produced a son named Harthacnut, who was dispatched to rule Denmark. Later writers assumed from these developments that Cnut intended for his empire to be divided, and had agreed a plan of succession. If this was the case, however, it collapsed within a few days of his departure.[16]

Immediately after Cnut's body had been laid to rest in Winchester, an assembly was held in Oxford. The *Anglo-Saxon Chronicle* calls it a *witan-gemot*, literally 'a meeting of the wise', employing for the first time a term that had been coined a generation earlier by Ælfric of Eynsham. The tradition of summoning national assemblies dated back as far as Æthelstan's reign a century before, but their constitutional significance is often overstated. The common assertion, for instance, that English kingship was 'elective' seems less impressive when one remembers that, until Cnut's accession, every candidate had been a member of the same royal family, directly descended from Alfred the Great. Nevertheless, the impression is that the influence of assemblies, and their ability to speak for the whole nation, had been increasing, and the use of the word *witan-gemot* may reflect this. The earls and thegns who met at Oxford in the closing days of 1035 knew they had come to decide who should be their next ruler.

It soon became clear that there was no consensus. 'Earl Godwine and all the chief men of Wessex', says the *Chronicle*, were in favour of Harthacnut, the son of Queen Emma. They were opposed, however, by the thegns north of the Thames, led by Earl Leofric. The son of a previous English ealdorman, Leofric hailed from a family that had fallen under a cloud at the start of Cnut's reign: his brother had been among those executed in the purge of 1017. But Leofric had laboured to restore their fortunes, and had latterly been promoted to the rank of earl of Mercia, replacing the Danes who had died or departed for Denmark. In Cnut's final charters he appears among the witnesses second only to Godwine, with whom he clearly did not see eye to eye. He and the men of his earldom rejected the claim of Harthacnut, and declared their support for Harold, the younger son of Cnut's first wife, Ælfgifu. (Her older son, Swein, had died by this point.)

The great difficulty for Harthacnut's supporters is that their man was still in Denmark, whereas Harold was in England, and probably present at the Oxford meeting. A final decision, it was agreed, would have to wait on Harthacnut's return. In the meantime, it was proposed that Harold should rule the whole kingdom as a regent. Godwine and his supporters objected strenuously to this suggestion, says the *Chronicle*, but could do nothing to prevent it. The only concession the earl was able to wring from his opponents was that Wessex should remain under the direct control of Harthacnut's mother, Queen Emma, who was to reside at Winchester with her late husband's housecarls.[17]

No one wanted Harthacnut to become king more than Emma. She had been queen of England for more than three decades and was determined not to relinquish her position merely because another royal husband had inconsiderately predeceased her. Her efforts on Harthacnut's behalf are described in a tract she commissioned a few years later, known today as the *Encomium of Queen Emma*. It claimed, conveniently but improbably, that Cnut had sworn at the time of their marriage that only her children would be permitted to succeed him. It also put forward the unsubtle slur that Harold was not actually the son of Cnut and Ælfgifu at all, but the child of one of their female servants. Ælfgifu, however, proved more than equal to the challenge of retaliating in this public relations war. In the spring of 1036, for instance, she set about winning over those English magnates who were undecided by inviting them to a big party and offering them bribes. Her approach was evidently a success, and greatly helped by the fact that Harthacnut had still not appeared. The longer he remained in Denmark, the stronger the support for Harold became.[18]

By the summer of 1036, Emma had become sufficiently desperate that she was ready to contemplate a radical change of plan. Harthacnut was the only son she had produced with Cnut, but she had other sons from her earlier marriage to Æthelred the Unready. These boys, Edward and Alfred, had escaped from England before the end of 1016, and thereby avoided the bloodletting at the start of Cnut's reign. Since that time they had lived as exiles in Normandy, their mother's homeland, as a guest of their kinsmen, the Norman dukes. As they had grown to manhood, the two brothers clearly entertained hopes of one day recovering their lost inheritance. Edward, the elder of the two, had already tried and failed to return to England a few years earlier, and witnessed charters as 'king'.[19]

With Harthacnut still tied down in Denmark, Emma turned to the sons she had abandoned twenty years earlier, and evidently encouraged them to believe that there was a groundswell of support for their return. In the autumn of 1036 both brothers set out for England in separate expeditions. Edward seems to have sailed first and made for Southampton, the obvious port for a rendezvous with his mother in Winchester. On arrival, however, he was disabused of his popularity by a large English army, who engaged his forces in battle and persuaded him to retire to Normandy. Alfred, meanwhile, set sail from Flanders and landed at Dover. He too intended to meet up with his mother, but soon after his arrival he was intercepted by Earl Godwine. The earl welcomed him, swore allegiance to him, and escorted his party to Guildford, where they were treated to a lavish homecoming feast.[20]

Godwine was not acting in good faith. In the days after Cnut's death, he and Emma had been staunch allies – the *Anglo-Saxon Chronicle* describes him as her most loyal supporter. But the queen's subsequent decision to abandon Harthacnut and to back the cause of Edward and Alfred must have appalled him. The earl owed everything to his enthusiastic support of the Danish Conquest. Matters were bound to go badly for him if either of the main surviving victims of that conquest succeeded to the throne. From his point of view, it was imperative that the new king should be a son of Cnut. If Harthacnut had ruled himself out of the running through tardiness, it followed that Godwine would have to make his peace with Harold. And having Harold's rival lodged under his roof at Guildford presented the earl with the perfect opportunity.

During the night after their feast, having drunk deeply and retired to bed, Alfred and his followers were attacked by Godwine's men. Some of them were killed, some of them mutilated, and others were sold into slavery. It was, says the *Anglo-Saxon Chronicle*, the worst atrocity in England since the Danish Conquest twenty years before. Alfred himself was seized and sent to London for an interview with Harold, who ordered him to be taken away and blinded. The unfortunate pretender was sent by ship into the fens of East Anglia, deprived of his sight while still on board, and then left in the care of the monks of Ely. A short time afterwards he died, presumably as a result of his traumatic injury.[21]

Although the chroniclers later made much of Alfred's death, at the time his removal resolved the political stand-off in England. In 1037, says the *Anglo-Saxon Chronicle*, 'Harold was everywhere chosen as king, and Harthacnut repudiated, because he remained too long in Denmark.' Godwine, having delivered Alfred into Harold's hands, had proved his commitment to the new regime and retained his power in Wessex. Emma, by contrast, having tried to set her exiled sons against the king, was deemed to have demonstrated her disloyalty. At that moment, says the *Chronicle*, the twice-widowed queen 'was driven from the country without mercy, to face the raging winter'.[22]

Harold's reign, however, was only brief: he died on 17 March 1040, aged no more than twenty-five, barely three years after his accession to the whole kingdom. What happened in England during this time is a mystery. The *Chronicle*, composed after the king's death, maintains a discreet silence, and none of the charters that he issued have survived. Even his colourful nickname, Harold Harefoot, tells us nothing. Later medieval writers claimed it was a description of his great agility, but since it is first recorded in a twelfth-century chronicle as 'Harefah', the more plausible explanation is that it arose from confusion with the Norwegian king, Harold Fairhair. The only certainty is that during Harold's reign fears of a fresh invasion from Scandinavia must have been mounting, for Harthacnut had not abandoned the hope of ruling all of their father's empire. Egged on by his mother from her exile in Flanders, the Danish king set sail for England in the spring of 1040, ready to fight his half-brother for possession of the crown. It was apparently only while he was en route that the news arrived of Harold's death, followed by an invitation from the English magnates to ascend to the throne peacefully.[23]

'They thought they were acting wisely', says the *Anglo-Saxon Chronicle*, but they were soon proved wrong. Harthacnut, the *Chronicle* continues, 'did nothing worthy of a king as long as he ruled'. In part this was because he and his mother returned to England bent on revenge. Soon after their arrival, Harthacnut had Harold's body removed from its resting place in Westminster and 'flung into a fen'. Godwine, now publicly accused for his part in the death of Alfred, managed to weather the storm of recrimination, swearing to the new king that he had only been obeying orders. Others were not so adroit. The earl of Northumbria was murdered at Harthacnut's command, presumably on suspicion of disloyalty. This might have been considered a legitimate political act, but the king had lured the earl south with a promise of safe conduct, prompting the *Chronicle* to brand him 'a breaker of his pledge'.

What really compromised Harthacnut's kingship, however, was his harsh taxation. Ever since 1012, when Æthelred the Unready had introduced it, English people had grown accustomed to paying the *heregeld*, a levy to subsidize a permanent mercenary fleet. Cnut had used it to retain the services of sixteen ships, and Harold had done the same. Harthacnut, though, had come to England with an invasion force of sixty-two ships, and demanded their crews be paid at the same established rate. The result, says the *Chronicle*, was 'a very severe tax, which was borne with difficulty': the price of wheat rocketed, and when two of the king's housecarls came to Worcester to demand payment, they were killed by an angry mob. In response, Harthacnut ordered the city to be harried, and his troops spent four days there looting and burning. 'All who had previously been zealous on his behalf', says the *Chronicle*, 'now became ill-disposed towards him.'[24]

The new king's plummeting popularity offers the best explanation of what happened next. At some point in the second year of his reign, Harthacnut invited his surviving half-brother, Edward, to return from Normandy and share in the rule of the kingdom – the *Anglo-Saxon Chronicle* says that Edward 'was sworn in as king'. According to the *Encomium of Queen Emma*, this was nothing more than an expression of brotherly love, an explanation which seems unlikely, given that the two men had almost certainly never met. A more plausible reason would be that Harthacnut's hand was forced by his magnates, and the demands of the wider political community. A twelfth-century legal treatise called *Quadripartitus* says that Edward was recalled to England at the initiative of Earl Godwine and the bishop of Winchester, and that when he arrived on the Hampshire coast, he was met by 'the thegns of all England'. Before he was allowed to proceed further, Edward was made to swear before what sounds like a large assembly of men that he would uphold 'the laws of Cnut'. Since Cnut's laws had explicitly harked back to those of King Edgar, this was essentially a demand for a return to the good old days, before the advent of extortionate royal taxation. The deal presented to Edward was reminiscent of the one made with his father back in 1014, when Æthelred's subjects had received him back from Norman exile on condition that he rule them better. Even more than the *witan-gemot* at Oxford in 1035, it demonstrates the collective bargaining power of England's thegnly class.[25]

From 1041, therefore, the country found itself in the strange position of having two kings, one a son of Æthelred, the other a son of Cnut, both of them sons of the same mother. Emma's *Encomium*, which she commissioned at this point to defend this extraordinary state of affairs, compares their triumvirate to the Holy Trinity, and insists that there was 'no disagreement between them'. Had that truly been the case, of course, such a statement would have been redundant, and the suspicion must be that in reality the two half-brothers, one the victim of the Danish Conquest, the other embodying its continuation, found it very difficult to work together.[26]

Fortunately, the problem did not last long. On 8 June 1042, the year after Edward's return, Harthacnut suddenly collapsed and died at Lambeth, near London, while attending the wedding of one of his men. Given the political tension at his court, we would be justified in suspecting foul play, and our sources drop heavy hints that it was indeed afoot. Harthacnut was in his early twenties, and reportedly 'in good health and great heart', yet according to the *Anglo-Saxon Chronicle*, he died 'standing at his drink', and fell to the floor 'with fearful convulsions'. Whether or not something had been slipped into his drinking horn, his swift end signalled the return to a more conventional form of government. Even before he was buried, says the *Chronicle*, 'the whole nation chose Edward to be king'.[27]

★

29. The author of the *Encomium* presents his work to Queen Emma. Her two sons, Harthacnut and Edward, appear to have been added to the picture, just as the text itself was revised to accord with changing political circumstances.

Today Edward is familiar to most people on account of his memorable byname, 'the Confessor'. This was awarded to him after 1161, at which point the pope promoted him to sainthood, having accepted the evidence that the king had worked miracles both before and after his death. Many of these were described in the so-called *Life of King Edward*, and while we may doubt that they were genuine, there is no doubt that Edward was genuinely pious. The *Life* tells us that he diligently attended Mass, was generous in his distribution of alms to the poor, and that he loved to converse with abbots and monks. From the start of his reign he was a devoted patron of the small and previously impoverished monastic community to the west of London, whose abbey was known as the West Minster, rebuilding their church on such a scale that by the time of his death it was the biggest in Britain.[28]

His posthumous sanctity, however, should not mislead us into thinking that he was unconcerned with secular affairs, or that he had no aptitude for the more muscular aspects of kingship. Pious he may have been, but the Confessor was neither a pacifist nor a pushover. In the second year of his reign, for instance, he responded vigorously to reports that his mother was plotting against him, riding with his earls and their military retinues to Winchester and depriving the former queen of all her property. Similarly, in 1044, and also in the year that followed, Edward reacted to threats of an imminent invasion from Norway by assembling ships at Sandwich and sailing out into the Channel, ready to fend off any attack.

What Edward lacked was not gumption, but political allies. A quarter of a century in foreign exile meant he had not had the opportunity to forge the kind of close relationships with his leading nobles that all kings needed in order to prosper. Unlike Cnut, he had not come to England as a conqueror, able to enforce his will with an invading army, ready to replace anyone who opposed or displeased him. The Confessor had arrived peacefully, by invitation, and was attended by only a handful of friends and followers from Normandy. Having fled his homeland as a boy, he had returned as a man approaching forty, to find that both he and the country had changed, and that he was now an outsider, more familiar with the affairs and customs of northern France than those of his place of birth.[29]

For all these reasons the new king needed Godwine. In the same twenty-five-year period the earl had become everything the king was not – rich, popular and well connected. As earl of Wessex, he essentially occupied the power base of Edward's royal ancestors, and to some extent must have usurped their position as a focus for loyalty. The earl's motivation for championing Edward's cause is harder to fathom, bearing in mind his fierce opposition to the return of Alfred only a few years earlier. It may be that, having deserted Harthacnut for Harold, he felt vulnerable when Harthacnut unexpectedly came to power and began revenging himself on those who had betrayed him. Although Edward was hardly likely to have been any more forgiving of his brother's murder, Godwine may have reckoned that he would be better able to deal with a powerless exile than a wrathful king of Denmark who could call on military support from his other dominions.

Edward's reign, then, was founded on this awkward alliance, which required him and Godwine to go through a public performance of reconciliation. The earl, for his part, swore he had never intended Alfred to come to any harm, and presented the king with the gift of a magnificent gilded warship, crewed with eighty warriors all decked out in gold. Edward responded by rewarding three of Godwine's kinsmen with earldoms. His eldest sons, Swein and Harold, were respectively placed in charge of the south-west Midlands and East Anglia in 1043, and his nephew Beorn was given the command of the south-east Midlands in 1045.[30]

It was also in 1045 that the king was married to Godwine's daughter, Edith. According to the *Life of King Edward*, which she commissioned herself, Edith was as close to perfection as could be imagined: beautiful, intelligent, articulate, affectionate, honest, artistic, generous and (self-evidently) modest. But even in listing her attractions and accomplishments at length, her hired author does not ignore the political reality that lay behind her pairing with Edward. The king, he says, 'agreed more readily to contract this marriage because he knew that, with the advice and help of Godwine, he would have a firmer hold on his hereditary rights in England'.[31]

As time wore on, though, Edward's relationship with his father-in-law began to grow fractious. This was in part because they had very different attitudes toward the legacy of the Danish Conquest. Soon after his marriage the king banished a niece of King Cnut named Gunhilda, who was residing in England with her two children, and the following year he drove out Osgod Clapa, one of Cnut's Danish followers. Godwine, by contrast, strove to maintain close relations with Denmark. When, in 1047, the new Danish king, Swein Estrithson, appealed to England for military assistance against Norway, Godwine – his uncle – was all in favour, and recommended dispatching a fleet of fifty ships. But Edward refused, backed by Leofric of Mercia and apparently the great majority of the wider political community. 'It seemed a foolish plan to everybody', says the *Anglo-Saxon Chronicle*.[32]

The two men also clashed over ecclesiastical appointments. When the archbishop of Canterbury resigned due to ill health in 1044, the selection of his stand-in had been carried out 'with the advice of the king and Earl Godwine'. But when the archbishop finally died in October 1050, Edward rejected Godwine's suggestion for a replacement and appointed his friend, Robert of Jumièges. Robert, as his name suggests, was a Norman, the former abbot of Jumièges, a monastery on the River Seine. He had come to England with Edward in 1041 and been made bishop of London three years later. In the words of the *Life of King Edward*, Robert was 'the most powerful confidential adviser of the king', which naturally made him a rival to Godwine, who objected strenuously to the promotion of a 'stranger' as archbishop. As with his foreign policy advice, however, the earl was overruled, and in March 1051 Robert's appointment was confirmed by the king's council.[33]

The final straw proved to be the issue of the succession. Godwine's plan was obviously that Edward and Edith would present him with a grandson who would in due course go on to become the next king. But by 1051, after six years of marriage, the royal couple had produced no children at all. Modern commentators tend to believe this was merely biological bad luck, but Edith herself insisted it was because her husband had never slept with her. The king, says his biographer, was a celibate who 'preserved the dignity of his consecration with holy chastity'.[34] Whatever the truth, the absence of offspring was deeply worrying for everyone, for there were no other obvious candidates for the throne. Edward was the last known representative of the ancient house of Wessex: his older half-brothers had been killed in the course of the Danish Conquest, and his younger brother Alfred had been betrayed to his death by Godwine. If the king failed to produce an heir, the country faced a return to the years of crisis that had preceded his accession.

Edward, however, had come up with an alternative solution. In the spring of 1051, probably in the same council that approved the appointment of Robert of Jumièges, the king apparently proposed that after his death the crown should pass to his cousin, Duke William of Normandy. From the king's perspective this made excellent sense. Born around 1027, William was a young, successful warrior who had established his authority in northern France in the face of repeated attempts to overthrow him. On a practical level, his accession would restore the alliance between England and Normandy that had been forged by the marriage of Edward's parents, Æthelred and Emma, almost half a century earlier. And there were almost certainly personal reasons on Edward's part for preferring William. The king had spent twenty-five years in Normandy as an exile, and clearly felt a debt of gratitude to its ducal family, who had raised him and supported his attempts at restoration.[35]

But the prospect of a Norman succession must have gone down very badly with Godwine, and, in the months that followed, his relationship with Edward rapidly deteriorated. In the summer of 1051 the earl clashed with the king's most intimate adviser, Robert of Jumièges, who accused him of invading some of Canterbury's lands, and apparently convinced Edward that Godwine was planning to attack him. Then, in the last days of August, the earl clashed with the king himself. The trigger was a visit to England of the count of Boulogne, who was married to Edward's sister, Godgifu. On his way back home the count's men squabbled with the citizens of Dover, and their dispute resulted in deaths on both sides. The count complained to his royal brother-in-law, and Edward responded by commanding Godwine to attack Dover in retribution. But Godwine refused. Kent was part of his earldom, and he reportedly declared that he would not injure his own people.[36]

With the rift between them finally exposed, the king and his father-in-law prepared to settle their differences by force. Godwine and his sons raised the men of their earldoms, and Edward summoned to his side Leofric of Mercia and Siward, the earl of Northumbria. But when the two armies were assembled in Gloucestershire that September, ready for battle, their commanders hesitated, fearing (says the *Chronicle*) that civil war would leave the country open to foreign invasion, and lead to their collective ruin. It was agreed instead that all parties would proceed to London, where Godwine would stand trial. As they made their way east, however, the earl's forces gradually melted away, while the king's army grew stronger and stronger. When they eventually reached London, Edward felt sufficiently empowered that he revealed his long-concealed hand, and told Godwine he could have peace 'when he gave him back his brother alive'.

Belatedly realizing that the king's hatred was deep-seated and implacable, the earl responded by running. Two of his sons rode west and took ship to Ireland, while Godwine and the rest of his family sailed across the Channel to Flanders. Only his daughter, Queen Edith, was unable to escape, and she was immediately banished by her husband to a nunnery. 'If any Englishman had been told that events would take this turn, he would have been very surprised,' said the *Anglo-Saxon Chronicle*, 'for Godwine had risen to such great eminence as if he ruled the king and all England.'[37]

Having successfully ousted his in-laws, Edward immediately took steps to shore up his position. The earldoms held by the Godwine family were seized and reassigned to others: East Anglia was awarded to Earl Leofric's son, Ælfgar, and the western shires of Wessex were given to Odda, who was probably a distant kinsman of the king. Edward also summoned his closer kinsman, Duke William of Normandy, who crossed the Channel to visit him at some point in the autumn of 1051 or during the winter that followed. The purpose was presumably to reaffirm the promise of the succession that had been made earlier in the year, and to bind William more closely to Edward's cause. The *Anglo-Saxon Chronicle*, noting the duke's presence in England, says that the king received him as a vassal. Edward's hope was evidently that by giving these men, native and Norman, a vested interest in safeguarding the revolution, they would rally to his aid in the event of a Godwine *revanche*.[38]

Their support was going to be all the more necessary because the king had recently abandoned his father's policy of maintaining a mercenary fleet. In 1049 he had dismissed nine of the fourteen ships in his pay, and the following year he did away with the remaining five. With the benefit of hindsight his decision to do this as his feud with Godwine was intensifying seems perverse, but two factors may have made it desirable. Firstly, the tax to subsidize the fleet – the *heregeld* – had always been hugely unpopular, to the extent that it may have cost Harthacnut his kingship. The *Anglo-Saxon Chronicle* reports its abolition in 1051 with evident relief. Secondly, the ships funded by the *heregeld* had traditionally been crewed by men of Scandinavian descent, and thus represented another legacy of the Danish Conquest that Edward wished to undo. Speculatively, there may have been sympathy among these men for Godwine and his interventionist approach to Scandinavian politics. If so, the king's wish to be rid of them becomes more readily understandable.[39]

The viability of Edward's plans was tested in 1052, when the Godwine family attempted an armed comeback. At first the king's position seemed promising. He commanded his newly promoted earls to raise a fleet, which succeeded in preventing Godwine from making a landfall, and forced him to return to Flanders. But the crews of these ships, being volunteers, soon declared their service was done, and sailed back to London, leaving Edward desperately casting around for replacements. This delay gave his enemies the opportunity they needed. In August Godwine sailed again, this time joining forces in the Channel with the sons he had sent to Ireland. Together they sailed around the south-east coast, seizing supplies and ships, and recruiting more and more supporters. Public opinion, so far as it can be judged, seems to have swung behind the exiled earl, possibly because news of the king's plan for a Norman succession had spread. By the time Godwine reached London he was at the head of a massive armada, whereas Edward was still waiting forlornly for reinforcements. 'The sea was covered with ships', says the author of the *Life of King Edward*, unable to contain his exultation. 'The sky glittered with the press of weapons.'

Outnumbered and outmanoeuvred, the king had no choice but to submit, though naturally his surrender was presented as a reconciliation. Through furiously gritted teeth Edward publicly forgave his father-in-law and reinstated him and his sons to their former earldoms. Queen Edith, packed off to a nunnery the previous year, was restored to the royal bedchamber. The king's Norman friends, realizing the peril of their position, fled in all directions. Some went north, says the *Chronicle*, and some went west, eventually ending up in Scotland, where they entered the service of its murderous king, Macbeth. Edward's principal adviser, Robert of Jumièges, rode east to the Essex coast and took a dangerously dilapidated ship back to Normandy. By any realistic assessment, the plan for a Norman succession was dead in the water.[40]

★

Godwine, it turned out, had little time to enjoy his triumph. Barely seven months later, on Easter Monday 1053, the earl suffered some kind of seizure while dining with the king at Winchester. 'He suddenly sank towards the foot-stool,' says the *Anglo-Saxon Chronicle*, 'bereft of speech and deprived of all of his strength.' Three days later he died, and was taken for burial at the Old Minster. At his funeral, says the *Life of King Edward*, the people showed great grief, weeping for the loss of 'the kingdom's protector'.[41]

But they were soon consoled, the same source continues, by the fact that Godwine was succeeded as earl of Wessex by 'his eldest and wisest son, Harold'. Strictly speaking Harold was the eldest *surviving* son: his older brother, Swein, had died a few months earlier, in September 1052, returning from a pilgrimage to Jerusalem. This was evidently something of a relief to the family, for Swein is not mentioned in the *Life of King Edward*, having repeatedly embarrassed them, first by abducting the abbess of Leominster, and later by murdering his cousin, Earl Beorn. Harold, by contrast, shared none of his deceased brother's defects, and was, in the opinion of his sister's hired pen, even better than Godwine himself. 'A true friend of his people and his country,' says the *Life*, 'he wielded his father's powers even more actively, and walked in his ways of patience and mercy.' Tall, handsome, strong in mind and body, kind to men of goodwill but ferocious in dealing with criminals, Harold is presented as little short of perfect – a king in waiting.[42]

This was just as well, for it is equally plain from the *Life* that Edward himself was not permitted to exercise much power after his in-laws' forceful return. Obviously the author presents this as a voluntary decision on the king's part. Edward, we are told, happily left the business of government to others, preferring to spend his days hunting and hawking, or practising his religious devotions. But it is hard not to conclude from the description of the king's activities that he was essentially a Godwine puppet after 1052, compliantly staying out of the way or doing as he was told. His wife, Edith, having returned from her humiliating banishment, clearly played a part in maintaining this control, stage-managing his public appearances. It was only on special occasions, says the *Life of King Edward*, 'that he displayed the pomp of royal finery in which the queen obligingly arrayed him'.[43]

The strongest indication that Edward was not exercising any real power after 1052 is the identity of the new archbishop of Canterbury. The king's own religious sympathies were predominately monastic and pro-reform. This was hardly surprising, for his exile in Normandy had coincided with the belated but enthusiastic embrace of Benedictine monasticism by the Norman dukes and their leading men. Edward's own enthusiasm is indicated by his friendship with Robert of Jumièges, whose abbey was one of the most important centres of reform in the duchy. Robert had begun rebuilding the church there in a fashionable new 'Romanesque' style before his departure for England, and after his accession Edward had done the same at Westminster, using Jumièges as his model. Both men, moreover, had responded positively when the reformers took over the papacy in 1048: Edward had sent English delegates to papal councils in the two years that followed, and when Robert was made archbishop of Canterbury in 1051, he had dutifully travelled to Rome to receive his pallium.[44]

In September 1052, however, after Godwine's return had caused Robert to flee, the archbishopric of Canterbury was awarded to Stigand. As his Norse name suggests, Stigand was part of the Anglo-Danish connection. Like Godwine, he first came to prominence under Cnut, who appointed him as priest of the church on the site of the Battle of *Assandun*. After Cnut's death he remained attached to the widowed Queen Emma: it was probably her influence, or that of Godwine, that secured him the bishopric of Winchester in 1047. Once the seat of the kings of Wessex, Winchester had become strongly associated with the memory of the Danish Conquest: Cnut was buried there, as was Harthacnut, and Emma herself was buried there after her death in 1052, soon to be followed by Godwine a year later. Edward's decision to rebuild Westminster Abbey, and to establish a new royal palace alongside it, was almost certainly determined by his distaste for what Winchester had become, and his desire for a fresh start.[45]

The installation of Stigand as archbishop of Canterbury therefore marked the promotion of a man who represented everything Edward was against, and can only be seen as an appointment dictated by the Godwine family in their moment of triumph. Stigand was not a monk but a secular priest – the first non-monk to be archbishop of Canterbury for almost a century. This in itself was not necessarily a problem – Wulfstan, the former archbishop of York, had probably not been a monk either – but Stigand was secular in the extreme, a worldly cleric who exhibited considerable contempt for the ideals of reform. After his promotion to Canterbury, he failed to surrender his position as bishop of Winchester, and continued to hold the two sees in plurality – a practice that reformers deplored. He was also, according to later writers, guilty of simony – the buying and selling of ecclesiastical offices. Vastly rich and powerful, Stigand had little time for the newly reformed papacy. Rather than travel to Rome to collect his pallium, as was customary, he simply used the one that Robert of Jumièges had left behind in his haste to depart. For these reasons, some English churchmen did not regard his appointment as legitimate. 'There was no archbishop in the land', said one version of the *Anglo-Saxon Chronicle* in 1053. In the years that followed, several newly elected bishops went overseas to be consecrated, anxious to avoid Stigand's taint.[46]

Stigand was clearly an extreme case, held in contempt by some of his episcopal colleagues, but it is worth stressing that most people, spiritual and lay, had no problem with secular priests per se. Edward the Confessor himself, for all his reported love of monks, employed secular clerics in his household and in some cases rewarded them with bishoprics. Clearly the king did not share the opinion of his grandfather, Edgar, that the prayers of such men were worthless. The success of zealous, puritanical reformers in Edgar's reign had proved highly damaging during the reign of Æthelred, inducing a self-flagellating mindset among

England's elite as they were struggling to deal with renewed viking invasions. After the Danish Conquest, their attitude towards religion appears to have been healthier. Led by the example of their self-confident Danish conquerors, the English were still pious, but no longer trapped in a vicious cycle of purges in pursuit of moral purity.[47]

This new Anglo-Danish attitude towards religion is well illustrated by Harold Godwineson. The new earl of Wessex was a generous benefactor to several Benedictine monasteries and friendly with their abbots – the abbot of Peterborough, Leofric, accompanied him on his march to Hastings. Harold's main spiritual investment, however, was a non-monastic church at Waltham in Essex. Waltham Holy Cross, as it was known, had been founded a generation earlier by one of Cnut's followers, Tovi the Proud, after he miraculously discovered a cross on one of his estates. Harold rebuilt the church on a lavish scale and re-founded it as a college of secular canons, a new type of institution that was fashionable on the Continent. The priests there were pious and learned, but also practical, and could serve in his household as administrators and clerks if required. Not all of them, perhaps, were quite as secular as Leofgar, a priest whom the earl promoted from his household in 1056 to become the new bishop of Hereford. 'He wore his moustaches during his priesthood,' says the *Anglo-Saxon Chronicle*, disapprovingly, 'and took up his spear and sword after his consecration as bishop.' Leofgar and his fellow fighting priests were killed in battle against the Welsh a few months later.[48]

Harold's heavy investment at Waltham was mirrored by that of his fellow earls. Leofric of Mercia and his wife, Godgifu, created a college of secular canons by re-endowing the church of St Mary Stow in Lincolnshire, and were probably responsible for the creation of what is now one of the largest surviving Anglo-Saxon churches. Siward, the earl of Northumbria, did something similar at York, founding a secular minster dedicated to St Olaf, a former king of Norway who earlier in life may have participated in Cnut's conquest of England. Earl Odda, who survived the revolution of 1052 but was given a much smaller earldom, commissioned a more modest chapel at Deerhurst in Gloucestershire, dedicated in 1056 – both the chapel and its dedication stone have survived. And where these earls led, others followed. All across the country in Edward's reign, prosperous thegns were either founding new parish churches on their estates, or rebuilding old wooden ones in stone. The towers at Barton-on-the-Humber in Lincolnshire, and Earls Barton in Northamptonshire (colour picture 23), are outstanding examples.[49]

This pious investment in stone was a good indication of England's return to prosperity. After long decades of war, invasion and uncertainty, the country at last seemed to be calm. The first decade of Edward's own reign had evidently not been easy. Throughout the 1040s the *Chronicle* makes repeated reference to harsh winters and storms, pestilence among people and animals, crop failures, inflation and famine, and during that same period the quality of the coinage was terrible. But as we move into the 1050s, the picture brightens. References to natural disasters disappear, and the coinage was reformed to a high standard. After the return of the Godwine family, says the *Life of King Edward*, 'the whole country settled down in peace and tranquillity'. The Confessor is compared to King Solomon, enjoying a reign of glory and abundance. 'A golden age', says the author, 'shone for his English race.'[50]

But beneath this economic success there were deep political divisions, an enduring legacy of the Danish Conquest. Some people in the country were committed to the ancient royal house of Wessex, and wanted to see it continue, in spite of Edward's failure to father a successor. The clearest evidence of this was a sustained effort to locate a long-lost relative of the king. Soon after the return of the Godwine family, if not earlier, Edward had discovered that he had a namesake nephew living on the other side of Europe. This Edward, known to historians as 'Edward the Exile', was one of the two sons of Edmund Ironside, who had been sent as small children to Sweden by Cnut with the request that they be quietly disappeared. But the Swedish king had apparently taken pity on the infants and sent them on to Hungary. One of them, named Edmund after his father, had subsequently died, but Edward had survived and grown to manhood. In 1054, the bishop of Worcester was sent overseas in the hope of persuading him to return. That particular mission failed, but three years later, presumably after more patient long-distance diplomacy, the exile prince landed in England, returning after an absence of more than forty years.[51]

Immediately after his arrival, he dropped dead, in circumstances that some regarded as suspicious. 'We do not know for what reason it was brought about that he was not allowed to visit his kinsman, King Edward', says one version of the *Chronicle*, strongly hinting that sinister forces were at work. 'Alas, that was a miserable fate, and grievous to all this people, that he so speedily ended his life after he came to England.' The Exile's death was not, in fact, the total disaster that the *Chronicle* implies, for he had fathered a son, named Edgar, aged no more than five, who took his place as the heir apparent. For those who wished to see the ancient royal line sustained, this young prince (*ætheling*) was their last remaining hope.[52]

The problem for such people, however, was that there were plenty of others who did not share their attachment. The Danish Conquest had dissolved long-established loyalties and destroyed the former political consensus, and at the same time created new dynasties that owed nothing to Edward and his ancestors. Chief among them, of course, was the family of Godwine, whose power in this same period was expanding rapidly. In 1055, when old Earl Siward of Northumbria died, he was succeeded not by his son, as expected, but by Harold's younger brother, Tostig. 'With no opposition from the king', says the *Life of King Edward*, suggesting some people thought otherwise. One of them was clearly Earl Ælfgar of East Anglia, the son of Leofric of Mercia, who was twice sent into exile during these years, almost certainly for protesting against the Godwine family's stranglehold over royal patronage. But Ælfgar's objections were in vain. When he inherited Mercia from his father in 1057, East Anglia was awarded to a third Godwine brother, Gyrth, and the following year a new south-eastern earldom was created for a fourth, Leofwine.[53]

With all but one of England's major earldoms under their control, the Godwinesons seemed unassailable. When the archbishop of York died in 1060 he was replaced by Bishop Ealdred of Worcester, a friend and supporter of Harold, meaning that both archdioceses were in Godwine-friendly hands. After the death of Ælfgar of Mercia in or soon after 1062, Harold and Tostig launched a devastating attack on his former ally, King Gruffudd of Wales, replacing him with a client ruler and sending his decapitated head back to England in triumph. Memorial stones were raised all over Wales to mark their victory, proclaiming Harold as the country's conqueror. Despite the existence of the young Edgar Ætheling, the earl of Wessex must have seemed a strong contender to replace the snowy-haired Edward the Confessor, who was now around sixty years old. It was only when Harold decided to pay a visit to Duke William of Normandy that his apparently unstoppable run of success was arrested.[54]

Harold's trip to Normandy, which probably took place in 1064, is well known because it is depicted at length on the Bayeux Tapestry. (Harold, indeed, is arguably the Tapestry's true subject – its narrative begins with his Norman adventure and ends with his death.) The opening scenes show the earl conversing with Edward the Confessor, riding with his retinue to Bosham, and then – after a final meal and a prudent prayer – setting out to sea.

But why did Harold embark upon this voyage? The Tapestry, whose captions are telegraphically brief, does not deign to tell us, and contemporary English authors do not mention it at all. According to Norman chroniclers, the earl went at the insistence of Edward the Confessor, to renew the king's earlier promise of the English throne to Duke William. This explanation, however, stretches credibility beyond its elastic limit. It beggars belief that the aged Confessor, so evidently in the grip of the Godwine family after 1052, could have commanded Harold to undertake a task that was so inimical to his own interests and ambitions.[55]

The most convincing explanation is offered by an English chronicler named Eadmer of Canterbury, writing in the early twelfth century, who says that Harold travelled to Normandy to retrieve two of his relatives who were being held as hostages. The existence of these hostages is not in doubt – even the Norman chroniclers cannot avoid mentioning them. They had been handed over to Edward during his tense stand-off with the Godwine family in 1051, and probably transferred to William's custody when the duke had visited England soon afterwards. Eadmer, whose account is well informed on detail, names them as Wulfnoth, another of Harold's younger brothers, and Hakon, the son of his older brother, the late Earl Swein.

The suggestion that Harold went on his own initiative to secure the release of these two close kinsmen fits far better with what we know of his position at this point. By the mid-1060s he was strong, successful and popular, effectively ruling the kingdom on Edward's behalf. To him and his supporters it must have seemed shameful that two members of his family were still being detained by William more than a dozen years after their surrender. Wulfnoth and Hakon had presumably been given to the duke as a way of guaranteeing the Confessor's promise of the English succession. If, as seems likely, Harold was already contemplating his own bid for the throne, it would have been essential for him to secure their release and put them beyond harm's reach. His hope must have been that he could somehow talk William round and purchase the hostages' freedom. According to Eadmer, the earl embarked for Normandy 'taking with him his richest and most honourable men, equipped with a lordly provision of gold, silver, and costly raiment'.[56]

But the trip, alas, did not go to plan. In the first place Harold and his men sailed into a storm and were blown off course, ending up in Ponthieu, Normandy's north-eastern neighbour, and taken prisoner by its count. Eventually freed after William's intervention, they were brought to Normandy and treated with greater honour. The Tapestry shows the duke bestowing armour on Harold, and taking him on a military campaign in

Brittany – the earl demonstrates his heroism by rescuing some Norman soldiers from quicksand. When it came to the matter of the hostages, however, Harold was only partially successful, securing the release of his nephew, Hakon, but not his brother, Wulfnoth. William made it clear that he had no intention of abandoning his claim to the English throne, and evidently wanted to retain at least one hostage as security. Worse still, from Harold's point of view, the duke made him swear on holy relics that he would support his claim, and that he would work to ensure a smooth Norman succession when the time came. Unable to see any other way to escape, says Eadmer, Harold agreed to everything William wished.[57]

If Harold's visit to Normandy was a disappointment, what followed was a near disaster. Soon after his return to England there was a massive uprising in Northumbria against the rule of his brother, Tostig. The imposition of a Godwineson as their governor had displeased the Northumbrians from the start, and Tostig had done little to ameliorate matters in the intervening decade. According to unsympathetic chroniclers the earl had raised

30. The Bayeux Tapestry: Harold swears to uphold William's claim.

taxes, robbed the Church, killed his enemies and seized their lands. Even the *Life of King Edward*, composed to sing the Godwinesons' praises, admits that Tostig was 'occasionally a little too zealous in attacking evil', and reports that his critics charged him with being excessively cruel. In 1064 the earl had invited two of his northern rivals to a peace conference in York, only to have them treacherously slain. When their lord came south to complain at the Confessor's Christmas court, he was in turn murdered on the orders of Tostig's sister, Queen Edith.[58]

In the autumn of 1065, these accumulated resentments exploded. At the start of October a group of 200 armed men attacked York, killing Tostig's housecarls, smashing open his treasury and seizing all his weapons, silver and gold. The rebellion spread quickly across the whole region, with more slaughter in the streets of Lincoln, as well as in the surrounding countryside. Anyone who could be identified as a member of the earl's affinity, says the *Life of King Edward*, was dragged to death without trial. Driving this violence was a clear political agenda. The rebels' aim was to replace Tostig with Morcar, a son of the late Earl Ælfgar of Mercia. He and his older brother, Eadwine, who had inherited their father's earldom, were evidently part of the conspiracy from the start. They raised the men of the Midlands, and were soon joined by men from Wales. This was not merely a northern rising, but a broad coalition of all those who had suffered as a result of the Godwinesons' rise.[59]

Tostig was not in Northumbria at the time the tempest struck, but in Wiltshire, attending the rededication of Wilton Abbey. Wilton had been the childhood home of his sister, Queen Edith, and she had financed the rebuilding of its old wooden church in stone. Naturally the queen was also present for this ceremony, along with the king and a great crowd of nobles. Harold Godwineson was almost certainly among their number, for when news of the northern uprising broke, he was sent to negotiate. He met the rebels at Northampton and conveyed a message from the king, which was that they should stand down, and their grievances would be redressed. The rebels, predictably, rejected this suggestion, and said they would be satisfied only when Tostig was banished from the kingdom.[60]

When Harold returned to Edward's court as the bearer of this reply, the atmosphere was already acrimonious, with the other magnates accusing his brother of having brought the crisis on his own head. Once it became clear that the price of peace was to be his expulsion, not merely from Northumbria but from England as a whole, Tostig reacted furiously, and publicly accused Harold of plotting with the rebels to deprive him of his earldom. The charge of conspiracy against Harold seems very far-fetched, and the real cause of Tostig's wrath is likely to have been his brother's refusal to provide him with military backing. When the king commanded an army to be raised against the rebels, who had by now ravaged Northamptonshire and advanced as far as Oxford, excuses were made about the onset of winter, the difficulty of raising troops, and the general undesirability of civil war. Faced with this recalcitrance, Edward had no choice but to comply with the rebels' demands, and sent Tostig into exile.[61]

The queen, says the *Life of King Edward*, wept inconsolably at her brother's departure, and the whole court was plunged into mourning. But no one, it seems, was more distraught than Edward himself, who was so angered by his nobles' disobedience that he became ill. In the weeks that followed his condition worsened, and on Christmas Day he was too unwell to eat anything set before him during the festive banquet. Because of his rapid decline, the dedication of Westminster Abbey, still not quite finished, had been brought forward to 28 December, but in the event the king was too sick to attend. Eight days after the ceremony, surrounded by his closest companions, the Confessor died, and the following day – 6 January 1066 – his body was taken to the abbey for burial. Later that day, probably in the same sacred space, Harold was crowned as his replacement.[62]

The coronation of Harold as England's new king can have come as a surprise to very few people. To many, it must have seemed the inevitable conclusion of a story that had begun half a century

31. The Bayeux Tapestry: The coronation of Harold Godwineson.

earlier, when his father had been plucked from obscurity by Cnut and promoted to be the country's leading nobleman. Godwine himself had been content with the marriage of his daughter to Edward the Confessor, expecting that from their match a new royal line would eventually blossom. When Edward frustrated this scheme and tried in vain to eject his in-laws, they had responded by reducing him to a cipher and taking over the running of his kingdom. It must have seemed unlikely that they were going to risk losing that power merely because in the meantime a candidate had been found with a stronger claim by blood. Whatever residual attachment there may have been in some quarters to the old house of Wessex, there was no one sufficiently powerful in 1066 to insist on the superior hereditary right of young Edgar Ætheling, a boy barely into his teens, and plenty of people willing to take a pragmatic view that the throne should pass to a grown man with a proven track record in war and government.

Against this background, the mechanisms by which Harold and his many supporters affected this coup hardly matter. According to pro-Godwine sources, the earl was nominated by Edward the Confessor in his dying moments, a scene also depicted on the Bayeux Tapestry. Other sources are more sceptical, saying that the old king merely 'entrusted' Harold with the kingdom, or that the earl had seized it 'with cunning force'. William of Malmesbury, writing half a century later, noted that in his own day many English people claimed that the Confessor had bequeathed the throne to Harold, but Malmesbury himself was not convinced. 'I think this claim rests more on goodwill than judgement,' he said, 'for it makes him pass on his inheritance to a man of whose influence he had always been suspicious.'[63]

What mattered a great deal more than any debatable last-minute change of heart from the dying Confessor was the backing of the majority of the kingdom's magnates, and here there can be no doubt that Harold secured the necessary support. He already had the blessing of both archbishops and a huge affinity of followers across southern and eastern England. What he required additionally was the endorsement of the new earls of Mercia and Northumbria, Eadwine and Morcar, who had led the recent rebellion. At some point in the autumn of 1065, Harold must have struck a deal with the two brothers, and convinced them to consent to his elevation when the time came. Both of them were present at court that Christmas, and presumably agreed to his coronation a few days later. The existence of such a pact between them is indicated by Harold's marriage around this time to their sister, Ealdgyth. The only person perhaps unhappy with this arrangement was the earl's existing wife, the fabled Edith Swan-Neck.[64]

Harold was taking no real risks in pushing aside a powerless teenager, or disappointing the mother of his children. His much greater gamble was that Duke William would not react to the news of his betrayal by executing his brother, Wulfnoth. In the event Wulfnoth's life was spared, and William responded in the first instance by sending messengers to Harold urging him to honour his recent oath. Unsurprisingly, these had no effect on Harold, whose strategy evidently rested on calling his opponent's bluff. Having met William in person, and seen him conduct a cautious military campaign against the Bretons, he must have hoped that the duke would be unwilling to go to the extreme of launching a dangerous cross-Channel invasion. The Normans, in spite of their viking roots, were not famed as a seafaring nation. Within a few weeks, however, the king would have discovered that William was making preparations to do just that, and assembling a great armada.[65]

Through the spring of 1066, therefore, the tension in England began to mount. People's fears were not helped by the appearance of Halley's Comet, which blazed across the night sky during the last week of April, prompting many to say that it portended some great and terrible change in the kingdom. And, sure enough, a short time later, the kingdom did come under attack — but not by the duke of Normandy. The assault was led by Harold's embittered brother, Tostig, who plundered the Isle of Wight, and then raided along the south coast as far as Sandwich. What he was hoping to achieve is unclear, but since his tactics were virtually identical to those employed by his father in 1052, his plan may have been to force his readmission by similar means. Harold, who was already making preparations against a Norman invasion, moved swiftly to the Kent coast, prompting his brother to sail north as far as the Humber. There the renegade earl was confronted by his rivals, Eadwine and Morcar, who likewise successfully expelled him. Tostig limped away with only twelve ships from an original fleet of sixty, and took refuge with the king of Scots.[66]

Harold, meanwhile, remained at Sandwich, and was assembling an army and a fleet against the anticipated attack from Normandy. This evidently took some time, but the end results were impressive. 'He gathered together greater naval and land levies than any king in this country had ever gathered before', said the *Anglo-Saxon Chronicle*. It would have been impractical to keep thousands of men in the same place for weeks on end, so at the start of the summer Harold took the decision to split them up, and stationed them at various points along the length of the south coast. He then sailed to the Isle of Wight, and waited for the sight of Norman sails.[67]

All through the summer the English king and his vast army waited, but no enemy materialized. William, it seems, had been ready to embark in August, but was held in check by bad weather in the Channel, and a wind that was blowing in the wrong direction. As the weeks wore on, and the onset of autumn approached, both commanders must have grown increasingly anxious, knowing they could not hope to hold their huge armies together for very much longer. At last, on 8 September, the waiting game ended when Harold reluctantly disbanded his forces. 'The men's provisions had run out,' says the *Chronicle*, 'and no one could keep them there any longer.' The troops, raised from all over the country, were sent home, and the king returned to London. His timing, it turned out, was terrible. As soon as he arrived in the city, news reached him that enemy forces had landed. But they were not in southern England, and it was not the enemy he had been expecting. It was his troublesome brother Tostig, who had returned to Northumbria, accompanied by a horde of vikings.[68]

At some stage during his exile, Tostig had travelled to Norway and befriended its king, Harold Sigurdson. Even in his own lifetime, this alternate King Harold was regarded as a legend. Adam of Bremen, writing in the 1070s, dubbed him 'the Thunderbolt of the North', and another chronicler described him as 'the strongest living man under the sun'. Born around 1015, he had spent his younger days fighting for the rulers of Russia and Constantinople, earning a fortune and a fearsome reputation, before returning to Norway in 1045 and making himself its king. By the thirteenth century, if not before, Scandinavians remembered him as 'the hard ruler', or Hardrada.

Despite the claims of many modern historians, there is no indication that Hardrada had any designs on England prior to 1066. The only earlier reference to him in the *Anglo-Saxon Chronicle* occurs in 1047, when he concluded a peace with Edward the Confessor, and since then he had been preoccupied with battling against his neighbours in Scandinavia. It was only the appearance of Tostig Godwineson that persuaded the grizzled king, now around fifty years old, that England was ripe to be plucked. The exiled earl assured his new friend that Northumbria would welcome the return of viking rule, and that a conquest of the south would pose no problem for a warrior of such great prowess. The temptation proved irresistible, and in August Hardrada set sail with a fleet of 300 ships. Having joined forces with Tostig and his small flotilla on the Tyne, the Norwegian king proceeded southwards into the Humber, landing at Riccall in early September. The *Chronicle* describes his coming as *unwaran* – unexpected.[69]

This development took Harold Godwineson entirely by surprise. For months he had concentrated all his forces on the Channel coast, fearing invasion from Normandy, and then dispersed them just days before he learned about the Norwegian landing. Now, realizing the scale of his error, he rushed to reassemble an army, riding north as fast as he could, recalling the recently dismissed warriors to his side. By 24 September, around two weeks after his return to London, he had reached the Yorkshire town of Tadcaster. At that point, the news was not good. Four days earlier, the earls of Mercia and Northumbria, Eadwine and Morcar, had engaged the invaders in battle at a place called Fulford, a few miles south of York. Both sides had suffered heavy losses, but the Norwegians had held the field, and the English earls had fled. Hardrada and Tostig had afterwards entered York, and struck up an alliance with its citizens, who had promised to help conquer the rest of the country.

The very next morning, however, the English king received more encouraging intelligence. Unaware of his rapid advance and close proximity – Tadcaster is only ten miles from York – the Norwegians had left the city, and travelled to a place eight miles to the east called Stamford Bridge. Their pact with the citizens of York required the mutual handover of hostages, and this exposed location was to be the place of exchange. Better still, while they had taken their weapons with them, the vikings had decided not to wear their mail-shirts on account of the warm weather.[70]

It was an unmissable opportunity. At once Harold set out, marching his army the eighteen miles through York to Stamford Bridge, where they fell upon their unsuspecting enemies. A savage battle ensued, so bloody and decisive it was remembered in later Scandinavian sagas, full of exciting but invented detail. Reliable contemporary reports tell us only that the fighting was fierce and lasted until late in the day. Numberless men fell on both sides, says the *Anglo-Saxon Chronicle*, but the result was an undisputable victory for Harold Godwineson. His brother Tostig was among the fallen, as was his namesake adversary, the mighty Hardrada. When the Norwegians realized their leaders were lost they tried to flee back to their ships at Riccall, but the English pursued and slaughtered them as they ran. The River Ouse was choked with bodies, says the *Life of King Edward*, and the Humber ran red with viking blood. Only a handful of Norwegians were spared, including Hardrada's son, Olaf, who was allowed to depart in exchange for a promise never to return. According to the *Chronicle*, it took just twenty-four of their 300 ships to transport them home.[71]

For the author of the *Life*, a Godwine family saga, this was all a terrible tragedy. Harold and Tostig, his luminous heroes, had fallen out and fought each other to the death. 'Alas, those brothers' hearts too hard!' he lamented. 'This murderous page will hardly please their sister, the queen.' But for many others, including Harold himself, the outcome of the battle must have been a cause of celebration rather than mourning. He had been elected as king at the start of the year on the strength of his supposed virtue, and the belief that it was more important than blood. Ever since then the country had been in a state of high tension, prompting the *Chronicle* to remark that his reign saw 'lytle stilnesse'. Now

Harold's virtue had been vindicated. God had favoured him in battle. By acting decisively and boldly, he had defeated and killed a formidable adversary, famed as the greatest warrior of the age. While some wept for the loss of Tostig, others must have been composing songs in honour of their heroic king, and hopefully anticipating the glorious years that lay ahead.

Three days later, the duke of Normandy landed in Sussex, and advanced his army to Hastings.[72]

CONCLUSION

The sun rose on the morning after the battle to reveal a scene of sickening carnage. 'Far and wide,' wrote William the Conqueror's chaplain, William of Poitiers, 'the earth was covered with the flower of the English nobility and youth, drenched in blood.' The most notable casualty was King Harold, who had been hacked to death by a group of Norman knights, his body mutilated almost beyond recognition.[1]

This, alas, was only the beginning. When the surviving English refused to submit to William and chose instead to elect the young Edgar Ætheling as their new ruler, the duke marched his army towards London, subjecting the surrounding shires to a campaign of terror. Eventually the diehards surrendered, enabling the Conqueror to be crowned on Christmas Day, an event marred by his men burning down the houses around Westminster Abbey. But in the months that followed, his new English subjects tried repeatedly to reverse the verdict of Hastings, and William put down their rebellions with increasing prejudice. When the Northumbrians rose against him for a third time in 1069, supported by an invading army from Denmark, the king's retribution was terrible, and on his orders all the land beyond the Humber was laid to waste. One writer described how the livestock and carefully harvested crops in every settlement were brought together and burned, and stated that as a result more than 100,000 people perished from famine. The data in Domesday Book suggests that the true death toll was probably even higher.[2]

The Harrying of the North, as it was dubbed in modern times, is deservedly notorious, and was regarded by contemporaries as a heinous crime for which William would have to answer before God. But in percentage terms, the Conquest was even more devastating for the aristocracy than it was for innocent peasants. The Godwinesons – Harold, Tostig, Leofwine and Gyrth – died in the battles of 1066, and their grieving mother Gytha ended her days in foreign exile. Eadwine and Morcar, the brother earls of Mercia and Northumbria, joined a final desperate English rebellion in 1071, and fell as a result – Eadwine betrayed and killed by his own men, Morcar captured and imprisoned for the rest of his life. Archbishop Stigand, meanwhile, was deposed in 1070 and died in captivity two years later, and many other bishops and abbots were removed at the same moment. The almost total eclipse of the Old English elite is revealed in the pages of Domesday. Of the thousand or so individuals who held their lands directly from the king in 1086, only thirteen were English. All the rest were foreign newcomers.[3]

This replacement of England's ruling class had profound consequences, for the Normans had different ideas about the way society should be regulated. One major innovation was the castle, a new and brutally effective form of fortification that had been developing in Francia since the turn of the millennium. 'They built castles far and wide throughout the land', said the *Anglo-Saxon Chronicle* in 1067, 'oppressing the unhappy people.' In every major town and city, huge areas were cleared and dozens of houses destroyed to make way for these looming monstrosities of earth and timber, from which the occupiers could keep watch over the resentful citizens. Across the rest of the country, wherever a new Norman lord took control, a castle would rise as a means of safeguarding his investment. Within a generation or two of 1066, something like 500 were planted in England and Wales as a means of keeping the population in check.[4]

Not every new idea, however, led to an increase in oppression. Even as the Normans were imposing greater burdens on people who were formerly considered free, they were simultaneously liberating those who were classed as slaves. William the Conqueror banned the export of slaves out of Bristol and emancipated those he encountered in Wales. Domesday suggests that during his reign the unfree population fell by a quarter, and by the mid-twelfth century it had dwindled to almost nothing. 'In this respect,' wrote one chronicler in the 1130s, 'the English found foreigners treated them better than they had treated themselves.' In a similar fashion, the Normans ended the culture of political killing that had prevailed in England prior to the Conquest. For all their savagery in warfare, William and his followers were chivalrous in their treatment of defeated enemies, preferring to imprison them, and sometimes to release them in exchange for ransom. Bloody purges of the kind carried out at the courts of Æthelred and Cnut were not repeated after 1066, and were not heard of again until the fourteenth century.[5]

As these more benign aspects of the Conquest suggest, the Normans had to a large extent transcended their viking roots. When their distant ancestors had attacked and invaded England in earlier centuries, they had spared nothing, torching churches and rounding up slaves in their lust for blood and plunder. The Normans were equally avaricious, and had the same aptitude for violence, but their appetite for destruction was less wanton. When it came to churches, they destroyed in order to rebuild, ripping down the ancient minsters that had grown incrementally over the centuries, and replacing them with pristine new Romanesque structures of uniform style and massive dimensions. In the north, where monasticism had been wiped out by the vikings, they refounded famous houses, including St Hild's abbey at Whitby and Bede's beloved Wearmouth–Jarrow. Contemporary chroniclers rightly regarded this as a religious and architectural renaissance.[6]

The Norman attitude towards the English Church is crucial, for it determined how much written evidence survived its takeover. On the one hand, the Normans were unsympathetic reformers, with little use for charters and chronicles written in Old English. Much material must have been lost after 1066 by a process of slow attrition, as ancient texts that were no longer comprehensible were casually discarded. On the other hand, the fact that the conquerors were conscientious Christians meant that libraries were not indiscriminately destroyed. The vikings had effectively obliterated the written history of Northumbria and East Anglia. The Normans, by contrast, conserved at least some of what they found. *Beowulf* and Bede; Asser and the *Anglo-Saxon Chronicle*; the lives of Wilfrid, Dunstan, Oswald and Æthelwold – all survived the cultural revolution of 1066.

In addition, by commissioning the Domesday Survey, William the Conqueror created a source that preserved more information about Anglo-Saxon England than any other. The great inquest, it is true, could not have been carried out without the machinery of government introduced by England's tenth-century kings. Here too the Normans were building on solid Anglo-Saxon foundations. But the scale of the survey, to judge from the awe of contemporaries, was new. Its principal output, Domesday Book, is the most comprehensive survey of any human society before the nineteenth century (colour picture 24). A hoard of almost 2 million words, it preserves a composite picture of Anglo-Saxon England at its sunset – its cities and *burhs*, its shires and hundreds, its earls, *ceorls*, priests, monks and ploughmen.[7]

Much of that England is now gone forever. The Anglo-Saxons never truly believed, as the Romans did, that they were building for eternity. Their timber halls and hunting lodges burned long ago, as their owners anticipated. Their churches, too, have been for the most part replaced by later reformers, whether Norman or Victorian. Wilfrid's crypt at Hexham might excite our imagination, but it will never provoke the same degree of wonder as nearby Hadrian's Wall. With one or two notable exceptions – Offa's Dyke, or the church he built at Brixworth – the physical legacy of the Anglo-Saxons is thin, their surviving monuments few.

Some of that England had never really existed in the first place. A lot of what is often touted as the enduring legacy of the Anglo-Saxons proves on closer inspection to be mythological. The claim that they invented representative government because their kings held large assemblies ignores the fact that other rulers in contemporary Europe did the same. The belief that they were pioneering in their love of freedom requires us to forget that their nearest continental neighbours called themselves the Franks – that is, the free people. Their laws and legal concepts were mostly gone by the twelfth century, replaced with newly drafted Norman ones. The notion that they considered themselves uniquely favoured by God has lately been discredited on the grounds that no surviving document actually claims that distinction on their behalf.[8]

And yet, although their buildings are mostly gone, and their myths have been dispelled, a great deal of the Anglo-Saxon inheritance remains. The head of the English Church is still based at Canterbury because it was the principal city of King Æthelberht when he welcomed St Augustine over 1,400 years ago. Westminster is the political heart of the kingdom because Edward the Confessor added a royal palace when he rebuilt its ancient abbey. The shires of England, although tinkered with in the late twentieth century, are essentially the same as they were at the time of their creation more than 1,000 years ago. Most English villages can boast that they are first mentioned in Domesday Book, but their names often indicate a history that began centuries earlier. Woodnesborough in Kent, near to the fifth-century burial ground at Finglesham, preserves the memory of the pagan god Woden, and hence a story that stretches all the way back to the pre-Christian past. The fact that so much of this is unchanged is remarkable. Roman Britannia, despite the grandeur of its ruins, lasted barely 400 years, and was over by the mid-fifth century. England is still a work in progress.

The fact that the Norman Conquest left these foundations intact should not blind us to its human tragedy. 'Woe is to you, England', wrote the author of the *Life of King Edward*, whose work had been derailed by the destruction of the Godwine family. 'You have lost your native king and suffered defeat, with much spilling of blood of many of your men, in a war against a foreigner.' He did not wish to discuss the traumatic events of

1066, and neither did most of his contemporaries. 'William became king', said Eadmer of Canterbury, writing at the close of the eleventh century. 'What treatment he meted out to those who managed to survive the great slaughter, I forbear to tell.'[9]

When a new generation tried to make sense of their past in the twelfth century, therefore, they found there was much work to be done. In the 1120s William of Malmesbury began his *Deeds of the Kings of the English*, and in the 1130s Henry of Huntingdon embarked on his *History of the English*. Both men were of mixed Anglo-Norman parentage, but regarded themselves as Englishmen, and both wrote partly in the hope of healing the rift the Conquest had created – 'to mend the broken chain of our history', as Malmesbury put it. In each case their ambitious books began with the coming of the English in the fifth century and continued to their own present. For them, the coming of the Normans was simply a new chapter. It was not the end of the story.[10]

32. Great Domesday and Little Domesday.

Abbreviations

Æthelweard	*The Chronicle of Æthelweard*, ed. A. Campbell (1962).
Annals of St Bertin	*The Annals of St Bertin*, ed. J. L. Nelson (Manchester, 1991).
ASE	*Anglo-Saxon England*
ASSAH	*Anglo-Saxon Studies in Archaeology and History*
Asser	Asser's *Life of King Alfred* in Keynes and Lapidge (see below).
Bede	Bede's *Ecclesiastical History of the English People*, ed. B. Colgrave and R. A. B. Mynors (Oxford, 1969).
Blair, *Building*	J. Blair, *Building Anglo-Saxon England* (Princeton and Oxford, 2018).
Early Lives	*The Early Lives of St Dunstan*, ed. and trans. M. Winterbottom and M. Lapidge (Oxford, 2012).
EHD	*English Historical Documents*
EHR	*English Historical Review*
Encomium	*Encomium Emmae Reginae*, ed. A. Campbell and S. Keynes (Cambridge, 1998).
Encyclopedia	*The Wiley Blackwell Encyclopedia of Anglo-Saxon England*, ed. M. Lapidge,

	J. Blair, S. Keynes, and D. Scragg (2nd edn, Oxford, 2014).
Gildas,	*The Ruin of Britain and Other Works*, ed. and trans. M. Winterbottom (1978).
Halsall, *Worlds*	G. Halsall, *Worlds of Arthur: Facts & Fictions of the Dark Ages* (Oxford, 2013).
HBC	*Handbook of British Chronology*, ed. E. B. Fryde, D. E. Greenway, S. Porter and I. Roy (3rd edn, Cambridge, 1986).
Higham and Ryan	N. J. Higham and M. J. Ryan, *The Anglo-Saxon World* (2013).
John of Worcester	*The Chronicle of John of Worcester*, II, ed. R. R. Darlington and P. McGurk, trans. J. Bray and P. McGurk (Oxford, 1995).
Keynes and Lapidge	*Alfred the Great: Asser's Life of King Alfred and other Contemporary Sources*, ed. and trans. S. Keynes and M. Lapidge (1983).
Life of King Edward	*The Life of King Edward Who Rests at Westminster*, ed. F. Barlow (2nd edn, Oxford, 1992).
Life of St Æthelwold	Wulfstan of Winchester, *Life of St Æthelwold*, ed. and trans. M. Lapidge and M. Winterbottom (Oxford, 1991).
Lives of St Oswald	Byrhtferth of Ramsey, *The Lives of St Oswald and St Ecgwine*, ed. and trans. M. Lapidge (Oxford, 2009).
Life of Wilfrid	Eddius Stephanus, 'The Life of Wilfrid', *The Age of Bede*, trans. J. F. Webb, ed. D. H. Farmer (revised edn, 1983).

Malmesbury	William of Malmesbury, *Gesta Regum Anglorum*, I, ed. and trans. R. A. B. Mynors, R. M. Thomson and M. Winterbottom (Oxford, 1998).
Molyneaux, *Formation*	G. Molyneaux, *The Formation of the English Kingdom in the Tenth Century* (Oxford, 2015).
ODNB	www.oxforddnb.com (entries cited by author and subject). For the printed text, see *The Oxford Dictionary of National Biography*, ed. H. C. G. Matthews and B. Harrison (60 vols., Oxford, 2004).
Sawyer	The Electronic Sawyer: esawyer.lib. cam.ac.uk (cited by charter number).
TRHS	*Transactions of the Royal Historical Society*

Notes

Unless otherwise indicated, the place of publication is London

Introduction

1. D. M. Stenton, *The English Woman in History* (1956), 348.
2. P. Stafford, 'Women and the Norman Conquest', *TRHS*, 6th ser., 4 (1994), 221–49. Stafford also dismantles the claim that Anglo-Saxon women had greater rights as landholders. Only five per cent of the land recorded in Domesday Book was held by women, and only one per cent by women other than queens and countesses. Ibid., 226.
3. Higham and Ryan, 13–15.

1 The Ruin of Britain: The Fall of Rome and the Coming of the Saxons

1. 'Eric Lawes: Obituary', *Guardian* (23 July 2015); C. Johns and R. Bland, 'The Hoxne Late Roman Treasure', *Britannia*, 25 (1994), 165–73; R. Bland, 'Hoarding in the Iron Age and Roman Britain: The Puzzle of the Late Roman Period', *British Numismatic Journal*, 84 (2014), 30–6.
2. R. Bland, *Coins Hoards and Hoarding in Roman Britain AD 43–c.498* (2018), 12–14, 113–16; Johns and Bland, 'Hoxne Late

Roman Treasure', 165; J. R. Maddicott, 'Prosperity and Power in the Age of Bede and Beowulf', *Proceedings of the British Academy*, 117 (2003), 58.

3 P. Salway and J. Blair, *Roman and Anglo-Saxon Britain* (new edn, Oxford, 1992), 1–24; R. Fleming, *Britain After Rome: The Fall and Rise, 400 to 1070* (2010), 1–6; *The Anglo-Saxons*, ed. J. Campbell (2nd edn, 1991), 10; Higham and Ryan, 26.

4 Fleming, *Britain After Rome*, 17–20; D. Mattingly, *An Imperial Possession: Britain in the Roman Empire, 54 BC–AD 409* (2006), 20.

5 B. Ward-Perkins, *The Fall of Rome and the End of Civilization* (Oxford, 2005), 88–100; Fleming, *Britain After Rome*, 6–7, 16–17; H. Härke, 'Anglo-Saxon Immigration and Ethnogenesis', *Medieval Archaeology*, 55 (2011), 8; Salway and Blair, *Roman and Anglo-Saxon Britain*, 2.

6 Halsall, *Worlds*, 92; P. J. Casey, 'The Fourth Century and Beyond', *The Roman Era*, ed. P. Salway (Oxford, 2002), 76–7.

7 Higham and Ryan, 22–5; D. J. Breeze and B. Dobson, *Hadrian's Wall* (4th edn, 2000), 1; Fleming, *Britain After Rome*, 3–5; Mattingly, *Imperial Possession*, 239.

8 N. Faulkner and R. Reece, 'The Debate About the End: A Review of Evidence and Methods', *Archaeological Journal*, 159 (2002), 68; T. Wilmott, *Richborough and Reculver* (2012), 32–41; A. Pearson, *The Roman Shore Forts: Coastal Defences of Southern Britain* (Stroud, 2002), *passim*; Fleming, *Britain After Rome*, 5–6.

9 A. R. Birley, *The Roman Government of Britain* (Oxford, 2005), 415–16, 428–9, 430–40.

10 Faulkner and Reece, 'Debate About the End', 59–76.

11 P. Heather, 'The Huns and the End of the Roman Empire in Western Europe', *EHR*, 110 (1995), 4–41; C. Freeman, *Egypt, Greece and Rome: Civilizations of the Ancient Mediterranean* (3rd edn, Oxford, 2014), 611.

12 Halsall, *Worlds*, 177–8; M. A. McEvoy, *Child Emperor Rule in the Late Roman West, AD 367–455* (Oxford, 2013), 85.

13 Birley, *Roman Government*, 423–4, 449.

14 Ibid., 449; Casey, 'Fourth Century and Beyond', 93.

[15] G. Halsall, *Barbarian Migrations and the Roman West, 376–568* (Cambridge, 2007), 187–8, 201–2.

[16] Bland, 'Hoarding in the Iron Age', 28–30; Higham and Ryan, 41.

[17] P. Guest, 'The Hoarding of Roman Metal Objects in Fifth-Century Britain', *AD 410: The History and Archaeology of Late and Post-Roman Britain*, ed. F. K. Haarer et al. (Soc. for the Promotion of Roman Studies, 2014), 122–4.

[18] Halsall, *Worlds*, 12–13; Birley, *Roman Government*, 456–60.

[19] Ibid., 460; Ward-Perkins, *Fall of Rome*, 48–9; Zosimus, *New History*, ed. R. T. Ridley (Canberra, 1982), 128–9.

[20] Fleming, *Britain After Rome*, 27; Halsall, *Worlds*, 97, 174–7.

[21] For further discussion, see S. Esmonde-Cleary, 'Introduction: the Roman Society and the Study of AD 410', *AD 410: The History and Archaeology of Late and Post-Roman Britain*, ed. Haarer et al., 1–10; idem, 'The Ending(s) of Roman Britain', *The Oxford Handbook to Anglo-Saxon Archaeology*, ed. H. Hamerow, D. A. Hinton and S. Crawford (Oxford, 2011), 13–29.

[22] Guest, 'Hoarding of Roman Metal Objects', 119; Higham and Ryan, 50.

[23] Sidonius, *Poems and Letters*, trans. W. B. Anderson, vol. 1 (1963), 150–1.

[24] Sidonius Apollinaris, *Letters*, trans. O. M. Dalton, vol. 2 (1915), 149.

[25] P. Salway, *The Oxford Illustrated History of Roman Britain* (Oxford, 1993), 236–9. For a short summary of Sidonius' career, see M. P. Hanaghan, *Reading Sidonius' Epistles* (Cambridge, 2019), 2–8.

[26] Sidonius Apollinaris, *Letters*, 149–50.

[27] 'The Life of St Germanus of Auxerre', *Soldiers of Christ: Saints and Saints' Lives from Late Antiquity and the Early Middle Ages*, ed. T. F. X. Noble and T. Head (Pennsylvania University Press, 1995), 85–91.

[28] Bede, 40–1, 48–53.

[29] Halsall, *Worlds*, 15, 60; P. Heather, *Empires and Barbarians* (2009), 124, 282; B. Yorke, 'Anglo-Saxon Origin Legends', *Myth,*

Rulership, Church and Charters: Essays in Honour of Nicholas Brooks, ed. J. Barrow and A. Wareham (Aldershot, 2008), 15–18.

[30] The key passage is Gildas, 28, but the translation given is debatable. For a different interpretation – the one understood by Bede – see H. Wiseman, 'The Derivation of the Date of the Badon Entry in the *Annales Cambriae* from Bede and Gildas', *Parergon*, 17 (2000), 1–10. See below, n. 59.

[31] Gildas, 17, 22.

[32] Ibid., 26–7.

[33] Yorke, 'Anglo-Saxon Origin Legends', 19–20; Gildas, 25–6.

[34] Mattingly, *Imperial Possession*, 230; M. Welch, *Anglo-Saxon England* (1993), 100–1; P. Salway, 'Conclusion', *The Roman Era*, ed. Salway, 231–2.

[35] Bede, 49; Gildas, 23–4, 149. Marcian's reign as emperor actually began in 450.

[36] Higham and Ryan, 76–8; Halsall, *Worlds*, 104. The dating of evidence of Saxon settlement before 430 has now been rejected. See e.g. Welch, *Anglo-Saxon England*, 101–2. For the Gallic Chronicle, see Birley, *Roman Government*, 464. I have not used his translation.

[37] Gildas, 27–8. Gildas gives no indication how much time elapsed between the Saxon revolt and the resistance of Ambrosius. He does, however, indicate that the grandchildren of Ambrosius were alive in his own day, and says they were inferior, implying they were adult rulers. Ambrosius thus probably lived at least half a century before Gildas, and possibly longer. Bede places his resistance in the reign of Zeno (474–91), but this was evidently just a guess. Wiseman, 'Derivation of the Date', 7, 9.

[38] Fleming, *Britain After Rome*, 45, 142–4; Halsall, *Worlds*, 26–30, 104, 223–34; Higham and Ryan, 112–19.

[39] H. Williams, 'Cemeteries as Central Places – Place and Identity in Migration Period Eastern England', *Central Places in the Migration and Merovingian Periods*, ed. L. Larsson and B. Hårdh (Stockholm, 2002), 341–62; Halsall, *Worlds*, 260–5.

[40] J. C. Mann, 'The Creation of Four Provinces in Britain by Diocletian', *Britannia*, 29 (1998), 339–41.

41 B. Yorke, 'Anglo-Saxon *Gentes* and *Regna*', *Regna and Gentes*, ed. H.-W. Goetz, J. Jarnut and W. Pohl (Leiden, 2003), 395–7.

42 B. Ward-Perkins, 'Why Did the Anglo-Saxons Not Become More British?', *EHR*, 115 (2000), 518–21.

43 Halsall, *Worlds*, 103–13.

44 Ibid., 112–13, 242–5; Higham and Ryan, 87–91.

45 Halsall, *Worlds*, 111–12.

46 Cf. M. E. Jones, *The End of Roman Britain* (Cornell, 1996), 73–99.

47 See similar calculations in Härke, 'Anglo-Saxon Immigration', 9.

48 Ward-Perkins, 'Why Did the Anglo-Saxons Not Become More British?', 521–3; Higham and Ryan, 70; F. M. Stenton, *Anglo-Saxon England* (3rd edn, Oxford, 1971), 98–101.

49 Ward-Perkins, 'Why Did the Anglo-Saxons Not Become More British?', 517, 528–9; Salway, *Oxford Illustrated History of Roman Britain*, 513–29. For the persistence of Roman field boundaries, see S. Rippon, C. Smart and B. Pears, *The Fields of Britannia* (Oxford, 2015).

50 Härke, 'Anglo-Saxon Immigration', 13–14.

51 Ward-Perkins, 'Why Did the Anglo-Saxons Not Become More British?', 514; Heather, *Empires and Barbarians*, 283–5.

52 Bede, 50–1.

53 J. Hines, 'The Becoming of the English: Identity, Material Culture and Language in Early Anglo-Saxon England', *ASSAH*, 7 (1994), 50–2; Bede, 476–7.

54 Hines, 'Becoming of the English', 52–3; Halsall, *Worlds*, 267–9.

55 Fleming, *Britain After Rome*, 32–5; Ward-Perkins, *Fall of Rome*, 117–20.

56 Halsall, *Worlds*, 41–2.

57 Gildas, 28, but cf. Wiseman, 'Derivation of the Date', 6.

58 For a dissection of the Arthur legend, see N. J. Higham, *King Arthur: Myth-Making and History* (2002).

59 Gildas, 13, 28; Wiseman, 'Derivation of the Date', 6. Gildas says he was born forty-three years after the victory of Ambrosius Aurelianus, which took place 'some time' after the Saxon revolt, which is datable to *c*.440.

[60] Gildas, 28; Fleming, *Britain After Rome*, 28; R. Naismith, *Citadel of the Saxons: The Rise of Early London* (2019), 43; K. Leahy, *The Anglo-Saxon Kingdom of Lindsey* (Stroud, 2007), 25–6.

[61] Gildas, 28–9.

2 War-Wolves and Ring-Givers: The Emergence of Kings and Kingdoms

[1] *Encyclopedia*, 65–6. For a recent summary of the debate, see *The Dating of Beowulf: A Reassessment*, ed. L. Neidorf (Cambridge, 2014).

[2] S. Newton, *The Origins of Beowulf and the Pre-Viking Kingdom of East Anglia* (Woodbridge, 1993), 27–8.

[3] J. R. R. Tolkien, *Beowulf: A Translation and Commentary*, ed. C. Tolkien (2015); C. Tolley, 'Old English Influence on *The Lord of the Rings*', *Beowulf and Other Stories: A New Introduction to Old English, Old Icelandic and Anglo-Norman Literatures*, ed. R. North and J. Allard (2nd edn, 2012), 38–62.

[4] *Beowulf*, trans. S. Heaney (1999), 46, 50, 78.

[5] Henry, Archdeacon of Huntingdon, *Historia Anglorum: The History of the English People*, ed. D. Greenway (Oxford, 1996), 16–17.

[6] D. P. Kirby, *The Earliest English Kings* (revised edn, 2000), 4–7.

[7] *EHD*, i, 152–5.

[8] B. Yorke, 'The Jutes of Hampshire and Wight and the Origins of Wessex', *The Origins of Anglo-Saxon Kingdoms* (Leicester, 1989), 85–7.

[9] Above, 37–9; Higham and Ryan, 91–5.

[10] T. M. Charles-Edwards, 'Kinship, Status and the Origins of the Hide', *Past & Present*, 56 (1972), 6–7; Härke, 'Anglo-Saxon Immigration', 6–7.

[11] J. Hines, 'A New Chronology and New Agenda: The Problematic Sixth Century', *Transformation in Anglo-Saxon Culture: Toller Lectures on Art, Archaeology and Text*, ed. C. Insley and G. R. Owen-Crocker (Oxford, 2017), 1–22; Higham and

Ryan, 128–33; Fleming, *Britain After Rome*, 89–90, 93–7; Blair, *Building*, 114–25.

[12] J. M. Dodgson, 'The Significance of the Distribution of the English Place-Name in *-ingas, -inga-*, in South-East England', *Medieval Archaeology*, 10 (1966), 1–29; *Encyclopedia*, 257.

[13] *Beowulf*, trans. Heaney, 3–5.

[14] Fleming, *Britain After Rome*, 102–9; *EHD*, i, 406; S. Bassett, 'In Search of the Origins of Anglo-Saxon Kingdoms', *Origins of Anglo-Saxon Kingdoms*, ed. Bassett, 3–27.

[15] B. Yorke, *Kings and Kingdoms of Early Anglo-Saxon England* (1990).

[16] Bassett, 'In Search of the Origins', 24.

[17] T. P. Newfield, 'The Climate Downturn of 536–50', *The Palgrave Handbook of Climate History*, ed. S. White, C. Pfister, and F. Mauelshagen (2018), 450; *EHD*, i, 155–6.

[18] A. Gibbons, 'Why 536 was "the Worst Year to Be Alive"', *Science*, 362 (Nov. 2018), 733–4; cf. Newfield, 'Climate Downturn', 448.

[19] Ibid., 469, 471; above, 39; J. R. Maddicott, 'Two Frontier States: Northumbria and Wessex, *c.*650–750', *The Medieval State*, ed. J. R. Maddicott and D. M. Palliser (2000), 42–3; J. Morris, *The Age of Arthur* (1973), 222–3, suggests the plague did not affect the Anglo-Saxons.

[20] J. R. Maddicott, 'Plague in Seventh-Century England', *Past & Present*, 156 (1997), 10–11; idem, 'Two Frontier States', 43–5.

[21] Bede, 148–9.

[22] Ibid., 148–9, 232–3; *EHD*, i, 157–8; Yorke, 'Anglo-Saxon Origin Legends', 17–18; B. Yorke, 'Ceawlin', *ODNB*.

[23] Bede, 148–51.

[24] Above, 37; M. Welch, 'Anglo-Saxon Kent to AD 800', *The Archaeology of Kent to AD 800* (Woodbridge, 2007), 209–20; cf. C. Behr, 'The Origins of Kingship in Early Medieval Kent', *Early Medieval Europe*, 9 (2000), 25–52, and idem, 'New Bracteate Finds from Early Anglo-Saxon England', *Medieval Archaeology*, 54 (2010), 34–88.

25 Welch, 'Anglo-Saxon Kent', 191–2, 220–3; *Anglo-Saxons*, ed. Campbell, 24–5; Behr, 'Origins of Kingship', 48.

26 Higham and Ryan, 131; Heather, *Empires and Barbarians*, 306–10. Childeric's tomb was rediscovered in 1653, but most of the treasure it had contained was stolen in 1831 and melted down, so only a few pieces remain today.

27 Welch, 'Anglo-Saxon Kent', 190–1.

28 N. Brooks, *The Early History of the Church of Canterbury* (Leicester, 1984), 5–6, 21–5.

29 Ibid., 3–4; *EHD*, i, 790; Bede, 132–5.

30 Ibid., 72–9; Brooks, *Early History*, 4–8.

31 Bede, 110–11, 114–15, 150–1. For Æthelberht's law-code, see *EHD*, i, 391–4.

32 L. Webster, *Anglo-Saxon Art* (2012), 55–67.

33 Ibid., 61–7; Welch, 'Anglo-Saxon Kent', 190, 193, 209, 244; Bede, 72–3.

34 Ibid., 104–7, 142–3; Brooks, *Early History*, 9–11.

35 Bede, 116–17; Yorke, *Kings and Kingdoms*, 74.

36 Ibid., 74–7; Kirby, *Earliest English Kings*, 57; Bede, 116–17, 230–1, 262–3, 562–3; *EHD*, i, 156.

37 Bede, 116–17; Kirby, *Earliest English Kings*, 59.

38 Ibid., 60; Yorke, *Kings and Kingdoms*, 77.

39 Bede, 174–81.

40 Ibid., 148–51, 179–80, 212–13.

41 Ibid., 190–1, 284–5; Yorke, *Kings and Kingdoms*, 61; M. Carver, *The Sutton Hoo Story: Encounters with Early England* (Woodbridge, 2017), 38–9, 191; C. Scull, F. Minter and J. Plouviez, 'Social and Economic Complexity in Early Medieval England: A Central Place Complex of the East Anglian Kingdom at Rendlesham, Suffolk', *Antiquity*, 90 (2016), 1594–1612.

42 Bede, 188–91.

43 L. Blackmore, I. Blair, S. Hirst and C. Scull, *The Prittlewell Princely Burial: Excavations at Priory Crescent, Southend-on-Sea, Essex, 2003* (2019).

44 Henry, Archdeacon of Huntingdon, *Historia Anglorum*, ed. Greenway, 17; Carver, *Sutton Hoo Story*, 120–51.

45 Ibid., 2–28, tells the story of the original excavation, and describes the treasure at 29–55.

46 Ibid., 38–9, 195–6; Halsall, *Worlds*, 36–7.

47 Carver, *Sutton Hoo Story*, 8–14, 129–34, 191, 195. Another boat burial was found at nearby Snape in 1862: Higham and Ryan, 133.

48 Cf. Newton, *Origins of Beowulf*, *passim*; *Beowulf*, trans. Heaney, 4, 99 (lines 34–42, 3158).

49 Bede, 162–3.

50 Ibid., 192–3; Carver, *Sutton Hoo Story*, 31–2; *EHD*, i, 186.

51 P. Wormald, 'Bede, the Bretwaldas and the Origin of the *Gens Anglorum*', *Ideal and Reality in Frankish and Anglo-Saxon Society*, ed. P. Wormald et al. (Oxford, 1983), 99–129; B. Yorke, 'The Bretwaldas and the Origins of Overlordship in Anglo-Saxon England', *Early Medieval Studies in Memory of Patrick Wormald*, ed. S. Baxter, C. Karkov, J. L. Nelson and D. Pelteret (Farnham, 2009), 81–95.

52 Bedae, *Opera de Temporibus*, ed. C. W. Jones (Cambridge, Mass., 1943), 213; A. S. Dobat, 'The King and his Cult: The Axe-Hammer from Sutton Hoo and its Implications for the Concept of Sacral Leadership in Early Medieval Europe', *Antiquity*, 80 (2006), 880–93.

53 Maddicott, 'Two Frontier States', 32–3.

54 *Beowulf*, trans. Heaney, 5–7.

55 Bede, 188–9; B. Hope-Taylor, *Yeavering: An Anglo-British Centre of Early Northumbria* (revised edn, 2009).

56 Maddicott, 'Two Frontier States', 32; Higham and Ryan, 136. See also *Yeavering: People, Power & Place*, ed. P. Frodsham and C. O'Brien (2005).

57 *Anglo-Saxons*, ed. Campbell, 57; Carver, *Sutton Hoo Story*, 187.

58 *Beowulf*, ed. Heaney, 5 (lines 82–5); Bede, 188–9. For a general discussion of great halls, see Blair, *Building*, 114–31.

59 Bede, 182–5.

60 Ibid., 150–7.

61 Ibid., 106–9, 162–75.

62 Ibid., 186–9.

63 Ibid., 164–7.

[64] Ibid., 148–9, 162–3, 202–5.

[65] Ibid., 202–5; *Beowulf*, trans. Heaney, 98 (lines 3152–5).

[66] Bede, 212–17.

[67] Ibid., 150–1, 212–13, 230–1.

[68] Ibid., 204–5, 246–7; Kirby, *Earliest English Kings*, 75–6.

[69] Bede, 294–5; N. Brooks, 'The Formation of the Mercian Kingdom', *Origins of Anglo-Saxon Kingdoms*, ed. Bassett, 159–70; Yorke, *Kings and Kingdoms*, 101–2.

[70] Ibid.; *EHD*, i, 161–2; Bede, 202–3; J. M. Wallace-Hadrill, Bede's *Ecclesiastical History of the English People: A Historical Commentary* (Oxford, 1988), 84.

[71] Bede, 240–3, 250–3; D. J. Craig, 'Oswald, King of Northumbria', *ODNB*.

[72] Bede, 148–51, 232–5, 268–9.

[73] Ibid., 254–7; 262–3; 278–81; S. E. Kelly, 'Penda', *ODNB*.

[74] Bede, 288–91; Kirby, *Earliest English Kings*, 80.

[75] Bede, 288–93; Wallace-Hadrill, *Historical Commentary*, 122–3.

[76] Kelly, 'Penda' (see also Brooks, 'Formation of the Mercian Kingdom', 169: 'Penda of Mercia bestrode the political stage like a Colossus'); Bede, 292–3; Blair, *Building*, 94–5.

[77] J. Campbell, 'Bede I', *Essays in Anglo-Saxon History* (1986), 13.

[78] *The Staffordshire Hoard: An Anglo-Saxon Treasure*, ed. C. Fern, T. Dickinson and L. Webster (2019), *passim*; Carver, *Sutton Hoo Story*, 194–5.

[79] *Beowulf*, ed. Heaney, 71–2 (lines 2248–53).

3 God's Chosen Instrument: St Wilfrid and the Establishment of Christianity

[1] P. T. Bidwell, 'A Survey of the Anglo-Saxon Crypt at Hexham and Its Reused Roman Stonework', *Archaeologia Aeliana*, 5th ser., 39 (2010), 53–5, 84, 86; *Life of Wilfrid*, 128.

[2] Ibid., 106; Bede, 202–5, 212–17; above, 75–7. Wilfrid was particularly devoted to Oswald's cult, and it may be that one of the reasons he chose to build a church at Hexham was its proximity to Heavenfield. Bede, 216–17, 378–9.

3   H. Mayr-Harting, *The Coming of Christianity to Anglo-Saxon England* (2nd edn, 1977), 78–93.

4   M. Herbert, 'Columba', *ODNB*.

5   Craig, 'Oswald', *ODNB*; Bede, 218–21. Aidan's church burned down twice, but his successor Finan rebuilt it 'after the Irish method, not of stone but of hewn oak, thatching it with reeds'. Ibid. 264–5, 294–5.

6   *Life of Wilfrid*, 107–8.

7   Ibid., 108–9. Stephen of Ripon calls Annemund 'Dalfinus'.

8   G. S. Aldrete, *Daily Life in the Roman City: Rome, Pompei, and Ostia* (2004), 21–3; R. Krautheimer, *Rome: Profile of a City, 312–1308* (Princeton, 2000), 62–4; P. Hetherington, *Medieval Rome: A Portrait of the City and its Life* (1994), 30–5.

9   Ibid., 52; R. H. C. Davis, *A History of Medieval Europe* (revised edn, 1970), 72–4, 85–9, 94; *Life of Wilfrid*, 110.

10 Ibid.; Hetherington, *Medieval Rome*, 51–2.

11 C. Corning, *The Celtic and Roman Traditions: Conflict and Consensus in the Early Medieval Church* (2006), 13–14; *Life of Wilfrid*, 111.

12 Ibid.; Bede, 258–9; Davis, *History of Medieval Europe*, 83, 118–19.

13 *Life of Wilfrid*, 111–12.

14 Bede, 196–7, 262–5, 276–83, 290–3.

15 Ibid., 232–6; *Life of Wilfrid*, 112.

16 Ibid., 112–13, 120, 156; Bede, 'Life of Cuthbert', *The Age of Bede*, trans. J. F. Webb, ed. D. H. Farmer (revised edn, 1983), 51, 53; Mayr-Harting, *Coming of Christianity*, 148; S. Foot, *Monastic Life in Anglo-Saxon England, c. 600–900* (Cambridge, 2006), 1–4.

17 Bedae, *Opera de Temporibus*, ed. Jones, 212. Bede is the only contemporary writer to refer to Eostre, so this is all we know about her. There is no evidence to connect her to Ishtar, eggs or bunnies.

18 Mayr-Harting, *Coming of Christianity*, 103–5; Corning, *Celtic and Roman Traditions*, 4–13.

19 Bede, 294–7.

20 Ibid., 292–3, 404–15; Mayr-Harting, *Coming of Christianity*, 150–1.

21 *Life of Wilfrid*, 114; Bede, 234–5, 296–9.

22 Ibid., 298–301.

23 *Life of Wilfrid*, 114–15; Bede, 300–7.

24 Ibid., 306–9.

25 Ibid., 298–9, 308–9; Mayr-Harting, *Coming of Christianity*, 109–10.

26 Bede, 288–9, 310–13, 328–9, 322–3. For an extended discussion, see Maddicott, 'Plague in Seventh-Century England'.

27 Bede, 86–7, 336–7; *Life of Wilfrid*, 117–18; Maddicott, 'Plague in Seventh-Century England', 15.

28 Bede, 308–9, 314–15; *Life of Wilfrid*, 118.

29 Ibid., 118–20; Bede, 314–17.

30 Ibid., 254–5, 314–17; Maddicott, 'Plague in Seventh-Century England', 16; Bede, 'Lives of the Abbots of Wearmouth and Jarrow', *Age of Bede*, trans. and ed. Farmer, 186; R. Cramp, 'Alchfrith', *ODNB*.

31 *Life of Wilfrid*, 120.

32 Bede, 318–23, 328–33.

33 Ibid., 236–7, 332–7. Theodore's involvement in the appointment of Bisi to East Anglia in 669/70 is assumed on the basis of the date. *HBC*, 216.

34 *Life of Wilfrid*, 122.

35 Foot, *Monastic Life*, 12–13.

36 Stenton, *Anglo-Saxon England*, 148–51; Webster, *Anglo-Saxon Art*, 86–90.

37 Bede, 236–7; *Two Lives of St Cuthbert*, ed. B. Colgrave (1940), 163–5.

38 Fleming, *Britain After Rome*, 161–2; Bede, 336–7.

39 Above, 60–1.

40 Bede, 332–3, 348–53.

41 Ibid., 348–9, 370–1; *Life of Wilfrid*, 123–4, 126; J. R. Maddicott, 'Ecgfrith', *ODNB*.

42 *Life of Wilfrid*, 123–4. As at Hexham, Wilfrid's crypt at Ripon has survived.

43 Ibid.,128; Bede, 352–3, 390–3. Wilfrid may have tried to dissolve the marriage on the grounds it had never been

consummated, for he insisted Æthelthryth had remained a virgin. This seems unlikely, since she was married to Ecgfrith for over a decade, and had been married once before that. Bede confides that people doubted Wilfrid's claim.

44 *Life of Wilfrid*, 127–30.
45 Ibid., 133–4; Bede, 352–5; Stenton, *Anglo-Saxon England*, 134.
46 *Life of Wilfrid*, 130; Bede, 370–1.
47 *Life of Wilfrid*, 130–4, 137.
48 Ibid., 135–8; Bede, 370–1. The three new bishops were Bosa, Eata and Eadhæd.
49 *Life of Wilfrid*, 138–40.
50 Ibid., 140–2.
51 Ibid., 146–9.
52 Ibid., 148–9; cf. Bede, 372–3.
53 Ibid., 338–9, 356–9, 372–8, 392–3; Maddicott, 'Plague in Seventh-Century England', 12–14.
54 Bede, 380–1; Yorke, *Kings and Kingdoms*, 137.
55 Bede, 382–3. Eadwine of Northumbria had similarly promised to convert if God granted him victory over Wessex. Ibid., 164–7.
56 Maddicott, 'Plague in Seventh-Century England', 13–14.
57 Bede, 370–1, 428–9, 436–9.
58 Ibid., 430–9; D. Rollason and R. Dobson, 'Cuthbert', *ODNB*.
59 Bede, 426–9; Bede, 'Life of Cuthbert', ed. Farmer, 77–9.
60 *EHD*, i, 167–8; B. Yorke, 'Cædwalla', *ODNB*.
61 *Life of Wilfrid*, 150–1. Cædwalla was reportedly wounded during his conquest of the Isle of Wight, and it may be that his star was already waning. Two years later he would set out for Rome, where he died soon after his arrival, having been baptized by the pope.
62 R. Cramp, 'Aldfrith, king of Northumbria', *ODNB*; A. Thacker, 'Ælfflæd', *ODNB*; *Life of Wilfrid*, 151.
63 Ibid., 152; Bede, 442–3. Soon after his consecration in 685 Cuthbert had swapped dioceses with Eata. Ibid., 438–9.
64 Maddicott, 'Plague in Seventh-Century England', 13–14, 45, 47–8.

65 *Abbots of Wearmouth and Jarrow*, ed. C. Grocock and I. N. Wood (Oxford, 2013), xxix–xxxii; S. J. Coates, 'Ceolfrith', *ODNB*; idem, 'Benedict Biscop', *ODNB*.

66 Bede, xx, xxv; R. L. S. Bruce-Mitford, 'The Art of the Codex Amiatinus', *Journal of the British Archaeological Association*, 3rd ser., 32 (1969), 2. The Codex Amiatinus, one of the three Bibles commissioned by Ceolfrith, still survives. Almost half a metre tall, and weighing a monumental thirty-four kilograms, it was produced as a gift for the pope, and carried to the Continent by a large party of monks from Wearmouth–Jarrow, led by Ceolfrith himself. The elderly abbot, alas, died en route to Rome, and the Codex somehow ended up in the monastery of Mount Amiata in Tuscany, hence its misleading modern name. It remained there for over a millennium, until it was acquired by the Laurentian Library in Florence. In 2018 it was lent to the British Library for an exhibition of Anglo-Saxon manuscripts, returning to Britain for the first time in more than 1,000 years.

67 M. P. Brown, *Painted Labyrinth: The World of the Lindisfarne Gospels* (revised edn, 2004), 4, 10; Coates, 'Aldfrith', *ODNB*; *Life of Wilfrid*, 152.

68 Ibid., 150–3; *HBC*, 217, 219; Bede, 472–5.

69 *Life of Wilfrid*, 153. Wilfrid's appeal to Rome during his time in Mercia is apparent from the ruling of Pope Sergius (687–701) mentioned in ibid., 154, 159, 161, 165.

70 Ibid., 153–6.

71 Ibid., 158–65.

72 Ibid., 165–7.

73 Ibid., 168–71.

74 Ibid., 171–3.

75 Ibid., 173–4; Bede, 458–61.

76 *Life of Wilfrid*, 174–6.

77 Ibid., 178–80; A. Thacker, 'Wilfrid', *ODNB*.

78 *Life of Wilfrid*, 179; Bede, 528–31.

79 *Life of Wilfrid*, 180.

Notes to pages 129–39

80 Ibid., 162, 164–6; A. Thacker, 'England in the Seventh Century', *The New Cambridge Medieval History, I: c.500–c.700*, ed. P. Fouracre (Cambridge, 2005), 482; Stenton, *Anglo-Saxon England*, 145–6.

81 Bede, 558–61.

4 An English Empire?: King Offa and the Domination of the South

1 R. R. Davies, *The Age of Conquest: Wales 1063–1415* (Oxford, 2000), 3–4.

2 K. Ray and I. Bapty, *Offa's Dyke: Landscape and Hegemony in Eighth-Century Britain* (Oxford, 2016), 56, 127–8; M. Worthington, 'Offa's Dyke', *Æthelbald and Offa: Two Eighth-Century Kings of Mercia* (BAR British Series, 383, 2005), 91; P. Squatriti, 'Digging Ditches in Early Medieval Europe', *Past & Present*, 176 (2002), 21.

3 D. J. Tyler, 'Offa's Dyke: A Historiographical Reappraisal', *Journal of Medieval History*, 37 (2011), 147–9.

4 Asser, 71; Ray and Bapty, *Offa's Dyke*, 23–5.

5 Ibid., 25–9; Higham and Ryan, 52–4. On the Wansdyke, see T. Malim, 'Grim's Ditch, Wansdyke and the Ancient Highways of England: Linear Monuments and Political Control', *Proceedings of the Clifton Antiquarian Club*, 9 (2010), 148–79.

6 Above, 79–81, 115–19.

7 Naismith, *Citadel of the Saxons*, 40–55; *A Choice of Anglo-Saxon Verse*, ed. and trans. R. Harmer (1970), 26–7, 110–11, 180–1.

8 Naismith, *Citadel of the Saxons*, 2, 10, 14.

9 Maddicott, 'Prosperity and Power', 58–9; P. Sawyer, *The Wealth of Anglo-Saxon England* (Oxford, 2013), 52–60.

10 R. Cowie, 'Mercian London', *Mercia: An Anglo-Saxon Kingdom in Europe*, ed. M. P. Brown and C. A. Farr (Leicester, 2001), 195, 198–201; Naismith, *Citadel of the Saxons*, 80–9.

11 Maddicott, 'Prosperity and Power', 53–4, 57–60; K. Ulmschneider, 'Settlement, Economy, and the "Productive" Site: Middle

Anglo-Saxon Lincolnshire AD 650–780', *Medieval Archaeology*, 44 (2000), 68.

12 Bede, 142–3; Naismith, *Citadel of the Saxons*, 73–6, 80–1.

13 J. R. Maddicott, 'London and Droitwich, *c.*650–750: Trade, Industry and the Rise of Mercia', *ASE*, 34 (2005), 16–23.

14 Ibid., 21–4, 49–50, 57–8; *Anglo-Saxons*, ed. Campbell, 95–8.

15 Maddicott, 'London and Droitwich', 13, 16; *EHD*, i, 173–5, 266.

16 S. E. Kelly, 'Æthelbald', *ODNB*; *EHD*, i, 492–4; Bede, 558–9.

17 Mayr-Harting, *Coming of Christianity*, 262–74.

18 I. N. Wood, 'Boniface', *ODNB*.

19 *EHD*, i, 816–17.

20 Ibid., 820.

21 Ibid., 804–6; Yorke, *Kings and Kingdoms*, 91, 163–4.

22 *S. Bonifatii et S. Lullii Epistolae,* ed. M. Tangl (Monumenta Germaniae Historica: *Epistolae Selectae*, i, Berlin, 1916), 171 (no. 78).

23 Ray and Bapty, *Offa's Dyke*, 108; L. Hayes and T. Malim, 'The Date and Nature of Wat's Dyke: A Reassessment in the Light of Recent Investigations at Gobowen, Shropshire', *ASSAH*, 15 (2008), 147–79.

24 S. Keynes, 'The Reconstruction of a Burnt Cottonian Manuscript: The Case of MS. Otho A. I', *British Library Journal*, 22 (1996), 137; Sawyer 92.

25 Blair, *Building*, 189–91.

26 N. Brooks, 'The Development of Military Obligations in Eighth-and Ninth-Century England', *England Before the Conquest: Studies in primary sources presented to Dorothy Whitelock*, ed. P. Clemoes and K. Hughes (Cambridge, 1971); Blair, *Building*, 114–15, 190–3.

27 *EHD*, i, 173–5, 266.

28 Ibid., 771–5.

29 Mercia and Northumbria, for example, had violently contested the control of the lesser kingdom of Lindsey in the mid-seventh century, but ceased to do so after 679, when it was permanently annexed to Mercia. In 743 Æthelbald allied with Cuthred of Wessex to fight against the Britons. Yorke, *Kings and Kingdoms*, 79, 105; *EHD*, i, 174.

30 Halsall, *Worlds*, 303; Maddicott, 'Two Frontier Kingdoms', 42–3; T. M. Charles-Edwards, *Wales and the Britons, 350–1064* (Oxford, 2013), 27.

31 *EHD*, i, 266, 286.

32 *Encyclopedia*, 204–6; Charles-Edwards, *Wales and the Britons*, 419, 434–5.

33 Sawyer 105; Stenton, *Anglo-Saxon England*, 206–7; Brooks, *Early History*, 111–12.

34 Ibid., 112–13; *EHD*, i, 268; Sawyer 108; Stenton, *Anglo-Saxon England*, 208–9.

35 Ibid., 207; Brooks, *Early History*, 113; *EHD*, i, 178.

36 Charles-Edwards, *Wales and the Britons*, 414–19. If Cyngen had been born before 780, he would have been over seventy-four at his death. Had he been born after 790 he would have been under eighteen at his accession. Neither scenario is impossible, but a date of birth at some point between these two dates seems likelier.

37 D. Hill, 'Offa's Dyke: Pattern and Purpose', *The Antiquaries Journal*, 80 (2000), 200–1.

38 Ibid., 195–206; Worthington, 'Offa's Dyke', 91–5.

39 Ray and Bapty, *Offa's Dyke*, 270.

40 E.g. M. Wood, *In Search of the Dark Ages* (new edn, 2006), 101. Cf. Tyler, 'Offa's Dyke', 153, 157.

41 S. Keynes, 'The Kingdom of the Mercians in the Eighth Century', *Æthelbald and Offa: Two Eighth-Century Kings of Mercia*, 10; *Anglo-Saxons*, ed. Campbell, 119; Worthington, 'Offa's Dyke', 91–5; Tyler, 'Offa's Dyke', 152–3.

42 Stenton, *Anglo-Saxon England*, 217–18; Brooks, *Early History*, 113–14.

43 D. M. Metcalf, 'Betwixt Sceattas and Offa's Pence: Mint-Attributions and the Chronology of a Recession', *British Numismatic Journal*, 79 (2009), 1–33.

44 Maddicott, 'Prosperity and Power', 52, 65; R. Naismith, 'The Coinage of Offa Revisited', *British Numismatic Journal*, 80 (2010), 77–9.

45 Ibid., 84–5; R. Naismith, *Money and Power in Anglo-Saxon England: The Southern English Kingdoms, 757–865* (Cambridge, 2012), 8, 54–8, 100–1, 206.

46 Ibid., 62–4; *EHD*, i, 817, 820; Kelly, 'Offa', *ODNB*.

47 Ibid.; *EHD*, i, 773.

48 Wickham, *Inheritance of Rome*, 376–8; Keynes, 'Kingdom of the Mercians', 15.

49 *EHD*, i, 860; Brooks, *Early History*, 114–17.

50 Ibid., 117–18; *EHD*, i, 836–40.

51 Ibid., 180, 860, 862; Brooks, *Early History*, 118–20.

52 H. Edwards, 'Cynewulf', *ODNB*; *EHD*, i, 175–6, 179–80, 837.

53 Ibid., 175–6. For discussion, see e.g. H. Kleinschmidt, 'The Old English Annal for 757 and West Saxon Dynastic Strife', *Journal of Medieval History*, 22 (1996); B. Yorke, 'The Representation of Early West Saxon History in the Anglo-Saxon Chronicle', *Reading the Anglo-Saxon Chronicle: Language, Literature, History*, ed. A. Jorgensen (Turnhout, 2010), 142–8.

54 H. Edwards, 'Beorhtric', *ODNB*; S. E. Kelly, 'Offa', *ODNB*; *EHD*, i, 180, 187.

55 S. Allott, *Alcuin of York: His Life and Letters* (York, 1974), 16, 43 (nos. 10 and 31); *EHD*, i, 341.

56 Ibid., 180, 187, 848.

57 Ibid., 848–9; J. L. Nelson, 'Carolingian Contacts', *Mercia: An Anglo-Saxon Kingdom in Europe*, ed. M. P. Brown and C. A. Farr (Leicester, 2001), 142.

58 Ibid., 129; *EHD*, i, 181, 849; Naismith, 'Coinage of Offa Revisited', 79; G. Williams, 'Mercian Coinage and Authority', *Mercia: An Anglo-Saxon Kingdom in Europe*, ed. Brown and Farr, 215.

59 *EHD*, i, 848–9; D. P. S. Peacock, 'Charlemagne's Black Stones: The Re-Use of Roman Columns in Early Medieval Europe', *Antiquity*, 71 (1997), 709–15; R. Prien, 'The Copy of an Empire? Charlemagne, the Carolingian Renaissance and Early Medieval Perception of Late Antiquity', *The Transformative Power of the Copy*, ed. C. Forberg and P. Stockhammer (Heidelberg, 2017), 309–29.

[60] D. Parsons and D. Sutherland, *The Anglo-Saxon Church of All Saints, Brixworth, Northamptonshire: Survey, Excavation and Analysis, 1972–2010* (Oxford, 2013), xxii–xxiii, 232–3; J. Blair, *The Church in Anglo-Saxon Society* (Oxford, 2005), 274–7.

[61] Squatriti, 'Digging Ditches', 11–65; Tyler, 'Offa's Dyke', 159–61.

[62] T. M. Charles-Edwards, 'The Making of Nations in Britain and Ireland in the Early Middle Ages', *Lordship and Learning: Studies in Memory of Trevor Aston* (Woodbridge, 2004), 17–18; *EHD*, i, 494, 812–13, 816.

[63] Above, 36–7; Charles-Edwards, 'Making of Nations', 13–14, 20; idem, *Wales and the Britons*, 1–2, 424; *EHD*, i, 398–407.

[64] Charles-Edwards, 'Making of Nations', 20; idem, *Wales and the Britons*, 226–41, 424, 427; Bede, 140–3, 552–5, 560–1; *EHD*, i, 773.

[65] Above, 78; Charles-Edwards, *Wales and the Britons*, 421–2.

[66] Keynes, 'Kingdom of the Mercians', 3–6. Cf. Kelly, 'Offa', *ODNB*, and Brooks, *Early History*, 113.

[67] Kelly, 'Offa', *ODNB*. Alcuin, for example, lamented the killing of King Æthelred of Northumbria in 796, but made no similar complaint about Offa's passing.

[68] *EHD*, i, 846, 855.

[69] Ibid., 855; Keynes, 'Kingdom of the Mercians', 17.

[70] Allott, *Alcuin of York*, 10, 65–6 (nos. 7 and 50).

5 Storm from the North: The Viking Assault on Britain and Francia

[1] *EHD*, i, 181, 842–6; Sawyer 134.

[2] J. D. Richards, *The Vikings: A Very Short Introduction* (Oxford, 2005), 2–4; P. Sawyer, 'The Age of the Vikings and Before', *The Oxford Illustrated History of the Vikings*, ed. P. Sawyer (Oxford, 1997), 2; T. Williams, *Viking Britain: An Exploration* (2017), 37–42.

[3] *EHD*, i, 843; Sawyer, 'Age of the Vikings', 3–7.

[4] M. Arnold, *The Vikings: Culture and Conquest* (2006), 67–78, 80; D. M. Hadley, *The Vikings in England: Settlement, Society and Culture* (Manchester, 2006), 17.

5   Above, 165; Williams, *Viking Britain*, 67–9, 75–6.
6   Ibid., 32–5, 48–9; G. Halsall, 'Playing By Whose Rules? A Further Look at Viking Atrocity in the Ninth Century', *Medieval History*, 2 (1992), 3–12; Arnold, *Vikings*, 29–32, 49–50.
7   Sawyer, 'Age of the Vikings', *Oxford Illustrated History of the Vikings*, 3; *EHD*, i, 180, 273. For the Great Glen, see B. E. Crawford, 'The Making of a Frontier: The Firthlands from the Ninth to the Twelfth Centuries', *Firthlands of Ross and Sutherland*, ed. J. R. Baldwin (Scottish Soc. for Northern Studies, 1986), 33–46.
8   Sawyer, 'Age of the Vikings', 3; J. L. Nelson, *King and Emperor: A New Life of Charlemagne* (2019), 376; *EHD*, i, 272–6; Sawyer 134.
9   Above, 154–8, 169; M. K. Lawson, 'Cenwulf', *ODNB*; Brooks, *Early History*, 114, 121–7; Hayes and Malim, 'Date and Nature of Wat's Dyke', 173–6.
10 *EHD*, i, 183, 187. The claim that Egbert was related to the kings of Kent has been discredited. R. Naismith, 'The Origins of the Line of Egbert, King of the West Saxons, 802–839', *EHR*, 126 (2011) 1–16. Cf. Keynes, 'Kingdom of the Mercians', 16–17; H. Edwards, 'Ecgberht', *ODNB*.
11 Sawyer 1435; S. Keynes, 'Mercia and Wessex in the Ninth Century', *Mercia: An Anglo-Saxon Kingdom in Europe*, ed. Brown and Farr, 311–13; *EHD*, i, 185–6.
12 Ibid., 186.
13 C. Downham, 'The Earliest Viking Activity in England?', *EHR*, 132 (2017), 5–10.
14 J. L. Nelson, 'The Frankish Empire', *Oxford Illustrated History of the Vikings*, 23–4; *Annals of St Bertin*, 30. For Dorestad, see *The Oxford Encyclopedia of Medieval Warfare and Military Technology*, vol. 1, ed. C. J. Rogers (Oxford, 2010), 543–4; S. Coupland, 'Dorestad in the Ninth Century: The Numismatic Evidence', *Jaarboek voor Munt en Penningkunde*, 75 (1988), 5–26.
15 Arnold, *Vikings*, 82–4; D. Ó Corráin, 'Ireland, Wales, Man, and the Hebrides', *Oxford Illustrated History of the Vikings*, 83–5.

16 S. McGrail, *Ancient Boats in North-West Europe: The Archaeology of Water Transport to* AD *1500* (new edn, 1998), 216; *EHD*, i, 186. For later raids on the Somerset coast launched from Ireland, see *EHD*, ii, 127, 149–50.

17 *EHD*, i, 187; J. L. Nelson, 'Æthelwulf', *ODNB*.

18 *Annals of St Bertin*, 42–3. *Pace* the editor's note, the king who sent the messengers in the spring of 839 must have been Egbert, not Æthelwulf.

19 *EHD*, i, 187; Nelson, 'Frankish Empire', 24–6; *Annals of St Bertin*, 50–1.

20 *EHD*, i, 187; *Encyclopedia*, 156, 434; A. R. Rumble, 'Hamtun *alias* Hamwic (Saxon Southampton): The Place-Name Traditions and their Significance', *Excavations at Melbourne Street Southampton, 1971–76*, ed. P. Holdsworth (Council for British Archaeology, 1980), 7–20.

21 *EHD*, i, 187.

22 Above, 180–1; Naismith, *Citadel of the Saxons*, 102–4; Higham and Ryan, 247.

23 B. Yorke, *Wessex in the Early Middle Ages* (Leicester, 1995), 47, 58; Brooks, 'Development of Military Obligations', 81; Sawyer 292; Nelson, 'Æthelwulf', *ODNB*; S. Keynes, 'The West Saxon Charters of King Æthelwulf and His Sons', *EHR*, 109 (1994), 1116.

24 Nelson, 'Frankish Empire', 25–6; *Annals of St Bertin*, 55–6, 60, 62, 65, 68.

25 *EHD*, i, 188.

26 Ibid.; Ó Corráin, 'Ireland, Wales, Man, and the Hebrides', 87–8; *Annals of St Bertin*, 56.

27 *EHD*, i, 188; N. P. Brooks, 'England in the Ninth Century: The Crucible of Defeat', *TRHS*, 5th ser., 29 (1979), 5–6.

28 *EHD*, i, 188; *Annals of St Bertin*, 69. When London was attacked in 842 the *Chronicle* calls it Lundenne, but 851 it calls it Lundenburg, suggesting the walled city.

29 *EHD*, i, 189; Asser, 69; R. Abels, *Alfred the Great: War, Kingship and Culture in Anglo-Saxon England* (1998), 68–70.

30 Ibid., 70–1; *EHD*, i, 187–8.

31 Ibid., 189; *Annals of St Bertin*, 80.

[32] Abels, *Alfred the Great*, 72–7.

[33] Ibid., 71, 78; *Annals of St Bertin*, 83.

[34] Ibid.; Asser, 70–1.

[35] Ibid. I am unpersuaded by the argument that Æthelberht remained as king of Kent, Sussex and Essex, and the heartlands of Wessex were split between Æthelbald and his father. Apart from anything else, it fails to account for Æthelwulf's burial at Steyning in Sussex in 858, and his later translation to Winchester after Æthelbald's death. Abels, *Alfred the Great*, 89. Cf. Kirby, *Earliest English Kings*, 166–7.

[36] Asser, 72–3.

[37] Nelson, 'Æthelwulf', *ODNB*; *EHD*, i, 187.

[38] Asser, 73.

[39] Ibid.; Keynes and Lapidge, 174; Abels, *Alfred the Great*, 93–4.

[40] *EHD*, i, 190–1; Asser, 73–4.

[41] *Annals of St Bertin*, 82–6, 90–1, 94.

[42] Ibid., 100, 118, 131; S. Coupland, 'The Fortified Bridges of Charles the Bald', *Journal of Medieval History*, 17 (1991), 1–12.

[43] *EHD*, i, 190–1.

[44] Ibid., 190; C. Downham, *Viking Kings of Britain and Ireland: The Dynasty of Ívarr to AD 1014* (Edinburgh, 2008), 15–16, 64–5; S. Keynes, 'Vikings in England', *Oxford Illustrated History of the Vikings*, 54.

[45] *EHD*, i, 191; Brooks, 'England in the Ninth Century', 9–10.

[46] *EHD*, i, 191; Abels, *Alfred the Great*, 117–18; Williams, *Viking Britain*, 110–13.

[47] *EHD*, i, 192.

[48] Ibid., 187–9, 527.

[49] Ibid., 192; Asser, 77.

[50] Ibid., 78; *EHD*, i, 192; A. Gransden, 'Edmund [St Edmund]', *ODNB*.

[51] *EHD*, i, 192; Asser, 78.

[52] Ibid., 78–80.

[53] Ibid., 80; *EHD*, i, 193; Downham, *Viking Kings*, 66–7.

[54] Asser, 80–1; *EHD*, i, 193.

[55] Ibid., 190–1, 193.

6 Resurrection: Alfred the Great and the Forging of Englishness

1   *A History of the County of Berkshire*, iv, ed. W. Page and P. H. Ditchfield (1924), 320; *Jackson's Oxford Journal*, nos. 542 and 543 (17 September and 24 September 1763); C. R. Cocherell, *Iconography of the West Front of Wells Cathedral* (1851), 75, suggested one of the statues in the cathedral's thirteenth-century facade was Alfred, but more recent writers have rejected this. Cf. C. M. Malone, *Facade as Spectacle: Ritual and Ideology at Wells Cathedral* (Leiden, 2004), 61–4.

2   O. J. W. Cox, 'Frederick, Prince of Wales, and the First Performance of "Rule Britannia!"', *Historical Journal*, 56 (2013), 931–54; S. Keynes, 'The Cult of King Alfred the Great', *ASE*, 28 (1999), 278–9. For later eighteenth-century follies dedicated to Alfred, ibid., 286, 320–2, and for the development of his cult thereafter, 281–356; Abels, *Alfred the Great*, 2.

3   Keynes and Lapidge, 44; Keynes, 'Cult of King Alfred', 231–2, 239, 254, 268.

4   Keynes and Lapidge, 48–58, 201–2, 223–7.

5   Abels, *Alfred the Great*, 318–19; idem, 'Alfred and his Biographers: Images and Imagination', *Writing Medieval Biography, 750–1250: Essays in Honour of Frank Barlow*, ed. D. Bates, J. Crick and S. Hamilton (Woodbridge, 2006), 70. The forgery argument was most recently put by A. Smyth, *King Alfred the Great* (Oxford, 1995). See the review by D. R. Howlett, *EHR*, 112 (1997), 942–4.

6   James I was the next *published* royal author in Britain after Alfred, but earlier monarchs had written and translated for their own edification. Elizabeth I, for example, translated Boethius' *The Consolation of Philosophy*, one of the texts translated by Alfred.

7   M. Godden, 'Did King Alfred Write Anything?', *Medium Ævum*, 76 (2007), 1–23.

8   M. Biddle, *Winchester in the Early Middle Ages: An Edition and Discussion of the Winton Domesday* (Oxford, 1976), 277–82;

B. M. Ford and S. Teague, *Winchester: A City in the Making* (Oxford, 2011), 76–9, 189, 232–6, suggest the streets were laid out between 840 and 880. M. Biddle, *The Search for Winchester's Anglo-Saxon Minsters* (Oxford, 2018), 1, 6–7, accepts this revised date range.

[9] *Historia Ecclesie Abbendonensis: The History of the Church of Abingdon*, ed. J. Hudson (2 vols., Oxford, 2002, 2007), i, 272–5.

[10] Abels, *Alfred the Great*, 45–6; Asser, 74–5, 80–1.

[11] Ibid., 69–70; *EHD*, i, 880; Abels, *Alfred the Great*, 57–67.

[12] Asser, 76, 88–91, 101; D. Pratt, 'The Illnesses of King Alfred the Great', *ASE*, 30 (2001), 73–4.

[13] Above, 195–201; Asser, 79.

[14] Ibid., 106; *EHD*, i, 192; *Encyclopedia*, 459–61.

[15] Asser, 81; J. R. Maddicott, 'Trade, Industry and the Wealth of King Alfred', *Past & Present*, 123 (1989), 12.

[16] *EHD*, i, 277, 282–3.

[17] Ibid., 194; D. M. Hadley, J. D. Richards, et al., 'The Winter Camp of the Viking Great Army, AD 872–3, Torksey, Lincolnshire', *Antiquaries Journal,* 96 (2016), 26, 39, 43, 50, 54, 62.

[18] Ibid., 43; *EHD*, i, 194; Williams, *Viking Britain*, 147; C. L. Jarman, M. Biddle, T. Higham and C. Bronk Ramsey, 'The Viking Great Army in England: New Dates from the Repton Charnel', *Antiquity*, 92 (2018), 1–17.

[19] *EHD*, i, 194, 200. Cf. S. Keynes, 'King Alfred and the Mercians', *Kings, Currency and Alliances*, ed. M. A. S. Blackburn and D. N. Dumville (Woodbridge, 1998), 12–19.

[20] *EHD*, i, 192, 194; Williams, *Viking Britain*, 155–61.

[21] *EHD*, i, 194–5; Blair, *Building*, 245–6; Asser, 82–3.

[22] *EHD*, i, 195, 283.

[23] Ibid., 195; Asser, 69; G. Halsall, *Warfare and Society in the Barbarian West, 450–900* (2003), 156.

[24] *EHD*, i, 195; Asser, 83. See C. Konshuh, 'Fighting with a *Lytlewerode*: Alfred's Retinue in the *Anglo-Saxon Chronicle*', *The Medieval Chronicle X* (Leiden, 2016), 106–8.

[25] Keynes and Lapidge, 197–202.

[26] Asser, 83–4; *EHD*, i, 195.

[27] Asser, 84, 103.

[28] Ibid., 84–5; *EHD*, i, 196. Some writers state that the vikings fled to the Iron Age hillfort at Bratton Camp, two miles from Edington. This tradition dates to the eighteenth century – e.g. *Archaeologia*, vol. 7 (1785), 22 – but there is nothing in the contemporary sources to support it. Earlier references in Asser's account to the vikings making camp at Chippenham, and subsequent ones to them leaving from Chippenham, make it more likely that this was the location Alfred besieged.

[29] Asser, 85; Abels, *Alfred the Great*, 164.

[30] Asser, 85; *EHD*, i, 196, 200.

[31] R. Naismith, *Medieval European Coinage 8: Britain and Ireland c. 400–1066* (Cambridge, 2017), 169–70. Cf. S. Keynes, 'Alfred the Great and the Kingdom of the Anglo-Saxons', *A Companion to Alfred the Great*, ed. N. Guenther Discenza and P. E. Szarmach (Leiden, 2015), 20–1.

[32] Ibid., 22; *EHD*, i, 196.

[33] Ibid., 416–17. John of Worcester says 'after the death of Ceolwulf, Alfred, king of the West Saxons, in order to expel the army of the pagan Danes from his kingdom, recovered London and the surrounding area by his activity, and acquired part of the kingdom of the Mercians which Ceolwulf had held'. *EHD*, i, 199, n. 4.

[34] Abels, *Alfred the Great*, 180–2; Naismith, *Medieval European Coinage*, 165–6.

[35] Ibid., 169; S. Foot, 'The Making of *Angelcynn*: English Identity Before the Norman Conquest', *TRHS*, 6th ser., 6 (1996), 27, 29–30; Asser, 86–8, 97, 99.

[36] Ibid., 85–6; *EHD*, ii, 196–7. The *Chronicle*'s entry for 883 has long puzzled historians. A successful stand-off against the vikings at Fulham in 879, which prompted Alfred to promise alms to Rome, seems to me the likeliest explanation. Cf. Abels, *Alfred the Great*, 171; *EHD*, i, 197, n. 6.

[37] Halsall, *Warfare and Society*, 1–19; G. Williams, 'Military Institutions and Royal Power', *Mercia: An Anglo-Saxon Kingdom in Europe*, ed. Brown and Farr, 295–309.

[38] Halsall, *Warfare and Society*, 223–7.

[39] T. Reuter, 'Plunder and Tribute in the Carolingian Empire', *TRHS*, 35 (1985). 87–91; Sawyer 134.

[40] *Anglo-Saxons*, ed. Campbell, 152–3, for example, presents a conventional view, based on M. Biddle and D. Hill, 'Late Saxon Planned Towns', *Antiquaries Journal*, 51 (1971), 70–85.

[41] Keynes and Lapidge, 193–4, 339–4; Asser, 101–2. J. Haslam, 'The Burghal Hidage and the West Saxon Burhs: A Reappraisal', *ASE*, 45 (2016), is the most recent attempt by the same author to argue that all the burhs were created simultaneously by Alfred in 878–9. Buckingham, however, remains a stumbling block.

[42] Above, 144–6, 186; Blair, *Building*, 245–6; Asser, 82.

[43] Royal Commission on the Historical Monuments of England, 'Wareham West Walls', *Medieval Archaeology*, 3 (1959), 120; Blair, *Building*, 232–46.

[44] Asser, 101–3; Keynes and Lapidge, 340; *EHD*, i, 203–4.

[45] Abels, *Alfred the Great*, 203.

[46] Keynes and Lapidge, 193–4, 341; Yorke, *Wessex in the Early Middle Ages*, 116.

[47] Ibid., 194, 341.

[48] The *Chronicle* for 892–3 says Alfred 'had divided his army in two, so that always half were at home, half on service, apart from the men who guarded the *burhs*'. It is not clear whether this was an arrangement introduced that year or earlier in the reign. Asser describes how those who served in the royal household were divided into three groups that worked in monthly rotation, but does not say that this system was introduced by Alfred. *EHD*, i, 202; Asser, 106. Cf. Abels, *Alfred the Great*, 196–8.

[49] Brooks, 'England in the Ninth Century', 20; Abels, *Alfred the Great*, 207; Asser, 101; *Historia Ecclesie Abbendonensis*, i, ed. Hudson, 272–5.

[50] Asser, 86–7; *EHD*, i, 197–8.

[51] E.g. Keynes and Lapidge, 24–5. Cf. R. Holt, 'The Urban Transformation in England, 900–1100', *Anglo-Norman Studies*, 32 (2010), 57–78.

52 Ford and Teague, *Winchester: A City in the Making*, 76–9, 189, 232–6.
53 Asser, 97–8; above, 186.
54 Naismith, *Citadel of the Saxons*, 119–23; *EHD*, i, 199; Keynes, 'King Alfred and the Mercians', 27–8.
55 Asser, 97–8, 101.
56 M. Atherton, *The Making of England: A New History of the Anglo-Saxon World* (2017), 66–7.
57 Keynes and Lapidge, 124–6; Brooks, 'England in the Ninth Century', 12–16.
58 *EHD*, i, 845; above, 183–4, 189–90, 207.
59 *EHD*, i, 197, 200; Naismith, *Medieval European Coinage*, 172–3; Asser, 102–5.
60 Keynes and Lapidge, 125; Asser, 92–4.
61 Ibid., 75–6, 99–100.
62 Keynes and Lapidge, 125–6.
63 Ibid., 28–9.
64 Asser, 92; J. Bately, 'Alfred as Author and Translator', *Companion to Alfred the Great*, ed. Guenther Discenza and Szarmach, 115–18; Godden, 'Did King Alfred Write Anything?', 1–23.
65 Keynes and Lapidge, 126, 203–6.
66 Cf. Godden, 'Did King Alfred Write Anything', 1–23, and J. Bately, 'Did King Alfred Actually Translate Anything? The Integrity of the Alfredian Canon Revisited', *Medium Ævum*, 78 (2009), 189–215.
67 Asser, 90, 107, 110; Keynes and Lapidge, 126; Foot, 'Making of *Angelcynn*', 35; Abels, *Alfred the Great*, 14–18, 192.
68 Keynes and Lapidge, 283–4; *EHD*, i, 201; Asser, 102.
69 *EHD*, i, 202.
70 Ibid.; Keynes and Lapidge, 189–90.
71 Ibid., 190; *EHD*, i, 201–3.
72 Ibid., 202–3.
73 Ibid., 203–4.
74 Ibid., 204–5; above, 194.
75 *EHD*, i, 205–6.
76 Ibid., 206–7; Keynes, 'Cult of King Alfred', 231.

[77] Abels, *Alfred the Great*, 5.

[78] N. Marafioti, *The King's Body: Burial and Succession in Late Anglo-Saxon England* (Toronto, 2014), 26.

7 Imperial Overstretch? King Æthelstan and the Conquest of the North

[1] Above, 173–4; *Historia de Sancto Cuthberto*, ed. and trans. T. Johnson South (Woodbridge, 2002), 1–2, 84, 96.

[2] Ibid., 64–7. The king's donation is recorded in the form of a charter, but strictly speaking it is a *testamentum*, and the book containing the lives of St Cuthbert must have been donated at some point after the king's visit. S. Foot, *Æthelstan* (2011), 122; S. Keynes, 'King Æthelstan's Books', *Learning and Literature in Anglo-Saxon England*, ed. M. Lapidge and H. Gneuss (Cambridge, 1985), 180–5.

[3] *Encyclopedia*, 135; Rollason and Dobson, 'Cuthbert', *ODNB*; Foot, *Æthelstan*, 122–3.

[4] Ibid., 121–2; M. Brown, *The Lindisfarne Gospels: Society, Spirituality and the Scribe* (2003), 122–3, 134–9; C. E. Karkov, *The Ruler Portraits of Anglo-Saxon England* (Woodbridge, 2004), 53–83.

[5] Keynes, 'King Æthelstan's Books', 174; Foot, *Æthelstan*, 212–16.

[6] Ibid., 243; *Historia de Sancto Cuthberto*, ed. Johnson South, 64–7; *EHD*, i, 307.

[7] Ibid., 305; Foot, *Æthelstan*, 251–8; M. Lapidge, 'Some Latin Poems as Evidence for the Reign of Athelstan', *ASE*, 9 (1980), 62–71; M. Wood, 'The Lost Life of King Athelstan', idem, *In Search of England* (1999), 149–68.

[8] *EHD*, i, 305; Lapidge, 'Some Latin Poems', 72–83; above, 207.

[9] *Life of St Æthelwold*, 2–3; S. Miller, 'Edward [*called* Edward the Elder]', *ODNB*; Asser, 90–1; Malmesbury, 196–7; N. J. Higham, 'Edward the Elder's Reputation: An Introduction', *Edward the Elder, 899–924*, ed. N. J. Higham and D. H. Hill (Abingdon, 2001), 2.

[10] Keynes and Lapidge, 173–8; Abels, *Alfred the Great*, 178–80.

11 Hadley, *Vikings in England*, 1–9, 92; *Encyclopedia*, 145, 192; J. Kershaw and E. C. Røyrvik, 'The "People of the British Isles" Project and Viking Settlement in England', *Antiquity*, 90 (2016), 1670–5.

12 Ibid., 1675–9.

13 L. Abrams, 'Edward the Elder's Danelaw', *Edward the Elder*, ed. Higham and Hill, 128–43; C. Hart, *The Danelaw* (1992), 3–24.

14 Above, 240; Molyneaux, *Formation*, 45–7.

15 *EHD*, i, 209.

16 Ibid., 210–11.

17 Keynes, 'King Alfred and the Mercians', 27–8; *Annals of Ireland: Three Fragments*, ed. and trans. J. O'Donovan (Dublin, 1860), 226–37; *EHD*, i, 211.

18 Ibid., 211–12.

19 Ibid., 212–13.

20 Ibid., 214–16.

21 Ibid., 216–17.

22 Ibid., 217; M. R. Davidson, 'The (Non) Submission of the Northern Kings in 920', *Edward the Elder*, ed. Higham and Hill, 200–11.

23 *EHD*, i, 218.

24 Foot, *Æthelstan*, xv, 29–44.

25 Ibid., 38–40; *EHD*, i, 218, 305; Biddle, *Search for Winchester's Anglo-Saxon Minsters*, 47, 66–7.

26 Sawyer 395; Foot, *Æthelstan*, 43, 56–61, 73.

27 Ibid., 73–7, 216–23.

28 *EHD*, i, 218, 307.

29 Lapidge, 'Some Latin Poems', 83. The author has translated *Saxonum* and *Saxonia* as 'English' and 'England'.

30 Foot, *Æthelstan*, 25–8, 154–5, 212–13, 216.

31 *EHD*, i, 306; Naismith, *Medieval European Coinage*, 168; Maddicott, 'Trade, Industry and the Wealth of King Alfred', 4, 14–17.

32 *EHD*, i, 307.

33 Above, 52; J. R. Maddicott, *The Origins of the English Parliament, 924–1327* (Oxford, 2010). For a detailed discussion of Æthelstan's itinerary, see Foot, *Æthelstan*, 77–91.

34 Maddicott, *Origins of the English Parliament*, 1–11.

35 Ibid., 12–32. For a wider discussion, see L. Roach, *Kingship and Consent in Anglo-Saxon England, 871–978* (Cambridge, 2013).

36 B. T. Hudson, 'Ealdred', *ODNB*; A. Woolf, *From Pictland to Alba, 789–1070* (Edinburgh, 2007), 161–5, discusses some possible causes of the invasion.

37 Sawyer 407, 425; *EHD*, i, 219, 278, 548–51. The *Chronicle's* entry for 934 contains its first mention of Scotland. Its entry for 920 contains its first reference to the king of Scots. Why the Scots had replaced the Picts is by no means clear. See Woolf, *From Pictland to Alba*, 320–2.

38 D. Brown, 'Constantine II', *ODNB*; Woolf, *From Pictland to Alba*, 166; Sawyer 426, 1792.

39 Above, 165–8. The author of *The History of the Britons* was traditionally known as Nennius. For his context and purpose, see Higham, *King Arthur*, 119–66.

40 Abels, *Alfred the Great*, 182–3, 186–7; A. Breeze, '*Armes Prydein*, Hywel Dda, and the Reign of Edmund of Wessex', *Études Celtiques*, 33 (1997), 210–15.

41 B. T. Hudson, 'Óláf Guthfrithson', *ODNB*; *EHD*, i, 279, 309.

42 Ibid., 309; Woolf, *From Pictland to Alba*, 169–71; Downham, *Viking Kings*, 104. Cf. M. Wood, 'Searching for Brunanburh: The Yorkshire Context of the "Great War" of 937', *Yorkshire Archaeological Journal*, 85 (2013), 138–59.

43 Woolf, *From Pictland to Alba*, 169; *EHD*, i, 219–20, 309.

44 Æthelweard, 54.

45 *EHD*, i, 220, 214–15; Malmesbury, 228–9.

46 Ibid., 216–17, 228–9; M. Morris, *A Great and Terrible King: Edward I and the Forging of Britain* (2008), *passim*.

47 *EHD*, i, 220.

8 One Nation Under God: St Dunstan and the Pursuit of Uniformity

1 Higham, *King Arthur*, 230–2; V. M. Lagorio, 'The Evolving Legend of St Joseph of Glastonbury', *Glastonbury Abbey and the Arthurian Tradition*, ed. J. P. Carley (Cambridge, 2001), 55–75.

The story that Jesus came to Glastonbury as a boy in the company of Joseph of Arimathea, a merchant drawn to Britain because of the tin trade, appears no earlier than the last decade of the nineteenth century. It is therefore unlikely that William Blake was alluding to it when he composed his famous poem 'Jerusalem' in 1808, as is often claimed. See A. W. Smith, '"And Did Those Feet … ?": The "Legend" of Christ's Visit to Britain', *Folklore*, 100 (1989), 63–83.

2   Malmesbury, 802–5; R. Gilchrist and C. Green, *Glastonbury Abbey: Archaeological Investigations 1904–79* (2015), 6, 57, 102, 124, 145.

3   *Early Lives*, xiii, 14–17, 54–7; M. Lapidge, 'Dunstan', *ODNB*.

4   *Early Lives*, 10–13; N. Brooks, 'The Career of St Dunstan', *St Dunstan: His Life, Times and Cult*, ed. N. Ramsey, M. Sparks and T. Tatton-Brown (Woodbridge, 1992), 3–7. 'B' clearly errs in placing Dunstan's birth in the reign of Æthelstan. Most scholars prefer a date of *c*.909. See e.g. M. Gretsch, *The Intellectual Foundations of the English Benedictine Reform* (Cambridge, 1999), 256–7, n. 94.

5   P. Rahtz, *Glastonbury* (1993), 12–18; *Early Lives*, 12–19.

6   Ibid., 16–17; Foot, *Monastic Life*, 5–7; above, 96, 98; *Encyclopedia*, 327–8, 363–4.

7   L. Abrams, 'The Conversion of the Danelaw', *Vikings and the Danelaw*, ed. J. Graham-Campbell et al. (2001), 31–44; Stenton, *Anglo-Saxon England*, 434.

8   Ibid., 438–9; Brooks, 'England in the Ninth Century', 12; above, 229; Fleming, *Britain After Rome*, 318–21.

9   *Early Lives*, xxiv–xxv.

10   D. Iogna-Prat, 'Cluny, 909–910, ou l'Instrumentalisation de la Mémoire des Origines', *Revue Mabillon*, 11 (2000), 161–85; *Anglo-Saxons*, ed. Campbell, 181, 184; L. Roach, *Æthelred the Unready* (2016), 33–4; Higham and Ryan, 311.

11   Foot, *Æthelstan*, 22, 44–52, 100–2; C. Cubitt and M. Costambeys, 'Oda', *ODNB*; *Encyclopedia*, 279.

12   *Early Lives*, xviii, 18–29. The text does not support the editors' belief that Dunstan was expelled from Æthelstan's court. Cf. Brooks, 'Career of St Dunstan', 5; Foot, *Æthelstan*, 108.

13 *Encyclopedia*, 6–7; *Early Lives*, 26–7.

14 Ibid., 34–43; M. A. Meyer, 'Women and the Tenth-Century English Monastic Reform', *Revue Bénédictine*, 87 (1977), 34–61.

15 *Early Lives*, 40–1; P. Stafford, 'Eadgifu', *ODNB*.

16 *Early Lives*, 42–7.

17 Ibid., 48–9.

18 Ibid., 48–51, 58–9.

19 Ibid., 50–1; Brooks, 'Career of St Dunstan', 11–12; *Life of St Æthelwold*, 14–17.

20 *EHD*, i, 220; Downham, *Viking Kings*, 43; Olaf Cuaran is often confused and conflated with Æthelstan's opponent at *Brunanburh*, Olaf Guthfrithson, who invaded Britain the previous year, but was probably not king of York, as is usually claimed. See K. Halloran, 'Anlaf Guthfrithson at York: A Non-Existent Kingship?', *Northern History*, 50 (2013), 180–5.

21 *EHD*, i, 221, 279; K. Halloran, 'The War for Mercia, 942–943', *Midland History*, 41 (2016), 96–105; C. Downham, '"Hiberno-Norwegians" and "Anglo-Danes": Anachronistic Ethnicities in Viking-Age England', *Mediaeval Scandinavia*, 19 (2009), 148, offers a preferable translation of the *Chronicle*'s poem.

22 *EHD*, i, 221–2; Halloran, 'War for Mercia', 105–6; *Early Lives*, xxix; Malmesbury, 820–1.

23 *EHD*, i, 222; *Early Lives*, 60–1, 92–7, 124–5; K. Halloran, 'A Murder at Pucklechurch: The Death of King Edmund, 26 May 946', *Midland History*, 40 (2015), 120–9.

24 Ibid., 60–1; A. Williams, 'Eadred', *ODNB*; Brooks, 'Career of St Dunstan', 13; *Lives of St Oswald*, 84–5.

25 *EHD*, i, 222–4, 280; Cubitt and Costambeys, 'Oda', *ODNB*. For debate on the events of these years, and the identity of Erik, see P. Sawyer, 'The Last Scandinavian Kings of York', *Northern History*, 31 (1995), 39–44; C. Downham, 'The Chronology of the Last Scandinavian Kings of York, AD 937–954', *Northern History*, 40 (2003), 25–51; A. Woolf, 'Erik Bloodaxe Revisited', *Northern History*, 35 (1998), 189–93; C. Downham, 'Eric Bloodaxe – Axed? The Mystery of the Last Scandinavian King of York', *Medieval Scandinavia*, 14 (2004), 51–77.

[26] *Life of St Æthelwold*, 10–17.

[27] Ibid., 18–25.

[28] *Early Lives*, 64–5; *EHD*, i, 224; *Life of St Æthelwold*, 16–19.

[29] S. Keynes, 'Eadwig', *ODNB*; Æthelweard, 55.

[30] *Early Lives*, 66–9.

[31] Ibid., 68–73; Brooks, 'Career of St Dunstan', 15.

[32] *Early Lives*, 76n, 92–3; Sawyer 1211; C. Hart, 'Æthelstan Half-King', *ODNB*; S. Jayakumar, 'Eadwig and Edgar: Politics, Propaganda, Faction', *Edgar, King of the English, 959–975: New Interpretations*, ed. D. Scragg (Woodbridge, 2008), 93–4; B. Yorke, 'Æthelwold and the Politics of the Tenth Century', *Bishop Æthelwold: His Career and Influence*, ed. idem (Woodbridge, 1988), 74–5.

[33] Jayakumar, 'Eadwig and Edgar', 84–9.

[34] Ibid., 89–91; Yorke, 'Æthelwold and the Politics of the Tenth Century', 79–80.

[35] E. John, 'The King and the Monks in the Tenth-Century Reformation', idem, *Orbis Britanniae and other Studies* (Leicester, 1966), 157–8; Maddicott, *Origins of the English Parliament*, 25; A. Williams, 'Edgar', *ODNB*; cf. Keynes, 'Eadwig', *ODNB*.

[36] Ibid.; *Early Lives*, 74–5.

[37] Ibid., xxxv–xxxvii, 76–9. Dunstan had been offered the bishopric of Crediton by King Eadred, but had refused: ibid., 62–3.

[38] Ibid., 76–7; *EHD*, i, 225; Jayakumar, 'Eadwig and Edgar', 88; Yorke, 'Æthelwold and the Politics of the Tenth Century', 77–8; Keynes, 'Eadwig', *ODNB*.

[39] Williams, 'Eadred', *ODNB*; idem, 'Edgar', *ODNB*.

[40] *Early Lives*, 78–81; Brooks, *Early History*, 243–4.

[41] *Early Lives*, xxxviii–xxxix, 82–5; *HBC*, 220; *Lives of St Oswald*, 8–11, 38–9, 50–9.

[42] *Early Lives*, xxxix–xl.

[43] *Lives of St Oswald*, 76–9; *EHD*, i, 921; John, 'The King and the Monks', 160; *Life of St Æthelwold*, 24–9.

[44] Ibid., 28–33; Lapidge, 'Dunstan', *ODNB*; *EHD*, i, 226.

[45] *Lives of St Oswald*, 72–9.

[46] Ibid., 78–81; Fleming, *Britain After Rome*, 323.

[47] *Lives of St Oswald*, 88–95, 100–1, 112–13; *Life of St Æthelwold*, 43n; Lapidge, 'Dunstan', *ODNB*; N. P. Brooks, 'Oswald [St Oswald]', *ODNB*.

[48] Yorke, 'Æthelwold and the Politics of the Tenth Century', 68; *Life of St Æthelwold*, 38–41; Brooks, *Early History*, 224; D. Knowles, *The Monastic Order in England* (2nd edn, Cambridge, 1963), 50–1.

[49] *Life of St Æthelwold*, 44–5; *Regularis Concordia*, ed. and trans. T. Symons (1953), 1–4.

[50] Ibid., 2, 7; Gretsch, *Intellectual Foundations*, 14–15, 272–3, 335; J. Barrow, 'The Chronology of the Benedictine "Reform"', *Edgar, King of the English*, ed. Scragg, 212, 218.

[51] *Regularis Concordia*, ed. Symons, 5; *Anglo-Saxon Kingdoms: Art, Word, War*, ed. C. Breay and J. Story (2018), 286–7; E. John, 'The Newminster Charter', idem, *Orbis Britanniae*, 271–5; Sawyer 745; D. Pratt, 'The Voice of the King in "King Edgar's Establishment of Monasteries"', *ASE*, 41 (2012), 145–204; Karkov, *Ruler Portraits*, 85–93.

[52] *Anglo-Saxon Kingdoms*, ed. Breay and Story, 280, 290–1; *EHD*, i, 922.

[53] Higham and Ryan, 320; C. Cubitt, 'The Tenth-Century Benedictine Reform in England', *Early Medieval Europe*, 6 (1997), 88–90; Gretsch, *Intellectual Foundations*, 2; Atherton, *Making of England*, 262–6.

[54] *EHD*, i, 433, 920; Molyneaux, *Formation*, 155–65.

[55] Ibid., 141–55; T. Lambert, *Law and Order in Anglo-Saxon England* (Oxford, 2017), 133, 242–50.

[56] *EHD*, i, 226, 434; A. R. Rumble, 'The Laity and the Monastic Reform in the Reign of Edgar', *Edgar, King of the English*, ed. Scragg, 246–7, 251; H. Gittos, *Liturgy, Architecture and Sacred Places in Anglo-Saxon England* (Oxford, 2013), 103.

[57] *Early Lives*, 120–1; *EHD*, i, 227–8, 284; *Lives of St Oswald*, 74–5; P. Wormald, *The Making of English Law: King Alfred to the Twelfth Century* (Oxford, 1999), 125.

58 Stenton, *Anglo-Saxon England*, 455–6; Brooks, 'Oswald [St Oswald]', *ODNB*.
59 *Encyclopedia*, 488; *EHD*, i, 435; Wormald, *Making of English Law*, 318. For discussion, see L. Abrams, 'King Edgar and the Men of the Danelaw', *Edgar, King of the English*, ed. Scragg, 171–91.
60 *EHD*, i, 435; Molyneaux, *Formation*, 116–41; *Regularis Concordia*, ed. Symons, 3.
61 Keynes, 'Vikings in England', 70–3; idem, 'Edgar, *rex admirabilis*', *Edgar, King of the English*, ed. Scragg, 25; N. Banton, 'Monastic Reform and the Unification of Tenth-Century England', *Studies in Church History*, 18 (1992), 81.
62 Cubitt, 'Tenth-Century Benedictine Reform', 79–80; Molyneaux, *Formation*, 190, 257; C. Insley, 'Charters, Ritual and Late Tenth-Century English Kingship', *Gender and History*, ed. S. Reynolds, J. Nelson and S. Johns (2012), 86–7; Davis, *History of Medieval Europe*, 225.
63 Ibid., 152, 215; *EHD*, i, 227–8; Molyneaux, *Formation*, 187–8; C. E. Karkov, 'The Frontispiece to the New Minster Charter and the King's Two Bodies', *Edgar, King of the English*, ed. Scragg, 235; idem, *Ruler Portraits*, 86–7.
64 *Lives of St Oswald*, 104–11; Molyneaux, *Formation*, 188, 191; Banton, 'Monastic Reform', 81–2.
65 *EHD*, i, 225, 228, 927; Keynes, 'Edgar, *rex admirabilis*', 50–1; *Lives of St Oswald*, 108–9.
66 Keynes, 'Edgar, *rex admirabilis*', 51; *Lives of St Oswald*, 120–1.
67 Ibid., 122–3; *Regularis Concordia*, ed. Symons, 2.

9 The Ill-Counselled King: Æthelred the Unready and the Fear of Apocalypse

1 Malmesbury, 268–75; William of Malmesbury, *Gesta Regum Anglorum*, II, ed. and trans. R. A. B. Mynors, R. M. Thomson and M. Winterbottom (Oxford, 1999), 146.
2 Roach, *Æthelred*, 6–7.

3   Æthelweard, 9; *Aelfric's Lives of Saints*, ed. W. W. Skeat (1881), 414–15, 422–5, 454–5. 'Engla londe' had previously been used in a translation of Bede's *Ecclesiastical History* of *c*.900, but in the looser sense of 'English territory'. Molyneaux, *Formation*, 6.

4   Roach, *Æthelred*, 3–15.

5   Ibid., 43–4; C. Hart, 'Edward the Martyr', *ODNB*.

6   Roach, *Æthelred*, 45–55.

7   Ibid., 61–3.

8   D. J. V. Fisher, 'The Anti-Monastic Reaction in the Reign of Edward the Martyr', *The Cambridge Historical Journal*, 10 (1952), 262–5; Roach, *Æthelred*, 102.

9   *Lives of St Oswald*, 122–5.

10 Ibid., 122–31, 136–7.

11 Ibid., 138–41; *EHD*, i, 230.

12 Stafford, 'Ælfthryth', *ODNB*; R. Abels, *Æthelred the Unready* (2018), 14–19; Roach, *Æthelred*, 68–80.

13 Abels, *Æthelred*, 21–2; *Lives of St Oswald*, 140–3. Doubt about the identity of the body exists because Archbishop Wulfstan later stated that Edward's corpse had been burned: *EHD*, i, 931.

14 *EHD*, i, 231; Maddicott, *Origins of the English Parliament*, 34–5.

15 Roach, *Æthelred*, 86–8; Biddle, *Search for Winchester's Anglo-Saxon Minsters*, 42–3, 48–51; *Life of St Æthelwold*, 60–3.

16 Holt, 'Urban Transformation', 67, 70, 73–6; Blair, *Building*, 269–74, 339–50.

17 Fleming, *Britain After Rome*, 276–8; C. Dyer, *Making a Living in the Middle Ages: The People of Britain, 850–1520* (2002), 26–35; Blair, *Building*, 354–5.

18 Ibid., 311–17, 355–62; C. Insley, 'Southumbria', *A Companion to the Early Middle Ages: Britain and Ireland, c.500–c.1100*, ed. P. Stafford (Oxford, 2009), 332–3; Holt, 'Urban Transformation', 67; *EHD*, i, 230.

19 Blair, *Building*, 78, 375–6.

20 Ibid., 282–302, 316.

21 Sawyer, *Wealth of Anglo-Saxon England*, 58, 98–105; Molyneaux, *Formation*, 120–1; M. R. Godden, 'Money, Power and Morality in Late Anglo-Saxon England', *ASE*, 19 (1990), 48–50.

22 D. Wyatt, *Slaves and Warriors in Medieval Britain and Ireland, 800–1200* (Brill, 2009), 31; H. G. Richardson and G. O. Sayles, *Law and Legislation from Æthelberht to Magna Carta* (Edinburgh, 1966), 10, 16, 20–1; D. A. E. Pelteret, *Slavery in Early Mediæval England* (Woodbridge, 1995), 65. Cf. above, n. 3.

23 Blair, *Building*, 303–5, 314.

24 Roach, *Æthelred*, 91–5, 100–2; S. Keynes, 'Æthelred II', *ODNB* (quoting Sawyer 876); *EHD*, i, 233.

25 Roach, *Æthelred*, 101–3.

26 *EHD*, i, 228, 232.

27 Ibid., 232–3; *Lives of St Oswald*, 154–7.

28 *EHD*, i, 234, 319–24. It is possible that Swein Forkbeard participated in this attack: ibid., 579–80.

29 Ibid., 225; Roach, *Æthelred*, 95, 129–31.

30 *EHD*, i, 234; Malmesbury, 270–1; S. Keynes, 'A Tale of Two Kings: Alfred the Great and Æthelred the Unready', *TRHS*, 36 (1986), 203–5.

31 Asser, 79; *EHD*, i, 234; Malmesbury, 272–5; Abels, *Æthelred*, 45–8; Roach, *Æthelred*, 166.

32 Ibid., 137–40; *EHD*, i, 234; Abels, *Æthelred*, 63.

33 Roach, *Æthelred*, 138, 159–61.

34 Ibid., 136–67, 241–51; Keynes, 'Æthelred II', *ODNB*.

35 Ibid.; *EHD*, i, 235.

36 Roach, *Æthelred*, 175–7; *EHD*, i, 225.

37 Ibid., 236, 437–9.

38 Ibid., 438.

39 Molyneaux, *Formation*, 179–82; Lambert, *Law and Order*, 251–3, 306–10, 342–8.

40 *EHD*, i, 236–8; Abels, *Æthelred*, 53, suggests a new fleet attacked England in 997, but cf. John of Worcester, 446–7.

41 *EHD*, i, 237–8.

42 Ibid., 238; M. Morris, *The Norman Conquest* (2012), 15–16; Keynes, 'Emma [Ælfgifu]', *ODNB*; P. Stafford, *Queen Emma and Queen Edith* (Oxford, 1997), 174–5.

43 *EHD*, i, 238–9; Roach, *Æthelred*, 187–200.

44 Ibid., 200–1; P. H. Sawyer, 'Swein', *ODNB*; above, n. 28.

45 *EHD*, i, 239–40; Roach, *Æthelred*, 180–2.

46 Ibid., 202–3; *EHD*, i, 240.

47 P. Wormald, 'Æthelweard', *ODNB*; *EHD*, i, 240; Roach, *Æthelred*, 188, 203–7.

48 Ibid., 210–11; P. Wormald, 'Wulfstan [Lupus]', *ODNB*; S. Keynes, 'Eadric Streona', *ODNB*; *EHD*, i, 240n.

49 Roach, *Æthelred*, 201–2; *EHD*, i, 240–1.

50 Ibid., 241, 442–6; Roach, *Æthelred*, 227–35; Abels, *Æthelred*, 90–1.

51 Keynes, 'Eadric Streona', *ODNB*; *EHD*, i, 242.

52 Ibid., 242, 447–8; Roach, *Æthelred*, 267–79.

53 *EHD*, i, 242–4, 246.

54 Ibid., 245.

55 Abels, *Æthelred*, 34; Roach, *Æthelred*, 265; *EHD*, i, 245.

56 Ibid.

57 Ibid.

58 P. Stafford, 'The Laws of Cnut and the History of Anglo-Saxon Royal Promises', *ASE*, 10 (1982), 176–82; Lambert, *Law and Order*, 252–3, 308–10; Molyneaux, *Formation*, 220–1; *EHD*, ii, 120.

59 *EHD*, i, 245; Stenton, *Anglo-Saxon England*, 384–5; Higham and Ryan, 351; P. Stafford, 'Ælfgifu of Northampton', *ODNB*.

60 *EHD*, i, 245–6.

61 Ibid., 246; Roach, *Æthelred*, 287, 291.

62 *EHD*, i, 246.

63 Ibid.; *Chronicle of John of Worcester*, II, ed. Darlington, McGurk and Bray, 476–7.

64 *EHD*, i, 246–7, 925–6; J. Wilcox, 'Wulfstan's *Sermo Lupi ad Anglos* as Political Performance: 16 February 1014 and Beyond', *Wulfstan, Archbishop of York: The Proceedings of the Second Alcuin Conference*, ed. M. O. Townend (Turnhout, 2004), 375–96. Cf. Roach, *Æthelred*, 279–83.

65 Ibid.; *EHD*, i, 929–34.

66 Ibid., 246.

67 M. Morris, *King John: Treachery, Tyranny and the Road to Magna Carta* (2015), 94–6, 127–30, 254–6, 271–5, 290–4.

68 *EHD*, i, 246–7. Stafford, 'Laws of Cnut', 176–82, argues that the terms put to Æthelred in 1014 were repeated in clauses

69 to 83 of the second law code of King Cnut (for which see *EHD*, i, 465–7).

69 *EHD*, i, 247; Roach, *Æthelred*, 294.

70 *EHD*, i, 247, 451; Roach, *Æthelred*, 297–8.

71 Ibid., 298–300; *EHD*, i, 247, 593–6.

72 Ibid., 247–8.

73 Ibid., 248–9.

74 Ibid., 249; H. Summerson, 'George [St George]', *ODNB*; *An Anglo-Saxon Passion of St George*, ed. and trans. C. Hardwick (1850), 2–3.

75 *EHD*, i, 244.

76 Ibid., 249–51. 'Ironside' had been coined by 1057: *EHD*, ii, 135.

10 Twilight: The Rise of the House of Godwine

1 M. Morris, *The Norman Conquest* (2012), 176–88.

2 Ibid., 198–9, 327–53.

3 R. Fleming, 'Harold II', *ODNB*.

4 Henry, Archdeacon of Huntingdon, *Historia Anglorum*, ed. Greenway, 366–9; D. Hume, *The History of England*, vol. 1 (1763), 163–4.

5 Morris, *Norman Conquest*, 24, 28; E. Treharne, *Living Through Conquest: The Politics of Early English, 1020–1220* (Oxford, 2012), 9–14.

6 *EHD*, i, 252–4, 896; M. K. Lawson, *Cnut: England's Viking King, 1016–35* (new edn, 2011), 129, 146.

7 Keynes, 'Emma [Ælfgifu]', *ODNB*; *EHD*, i, 251; *Encomium*, [xxii–xxiv], 32–5; Treharne, *Living Through Conquest*, 14–15.

8 *EHD*, i, 247, 250–1; John of Worcester, ii, 502–3.

9 *EHD*, i, 250; S. Baxter, *The Earls of Mercia: Lordship and Power in Late Anglo-Saxon England* (Oxford, 2007), 26–8.

10 A. Williams, 'Godwine', *ODNB*; *Life of King Edward*, 9–11.

11 Ibid., 11; Morris, *Norman Conquest*, 29; M. K. Lawson, 'Cnut [Canute]', *ODNB*.

12 *EHD*, i, 335–6; M. Townend, 'Contextualizing the *Knútsdrápur*: Skaldic Praise-Poetry at the Court of Cnut', *Anglo-Saxon England*, 30 (2001), 145–79.

13 J. F. Kershaw, *Viking Identities: Scandinavian Jewellery in England* (Oxford, 2013), 177; Wormald, '*Engla Lond*: the Making of an Allegiance', *Journal of Historical Sociology*, 7 (1994), 18; *EHD*, i, 895–6.

14 Ibid., 452–4; Treharne, *Living Through Conquest*, 16–21, 26, 61–4.

15 Ibid., 64; *EHD*, i, 931; William of Malmesbury, *Saints' Lives*, ed. M. Winterbottom and R. M. Thomson (Oxford, 2002), 100–3; Malmesbury, 362–3; D. Wyatt, 'The Significance of Slavery: Alternative Approaches to Anglo-Saxon Slavery', *Anglo-Norman Studies*, 23 (2001), 327–47.

16 Morris, *Norman Conquest*, 23, 30–1.

17 *EHD*, i, 256–7; Maddicott, *Origins of the English Parliament*, 49–56; Baxter, *Earls of Mercia*, 33–5.

18 *Encomium*, [xxxii–xxxiii], 32–5, 38–41.

19 Morris, *Norman Conquest*, 19–22.

20 Ibid., 34–7.

21 *EHD*, i, 257–8; *Encomium*, [xxx], 42–7.

22 *EHD*, i, 258.

23 Morris, *Norman Conquest*, 37–8.

24 Ibid., 39–40; *EHD*, i, 259–60.

25 Ibid., 260; *Encomium*, 52–3; J. R. Maddicott, 'Edward the Confessor's Return to England in 1041', *EHR*, 119 (2004), 650–66; above, 352–3.

26 *Encomium*, 52–3.

27 *EHD*, i, 260; John of Worcester, 532–3.

28 E. Bozoky, 'The Sanctity and Canonisation of Edward the Confessor', *Edward the Confessor: The Man and the Legend*, ed. R. Mortimer (Woodbridge, 2009), 173–86; *Life of King Edward*, 62–71, 92–127; E. Fernie, 'Edward the Confessor's Westminster Abbey', *Edward the Confessor*, ed. Mortimer, 139–50.

29 Morris, *Norman Conquest*, 59–61, 63.

30 Ibid., 39, 62–3; *Life of King Edward*, 20–1. For the full text of the poem, see H. Summerson, 'Tudor Antiquaries and the *Vita Ædwardi regis*', *Anglo-Saxon England*, 38 (2009), 170–2. For comment, see S. Keynes and R. Love, 'Earl Godwine's Ship', *Anglo-Saxon England*, 38 (2009), 185–223.

31 *Life of King Edward*, 22–5.
32 *EHD*, ii, 112, 114–5; John of Worcester, 544–5.
33 *EHD*, ii, 112, 119–20; *Life of King Edward*, 28–31; H. E. J. Cowdrey, 'Robert of Jumièges', *ODNB*.
34 *Life of King Edward*, lxxiii–lxxviii, 14–15, 92–3. For discussion, see Morris, *Norman Conquest*, 64, 365.
35 Ibid., 19–22, 34, 43–4, 51–8, 69–70.
36 *Life of King Edward*, 30–3; *EHD*, ii, 120–2.
37 Ibid., 121–5; *Life of King Edward*, 34–7.
38 Morris, *Norman Conquest*, 72–5.
39 *EHD*, ii, 118–20.
40 Ibid., 125–30; *Life of King Edward*, 42–5; John of Worcester, 572–5.
41 *EHD*, ii, 130–1; *Life of King Edward*, 46–7.
42 Ibid., 46–9; *EHD*, ii, 114, 118, 127.
43 *Life of King Edward*, 60–5.
44 Morris, *Norman Conquest*, 86–90, 96–8.
45 Ibid., 96–7; H. E. J. Cowdrey, 'Stigand', *ODNB*.
46 Morris, *Norman Conquest*, 99–100, 107–8.
47 F. Barlow, *Edward the Confessor* (new edn, 1997), 180; Roach, *Æthelred*, 209–10.
48 Fleming, 'Harold II', *ODNB*; idem, *Britain After Rome*, 333; *EHD*, ii, 134–5, 143.
49 Baxter, *Earls of Mercia*, 182–8; J. Barrow, 'Wulfwig', *ODNB*; W. M. Aird, 'Siward, Earl of Northumbria', *ODNB*; A. Williams, 'Odda', *ODNB*; *Encyclopedia*, 138–9; Blair, *Building*, 402–5.
50 Barlow, *Edward the Confessor*, 139; R. Fleming, *Kings and Lords in Conquest England* (Cambridge, 1991), 53; *Life of King Edward*, 6–7, 18–19, 46–7.
51 Morris, *Norman Conquest*, 102–3, 105.
52 Ibid., 105–6; *EHD*, ii, 135–6.
53 Fleming, *Kings and Lords*, 48–52; *Life of King Edward*, 48–9; Morris, *Norman Conquest*, 103–7.
54 Ibid., 107–9.
55 *EHD*, ii, 239–41; Morris, *Norman Conquest*, 115, 117.
56 Ibid., 115–16; *Eadmer's History of Recent Events in England*, ed. G. Bosanquet (1964), 6.

57 Ibid., 6–8; *EHD*, ii, 248–51; Morris, *Norman Conquest*, 113–14, 116–18.

58 Ibid., 122–7; *Life of King Edward*, 48–9, 78–9.

59 Ibid., 76–7; Morris, *Norman Conquest*, 128.

60 Ibid., 129; *Life of King Edward*, 70–7.

61 Ibid., 78–81; *EHD*, ii, 140.

62 Ibid., 140–1; *Life of King Edward*, 80–3, 110–13; Summerson, 'Tudor Antiquaries', 8–9, 21–2.

63 *EHD*, ii, 141–2, 254; Malmesbury, 420–3; Morris, *Norman Conquest*, 132–41.

64 Ibid., 107–8, 136–7.

65 Ibid., 142–6.

66 Ibid., 146–8.

67 *EHD*, ii, 142–3.

68 Ibid., 143–4; Morris, *Norman Conquest*, 152–4.

69 Ibid., 155–61.

70 Ibid., 161–4.

71 Ibid., 164–5; *EHD*, ii, 143–5; *Life of King Edward*, 88–9.

72 Ibid., 84–5, 88–9; *EHD*, ii, 141, 144.

Conclusion

1 *The Gesta Guillelmi of William of Poitiers*, ed. R. H. C. Davis and M. Chibnall (Oxford, 1998), 139–41; Morris, *Norman Conquest*, 186.

2 Ibid., 189–231, 313–14.

3 Ibid., 189, 225, 238–40, 247–50, 320.

4 *EHD*, ii, 146; Morris, *Norman Conquest*, 333–4.

5 Ibid., 294–6, 338–9.

6 Ibid., 339–40.

7 Ibid., 307.

8 Molyneaux, *Formation*, 233–45; Wickham, *Inheritance of Rome*, 100–1; Lambert, *Law and Order*, 349–63; G. Molyneaux, 'Did the English Really Think They Were God's Elect in the Anglo-Saxon Period?', *Journal of Ecclesiastical History*, 65 (2014), 721–37;

idem, 'The Old English Bede: English Ideology or Christian Instruction?', *EHR*, 124, (2009), 1289–323.

9   *Life of King Edward*, 108–11; *Eadmer's History*, ed. Bosanquet, 9.

10 A. Gransden, *Historical Writing in England, c. 550 to c. 1307* (1974), 172, 194; Malmesbury, 14–15.

Bibliography

Unless otherwise indicated, the place of publication is London

PRIMARY SOURCES:

Abbots of Wearmouth and Jarrow, ed. C. Grocock and I. N. Wood (Oxford, 2013).

Aelfric's Lives of Saints, ed. W. W. Skeat (1881).

Alfred the Great: Asser's Life of King Alfred and other Contemporary Sources, ed. and trans. S. Keynes and M. Lapidge (1983).

An Anglo-Saxon Passion of St George, ed. and trans. C. Hardwick (1850).

Annals of Ireland: Three Fragments, ed. and trans. J. O'Donovan (Dublin, 1860).

Annals of St Bertin, ed. J. L. Nelson (Manchester, 1991).

Bedae, *Opera de Temporibus*, ed. C. W. Jones (Cambridge, Mass., 1943).

Bede, *Ecclesiastical History of the English People*, ed. B. Colgrave and R. A. B. Mynors (Oxford, 1969).

Bede, 'Life of Cuthbert', and 'Lives of the Abbots of Wearmouth and Jarrow', *The Age of Bede*, trans. J. F. Webb, ed. D. H. Farmer (revised edn, 1983).

Beowulf, trans. S. Heaney (1999).

Byrhtferth of Ramsey, *The Lives of St Oswald and St Ecgwine*, ed. and trans. M. Lapidge (Oxford, 2009).

A Choice of Anglo-Saxon Verse, ed. and trans. R. Harmer (1970).

The Chronicle of Æthelweard, ed. A. Campbell (1962).

The Chronicle of John of Worcester, II, ed. R. R. Darlington and P. McGurk, trans. J. Bray and P. McGurk (Oxford, 1995).

Eadmer's History of Recent Events in England, ed. G. Bosanquet (1964).

The Early Lives of St Dunstan, ed. and trans. M. Winterbottom and M. Lapidge (Oxford, 2012).

Eddius Stephanus, 'The Life of Wilfrid', *The Age of Bede*, trans. J. F. Webb, ed. D. H. Farmer (revised edn, 1983).

Encomium Emmae Reginae, ed. A. Campbell and S. Keynes (Cambridge, 1998).

English Historical Documents, c.500–1042, ed. D. Whitelock (2nd edn, 1979).

English Historical Documents, 1042–1189, ed. D. C. Douglas and G. W. Greenaway (1953).

The Gesta Guillelmi of William of Poitiers, ed. R. H. C. Davis and M. Chibnall (Oxford, 1998).

Gildas, *The Ruin of Britain and Other Works*, ed. and trans. M. Winterbottom (1978).

Henry, Archdeacon of Huntingdon, *Historia Anglorum: The History of the English People*, ed. D. Greenway (Oxford, 1996).

Historia de Sancto Cuthberto, ed. and trans. T. Johnson South (Woodbridge, 2002).

The Life of King Edward Who Rests at Westminster, ed. F. Barlow (2nd edn, Oxford, 1992).

'The Life of St Germanus of Auxerre', *Soldiers of Christ: Saints and Saints' Lives from Late Antiquity and the Early Middle Ages*, ed. T. F. X. Noble and T. Head (Pennsylvania University Press, 1995).

Regularis Concordia, ed. and trans. T. Symons (1953).

S. Bonifatii et S. Lullii Epistolae, ed. M. Tangl (Monumenta Germaniae Historica: *Epistolae Selectae*, i, Berlin, 1916).

Sidonius, *Poems and Letters*, trans. W. B. Anderson, vol. 1 (1963).

Sidonius Apollinaris, *Letters*, trans. O. M. Dalton, vol. 2 (1915).

Two Lives of St Cuthbert, ed. B. Colgrave (1940).

William of Malmesbury, *Gesta Regum Anglorum*, ed. and trans. R. A. B. Mynors, R. M. Thomson and M. Winterbottom (2 vols., Oxford, 1998–9).

— *Saints' Lives*, ed. M. Winterbottom and R. M. Thomson (Oxford, 2002).

Wulfstan of Winchester, *Life of St Æthelwold*, ed. and trans. M. Lapidge and M. Winterbottom (Oxford, 1991).

Zosimus, *New History*, ed. R. T. Ridley (Canberra, 1982).

SECONDARY WORKS (CITED):

Abels, R., *Alfred the Great: War, Kingship and Culture in Anglo-Saxon England* (1998).

— 'Alfred and his Biographers: Images and Imagination', *Writing Medieval Biography, 750–1250: Essays in Honour of Frank Barlow*, ed. D. Bates, J. Crick and S. Hamilton (Woodbridge, 2006).

— *Æthelred the Unready* (2018).

Abrams, L., 'Edward the Elder's Danelaw', *Edward the Elder, 899–924*, ed. N. J. Higham and D. H. Hill (Abingdon, 2001).

— 'The Conversion of the Danelaw', *Vikings and the Danelaw*, ed. J. Graham-Campbell et al. (2001).

— 'King Edgar and the Men of the Danelaw', *Edgar, King of the English, 959–975: New Interpretations*, ed. D. Scragg (Woodbridge, 2008).

Aird, W. M., 'Siward, Earl of Northumbria', *ODNB*.

Aldrete, G. S., *Daily Life in the Roman City: Rome, Pompei, and Ostia* (2004).

Allott, S., *Alcuin of York: His Life and Letters* (York, 1974).

Anglo-Saxon Kingdoms: Art, Word, War, ed. C. Breay and J. Story (2018).

The Anglo-Saxons, ed. J. Campbell (2nd edn, 1991).

Arnold, M., *The Vikings: Culture and Conquest* (2006).

Atherton, M., *The Making of England: A New History of the Anglo-Saxon World* (2017).

Banton, N., 'Monastic Reform and the Unification of Tenth-Century England', *Studies in Church History*, 18 (1992).

Barlow, F., *Edward the Confessor* (new edn, 1997).

Barrow, J., 'The Chronology of the Benedictine "Reform"', *Edgar, King of the English, 959–975: New Interpretations*, ed. D. Scragg (Woodbridge, 2008).

— 'Wulfwig', *ODNB*.

Bassett, S., 'In Search of the Origins of Anglo-Saxon Kingdoms', *The Origins of Anglo-Saxon Kingdoms*, ed. S. Bassett (Leicester, 1989).

Bately, J., 'Did King Alfred Actually Translate Anything? The Integrity of the Alfredian Canon Revisited', *Medium Ævum*, 78 (2009).

— 'Alfred as Author and Translator', *Companion to Alfred the Great*, ed. N. Guenther Discenza and P. E. Szarmach (Leiden, 2015).

Baxter, S., *The Earls of Mercia: Lordship and Power in Late Anglo-Saxon England* (Oxford, 2007).

Behr, C., 'The Origins of Kingship in Early Medieval Kent', *Early Medieval Europe*, 9 (2000).

— 'New Bracteate Finds from Early Anglo-Saxon England', *Medieval Archaeology*, 54 (2010).

Biddle, M., *Winchester in the Early Middle Ages: An Edition and Discussion of the Winton Domesday* (Oxford, 1976).

— *The Search for Winchester's Anglo-Saxon Minsters* (Oxford, 2018).

Biddle, M., and Hill, D., 'Late Saxon Planned Towns', *Antiquaries Journal*, 51 (1971).

Bidwell, P. T., 'A Survey of the Anglo-Saxon Crypt at Hexham and Its Reused Roman Stonework', *Archaeologia Aeliana*, 5th ser., 39 (2010).

Birley, A. R., *The Roman Government of Britain* (Oxford, 2005).

Blackmore, L., Blair, I., Hirst, S., and Scull, C., *The Prittlewell Princely Burial: Excavations at Priory Crescent, Southend-on-Sea, Essex, 2003* (2019).

Blair, J., *The Church in Anglo-Saxon Society* (Oxford, 2005).

— *Building Anglo-Saxon England* (Princeton and Oxford, 2018).

Bland, R., 'Hoarding in the Iron Age and Roman Britain: The Puzzle of the Late Roman Period', *British Numismatic Journal*, 84 (2014).

Bland, R., *Coin Hoards and Hoarding in Roman Britain* AD *43–c. 498* (2018).

Bozoky, E., 'The Sanctity and Canonisation of Edward the Confessor', *Edward the Confessor: The Man and the Legend*, ed. R. Mortimer (Woodbridge, 2009).

Breeze, A., '*Armes Prydein*, Hywel Dda, and the Reign of Edmund of Wessex', *Études Celtiques*, 33 (1997).

Breeze, D. J., and Dobson, B., *Hadrian's Wall* (4th edn, 2000).

Brooks, N., 'The Development of Military Obligations in Eighth- and Ninth-Century England', *England Before the Conquest: Studies in primary sources presented to Dorothy Whitelock*, ed. P. Clemoes and K. Hughes (Cambridge, 1971).

— 'England in the Ninth Century: The Crucible of Defeat', *TRHS*, 5th ser., 29 (1979).

— *The Early History of the Church of Canterbury* (Leicester, 1984).

— 'The Formation of the Mercian Kingdom', *The Origins of Anglo-Saxon Kingdoms*, ed. S. Bassett (Leicester, 1989).

— 'The Career of St Dunstan', *St Dunstan: His Life, Times and Cult*, ed. N. Ramsey, M. Sparks and T. Tatton-Brown (Woodbridge, 1992).

— 'Oswald [St Oswald]', *ODNB*.

Brown, D., 'Constantine II', *ODNB*.

Brown, M., *The Lindisfarne Gospels: Society, Spirituality and the Scribe* (2003).

— *Painted Labyrinth: The World of the Lindisfarne Gospels* (revised edn, 2004).

Bruce-Mitford, R. L. S., 'The Art of the Codex Amiatinus', *Journal of the British Archaeological Association*, 3rd ser., 32 (1969).

Campbell, J., 'Bede I', idem, *Essays in Anglo-Saxon History* (1986).

Carver, M., *The Sutton Hoo Story: Encounters with Early England* (Woodbridge, 2017).

Casey, P. J., 'The Fourth Century and Beyond', *The Roman Era*, ed. P. Salway (Oxford, 2002).

Charles-Edwards, T. M., 'Kinship, Status and the Origins of the Hide', *Past & Present*, 56 (1972).

— 'The Making of Nations in Britain and Ireland in the Early Middle Ages', *Lordship and Learning: Studies in Memory of Trevor Aston* (Woodbridge, 2004).

— *Wales and the Britons, 350–1064* (Oxford, 2013).

Coates, S. J, 'Benedict Biscop', *ODNB.*

— 'Ceolfrith', *ODNB.*

Cocherell, C. R., *Iconography of the West Front of Wells Cathedral* (1851).

Corning, C., *The Celtic and Roman Traditions: Conflict and Consensus in the Early Medieval Church* (2006).

Coupland, S., 'Dorestad in the Ninth Century: The Numismatic Evidence', *Jaarboek voor Munt en Penningkunde*, 75 (1988).

— 'The Fortified Bridges of Charles the Bald', *Journal of Medieval History*, 17 (1991).

Cowdrey, H. E. J., 'Robert of Jumièges', *ODNB.*

— 'Stigand', *ODNB.*

Cowie, R., 'Mercian London', *Mercia: An Anglo-Saxon Kingdom in Europe*, ed. M. P. Brown and C. A. Farr (Leicester, 2001).

Cox, O. J. W., 'Frederick, Prince of Wales, and the First Performance of "Rule Britannia!"', *Historical Journal*, 56 (2013).

Craig, D. J., 'Oswald, king of Northumbria', *ODNB.*

Cramp, R., 'Alchfrith', *ODNB.*

— 'Aldfrith, king of Northumbria', *ODNB.*

Crawford, B. E., 'The Making of a Frontier: The Firthlands from the Ninth to the Twelfth Centuries', *Firthlands of Ross and Sutherland*, ed. J. R. Baldwin (Scottish Soc. for Northern Studies, 1986).

Cubitt, C., 'The Tenth-Century Benedictine Reform in England', *Early Medieval Europe*, 6 (1997).

Cubitt, C., and Costambeys, M., 'Oda', *ODNB.*

The Dating of Beowulf: A Reassessment, ed. L. Neidorf (Cambridge, 2014).

Davidson, M. R., 'The (Non) Submission of the Northern Kings in 920', *Edward the Elder, 899–924*, ed. N. J. Higham and D. H. Hill (Abingdon, 2001).

Davis, R. H. C., *A History of Medieval Europe* (revised edn, 1970).

Davies, R. R., *The Age of Conquest: Wales 1063–1415* (Oxford, 2000).

Dobat, A. S., 'The King and his Cult: The Axe-Hammer from Sutton Hoo and its Implications for the Concept of Sacral Leadership in Early Medieval Europe', *Antiquity*, 80 (2006).

Dodgson, J. M., 'The Significance of the Distribution of the English Place-Name in *-ingas, -inga-,* in South-East England', *Medieval Archaeology*, 10 (1966).

Downham, C., 'The Chronology of the Last Scandinavian Kings of York, AD 937–954', *Northern History*, 40 (2003).

— 'Eric Bloodaxe – Axed? The Mystery of the Last Scandinavian King of York', *Medieval Scandinavia*, 14 (2004).

— *Viking Kings of Britain and Ireland: The Dynasty of Ívarr to AD 1014* (Edinburgh, 2008).

— '"Hiberno-Norwegians" and "Anglo-Danes": Anachronistic Ethnicities in Viking-Age England', *Mediaeval Scandinavia*, 19 (2009).

— 'The Earliest Viking Activity in England?', *EHR*, 132 (2017), 5–10.

Dyer, C., *Making a Living in the Middle Ages: The People of Britain, 850–1520* (2002).

Edwards, H., 'Beorhtric', *ODNB*.

— 'Cynewulf', *ODNB*.

— 'Ecgberht', *ODNB*.

Esmonde-Cleary, S., 'The Ending(s) of Roman Britain', *The Oxford Handbook to Anglo-Saxon Archaeology*, ed. H. Hamerow, D. A. Hinton and S. Crawford (Oxford, 2011).

— 'Introduction: The Roman Society and the Study of AD 410', *AD 410: The History and Archaeology of Late and Post-Roman Britain*, ed. F. K. Haarer et al. (Soc. for the Promotion of Roman Studies, 2014).

Faulkner, N., and Reece, R., 'The Debate About the End: A Review of Evidence and Methods', *Archaeological Journal*, 159 (2002).

Fernie, E., 'Edward the Confessor's Westminster Abbey', *Edward the Confessor: The Man and the Legend*, ed. R. Mortimer (Woodbridge, 2009).

Fisher, D. J. V., 'The Anti-Monastic Reaction in the Reign of Edward the Martyr', *The Cambridge Historical Journal*, 10 (1952).

Fleming, R., *Kings and Lords in Conquest England* (Cambridge, 1991).

— *Britain After Rome: The Fall and Rise, 400 to 1070* (2010).

— 'Harold II', *ODNB*.

Foot, S., 'The Making of *Angelcynn*: English Identity Before the Norman Conquest', *TRHS*, 6th ser., 6 (1996).

— *Monastic Life in Anglo-Saxon England, c. 600–900* (Cambridge, 2006).

— *Æthelstan* (2011).

Ford, B. M., and Teague, S., *Winchester: A City in the Making* (Oxford, 2011).

Freeman, C., *Egypt, Greece and Rome: Civilizations of the Ancient Mediterranean* (3rd edn, Oxford, 2014).

Gibbons, A., 'Why 536 was "the Worst Year to Be Alive"', *Science*, 362 (Nov. 2018).

Gilchrist, R., and Green, C., *Glastonbury Abbey: Archaeological Investigations 1904–79* (2015).

Gittos, H., *Liturgy, Architecture and Sacred Places in Anglo-Saxon England* (Oxford, 2013).

Godden, M. R., 'Money, Power and Morality in Late Anglo-Saxon England', *ASE*, 19 (1990).

— 'Did King Alfred Write Anything?', *Medium Ævum*, 76 (2007).

Gransden, A., *Historical Writing in England, c 550 to c.1307* (1974).

— 'Edmund [St Edmund]', *ODNB*.

Gretsch, M., *The Intellectual Foundations of the English Benedictine Reform* (Cambridge, 1999).

Guest, P., 'The Hoarding of Roman Metal Objects in Fifth-Century Britain', *AD 410: The History and Archaeology of Late and Post-Roman Britain*, ed. F. K. Haarer et al. (Soc. for the Promotion of Roman Studies, 2014).

Hadley, D. M., *The Vikings in England: Settlement, Society and Culture* (Manchester, 2007).

Hadley, D. M., Richards, J. D., et al., 'The Winter Camp of the Viking Great Army, AD 872–3, Torksey, Lincolnshire', *Antiquaries Journal*, 96 (2016).

Halloran, K., 'Anlaf Guthfrithson at York: A Non-Existent Kingship?', *Northern History*, 50 (2013).

— 'A Murder at Pucklechurch: The Death of King Edmund, 26 May 946', *Midland History*, 40 (2015).

— 'The War for Mercia, 942–943', *Midland History*, 41 (2016).

Halsall, G., 'Playing By Whose Rules? A Further Look at Viking Atrocity in the Ninth Century', *Medieval History*, 2 (1992).

— *Warfare and Society in the Barbarian West, 450–900* (2003).

— *Barbarian Migrations and the Roman West, 376–568* (Cambridge, 2007).

— *Worlds of Arthur: Facts and Fictions of the Dark Ages* (Oxford, 2013).

Hanaghan, M. P., *Reading Sidonius' Epistles* (Cambridge, 2019).

Handbook of British Chronology, ed. E. B. Fryde, D. E. Greenway, S. Porter and I. Roy (3rd edn, Cambridge, 1986).

Härke, H., 'Anglo-Saxon Immigration and Ethnogenesis', *Medieval Archaeology*, 55 (2011).

Hart, C., *The Danelaw* (1992).

— 'Æthelstan Half-King', *ODNB*.

— 'Edward the Martyr', *ODNB*.

Haslam, J., 'The Burghal Hidage and the West Saxon Burhs: A Reappraisal', *ASE*, 45 (2016).

Hayes, L., and Malim, T., 'The Date and Nature of Wat's Dyke: A Reassessment in the Light of Recent Investigations at Gobowen, Shropshire', *ASSAH*, 15 (2008).

Heather, P., 'The Huns and the End of the Roman Empire in Western Europe', *EHR*, 110 (1995).

— *Empires and Barbarians* (2009).

Herbert, M., 'Columba', *ODNB*.

Hetherington, P., *Medieval Rome: A Portrait of the City and its Life* (1994).

Higham, N. J., 'Edward the Elder's Reputation: An Introduction', *Edward the Elder, 899–924*, ed. N. J. Higham and D. H. Hill (Abingdon, 2001).

— *King Arthur: Myth-Making and History* (2002).

Higham, N. J., and Ryan, M. J., *The Anglo-Saxon World* (2013).

Hill, D., 'Offa's Dyke: Pattern and Purpose', *The Antiquaries Journal*, 80 (2000).

Hines, J., 'The Becoming of the English: Identity, Material Culture and Language in Early Anglo-Saxon England', *ASSAH*, 7 (1994).

— 'A New Chronology and New Agenda: The Problematic Sixth Century', *Transformation in Anglo-Saxon Culture: Toller Lectures on Art, Archaeology and Text*, ed. C. Insley and G. R. Owen-Crocker (Oxford, 2017).

Historia Ecclesie Abbendonensis: The History of the Church of Abingdon, ed. J. Hudson (2 vols., Oxford, 2002, 2007).

A History of the County of Berkshire, iv, ed. W. Page and P. H. Ditchfield (1924).

Holt, R., 'The Urban Transformation in England, 900–1100', *Anglo-Norman Studies*, 32 (2010).

Hope-Taylor, B., *Yeavering: An Anglo-British Centre of Early Northumbria* (revised edn, 2009).

Hudson, B. T., 'Ealdred', *ODNB*.

— 'Óláf Guthfrithson', *ODNB*.

Hume, D., *The History of England*, vol. 1 (1763).

Insley, C., 'Southumbria', *A Companion to the Early Middle Ages: Britain and Ireland, c. 500–c. 1100*, ed. P. Stafford (Oxford, 2009).

— 'Charters, Ritual and Late Tenth-Century English Kingship', *Gender and History*, ed. S. Reynolds, J. Nelson and S. Johns (2012).

Iogna-Prat, D., 'Cluny, 909–910, ou l'Instrumentalisation de la Mémoire des Origines', *Revue Mabillon*, 11 (2000).

Jarman, C. L., Biddle, M., Higham, T., and Bronk Ramsey, C., 'The Viking Great Army in England: New Dates from the Repton Charnel', *Antiquity*, 92 (2018).

Jayakumar, S., 'Eadwig and Edgar: Politics, Propaganda, Faction', *Edgar, King of the English, 959–975: New Interpretations*, ed. D. Scragg (Woodbridge, 2008).

John, E., 'The King and the Monks in the Tenth-Century Reformation', idem, *Orbis Britanniae and other Studies* (Leicester, 1966).

— 'The Newminster Charter', idem, *Orbis Britanniae and other Studies* (Leicester, 1966).

Johns, C., and Bland, R., 'The Hoxne Late Roman Treasure', *Britannia*, 25 (1994).

Jones, M. E., *The End of Roman Britain* (Cornell, 1996).

Karkov, C. E., *The Ruler Portraits of Anglo-Saxon England* (Woodbridge, 2004).

— 'The Frontispiece to the New Minster Charter and the King's Two Bodies', *Edgar, King of the English, 959–975: New Interpretations*, ed. D. Scragg (Woodbridge, 2008).

Kelly, S. E., 'Æthelbald'.

— 'Offa', *ODNB*.

— 'Penda', *ODNB*.

Kershaw, J. F., *Viking Identities: Scandinavian Jewellery in England* (Oxford, 2013).

Kershaw, J. F., and Røyrvik, E. C., 'The "People of the British Isles" Project and Viking Settlement in England', *Antiquity*, 90 (2016).

Keynes, S., 'King Æthelstan's Books', *Learning and Literature in Anglo-Saxon England*, ed. M. Lapidge and H. Gneuss (Cambridge, 1985).

— 'A Tale of Two Kings: Alfred the Great and Æthelred the Unready', *TRHS*, 36 (1986).

— 'The West Saxon Charters of King Æthelwulf and His Sons', *EHR*, 109 (1994).

— 'The Vikings in England', *The Oxford Illustrated History of the Vikings*, ed. P. Sawyer (Oxford, 1997).

— 'The Reconstruction of a Burnt Cottonian Manuscript: The Case of MS. Otho A. I', *British Library Journal*, 22 (1996).

— 'King Alfred and the Mercians', *Kings, Currency and Alliances*, ed. M. A. S. Blackburn and D. N. Dumville (Woodbridge, 1998).

— 'The Cult of King Alfred the Great', *ASE*, 28 (1999).

— 'Mercia and Wessex in the Ninth Century', *Mercia: An Anglo-Saxon Kingdom in Europe*, ed. M. P. Brown and C. A. Farr (Leicester, 2001).

— 'The Kingdom of the Mercians in the Eighth Century', *Æthelbald and Offa: Two Eighth-Century Kings of Mercia* (BAR British Series, 383, 2005).

— 'Edgar, *rex admirabilis*', *Edgar, King of the English, 959–975: New Interpretations*, ed. D. Scragg (Woodbridge, 2008).

— 'Alfred the Great and the Kingdom of the Anglo-Saxons', *A Companion to Alfred the Great*, ed. N. Guenther Discenza and P. E. Szarmach (Leiden, 2015).

— 'Æthelred II', *ODNB*.

— 'Eadric Streona', *ODNB*.

— 'Eadwig', *ODNB*.

Keynes, S., and Love, R., 'Earl Godwine's Ship', *ASE*, 38 (2009).

Kirby, D. P., *The Earliest English Kings* (revised edn, 2000).

Kleinschmidt, H., 'The Old English Annal for 757 and West Saxon Dynastic Strife', *Journal of Medieval History*, 22 (1996).

Knowles, D., *The Monastic Order in England* (2nd edn, Cambridge, 1963).

Konshuh, C., 'Fighting with a *Lytlewerode*: Alfred's Retinue in the *Anglo-Saxon Chronicle*', *The Medieval Chronicle X* (Leiden, 2016).

Krautheimer, R., *Rome: Profile of a City, 312–1308* (Princeton, 2000).

Lagorio, V. M., 'The Evolving Legend of St Joseph of Glastonbury', *Glastonbury Abbey and the Arthurian Tradition*, ed. J. P. Carley (Cambridge, 2001).

Lambert, T., *Law and Order in Anglo-Saxon England* (Oxford, 2017).

Lapidge, M., 'Some Latin Poems as Evidence for the Reign of Athelstan', *ASE*, 9 (1980).

— 'Dunstan', *ODNB*.

Lawson, M. K., *Cnut: England's Viking King, 1016–35* (new edn, 2011).

— 'Cenwulf', *ODNB*.

— 'Cnut [Canute]', *ODNB*.

Leahy, K., *The Anglo-Saxon Kingdom of Lindsey* (Stroud, 2007).

Maddicott, J. R., 'Trade, Industry and the Wealth of King Alfred', *Past & Present*, 123 (1989).

— 'Plague in Seventh-Century England', *Past & Present*, 156 (1997).

— 'Two Frontier States: Northumbria and Wessex, *c.*650–750', *The Medieval State*, ed. J. R. Maddicott and D. M. Palliser (2000).

— 'Prosperity and Power in the Age of Bede and Beowulf', *Proceedings of the British Academy*, 117 (2003).

— 'Edward the Confessor's Return to England in 1041', *EHR*, 119 (2004).

— 'London and Droitwich, *c.*650–750: Trade, Industry and the Rise of Mercia', *ASE*, 34 (2005).

— *The Origins of the English Parliament, 924–1327* (Oxford, 2010).

— 'Ecgfrith', *ODNB*.

Malim, T., 'Grim's Ditch, Wansdyke and the Ancient Highways of England: Linear Monuments and Political Control', *Proceedings of the Clifton Antiquarian Club*, 9 (2010).

Malone, C. M., *Façade as Spectacle: Ritual and Ideology at Wells Cathedral* (Leiden, 2004).

Mann, J. C., 'The Creation of Four Provinces in Britain by Diocletian', *Britannia*, 29 (1998).

Marafioti, N., *The King's Body: Burial and Succession in Late Anglo-Saxon England* (Toronto, 2014).

Mattingly, D., *An Imperial Possession: Britain in the Roman Empire, 54 BC–AD 409* (2006).

Mayr-Harting, H., *The Coming of Christianity to Anglo-Saxon England* (2nd edn, 1977).

McEvoy, M. A., *Child Emperor Rule in the Late Roman West, AD 367–455* (Oxford, 2013).

McGrail, S., *Ancient Boats in North-West Europe: The Archaeology of Water Transport to AD 1500* (new edn, 1998).

Metcalf, D. M., 'Betwixt Sceattas and Offa's Pence: Mint-Attributions and the Chronology of a Recession', *British Numismatic Journal*, 79 (2009).

Meyer, M. A., 'Women and the Tenth-Century English Monastic Reform', *Revue Bénédictine*, 87 (1977).

Miller, S., 'Edward [called Edward the Elder]', *ODNB*.

Molyneaux, G., 'The Old English Bede: English Ideology or Christian Instruction?', *EHR*, 124, (2009).

— 'Did the English Really Think They Were God's Elect in the Anglo-Saxon Period?', *Journal of Ecclesiastical History*, 65 (2014).

— *The Formation of the English Kingdom in the Tenth Century* (Oxford, 2015).

Morris, J., *The Age of Arthur* (1973).

Morris, M., *A Great and Terrible King: Edward I and the Forging of Britain* (2008).

— *The Norman Conquest* (2012).

— *King John: Treachery, Tyranny and the Road to Magna Carta* (2015).

Naismith, R., 'The Coinage of Offa Revisited', *British Numismatic Journal*, 80 (2010).

— 'The Origins of the Line of Egbert, King of the West Saxons, 802–839, *EHR*, 126 (2011).

— *Money and Power in Anglo-Saxon England: The Southern English Kingdoms, 757–865* (Cambridge, 2012).

— *Medieval European Coinage 8: Britain and Ireland c.400–1066* (Cambridge, 2017).

— *Citadel of the Saxons: The Rise of Early London* (2019).

Nelson, J. L., 'The Frankish Empire', *The Oxford Illustrated History of the Vikings*, ed. P. Sawyer (Oxford, 1997).

— 'Carolingian Contacts', *Mercia: An Anglo-Saxon Kingdom in Europe*, ed. M. P. Brown and C. A. Farr (Leicester, 2001).

— *King and Emperor: A New Life of Charlemagne* (2019).

— 'Æthelwulf', *ODNB*.

Newfield, T. P., 'The Climate Downturn of 536–50', *The Palgrave Handbook of Climate History*, ed. S. White, C. Pfister, and F. Mauelshagen (2018).

Newton, S., *The Origins of Beowulf and the Pre-Viking Kingdom of East Anglia* (Woodbridge, 1993).

Ó Corráin, D., 'Ireland, Wales, Man, and the Hebrides', *The Oxford Illustrated History of the Vikings*, ed. P. Sawyer (Oxford, 1997).

The Oxford Dictionary of National Biography, ed. H. C. G. Matthews and B. Harrison (60 vols., Oxford, 2004).

The Oxford Encyclopedia of Medieval Warfare and Military Technology, vol. 1, ed. C. J. Rogers, (Oxford, 2010).

Parsons, D., and Sutherland, D., *The Anglo-Saxon Church of All Saints, Brixworth, Northamptonshire: Survey, Excavation and Analysis, 1972–2010* (Oxford, 2013).

Peacock, D. P. S., 'Charlemagne's Black Stones: The Re-Use of Roman Columns in Early Medieval Europe', *Antiquity*, 71 (1997).

Pearson, A., *The Roman Shore Forts: Coastal Defences of Southern Britain* (Stroud, 2002).

Pelteret, D. A. E., *Slavery in Early Mediæval England* (Woodbridge, 1995).

Pratt, D., 'The Illnesses of King Alfred the Great', *ASE*, 30 (2001).

— 'The Voice of the King in "King Edgar's Establishment of Monasteries"', *ASE*, 41 (2012).

Prien, R., 'The Copy of an Empire? Charlemagne, the Carolingian Renaissance and Early Medieval Perception of Late Antiquity', *The Transformative Power of the Copy*, ed. C. Forberg and P. Stockhammer (Heidelberg, 2017).

Rahtz, P., *Glastonbury* (1993).

Ray, K., and Bapty, I., *Offa's Dyke: Landscape and Hegemony in Eighth-Century Britain* (Oxford, 2016).

Reuter, T., 'Plunder and Tribute in the Carolingian Empire', *TRHS*, 35 (1985).

Richards, J. D., *The Vikings: A Very Short Introduction* (Oxford, 2005).

Richardson, H. G., and Sayles, G. O., *Law and Legislation from Æthelberht to Magna Carta* (Edinburgh, 1966).

Rippon, S., Smart, C., and Pears, B., *The Fields of Britannia* (Oxford, 2015).

Roach, L., *Kingship and Consent in Anglo-Saxon England, 871–978* (Cambridge, 2013).

— *Æthelred the Unready* (2016).

Rollason, D., and Dobson, R., 'Cuthbert', *ODNB*.

Royal Commission on the Historical Monuments of England, 'Wareham West Walls', *Medieval Archaeology*, 3 (1959).

Rumble, A. R., 'Hamtun *alias* Hamwic (Saxon Southampton): The Place-Name Traditions and their Significance', *Excavations* at *Melbourne Street Southampton, 1971–76*, ed. P. Holdsworth (Council for British Archaeology, 1980).

— 'The Laity and the Monastic Reform in the Reign of Edgar', *Edgar, King of the English, 959–975: New Interpretations*, ed. D. Scragg (Woodbridge, 2008).

Salway, P., and Blair, J., *Roman and Anglo-Saxon Britain* (new edn, Oxford, 1992).

— *The Oxford Illustrated History of Roman Britain* (Oxford, 1993).

— 'Conclusion', *The Roman Era*, ed. P. Salway (2002).

Sawyer, P., 'The Last Scandinavian Kings of York', *Northern History*, 31 (1995).

— 'The Age of the Vikings and Before', *The Oxford Illustrated History of the Vikings*, ed. P. Sawyer (Oxford, 1997).

— *The Wealth of Anglo-Saxon England* (Oxford, 2013).

— 'Swein', *ODNB*.

Scull, C., Minter, F., and Plouviez, J., 'Social and Economic Complexity in Early Medieval England: A Central Place Complex of the East Anglian Kingdom at Rendlesham, Suffolk', *Antiquity*, 90 (2016).

Smith, A. W., '"And Did Those Feet … ?": The "Legend" of Christ's Visit to Britain', *Folklore*, 100 (1989).

Smyth, A., *King Alfred the Great* (Oxford, 1995).

Squatriti, P., 'Digging Ditches in Early Medieval Europe', *Past & Present*, 176 (2002).

Stafford, P., 'The Laws of Cnut and the History of Anglo-Saxon Royal Promises', *ASE*, 10 (1982).

— 'Women and the Norman Conquest', *TRHS*, 6th ser., 4 (1994).

— *Queen Emma and Queen Edith* (Oxford, 1997).

— 'Ælfgifu of Northampton', *ODNB*.

— 'Eadgifu', *ODNB*.

The Staffordshire Hoard: An Anglo-Saxon Treasure, ed. C. Fern, T. Dickinson and L. Webster (2019).

Stenton, D. M., *The English Woman in History* (1956).

Stenton, F. M., *Anglo-Saxon England* (3rd edn, Oxford, 1971).

Summerson, H., 'Tudor Antiquaries and the *Vita Ædwardi regis*', *ASE*, 38 (2009).

— 'George [St George]', *ODNB*.

Thacker, A., 'England in the Seventh Century', *The New Cambridge Medieval History, I: c.500 – c.700*, ed. P. Fouracre (Cambridge, 2005).

— 'Ælfflæd', *ODNB*.

— 'Wilfrid', *ODNB*.

Tolkien, J. R. R., *Beowulf: A Translation and Commentary*, ed. C. Tolkien (2015).

Tolley, C., 'Old English Influence on *The Lord of the Rings*', *Beowulf and Other Stories: A New Introduction to Old English, Old Icelandic and Anglo-Norman Literatures*, ed. R. North and J. Allard (2nd edn, 2012).

Townend, M., 'Contextualizing the *Knútsdrápur*: Skaldic Praise-Poetry at the Court of Cnut', *ASE*, 30 (2001).

Treharne, E., *Living Through Conquest: The Politics of Early English, 1020–1220* (Oxford, 2012).

Tyler, D. J., 'Offa's Dyke: A Historiographical Reappraisal', *Journal of Medieval History*, 37 (2011).

Ulmschneider, K., 'Settlement, Economy, and the "Productive" Site: Middle Anglo-Saxon Lincolnshire AD 650–780', *Medieval Archaeology*, 44 (2000).

Wallace-Hadrill, J. M., Bede's *Ecclesiastical History of the English People: A Historical Commentary* (Oxford, 1988).

Ward-Perkins, B., 'Why Did the Anglo-Saxons Not Become More British?', *EHR*, 115 (2000).

— *The Fall of Rome and the End of Civilization* (Oxford, 2005).

Webster, L., *Anglo-Saxon Art* (2012).

Welch, M., *Anglo-Saxon England* (1993).

— 'Anglo-Saxon Kent to AD 800', *The Archaeology of Kent to AD 800* (Woodbridge, 2007).

Wilcox, J., 'Wulfstan's *Sermo Lupi ad Anglos* as Political Performance: 16 February 1014 and Beyond', *Wulfstan, Archbishop of York: The Proceedings of the Second Alcuin Conference*, ed. M. O. Townend (Turnhout, 2004).

The Wiley Blackwell Encyclopedia of Anglo-Saxon England, ed. M. Lapidge, J. Blair, S. Keynes, and D. Scragg (2nd edn, Oxford, 2014).

Williams, A., 'Eadred', *ODNB*.

— 'Edgar', *ODNB*.

— 'Godwine', *ODNB*.

— 'Odda', *ODNB*.

Williams, G., 'Mercian Coinage and Authority', *Mercia: An Anglo-Saxon Kingdom in Europe*, ed. M. P. Brown and C. A. Farr (Leicester, 2001).

— 'Military Institutions and Royal Power', *Mercia: An Anglo-Saxon Kingdom in Europe*, ed. M. P. Brown and C. A. Farr (Leicester, 2001).

Williams, H., 'Cemeteries as Central Places – Place and Identity in Migration Period Eastern England', *Central Places in the Migration and Merovingian Periods*, ed. L. Larsson and B. Hårdh (Stockholm, 2002).

Williams, T., *Viking Britain: An Exploration* (2017).

Wilmott, T., *Richborough and Reculver* (2012).

Wiseman, H., 'The Derivation of the Date of the Badon Entry in the *Annales Cambriae* from Bede and Gildas', *Parergon*, 17 (2000).

Wood, I. N., 'Boniface', *ODNB*.

Wood, M., 'The Lost Life of King Athelstan', idem, *In Search of England* (1999).

— *In Search of the Dark Ages* (new edn, 2006).

— 'Searching for Brunanburh: The Yorkshire Context of the "Great War" of 937', *Yorkshire Archaeological Journal*, 85 (2013).

Woolf, A., 'Erik Bloodaxe Revisited', *Northern History*, 35 (1998).

— *From Pictland to Alba, 789–1070* (Edinburgh, 2007).

Wormald, P., 'Bede, the Bretwaldas and the Origin of the *Gens Anglorum*', *Ideal and Reality in Frankish and Anglo-Saxon Society*, ed. P. Wormald et al. (Oxford, 1983).

— '*Engla Londe*: The Making of an Allegiance', *Journal of Historical Sociology*, 7 (1994).

— *The Making of English Law: King Alfred to the Twelfth Century* (Oxford, 1999).

— 'Æthelweard', *ODNB*.

— 'Wulfstan [Lupus]', *ODNB*.

Worthington, M., 'Offa's Dyke', *Æthelbald and Offa: Two Eighth-Century Kings of Mercia* (BAR British Series, 383, 2005).

Wyatt, D., 'The Significance of Slavery: Alternative Approaches to Anglo-Saxon Slavery', *Anglo-Norman Studies*, 23 (2001).

— *Slaves and Warriors in Medieval Britain and Ireland, 800–1200* (Brill, 2009).

Yeavering: People, Power & Place, ed. P. Frodsham and C. O'Brien (2005).

Yorke, B., 'Æthelwold and the Politics of the Tenth Century', *Bishop Æthelwold: His Career and Influence*, ed. idem (Woodbridge, 1988).

— 'The Jutes of Hampshire and Wight and the Origins of Wessex', *The Origins of Anglo-Saxon Kingdoms*, ed. S. Bassett (Leicester, 1989).

— *Kings and Kingdoms of Early Anglo-Saxon England* (1990).

— *Wessex in the Early Middle Ages* (Leicester, 1995).

— 'Anglo-Saxon *Gentes* and *Regna*', *Regna and Gentes*, ed. H.-W. Goetz, J. Jarnut and W. Pohl (Leiden, 2003).

— 'Anglo-Saxon Origin Legends', *Myth, Rulership, Church and Charters: Essays in Honour of Nicholas Brooks*, ed. J. Barrow and A. Wareham (Aldershot, 2008).

— 'The Bretwaldas and the Origins of Overlordship in Anglo-Saxon England', *Early Medieval Studies in Memory of Patrick Wormald*, ed. S. Baxter, C. Karkov, J. L. Nelson and D. Pelteret (Farnham, 2009).

— 'The Representation of Early West Saxon History in the *Anglo-Saxon Chronicle*', *Reading the Anglo-Saxon Chronicle: Language, Literature, History*, ed. A. Jorgensen (Turnhout, 2010).

— 'Cædwalla', *ODNB*.

— 'Ceawlin', *ODNB*.

SECONDARY WORKS (CONSULTED):

Backhouse, J., *The Lindisfarne Gospels: A Masterpiece of Book Painting* (1995).

Baker, J., and Brookes, S., 'Fulham 878–79: A New Consideration of Viking Manoeuvres', *Viking and Medieval Scandinavia,* 8 (2012).

— *Beyond the Burghal Hidage: Anglo-Saxon Civil Defence in the Viking Age* (Leiden, 2013).

The Battle of Maldon AD 991, ed. D. Scragg (Oxford, 1991).

Beech, G. T., 'How England Got Its Name (1014–1030)', *Nouvelle revue d'onomastique,* 51 (2009).

Blair, J., 'Introduction: From Minster to Parish Church', *Minsters and Parish Churches: The Local Church in Transition, 950–1200,* ed. idem (Oxford, 1988).

Breeze, A., 'Gildas: Renewed Approaches', *Northern History,* 47 (2010).

Brooks, N., 'English Identity from Bede to the Millennium', *Haskins Society Journal,* 14 (2003).

Brugmann, B., 'Migration and Endogenous Change', *Oxford Handbook of Anglo-Saxon Archaeology* (Oxford, 2011).

Campbell, J., 'Bede's *Reges* and *Principes*', idem, *Essays in Anglo-Saxon History* (1986).

— 'Bede II', idem, *Essays in Anglo-Saxon History* (1986).

— 'The First Century of Christianity in England', idem, *Essays in Anglo-Saxon History* (1986).

— 'Observations on the Conversion of England', idem, *Essays in Anglo-Saxon History* (1986).

— 'England, *c.*991', idem, *The Anglo-Saxon State* (2000).

— 'The Late Anglo-Saxon State: A Maximum View', idem, *The Anglo-Saxon State* (2000).

— 'Was it Infancy in England?', idem, *The Anglo-Saxon State* (2000).

— 'Some Agents and Agencies of the Late Anglo-Saxon State', idem, *The Anglo-Saxon State* (2000).

Charles-Edwards, T., 'Early Medieval Kingships in the British Isles', *The Origins of Anglo-Saxon Kingdoms.* ed. S. Bassett (Leicester, 1989).

— 'Wales and Mercia, 613–918', *Mercia: An Anglo-Saxon Kingdom in Europe,* ed. M. P. Brown and C. A. Farr (Leicester, 2001).

Chick, D., 'The Coinage of Offa in Light of Recent Discoveries', *Æthelbald and Offa: Two Eighth-Century Kings of Mercia* (BAR British Series, 383, 2005).

Collins, R., *Early Medieval Europe, 300–1000* (3rd edn, 2010).

Costen, M., 'Dunstan, Glastonbury and the Economy of Somerset in the Tenth Century', *St Dunstan: His Life, Times and Cult*, ed. N. Ramsey, M. Sparks and T. Tatton-Brown (Woodbridge, 1992).

Crawford, B. E., 'The Vikings', *From the Vikings to the Normans*, ed. W. Davies (Oxford, 2003).

Cubitt, C., 'Wilfrid's "Usurping Bishops": Episcopal Elections in Anglo-Saxon England, *c.*600–*c.*800, *Northern History*, 25 (1989).

Dales, D., *Dunstan: Saint and Statesman* (2nd edn, Cambridge, 2013).

Downham, C., '"Hiberno-Norwegians" and "Anglo-Danes": Anachronistic Ethnicities in Viking Age England', *Mediaeval Scandinavia*, 19 (2009).

Dumville, D. M., 'Between Alfred the Great and Edgar the Peaceable: Athelstan, the First King of England', idem, *Wessex and England from Alfred to Edgar* (Woodbridge, 1992).

— 'Gildas and Maelgwn: Problems of Dating', *Gildas: New Approaches*, ed. M. Lapidge and D. Dumville (Woodbridge, 1984).

— 'The Chronology of *De Excidio Britanniae*, Book 1', *Gildas: New Approaches*, ed. M. Lapidge and D. Dumville (Woodbridge, 1984).

— 'King Alfred and the Tenth-Century Reform of the English Church', idem, *Wessex and England from Alfred to Edgar* (Woodbridge, 1992).

Edwards, N., 'Rethinking the Pillar of Eliseg', *Antiquaries Journal*, 89 (2009).

Fleming, R., 'The New Wealth, the New Rich and the New Political Style in Late Anglo-Saxon England', *Anglo-Norman Studies*, 23 (2001).

— 'Lords and Labour', *From the Vikings to the Normans*, ed. W. Davies (Oxford, 2003).

Fraser, J. E., 'Bede, the Firth of Forth, and the Location of *Urbs Iudeu*', *Scottish Historical Review*, Volume 87 (2008).

Gelling, M., *The Landscape of Place-Names* (Stamford, 2000).

— *Signposts to the Past: Place-Names and the History of England* (3rd edn, Chichester, 1997).

Gerrard, J., *The Ruin of Roman Britain: An Archaeological Perspective* (Cambridge, 2013).

Gibbs, M., 'The Decrees of Agatho and the Gregorian Plan for York', *Speculum*, 48 (1973).

Godden, M., 'Ælfric of Eynsham', *ODNB*.

Griffiths, D., 'Exchange, Trade and Urbanization', *From the Vikings to the Normans*, ed. W. Davies (Oxford, 2003).

Hall, A., 'The Instability of Place-Names in Anglo-Saxon England and Early Medieval Wales, and the Loss of Roman Toponymy', *Sense of Place in Anglo-Saxon England*, ed. R. Jones and S. Semple (Donington, 2012).

Halsall, G., 'The Barbarian Invasions', *The New Cambridge Medieval History, I: c.500 – c.700*, ed. P. Fouracre (Cambridge, 2005).

Hamerow, H., 'The Earliest Anglo-Saxon Kingdoms', *The New Cambridge Medieval History, I: c.500 – c.700*, ed. P. Fouracre (Cambridge, 2005).

— *Rural Settlements and Society in Anglo-Saxon England* (Oxford, 2012).

Harrington, S., and Welch, M., *The Early Anglo-Saxon Kingdoms of Southern Britain, AD 450–650* (Oxford, 2014).

Haslam, J., 'Market and Fortress in England in the Reign of Offa', *World Archaeology*, 19 (1987).

— 'King Alfred, Mercia and London, 874–86: A Reassessment', *ASSAH*, 17 (2011).

Hedeager, L., 'Cosmological Endurance: Pagan Identities in Early Christian Europe', *European Journal of Archaeology*, 1 (1998).

Higham, N., *The Kingdom of Northumbria: AD 350–1100* (Stroud, 1993).

— *The English Conquest: Gildas and Britain in the Fifth Century* (Manchester, 1994).

Hill, D., *An Atlas of Anglo-Saxon England* (revised edn, Oxford, 1984).

— 'Mercians: Dwellers on the Boundary', *Mercia: An Anglo-Saxon Kingdom in Europe*, ed. M. P. Brown and C. A. Farr (Leicester, 2001).

— 'The Eighth-Century Urban Landscape', *Æthelbald and Offa: Two-Eighth Century Kings of Mercia* (BAR British Series, 383, 2005).

Hines, J., 'Cultural change and social organisation in early Anglo-Saxon England', *After Empire: Towards an Ethnology of Europe's Barbarians*, ed. G. Ausenda (Woodbridge, 1995).

Holland, T., *Athelstan: The Making of England* (2016).

Howe, N., *Writing the Map of Anglo-Saxon England* (Yale, 2008).

Hudson, J., *The Formation of the English Common Law: Law and Society in England from King Alfred to Magna Carta* (2nd edn, 2018).

Hunt, J., *Warriors, Warlords and Saints: The Anglo-Saxon Kingdom of Mercia* (Alcester, 2016).

Inker, P., 'Technology as Active Material Culture: The Quoit-Brooch Style', *Medieval Archaeology*, 44 (2000).

Jayakumar, S., 'Reform and Retribution: The "Anti-Monastic Reaction" in the Reign of Edward the Martyr', *Early Medieval Studies in Memory of Patrick Wormald* (2009).

John, E., *Reassessing Anglo-Saxon England* (Manchester, 1996).

Jones, M. A., 'A Chosen Missionary People? Willibrord, Boniface, and the Election of the *Angli*', *Medieval Worlds*, 3 (2016).

Keynes, S., 'England, 900–1016', *The New Cambridge Medieval History, III: c. 900 – c. 1024*, ed. T. Reuter (Cambridge, 1999).

— 'Mercia and Wessex in the Ninth Century', *Mercia: An Anglo-Saxon Kingdom in Europe*, ed. M. P. Brown and C. A. Farr (Leicester UP, 2001).

— 'Edward, King of the Anglo-Saxons', *Edward the Elder, 899–924*, ed. N. J. Higham and D. H. Hill (Abingdon, 2001).

Kirby, D. P., 'Bede, Eddius Stephanus, and the "Life of Wilfrid"', *EHR*, 98 (1983).

Kock, J. T., 'The Place of *Y Gododdin* in the History of Scotland', *Celtic Connections*, vol. 1, ed. R. Black, W. Gillies and R. Ó Maolalaigh (East Linton, 1999).

Lavelle, R., *Alfred's Wars: Sources and Interpretations of Anglo-Saxon Warfare in the Viking Age* (Woodbridge, 2010).

— *Cnut: The North Sea King* (2017).

Leahy, K., Bland, R., Hooke, D., Jones, A., and Okasha, E., 'The Staffordshire (Ogley Hay) Hoard: Recovery of a Treasure', *Antiquity*, 85 (2011).

Leyser, H., *Beda: A Journey Through the Seven Kingdoms in the Age of Bede* (2015).

— *A Short History of the Anglo-Saxons* (2017).

Manco, J., *The Origins of the Anglo-Saxons* (2018).

Miller, M., 'Bede's use of Gildas', *EHR*, 90 (1975).

Moisl, H., 'The Bernician Royal Dynasty and the Irish in the Seventh Century', *Peritia* 2 (1983).

Murray, A., 'Bede and the Unchosen Race', *Power and Identity in the Middle Ages*, ed. H. Pryce and J. Watts (Oxford, 2007).

Nelson, J. L., '"A King Across the Sea": Alfred in Continental Perspective', *TRHS*, 36 (1986).

— 'The Political Ideas of Alfred of Wessex', *Kings and Kingship in Medieval Europe*, ed. A. J. Duggan (1993).

— 'England and the Continent in the Ninth Century: II, The Vikings and Others', *TRHS*, 13 (2003).

Noble, T. F. X., 'Rome in the Seventh Century', *Archbishop Theodore: Commemorative Studies on His Life and Influence*, ed. M. Lapidge (Cambridge, 1995).

Parsons, D., 'The Mercian Church: Archaeology and Topography', *Mercia: An Anglo-Saxon Kingdom in Europe*, ed. M. P. Brown and C. A. Farr (Leicester, 2001).

Pelteret, D., 'Saint Wilfrid: Tribal Bishop, Civic Bishop or Germanic Lord', *The Community, the Family and the Saint*, ed. J. Hill and M. Swan (Turnhout, 1998).

Pollington, S., *Anglo-Saxon Burial Mounds: Princely Burials in the 6th and 7th centuries* (Swaffham, 2008).

Pratt, D., 'Persuasion and Invention at the Court of Alfred the Great', *Court Culture in the Early Middle Ages: The Proceedings of the First Alcuin Conference*, ed. C. E. Cubitt (Turnhout, 2003).

Reynolds, S., 'What Do We Mean by "Anglo-Saxon" and "Anglo-Saxons"?', *Journal of British Studies*, 24 (1985).

Richards, J. D., *Viking Age England* (new edn, Stroud, 2004).

Rollason, *Northumbria, 500–1100: Creation and Destruction of a Kingdom* (Cambridge, 2003).

Smyth, A. P., 'The Emergence of English Identity, 700–1000', *Medieval Europeans: Studies in Ethnic Identity and National Perspectives in Medieval Europe*, ed. idem (Basingstoke, 1998).

Snyder, C. A., *An Age of Tyrants: Britain and the Britons, AD 400–600* (Stroud, 1998).

Squatriti, P., 'Offa's Dyke Between Nature and Culture', *Environmental History*, 9 (2004).

Stafford, P., *Unification and Conquest: A Political and Social History of England in the Tenth and Eleventh Centuries* (1989).

Thompson, E. A., 'Gildas and the History of Britain', *Britannia*, 10 (1979).

Tolkien, J. R. R., *Beowulf: The Monsters and the Critics and Other Essays* (1983).

Tyler, D. J., 'Orchestrated Violence and the "Supremacy of the Mercian Kings"', *Æthelbald and Offa: Two Eighth-Century Kings of Mercia* (BAR British Series, 383, 2005).

Underwood, R., *Anglo-Saxon Weapons and Warfare* (Stroud, 1999).

Vince, A., 'Market Centres and Towns in the Mercian Hegemony', *Mercia: An Anglo-Saxon Kingdom in Europe*, ed. M. P. Brown and C. A. Farr (Leicester, 2001).

Webster, L., 'Anglo-Saxon Art: Tradition and Transformation', *Transformation in Anglo-Saxon Culture: Toller Lectures on Art, Archaeology and Text*, ed. C. Insley and G. R. Owen-Crocker (Oxford, 2017).

Webster, L., Sparey-Green, C., Périn, P., and Hills, C., 'The Staffordshire (Ogley Hay) Hoard: Problems of Interpretation', *Antiquity*, 85 (2011).

White, R. H., 'A Brave New World? The Archaeology of Western Britain in the Fifth and Sixth Centuries', *AD 410: The History and Archaeology of Late and Post-Roman Britain,* ed. F. K. Haarer et al. (Soc. for the Promotion of Roman Studies, 2014).

Wickham, C., *The Inheritance of Rome: A History of Europe from 400 to 1000* (2009).

Williams, G., 'Military Institutions and Royal Power', *Mercia: An Anglo-Saxon Kingdom in Europe*, ed. M. P. Brown and C. A. Farr (Leicester, 2001).

— 'Military Obligations and Mercian Supremacy in the Eighth Century', *Æthelbald and Offa: Two Eighth-Century Kings of Mercia* (BAR British Series, 383, 2005).

Wood, I., 'The End of Roman Britain: Continental Evidence and Parallels', *Gildas: New Approaches*, ed. M. Lapidge and D. Dumville (Woodbridge, 1984).

— 'Northumbrians and Franks in the Age of Wilfrid', *Northern History*, 31 (1995).

Wood, M., 'Glastonbury, the Grail and the Isle of Avalon', idem, *In Search of England* (1999).

Woods, D., 'Gildas and the Mystery Cloud of 536–7', *Journal of Theological Studies*, NS, 61 (2010).

Wormald, P., 'Bede, *Beowulf*, and the Conversion of the Anglo-Saxon Aristocracy', *Bede and Anglo-Saxon England*, ed. R. T. Farrell (Oxford, 1978).

Worthington, M., 'Wat's Dyke: An Archaeological and Historical Enigma', *Bulletin of the John Rylands Library*, 79 (1997).

Yorke, B., *The Conversion of Britain: Religion, Politics and Society in Britain, c.600–800* (Harlow, 2006).

— 'The Origins of Anglo-Saxon Kingdoms: The Contribution of Written Sources', *ASSAH*, 10 (1999).

— *Nunneries and the Anglo-Saxon Royal Houses* (2003).

Zaluckyj, S., *Mercia: The Anglo-Saxon Kingdom of Central England* (Almeley, 2001).

Index

Abbreviations: abp (archbishop); abt (abbot); bp (bishop); e. (ealdorman/earl)